Middle Age
Old Age

Short Stories, Poems, Plays, and Essays on Aging

Edited by
Ruth Granetz Lyell
San José State University

Harcourt Brace Jovanovich, Inc.

New York   San Diego   Chicago   San Francisco   Atlanta
London   Sydney   Toronto

This book is lovingly dedicated
to the memory of my uncle,
  Professor Meyer F. Nimkoff,
who introduced me to scholarship,
and to my children,
  Miriam Tanya Lyell,
  Sean Andrew Lyell,
  Deirdre Judith Lyell,
  and
  David Patrick Lyell,
who introduced me to the continuity of generations.

ISBN: 0-15-558660-2

Library of Congress Catalog Card Number: 79-91423

Printed in the United States of America

COPYRIGHTS AND ACKNOWLEDGMENTS

GEORGE ALLEN & UNWIN LTD. for "On Being Sixty" by Po Chü-i and "Seven Poems
    on Aging" by Yüan Mei, reprinted by permission of George Allen & Unwin, Pub-
    lishers.
MARGARET BEERNINK for "Gino Spinelli" by K. D. Beernink.
JONATHAN CAPE, LTD. for excerpts from *The Notebooks of Leonardo da Vinci*, trans-
    lated by Edward McCurdy.

Copyrights and acknowledgments continue on p. 387, which constitutes a continuation
of the copyright page.

Foreword

As I read the gerontological literature, I have the uncomfortable feeling that altogether too much of the current research on aging lacks sufficient perspective. Conclusions are drawn from research on contemporary samples, are evaluated against the results in published studies, and are then generalized to the whole phenomenon of aging everywhere. The entire emphasis in this process is on the contemporary.

I have the same uncomfortable feeling that the person's perception lacks sufficient perspective when I talk with someone who is working directly with the elderly. Both practitioner and researcher convey the impression that all that is true about aging is what is known right now.

This situation of course occurs because researchers and practitioners have access only to subjects, interviewees, respondents, and clients in the here and now. Research on aging prior to this century focused mainly on ways to achieve longevity and not on the broader range of topics that are of interest to today's gerontologists. Hence the depth of perspective that one needs with which to compare current gerontological research findings is lacking simply because this kind of research was not done in the past.

This is a lack that I have felt keenly in the course of reading a myriad of gerontological research studies while teaching courses in the psychology and sociology of aging over the past six years. While some of the studies were quite good, I have wondered if the characteristics of aging that were reported really typified aging in all times and in all places, or if they were not instead limited to aging in the second half of the twentieth century. The trouble with this limitation is that the characteristics discovered in the second half of the twentieth century have been reported and read as though they were the *universal* characteristics of all people who age everywhere. And that simply is not true.

Fortunately, we do have a resource from the past. Writers of fiction, drama, and poetry, as well as essayists, at times focused on their own aging experiences or on their observations of others. I have tried to include a cross-section of these writers in this anthology. Use of this resource, when combined with current research findings, should help the reader achieve much greater insight and perspective. Works of fiction have the added benefit of illustrating the various processes of aging with portraits of persons who are whole, and are thereby more complex than the limited pictures that research studies can offer.

The second issue that interests me and that also motivated me to develop this anthology is my concern that too many gerontologists, older adults, social workers, social scientists, and students believe that the sometimes painful experiences of aging have to do almost entirely with modern industrial society's treatment of the elderly. They think that American culture, because it is youth-oriented, productivity-oriented, and future-oriented, is guilty of disliking and deploring aging and aged persons—and that these negative attitudes have the effect on many elderly of making them feel depressed, insecure, bitter, lonely, and self-hating. With that analysis I agree to a point. I disagree with the idea that the negative cultural attitude is the *only* major source of the problems of the elderly. There is something about the aging process itself that *can* produce feelings of despair, depression, and loneliness, for the aging process is characterized by decline, loss, and greater proximity to death; this occurs quite apart from culture and regardless of the specific culture. It is true that the worship of youthfulness in American culture goes to an extreme, and the consequences of it punish those who look and grow older—it exacerbates the problem—but the basic problem is still there.

The evidence lies in the fact that throughout history, in a diversity of cultures, people have sought methods to retard or reverse the aging process. Indeed, rejuvenation has been a recurrent obsession in many different cultures. This obsession has occurred even in cultures with a strong tradition of veneration of ancestors—in which individuals have not necessarily been in a hurry to join their ancestors or be venerated by their descendants. They have wanted to continue to live, and they have wanted the vigor and zest of youth.

Thus the problem of aging cannot be hidden by the Pollyanna-like assertion one finds, both in and out of gerontology, that all would be well with the elderly if only society's attitudes would change. Each of us who is aging knows better than that.

There are some negative aspects to the aging process that are not just a matter of society's preference for the young and its contempt for the old. There are also the physical decline, the slowing, and the interpersonal and physical loss that occur as one ages that have little to do directly with one's culture. Indirectly culture can speed up aging, or slow it down, or alter some of the consequences, but the process itself is inevitable and gradual.

Writers from many centuries and from quite different cultures have recognized this. In fact, I found so many poems on the theme of loss with age (Part 4) that it was difficult to choose which ones to include in this anthology. When poets do deal with the topic of aging, loss appears to be their main concern— and they dislike the change.

To contrast with the theme of loss, I deliberately sought poems that emphasized the wisdom and the growth of perspective and insight that can increase with age. I did not find as many as I had expected. Fortunately, unlike poets, many writers of short stories do capture this growth. Because those stories also dramatize other issues, they have been included in various sections of the book. However, they can also be read as examples of the theme of Part 3, old age as wisdom and peace. Stories such as "Grandma," "Old Man Minick," "A Village Singer," and "The Odd Old Lady" are jewels of insight that reflect the older person's ability to cut through peripheral issues and get to the heart of a matter. The individuals in these stories are straightforward and clear-thinking, and they have considerable insight. They understand the issues at hand, and they are ruggedly honest. Loss occurs in the lives of each, but because of their understanding of themselves and their own situations, none is brought down by the loss. Perspective, wisdom, and awareness are among the characteristics that allow each to cope with loss.

This brief volume represents my attempt to learn about aging from essayists and writers of fiction, after having learned about aging from gerontologists. In the introductions to the sections of the book, I have tried to integrate the thoughts of gerontologists with the ideas of those writers. This volume also represents my attempt to make available in one place, to readers interested in aging—which should include all of us—what some writers and essayists, especially those from the past and, to the extent that they are available in translation, those from other cultures, have thought about aging. It is an attempt to get beyond our own ethnocentrism and to approach the more universal truths about the multifaceted processes of aging. But many poems and stories (such as "Morituri Salutamus" by Henry Wadsworth Longfellow, Tillie Olsen's "Tell Me a Riddle," Nathaniel Hawthorne's "Dr. Heidegger's Experiment," "The Law of Life" by Jack London), essays, and plays (*Death of a Salesman* by Arthur Miller, Shakespeare's *King Lear*) could not be included here. The reader who wants to look further will find suggestions in the Sources for Further Reading on page 390.

Each of these references is limited. The reader who wants a cross-cultural and historical perspective that is more extensive will have to dig, explore, and sift through much literature, as I did, to find additional writings on aging. The exploring is likely to be productive and rewarding. One does have to sift through a great deal of extraneous material to find the additional statements and sources on aging. But those statements and sources are there. After all, the topic of aging, in one form or another, has been of universal interest throughout human history.

Many people have generously shared with me a number of short stories, novels, poems, and songs that they thought most clearly reflected the aging processes. For instance, each time I have mentioned to a psychology of aging class that I enjoy reading fiction and poetry on aging, a large number of students of various ages have brought me poetry to read—either poetry they or a friend had written or poetry they had read and enjoyed. It especially interested me that many of these students were not majors in a humanities department. Rather, they were concentrating in psychology, nursing, occupational therapy, sociology, physical therapy, or leisure and recreation.

Those who were most instrumental in suggesting the literary sources from which I made my selections were Paula Breen, Art Rauch, Ann Krause, Klaus Krause, and my husband, Bill Lyell. I am also most grateful to Bill for his enthusiasm for this anthology as it developed and for his interest in discussing ideas about some of the selections.

Nettie Foster, Terry Olivas, Barbara Schmidt, and Maggie Way took part in a small, spirited seminar at San José State University, New College, based on the manuscript of this book. Their insights into the many issues in aging that we discussed, based on the fiction in this anthology as well as on several novels, enabled me to see that the book was an idea whose time had more than come.

That this anthology has been published is a tribute to the keen insight of Matt Milan, my editor at Harcourt Brace Jovanovich, who recognized the potential appeal of an anthology of literature on aging. In moving it to actual book form, I was assisted by a highly competent copy editor, Eleanor Lahn, and by designer Nancy Kirsh and production manager Nancy Kalal of the Harcourt Brace Jovanovich staff.

Throughout, the interest and enthusiasm of a great many people for the idea that this volume represents sustained me in completing the project.

Ruth Granetz Lyell

Contents

Part Four
Loss   231

Part One

Generational Relationships

THERE IS A SUBTLE ANTAGONISM BETWEEN YOUTH AND OLD AGE THAT INFLU-
ences and often makes difficult the relationships among persons of different
generations. The young are entering society as productive members, each with
an unknown future, each with individual hopes, dreams, and uncertainties,
while the elderly are disengaging from society, often reluctantly and painfully,
and with little ahead that is better. Whenever there is competition in the use of
skills that decline with age, youth pushes aside the elderly, while the elderly
hold on by attempting to control economic resources and make decisions. Even
in cultures in which the elderly remain productive and retain some power, they
frequently feel some jealousy and resentment toward the young—while the
young often are either indifferent toward them, view them as old-fashioned, or
view them with feelings of repressed hostility. I know of no culture in which
there is not some animosity among persons of different ages.

The elderly were extremely successful in their power struggle in traditional
China, for example, because of the value of filial piety, sanctioned by the Con-
fucian Classics and reinforced and implemented for two thousand years by the
examination system. The elders had the power to make decisions for and rule
the entire extended family in accordance with their own perceptions, wishes,
and needs, and the young suffered in silent anguish. In agricultural families
generally, where the family was a self-contained economic system, the eldest
male ruled the family, often in an autocratic fashion; and this produced rebellious and antagonistic feelings in the young, who were expected to be submis-
sive and subordinate toward the elders.

While attitudes and treatment are less extreme in industrial cultures, there is
nonetheless considerable competition for prestige, power, respect, and material
assets, though at a more subtle level. Elders don't have the same socially
approved control over the young, but they often attempt to dominate and demand nonetheless and are reluctant to give up their authority. They attempt to
wield power over the middle-aged also—whom they see as young—through
endless requests, guilt-inducing hints, outright demands, and subtle compari-
sons. In a given family, this may keep a middle-aged son or daughter in a state
of high anxiety. At times the power struggle is reversed, with the independent
son or daughter treating the dependent elderly person as a subordinate by making his or her decisions, by not taking him or her seriously, and by not relating
to that person as an equal. This is not as likely to occur when the elderly person
remains independent: economically, behaviorally, and attitudinally.

"A Village Singer" (published in 1891—retirement is not a new problem!)
by Mary Wilkins Freeman (1852–1930) is a superb illustration of the power
struggle that is often contained in the youth-versus-old-age relationship. Candace Whitcomb, the leading soprano and the only paid musician in the large
choir of the local church for all of forty years, is forcibly and deviously retired
after her audience believes that her voice has lost its earlier quality. They

2

replace her with a younger soprano, Alma Way. Their deception is insulting to Candace, a strong, proud, and shrewd woman. She responds with anger toward them and toward her replacement. Note that her attitude of defiance in the face of severe rejection is just the opposite of the helpless attitude and passive behavior of Sudarshan Sharma in "The Gold Watch" (in Part 4) when he is also forcibly retired, for she fights back fiercely. This difference is consistent with research[1] that has found that women tend to grow increasingly assertive, dominant, strong, forceful, and self-confident with age, while men tend to become introspective, quiet, mellow, and less active as they age.[2]

The younger woman, Alma, clearly feels intimidated by Candace but is understanding and sympathetic. Candace's nephew, Wilson, however, fights her; and with him she uses her power to withhold her house and her money by threatening to change her will. She is a shrewd woman who uses power unflinchingly in a way that is appropriate to each opponent (with her peer, the minister, she points out that he too has worked in the church for forty years and will as likely be put out to pasture as she has been). Her attempts to intimidate her nephew are, however, unsuccessful. She mellows as her health declines and as she takes care of her unfinished business; but even then she does not give in completely. She remains independent and assertive.

Edna Ferber's story "Old Man Minick" was first published in 1922. With George S. Kaufman, Ferber (1887–1968) later wrote a play, "Minick," which dramatized this short story. The 1932 film "The Expert" was also based on the short story.

In "Old Man Minick," as in "A Village Singer," we find the theme of competition between persons of different generations whose life-styles conflict. Pa Minick is a widower who, immediately after the death of his wife of forty years, moves in with his son and daughter-in-law. Unlike his wife, they are not at all prepared to accept his idiosyncrasies and habits, nor he theirs, and he feels distant from them and lonely. He is miserable until he discovers his peers in the park nearby, for his peers accept him, argue with him, take him seriously, and view him as a person who is important to them.

In contrast, his son does not want the old man to visit him at work; his daughter-in-law does not especially want him at home; neither welcomes him to their parties; none of their friends is interested in what he has to say. He is simply there, utilizing their limited space. The problem is mutual: Minick is not in any way able to satisfy their needs—especially since he does not care for those

---

[1] Bernice L. Neugarten and David L. Gutmann, "Age-Sex Roles and Personality in Middle Age: A Thematic Apperception Study," in *Middle Age and Aging: A Reader in Social Psychology*, ed. Bernice L. Neugarten (Chicago: Univ. of Chicago Press, 1968), pp. 58–71. Though derived from the Thematic Apperception Test rather than directly from behavior, the findings have both face validity and support from other research.

[2] The mellowing process does not occur in Tom Garrison ("I Never Sang For My Father") and Grandfather Zisskind ("The Name"), probably because of the intensity of their unresolved anger, as those stories describe it. Mellowing involves contentment, satisfaction, and acceptance of one's life, while they instead are bitter.

needs—and they are not able to understand or to satisfy his. The two generations live in separate worlds under the same roof. Moreover, Minick disturbs their lives and they disturb his. They have the power to make decisions for him: what and when to eat, what habits he can keep, what he can and cannot do. They see him as sexless and brainless. He feels independent and fully himself only when away from them, such as when he is on the L and in the park. He can joke and converse easily only with his equals—the washerwoman, the sewing woman, and his peers in the park.

This story illustrates an issue that gerontologists argue: Is it preferable for an elderly person to live in an age-integrated or an age-segregated environment? An age-integrated environment for the elderly is one in which the individual lives in a neighborhood, building, or cluster of buildings with others around who are of all ages throughout the life cycle; while an age-segregated environment is one in which the neighbors are other elderly persons only. Sociologist Irving Rosow has stated these opposing views as follows.

> Professional people (medical practitioners, gerontologists, social workers, etc.) who work directly with the elderly are convinced that neighbors of different ages develop viable social relationships and mutual support. Such friendships, they believe, sustain the morale of older people as well as contribute to their youthfulness and independence. They therefore conclude that residential proximity of the generations should maximize the social integration of the aged.
>
> Social theorists take the opposite view. They feel that informal association develops around similar statuses, of which age is one extremely powerful factor. Consequently, social structure reinforces age-grading, erects barriers to intergenerational relations, and focuses friendship within age groups. Accordingly, residential proximity should not integrate the old and the young. Local friendships should develop more *within* than *between* generations, and old people are more likely to have friends of their own age than they are to have younger ones.[3]

In his research, Rosow found that older persons chose their friends from among other older persons rather than from persons of other generations and that residential proximity was often important in this choice, with the consequence that those elderly who did not live near other elderly were severely limited in their opportunities for friendship. The involuntary absence of friends often results in loneliness, low morale, overall dissatisfaction, confusion, forgetting, depression, and feelings of isolation and alienation, as Pa Minick experiences until he discovers his peers in the park. In studying Merrill Court, an age-segregated environment, sociologist Arlie Russell Hochschild observed the beneficial results of social and emotional support when elderly unrelated peers lived in the same apartment building and formed close-knit relationships with each other.[4]

[3] Irving Rosow, "Housing and Local Ties of the Aged," in Neugarten, pp. 382–89.

[4] Arlie Russell Hochschild, *The Unexpected Community* (Englewood Cliffs, N.J.: Prentice-Hall, 1973).

Her term *social siblings* refers to the bond that developed among them, a bond involving reciprocal caring and assistance, relationships rich in rivalries, disagreements, humor, satisfying activities, and devoid of indifference and loneliness. That is precisely what Pa Minick hopes to experience at the Grant Home.

We find three age-integrated environments in "Grandma" by Thyra Samter Winslow (1893–1961). Throughout the story, Grandma refers to herself only as mother, grandmother, and great-grandmother, never by name, for these roles are the bases of her relationships with all other people. She has a clear idea of what she expects in each relationship, but this expectation is never quite realized. None of her sons' or daughter's life-styles or family styles enables her to participate and feel comfortable with them in a way that is totally satisfying to her, even though there are some interesting differences among them.

At Fred's she is respected, productive, loved, part of the family, not lonely, and not isolated. There, however, she works constantly, and Fred's lack of affluence annoys and tires her. At Mary's, she feels the conflict, the dissension, that permeates that family life. Each member of the family is critical of everyone else, and Grandma is included as an object of their criticism. This of course makes her feel uncomfortable and unwelcome. At Albert's, where the family style is affluent and formal, the coldness, distance, and emotional isolation make her feel uncomfortable. There is no place for her in the lives of these people; she feels lonely and isolated. She has nothing to do, while each of them is busy. As occurs with Pa Minick, the offspring do not consider it appropriate for Grandma to join them in their activities; and the few times that she (and he) do so, Grandma (like Pa Minick) finds the activities not to her (and his) liking.

Here we see the basis of one kind of loneliness that many elderly persons experience: even though they are physically together, the *styles* of the generations are so different that the elderly person who does not share that style cannot fit into the everyday lives of the offspring. Grandma, like Pa Minick, is a visitor, an outsider, their dependent. Had it been *her* home that *they* visited, she would have been able to set the style and involve *them* in *her* activities. Since she is visiting *them,* she lacks the power to establish the style, the atmosphere, and the involvement of each with her.

It is only on the train between visits that she has the power to control her own life, determine her own style, and be the kind of grandma that she really wants to be. It is there that she is happiest.

"May and January" from "The Gulistan" is prose-poetry written by Sa'di (Sheikh Muslih-Uddin, Persian, 1184–1291) around 1258. "Over the River and Through the Wood" by John O'Hara (1905–1970) was first published in 1934. Both involve a similar kind of put-down that some elderly men experience: severe and painful rejection and humiliation of an old man by a young woman. Though written in quite different cultures and some seven hundred years apart, both see youth as being more desirable, attractive, interesting, and beautiful than old age. In both instances, the man admires youth to an extreme degree. The elderly man in both is viewed as irrelevant; younger people are indifferent toward him, and he is defeated by the young and by youth.

In "May and January," the young woman is short-sighted and undiscerning, and the author seems to see her as a fool. In "Over the River," the granddaughter and her friends are self-centered, insensitive, and snobbish. Their attitude toward Mr. Winfield is one of indifference, and they do not want him to intrude. Mr. Winfield does not criticize them for this—he does not criticize them for anything—so caught up is he in his perception of them as magnificent simply because they are young. What is the basis of their appeal? To him they represent pure potential; freshness; an open, unblemished future that has not yet been tarnished with mistakes, conflicts, decisions, and uncertainties. Though he scarcely knows Miss Farnsworth, he attributes to her an abundance of outstanding characteristics, unhesitatingly thinking of her as an extraordinary person. In the process, he becomes severely self-critical, runs himself down, expresses regrets about his life, sees himself as a has-been who has made too many mistakes and as a failure. His is a story of continual defeat and disappointment over the years in which he has yielded to his family's wishes and needs rather than his own, without the family's having appreciated or even known about his sacrifices. Now he feels sorry for himself, and is thinking about his lost youth, unactualized, at the moment when he is destroyed by youth.

He imagines that Miss Farnsworth will be what he has not been. She is not the sort of person who makes mistakes, so he thinks. Then this person, whom he has put on a pedestal and idealized, completely destroys him—with his help. He has worshiped youth, and youth has rejected him because he is old.

I Never Sang For My Father by Robert Anderson (born 1917), published in 1968, raises two important points about generational relations. First, how can an adult son or daughter respond to and relate to an elderly parent in such a way as to satisfy both the elder's needs and his or her own needs—especially when the two sets of needs are incompatible, and the offspring has compromised but the elder refuses to do so? There are many sons and daughters, of various ages throughout adulthood, who have given themselves completely and without relief to a constantly demanding parent. Life passes them by—work, marriage, children, interests—one or more of which they have sacrificed to care for the parent. It is a problem that is less difficult to deal with when the parent is overtly hostile or demanding; it is more difficult when the message is a subtle one.

This contemporary play is a superb illustration of the hold the overtly rejecting parent has on his offspring. The domineering father, Tom, guilty of father-smother love (which, as it usually does, masks repressed as well as not-so-repressed rejection), demands that his widowed son not remarry and move away so that the son, Gene, can maintain the routine of relating to and serving the father. Enjoyment in this relationship has been minimal for Gene because his father is bitter about his early life and demands that his family of procreation make up for his prior unhappiness. Tom is not interested in anything that Gene wants to talk about or finds satisfying: his work, his books, his perceptions of life, his feelings about his late wife Carol and his fiancée Peggy. Yet Tom demands that Gene share *his* interests: attending Rotary luncheons, watching television, allowing him the pleasure of having a son who was a Marine—all of which Gene goes along with but does not enjoy. While Gene is a gentle person, Tom is a bigot—pompous, self-centered, and crass, who uses his power over his wife, daughter, and son unhesitatingly, making their lives with him unhappy. Gene finally recognizes that his father is too bitter and obsessed with the past to make room for Gene in his life, and he successfully extricates himself from his father's hold.

The second important point that this play raises and illustrates is that one person's unresolved anger can be so self-defeating that it only results in making life painful for that person and his family. Tom is so obsessed with his father's rejection of him that he cannot live in the present. He has so much self-pity and anger, as well as guilt, from his past experiences with his own father that he cannot form a giving and accepting relationship with his son, daughter, or wife; yet he desperately wants this kind of relationship. He is jealous and resentful of them because they have not been neglected. Many of his conversations include boring repetition of some aspect of his early experience that obsesses him. Paradoxically, were he able to change, and were he open to this new experience, he would find the love and acceptance that he craves and has not had in the past, for his wife, daughter, and son are loving toward him and accepting of him. He is unable to accept and experience their love, yet he yearns for love. Because of his past unresolved conflicts, he rejects them and makes life miserable for them and for himself. As he ages, he is unable to enjoy his inner thoughts and feelings because he is so angry, and he becomes increasingly bitter about his life.

Both Tom and Grandfather Zisskind, in "The Name," have not completed their grief work for the dead: both continually repeat their stories because they cannot achieve closure, they cannot resolve their past conflicts; and neither has been able to work through his guilt feelings toward the dead—all of which prevents both of them from relating in any positive way to the living.

Aharon Megged, author of "The Name," was born in Poland and moved to Israel in 1926 at the age of 6. In this story we find another bitter old man whose obsession with the past seriously interferes with his enjoyment of the present. Grandfather Zisskind's obsession with the painful loss of his son and grandson prevents him from appreciating, enjoying, finding worth in, or even noticing his daughter Rachel, his granddaughter, her husband, and his new great-grandson, all of whom are available to him now. He is fixated on the past and on tradition, so traumatic have the events of his past been—so much so that he ignores all the positive characteristics of Rachel, Raya, Yehuda, and Ehud. They too might represent the continuity with the past that he so desperately wants, were he not obsessed with his particular idea of continuity.

This complex story nicely illustrates the conflict between generations surrounding the use of power. Who holds the power in this family? The young couple have the power to name their son. The old man has the power to withhold affection and attention from them. It is a no-win situation. The young couple wants to create their own world, their own identity, while the old man seeks continuity with the past. They are not interested in the Ashkenazic Jewish custom of naming a baby after an admired dead family member in order to carry on the name and the memory of the beloved deceased. They see this as a custom that emanates from the past, from the ghetto, with which they are not familiar. To them it is a custom from the *Golah*—from outside Israel, from the time when the Jews were dispersed. It is as foreign, unpleasant, different, and old to them as Grandfather Zisskind's fermenting preserves. They were born in Israel and they want the new, the modern, the contemporary; so they want a Hebrew name for their son rather than a Yiddish name. It is a common characteristic of persons of different generations in a changing culture that the old favor the past, the tradition, while the young favor the present and future, the contemporary.

It is also noteworthy that while in his state of despair and depression, Grandfather Zisskind is severely confused and forgetful, bewildered, and repetitive—some of the symptoms of the syndrome called senility. Yet once he has a purpose, a cause that he deeply believes in and which is part of his total being, he blossoms. He argues logically, consistently, eloquently, passionately, and his thoughts are not at all confused. He is coherent and sharp, while his young grandson-in-law seems confused. Once he has lost what he thought was his battle, however, he again becomes confused, befuddled, slow, and repetitive, for he has lost hope.

The 1967 story "Search for a Future" by Arthur Miller (born 1915) presents quite a different type of relationship between generations from any of the preceding selections. Here the elderly man and his son have a close and warm relationship in which love and respect are mutual. Hence the elder is still a role model to his son during a period in which the son experiences self-doubt and ambivalence.

The son, a successful actor of over forty, feels that his life has become too stale, too routine. He feels unfulfilled because everything in his life is so habitual. Psychoanalyst Erik Erikson calls this a crisis of generativity versus stagnation[5]—in which the middle-aged person finds too much sameness and security in life and no challenges, but at the same time realizes that while his or her own life is finite, life itself will go on. This person might attempt to resolve the crisis by reaching out to help younger persons, the next generation, as Harry does in attending the antiwar rally and in being concerned about the young men who are being killed or mutilated in the war.

"Mid-life crisis" or "occupational menopause" are also terms to describe Harry's self-assessment and self-doubt, which occur to varying degrees in many men over a wide age range, from forty to sixty. They assess their accomplishments against their earlier hopes and aspirations and often feel that they have not done with their lives what earlier they really wanted to do. Frequently they hate themselves for the compromises they have made along the

[5] Erik H. Erikson, *Childhood and Society* (New York: W. W. Norton, 1950), p. 231.

way and for the security that they have settled for instead of continuing to pursue their dreams.

Harry's father, though seriously ill, becomes a role model to his son, which is possible because of the respect and love they have had for each other. His father has not given up, has not stagnated, still has hope, is spontaneous and fresh; and his son admires him. Harry wants to make his own life more real by re-experiencing the freshness and spontaneity that he has lost. In contrast to Tom Garrison, Harry's father is a role model of integrity, for he has enjoyed and accepted his life as he lived it. Because he has felt good about his life, he is able to have a beneficial influence on his son.

An elderly person also has a beneficial influence on Cress Delahanty in the 1953 story "Sixteen," the final chapter of the novel *Cress Delahanty,* by Jessamyn West (born 1907). Cress is a free spirit, enjoying life, independence, her freedom, and her own feelings and thoughts while away from home at college. Hers is the egocentric exuberance of youth, which makes her think that only she and her friends, her peers, can experience the beauty of nature. She is surprised to learn that her eighty-year-old dying grandfather also likes flowers, for years earlier he had thrown them out soon after her grandmother died. Cress had misunderstood that behavior and did not realize that she had misunderstood it at the time, and thought that he was both unappreciative of natural beauty and insensitive. Discovering his fondness for flowers makes her suddenly aware of the basic similarity of the two of them in life. It is a growth experience for her of considerable magnitude.

A Village Singer

Mary Wilkins Freeman

The trees were in full leaf, a heavy south wind was blowing, and there was a loud murmur among the new leaves. The people noticed it, for it was the first time that year that the trees had so murmured in the wind. The spring had come with a rush during the last few days.

The murmur of the trees sounded loud in the village church, where the people sat waiting for the service to begin. The windows were open; it was a very warm Sunday for May.

The church was already filled with this soft sylvan music—the tender harmony of the leaves and the south wind, and the sweet, desultory whistles of birds—when the choir arose and began to sing.

In the centre of the row of women singers stood Alma Way. All the people stared at her, and turned their ears critically. She was the new leading soprano. Candace Whitcomb, the old one, who had sung in the choir for forty years, had lately been given her dismissal. The audience considered that her voice had grown too cracked and uncertain on the upper notes. There had been much complaint, and after long deliberation the church-officers had made known their decision as mildly as possible to the old singer. She had sung for the last time the Sunday before, and Alma Way had been engaged to take her place. With the exception of the organist, the leading soprano was the only paid musician in the large choir. The salary was very modest, still the village people considered it large for a young woman. Alma was from the adjoining village of East Derby; she had quite a local reputation as a singer.

Now she fixed her large solemn blue eyes; her long, delicate face, which had been pretty, turned paler; the blue flowers on her bonnet trembled; her little thin gloved hands, clutching the singing-book, shook perceptibly; but she sang out bravely. That most formidable mountain-height of the world, self-distrust and timidity, arose before her, but her nerves were braced for its ascent. In the midst of the hymn she had a solo; her voice rang out piercingly sweet; the people nodded admiringly at each other; but suddenly there was a stir; all the faces turned toward the windows on the south side of the church. Above the din of the wind and the birds, above Alma Way's sweetly straining tones, arose another female voice, singing another hymn to another tune.

"It's her," the women whispered to each other; they were half aghast, half smiling.

Candace Whitcomb's cottage stood close to the south side of the church. She was playing on her parlor organ, and singing, to drown out the voice of her rival.

10

Alma caught her breath; she almost stopped; the hymn-book waved like a fan; then she went on. But the long husky drone of the parlor organ and the shrill clamor of the other voice seemed louder than anything else.

When the hymn was finished, Alma sat down. She felt faint; the woman next to her slipped a peppermint into her hand. "It ain't worth minding," she whispered, vigorously. Alma tried to smile; down in the audience a young man was watching her with a kind of fierce pity.

In the last hymn Alma had another solo. Again the parlor organ droned above the carefully delicate accompaniment of the church organ, and again Candace Whitcomb's voice clamored forth in another tune.

After the benediction, the other singers pressed around Alma. She did not say much in return for their expressions of indignation and sympathy. She wiped her eyes furtively once or twice, and tried to smile. William Emmons, the choir leader, elderly, stout, and smooth-faced, stood over her, and raised his voice. He was the old musical dignitary of the village, the leader of the choral club and the singing-schools. "A most outrageous proceeding," he said. People had coupled his name with Candace Whitcomb's. The old bachelor tenor and old maiden soprano had been wont to walk together to her home next door after the Saturday night rehearsals, and they had sung duets to the parlor organ. People had watched sharply her old face, on which the blushes of youth sat pitifully, when William Emmons entered the singing-seats. They wondered if he would ever ask her to marry him.

And now he said further to Alma Way that Candace Whitcomb's voice had failed utterly of late, that she sang shockingly, and ought to have had sense enough to know it.

When Alma went down into the audience-room, in the midst of the chattering singers, who seemed to have descended, like birds, from song flights to chirps, the minister approached her. He had been waiting to speak to her. He was a steady-faced, fleshy old man, who had preached from that one pulpit over forty years. He told Alma, in his slow way, how much he regretted the annoyance to which she had been subjected, and intimated that he would endeavor to prevent a recurrence of it. "Miss Whitcomb—must be—reasoned with," said he; he had a slight hesitation of speech, not an impediment. It was as if his thoughts did not slide readily into his words, although both were present. He walked down the aisle with Alma, and bade her good-morning when he saw Wilson Ford waiting for her in the doorway. Everybody knew that Wilson Ford and Alma were lovers; they had been for the last ten years.

Alma colored softly, and made a little imperceptible motion with her head; her silk dress and the lace on her mantle fluttered, but she did not speak. Neither did Wilson, although they had not met before that day. They did not look at each other's faces—they seemed to see each other without that—and they walked along side to side.

They reached the gate before Candace Whitcomb's little house. Wilson looked past the front yard, full of pink and white spikes on flowering bushes, at the lace-curtained windows; a thin white profile, stiffly inclined, apparently over a book, was visible at one of them. Wilson gave his head a shake. He was a stout man, with features so strong that they overcame his flesh. "I'm going up home with you, Alma," said he; "and then—I'm coming back, to give Aunt Candace one blowing up."

"Oh, don't, Wilson."

"Yes, I shall. If you want to stand this kind of a thing you may; I sha'n't."

"There's no need of your talking to her. Mr. Pollard's going to."

"Did he say he was?"

"Yes. I think he's going in before the afternoon meeting, from what he said."

"Well, there's one thing about it, if she does that thing again this afternoon, I'll go in there and break that old organ up into kindling-wood." Wilson set his mouth hard, and shook his head again.

Alma gave little side glances up at him, her tone was deprecatory, but her face was full of soft smiles. "I suppose she does feel dreadfully about it," said she. "I can't help feeling kind of guilty, taking her place."

"I don't see how you're to blame. It's outrageous, her acting so."

"The choir gave her a photograph album last week, didn't they?"

"Yes. They went there last Thursday night, and gave her an album and a surprise-party. She ought to behave herself."

"Well, she's sung there so long, I suppose it must be dreadful hard for her to give it up."

Other people going home from church were very near Wilson and Alma. She spoke softly that they might not hear; he did not lower his voice in the least. Presently Alma stopped before a gate.

"What are you stopping here for?" asked Wilson.

"Minnie Lansing wanted me to come and stay with her this noon."

"You're going home with me."

"I'm afraid I'll put your mother out."

"Put mother out! I told her you were coming, this morning. She's got all ready for you. Come along; don't stand here."

He did not tell Alma of the pugnacious spirit with which his mother had received the announcement of her coming, and how she had stayed at home to prepare the dinner, and make a parade of her hard work and her injury.

Wilson's mother was the reason why he did not marry Alma. He would not take his wife home to live with her, and was unable to support separate establishments. Alma was willing enough to be married and put up with Wilson's mother, but she did not complain of his decision. Her delicate blond features grew sharper, and her blue eyes more hollow. She had had a certain fine prettiness, but now she was losing it, and beginning to look old, and there was a prim, angular, old maiden carriage about her narrow shoulders.

Wilson never noticed it, and never thought of Alma as not possessed of eternal youth, or capable of losing or regretting it.

"Come along, Alma," said he; and she followed meekly after him down the street.

Soon after they passed Candace Whitcomb's house, the minister went up the front walk and rang the bell. The pale profile at the window had never stirred as he opened the gate and came up the walk. However, the door was promptly opened, in response to his ring. "Good-morning, Miss Whitcomb," said the minister.

"*Good*-morning." Candace gave a sweeping toss of her head as she spoke. There was a fierce upward curl to her thin nostrils and her lips, as if she scented an adversary. Her black eyes had two tiny cold sparks of fury in them, like an enraged bird's. She did not ask the minister to enter, but he stepped lumberingly into the entry, and she retreated rather than led the way into her little parlor. He settled into the great rocking-chair and wiped his face. Candace sat down again in her old place by the window. She was a tall woman, but very slender and full of pliable motions, like a blade of grass.

"It's a—very pleasant day," said the minister.

Candace made no reply. She sat still, with her head drooping. The wind stirred the looped lace-curtains; a tall rose-tree outside the window waved; soft shadows floated through the room. Candace's parlor organ stood in front of an open window that faced the church; on the corner was a pitcher with a bunch of white lilacs. The whole room was scented with them. Presently the minister looked over at them and sniffed pleasantly.

"You have—some beautiful—lilacs there."

Candace did not speak. Every line of her slender figure looked flexible, but it was a flexibility more resistant than rigor.

The minister looked at her. He filled up the great rocking-chair; his arms in his shiny black coat-sleeves rested squarely and comfortably upon the hair-cloth arms of the chair.

"Well, Miss Whitcomb, I suppose I—may as well come to—the point. There was—a little—matter I wished to speak to you about. I don't suppose you were—at least I can't suppose you were—aware of it, but—this morning, during the singing by the choir, you played and—sung a little too—loud. That is, with—the windows open. It—disturbed us—a little. I hope you won't feel hurt—my dear Miss Candace, but I knew you would rather I would speak of it, for I knew—you would be more disturbed than anybody else at the idea of such a thing."

Candace did not raise her eyes; she looked as if his words might sway her through the window. "I ain't disturbed at it," said she. "I did it on purpose; I meant to."

The minister looked at her.

"You needn't look at me. I know jest what I'm about. I sung the way I did on purpose, an' I'm goin' to do it again, an' I'd like to see you stop me. I guess I've got a right to set down to my own organ, an' sing a psalm tune on a Sabbath day, 'f I want to; an' there ain't no amount of talkin' an' palaverin' a-goin' to stop me. See there!'' Candace swung aside her skirts a little. ''Look at that!''

The minister looked. Candace's feet were resting on a large red-plush photograph album.

''Makes a nice footstool, don't it?'' said she.

The minister looked at the album, then at her; there was a slowly gathering alarm in his face; he began to think she was losing her reason.

Candace had her eyes full upon him now, and her head up. She laughed, and her laugh was almost a snarl. ''Yes; I thought it would make a beautiful footstool,'' said she. ''I've been wantin' one for some time.'' Her tone was full of vicious irony.

''Why, miss—'' began the minister; but she interrupted him:

''I know what you're a-goin' to say, Mr. Pollard, an' now I'm goin' to have my say; I'm a-goin' to speak. I want to know what you think of folks that pretend to be Christians treatin' anybody the way they've treated me? Here I've sung in those singin'-seats forty year. I ain't never missed a Sunday, except when I've been sick, an' I've gone an' sung a good many times when I'd better been in bed, an' now I'm turned out without a word of warnin'. My voice is jest as good as ever 'twas; there can't anybody say it ain't. It wa'n't ever quite so high-pitched as that Way girl's, mebbe; but she flats the whole durin' time. My voice is as good an' high today as it was twenty years ago; an' if it wa'n't, I'd like to know where the Christianity comes in. I'd like to know if it wouldn't be more to the credit of folks in a church to keep an old singer an' an old minister, if they didn't sing an' hold forth quite so smart as they used to, ruther than turn 'em off an' hurt their feelin's. I guess it would be full as much to the glory of God. S'pose the singin' an' the preachin' wa'n't quite so good, what difference would it make? Salvation don't hang on anybody's hittin' a high note, that I ever heard of. Folks are gettin' as high-steppin' an' fussy in a meetin'-house as they are in a tavern, nowadays. S'pose they should turn you off, Mr. Pollard, come an' give you a photograph album, an' tell you to clear out, how'd you like it? I ain't findin' any fault with your preachin'; it was always good enough to suit me; but it don't stand to reason folks'll be as took up with your sermons as when you was a young man. You can't expect it. S'pose they should turn you out in your old age, an' call in some young bob squirt, how'd you feel? There's William Emmons, too; he's three years older'n I am, if he does lead the choir an' run all the singin' in town. If my voice has gi'en out, it stan's to reason his has. It ain't, though. William Emmons sings jest as well as he ever did. Why don't they turn him out the way they have me, an' give him a photograph album? I dun know but it would be a good idea to send everybody, as soon as they get a little old an' gone by, an' young folks begin to push, onto some desert island, an' give 'em each a photograph album. Then they can sit down an' look at pictures the rest of their days. Mebbe government'll take it up.

''There they come here last week Thursday, all the choir, jest about eight o'clock in the evenin', an' pretended they'd come to give me a nice little surprise. Surprise! h'm! Brought cake an' oranges, an' was jest as nice as they could be, an' I was real tickled. I never had a surprise-party before in my life. Jenny Carr she played, an' they wanted me to sing alone, an' I never suspected a thing. I've been mad ever since to think what a fool I was, an' how they must have laughed in their sleeves.

"When they'd gone I found this photograph album on the table, all done up as nice as you please, an' directed to Miss Candace Whitcomb from her many friends, an' I opened it, an' there was the letter inside givin' me notice to quit.

"If they'd gone about it any decent way, told me right out honest that they'd got tired of me, an' wanted Alma Way to sing instead of me, I wouldn't minded so much; I should have been hurt 'nough, for I'd felt as if some that had pretended to be my friends wa'n't; but it wouldn't have been as bad as this. They said in the letter that they'd always set great value on my services, an' it wa'n't from any lack of appreciation that they turned me off, but they thought the duty was gettin' a little too arduous for me. H'm! I hadn't complained. If they'd turned me right out fair an' square, showed me the door, an' said, 'Here, you get out,' but to go an' spill molasses, as it were, all over the threshold, tryin' to make me think it's all nice an' sweet—

"I'd sent that photograph album back quick's I could pack it, but I didn't know who started it, so I've used it for a footstool. It's all it's good for, 'cordin' to my way of thinkin'. An' I ain't been particular to get the dust off my shoes before I used it neither."

Mr. Pollard, the minister, sat staring. He did not look at Candace; his eyes were fastened upon a point straight ahead. He had a look of helpless solidity, like a block of granite. This country minister, with his steady, even temperament, treading with heavy precision his one track for over forty years, having nothing new in his life except the new sameness of the seasons, and desiring nothing new, was incapable of understanding a woman like this, who had lived as quietly as he, and all the time held within herself the elements of revolution. He could not account for such violence, such extremes, except in a loss of reason. He had a conviction that Candace was getting beyond herself. He himself was not a typical New Englander; the national elements of character were not pronounced in him. He was aghast and bewildered at this outbreak, which was tropical, and more than tropical, for a New England nature has a floodgate, and the power which it releases is an accumulation. Candace Whitcomb had been a quiet woman, so delicately resolute that the quality had been scarcely noticed in her, and her ambition had been unsuspected. Now the resolution and the ambition appeared raging over her whole self.

She began to talk again. "I've made up my mind that I'm goin' to sing Sundays the way I did this mornin', an' I don't care what folks say," said she. "I've made up my mind that I'm goin' to take matters into my own hands. I'm goin' to let folks see that I ain't trod down quite flat, that there's a little rise left in me. I ain't goin' to give up beat yet a while; an' I'd like to see anybody stop me. If I ain't got a right to play a psalm tune on my organ an' sing, I'd like to know. If you don't like it, you can move the meetin'-house."

Candace had had an inborn reverence for clergymen. She had always treated Mr. Pollard with the utmost deference. Indeed, her manner toward all men had been marked by a certain delicate stiffness and dignity. Now she was talking to the old minister with the homely freedom with which she might have addressed a female gossip over the back fence. He could not say much in return. He did not feel competent to make headway against any such tide of passion; all he could do was to let it beat against him. He made a few expostulations, which increased Candace's vehemence; he expressed his regret over the whole affair, and suggested that they should kneel and ask the guidance of the Lord in the matter, that she might be led to see it all in a different light.

Candace refused flatly. "I don't see any use prayin' about it," said she. "I don't think the Lord's got much to do with it, anyhow."

It was almost time for the afternoon service when the minister left. He had missed his comfortable noontide rest, through this encounter with his revolutionary parishioner. After the minister had gone, Candace sat by the window and waited. The bell rang, and she watched the people file past. When her nephew Wilson Ford with Alma appeared, she grunted to herself. "She's thin as a rail," said she; "guess there won't be much left of her by the time Wilson gets her. Little softspoken nippin' thing, she wouldn't make him no kind of a wife, anyway. Guess it's jest as well."

When the bell had stopped tolling, and all the people entered the church, Candace went over to her organ and seated herself. She arranged a singing-book before her, and sat still, waiting. Her thin, colorless neck and temples were full of beating pulses; her black eyes were bright and eager; she leaned stiffly over toward the music-rack, to hear better. When the church organ sounded out she straightened herself; her long skinny fingers pressed her own organ-keys with nervous energy. She worked the pedals with all her strength; all her slender body was in motion. When the first notes of Alma's solo began, Candace sang. She had really possessed a fine voice, and it was wonderful how little she had lost it. Straining her throat with jealous fury, her notes were still for the main part true. Her voice filled the whole room; she sang with wonderful fire and expression. That, at least, mild little Alma Way could never emulate. She was full of steadfastness and unquestioning constancy, but there were in her no smouldering fires of ambition and resolution. Music was not to her what it had been to her older rival. To this obscure woman, kept relentlessly by circumstances in a narrow track, singing in the village choir had been as much as Italy was to Napoleon—and now on her island of exile she was still showing fight.

After the church service was done, Candace left the organ and went over to her old chair by the window. Her knees felt weak, and shook under her. She sat down, and leaned back her head. There were red spots on her cheeks. Pretty soon she heard a quick slam of her gate, and an impetuous tread on the gravel-walk. She looked up, and there was her nephew Wilson Ford hurrying up to the door. She cringed a little, then she settled herself more firmly in her chair.

Wilson came into the room with a rush. He left the door open, and the wind slammed it to after him.

"Aunt Candace, where are you?" he called out, in a loud voice.

She made no reply. He looked around fiercely, and his eyes seemed to pounce upon her.

"Look here, Aunt Candace," said he, "are you crazy?" Candace said nothing. "Aunt Candace!" She did not seem to see him. "If you don't answer me," said Wilson, "I'll just go over there and pitch that old organ out of the window!"

"Wilson Ford!" said Candace, in a voice that was almost a scream.

"Well, what say! What have you got to say for yourself, acting the way you have? I tell you what 'tis, Aunt Candace, I won't stand it."

"I'd like to see you help yourself."

"I will help myself. I'll pitch that old organ out of the window, and then I'll board up the window on that side of your house. Then we'll see."

"It ain't your house, and it won't never be."

"Who said it was my house? You're my aunt, and I've got a little lookout for the credit of the family. Aunt Candace, what are you doing this way for?"

"It don't made no odds what I'm doin' so for. I ain't bound to give my reasons to a young fellar like you, if you do act so mighty toppin'. But I'll tell you one thing, Wilson Ford, after the way you've spoke today, you sha'n't never have one cent of my money, an' you can't never marry that Way girl if you don't have it. You can't never take her home to live with your mother, an' this house would have been might nice an' convenient for you some day. Now you won't get it. I'm goin' to make another will. I'd made one, if you did but know it. Now you won't get a cent of my money, you nor your mother neither. An' I ain't goin' to live a dreadful while longer, neither. Now I wish you'd go home; I want to lay down. I'm 'bout sick."

Wilson could not get another word from his aunt. His indignation had not in the least cooled. Her threat of disinheriting him did not cow him at all; he had too much rough independence, and indeed his aunt Candace's house had always been too much of an air-castle for him to comtemplate seriously. Wilson, with his burly frame and his headlong common-sense, could have little to do with air-castles, had he been hard enough to build them over graves. Still, he had not admitted that he never could marry Alma. All his hopes were based upon a rise in his own fortunes, not by some sudden convulsion, but by his own long and steady labor. Some time, he thought, he should have saved enough for the two homes.

He went out of his aunt's house still storming. She arose after the door had shut behind him, and got out into the kitchen. She thought that she would start a fire and make a cup of tea. She had not eaten anything all day. She put some kindling-wood into the stove and touched a match to it; then she went back to the sitting-room, and settled down again into the chair by the window. The fire in the kitchen-stove roared, and the light wood was soon burned out. She thought no more about it. She had not put on the teakettle. Her head ached, and once in a while she shivered. She sat at the window while the afternoon waned and the dusk came on. At seven o'clock the meeting bell rang again, and the people flocked by. This time she did not stir. She had shut her parlor organ. She did not need to out-sing her rival this evening; there was only congregational singing at the Sunday-night prayer-meeting.

She sat still until it was nearly time for meeting to be done; her head ached harder and harder, and she shivered more. Finally she arose. "Guess I'll go to bed," she muttered. She went about the house, bent over and shaking, to lock the doors. She stood a minute in the back door, looking over the fields to the woods. There was a red light over there. "The woods are on fire," said Candace. She watched with a dull interest the flames roll up, withering and destroying the tender green spring foliage. The air was full of smoke, although the fire was half a mile away.

Candace locked the door and went in. The trees with their delicate garlands of new leaves, with the new nests of song birds, might fall, she was in the roar of an intenser fire; the growths of all her springs and the delicate wontedness of her whole life were going down in it. Candace went to bed in her little room off the parlor, but she could not sleep. She lay awake all night. In the morning she crawled to the door and hailed a little boy who was passing. She bade him go for the doctor as quickly as he could, then to Mrs. Ford's, and ask her to come over. She held on to the door while she was talking. The boy stood staring wonderingly at her. The spring wind fanned her face. She had drawn on a dress skirt and put her shawl over her shoulders, and her gray hair was blowing over her red cheeks.

She shut the door and went back to her bed. She never arose from it again. The doctor and Mrs. Ford came and looked after her, and she lived a week. Nobody but herself thought until the very last that she would die; the doctor called her illness merely a light run of fever; she had her senses fully.

But Candace gave up at the first. "It's my last sickness," she said to Mrs. Ford that morning when she first entered; and Mrs. Ford had laughed at the notion; but the sick woman held to it. She did not seem to suffer much physical pain; she only grew weaker and weaker, but she was distressed mentally. She did not talk much, but her eyes followed everybody with an agonized expression.

On Wednesday William Emmons came to inquire for her. Candace heard him out in the parlor. She tried to raise herself on one elbow that she might listen better to his voice.

"William Emmons come in to ask how you was," Mrs. Ford said, after he was gone.

"I—heard him," replied Candace. Presently she spoke again. "Nancy," said she, "where's that photograph album?"

"On the table," replied her sister, hesitatingly.

"Mebbe—you'd better—brush it up a little."

"Well."

Sunday morning Candace wished that the minister should be asked to come in at the noon intermission. She had refused to see him before. He came and prayed with her, and she asked his forgiveness for the way she had spoken the Sunday before. "I—hadn't ought to—spoke so," said she. "I was—dreadful wrought up."

"Perhaps it was your sickness coming on," said the minister smoothingly.

Candace shook her head. "No—it wa'n't. I hope the Lord will—forgive me."

After the minister had gone, Candace still appeared unhappy. Her pitiful eyes followed her sister everywhere with the mechanical persistency of a portrait.

"What is it you want, Candace?" Mrs. Ford said at last. She had nursed her sister faithfully, but once in a while her impatience showed itself.

"Nancy!"

"What say?"

"I wish—you'd go out when—meetin's done, an'—head off Alma an' Wilson, an'—ask 'em to come in. I feel as if—I'd like to—hear her sing."

Mrs. Ford stared. "Well," said she.

The meeting was now in session. The windows were all open, for it was another warm Sunday. Candace lay listening to the music when it began, and a look of peace came over her face. Her sister had smoothed her hair back, and put on a clean cap. The white curtain in the bedroom window waved in the wind like a white sail. Candace almost felt as if she were better, but the thought of death seemed easy.

Mrs. Ford at the parlor window watched for the meeting to be out. When the people appeared, she ran down the walk and waited for Alma and Wilson. When they came she told them what Candace wanted, and they all went in together.

"Here's Alma an' Wilson, Candace," said Mrs. Ford, leading them to the bedroom door.

Candace smiled. "Come in," she said, feebly. And Alma and Wilson entered and stood beside the bed. Candace continued to look at them, the smile straining her lips.

"Wilson!"

"What is it, Aunt Candace?"

"I ain't altered that—will. You an' Alma can—come here an'—live—when I'm—gone. Your mother won't mind livin' alone. Alma can have—all—my things."

"Don't, Aunt Candace." Tears were running over Wilson's cheeks, and Alma's delicate face was all of a quiver.

"I thought—maybe—Alma 'd be willin' to—sing for me," said Candace.

"What do you want me to sing?" Alma asked, in a trembling voice.

" 'Jesus, lover of my soul.' "

Alma, standing there beside Wilson, began to sing. At first she could hardly control her voice, then she sang sweetly and clearly.

Candace lay and listened. Her face had a holy and radiant expression. When Alma stopped singing it did not disappear, but she looked up and spoke, and it was like a secondary glimpse of the old shape of a forest tree through the smoke and flame of the transfiguring fire the instant before it falls. "You flatted a little on—soul," said Candace.

Old Man Minick

Edna Ferber

His wife had always spoiled him outrageously. No doubt of that. Take, for example, the matter of the pillows merely. Old man Minick slept high. That is, he thought he slept high. He liked two plump pillows on his side of the great, wide, old-fashioned cherry bed. He would sink into them with a vast grunting and sighing and puffing expressive of nerves and muscles relaxed and gratified. But in the morning there was always one pillow on the floor. He had thrown it there. Always, in the morning, there it lay, its plump, white cheek turned reproachfully up at him from the side of the bed. Ma Minick knew this, naturally, after forty years of the cherry bed. But she never begrudged him that extra pillow. Each morning when she arose, she picked it up on her way to shut the window. Each morning the bed was made up with two pillows on his side of it, as usual.

Then there was the window. Ma Minick liked it open wide. Old man Minick, who rather prided himself on his modernism (he called it being up to date), was distrustful of the night air. In the folds of its sable mantle lurked a swarm of dread things—cold, clammy miasmas, fevers.

"Night air's like any other air," Ma Minick would say, with some asperity. Ma Minick was no worm; and as modern as he. So when they went to bed the window would be open wide. They would lie there, the two old ones, talking comfortably about commonplace things. The kind of talk that goes on between a man and woman who have lived together in wholesome peace (spiced with occasional wholesome bickerings) for more than forty years.

"Remind me to see Gerson to-morrow about that lock on the basement door. The paper's full of burglars."

"If I think of it." She never failed to.

"George and Nettie haven't been over in a week now."

"Oh, well, young folks. . . . Did you stop in and pay that Koritz the fifty cents for pressing your suit?"

"By golly, I forgot again! First thing in the morning."

A sniff. "Just smell the yards." It was Chicago.

"Wind must be from the west."

Sleep came with reluctant feet, but they wooed her patiently. And presently she settled down between them and they slept lightly. Usually, some time during the night, he awoke, slid cautiously and with infinite stealth from beneath the covers, and closed the wide-flung window to within a bare two inches of the sill. Almost invariably she heard him; but she was a wise old woman; a philosopher of parts. She knew better than to allow a window to shatter the peace of their marital felicity. As she lay there, smiling a little grimly in the dark and giving no sign of being awake, she thought, "Oh, well, I guess a closed window won't kill me either."

Still, sometimes, just to punish him a little, and to prove that she was nobody's fool, she would wait until he had dropped off to sleep again and then she, too, would achieve a stealthy trip to the window and would raise it slowly, carefully, inch by inch.

"How did that window come to be open?" he would say in the morning, being a poor dissembler.

"Window? Why, it's just the way it was when we went to bed." And she would stoop to pick up the pillow that lay on the floor.

There was little or no talk of death between this comfortable, active, sound-appearing man of almost seventy and this plump, capable woman of sixty-six. But as always, between husband and wife, it was understood wordlessly (and without reason) that old man Minick would go first. Not that either of them had the slightest intention of going. In fact, when it happened they were planning to spend the winter in California and perhaps live there indefinitely if they liked it and didn't get too lonesome for George and Nettie and the Chicago smoke, and Chicago noise, and Chicago smells and rush and dirt. Still the solid sum paid yearly in insurance premiums showed clearly that he meant to leave her in comfort and security. Besides, the world is full of widows. Everyone sees that. But how many widowers? Few. Widows there are by the thousands; living alone; living in hotels; living with married daughters and sons-in-law or married sons and daughters-in-law. But of widowers in a like situation there are bewilderingly few. And why this should be no one knows.

So, then. The California trip never materialised. And the year that followed never was quite clear in old man Minick's dazed mind. In the first place, it was the year in which stocks tumbled and broke their backs. Gilt-edged securities showed themselves to be tinsel. Old man Minick had retired from active business just one year before, meaning to live comfortably on the fruit of a half-century's toil. He now saw that fruit rotting all about him. There was in it hardly enough nourishment to sustain them. Then came the day when Ma Minick went downtown to see Matthews about that pain right here and came home looking shrivelled, talking shrilly about nothing, and evading Pa's eyes. Followed months that were just a jumble of agony, X-rays, hope, despair, morphia, nothingness.

After it was all over: "But I was going first," old man Minick said, dazedly.

The old house on Ellis near Thirty-ninth was sold for what it would bring.

George, who knew Chicago real estate if anyone did, said they might as well get what they could. Things would only go lower, you'll see. And nobody's going to have any money for years. Besides, look at the neighbourhood!

Old man Minick said George was right. He said everybody was right. You would hardly have recognised in this shrunken and wattled figure the spruce and dressy old man whom Ma Minick used to spoil so delightfully. "You know best, George. You know best." He who used to stand up to George until Ma Minick was moved to say, "Now, Pa, you don't know everything."

After Ma when bills, and the hospital, and the nurses and the medicines and the thousand and one things were paid there was left exactly five hundred dollars a year.

"You're going to make your home with us, Father," George and Nettie said. Alma, too, said this would be the best. Alma, the married daughter, lived in Seattle. "Though you know Fred and I would be only too glad to have you."

Seattle! The ends of the earth. Oh, no. No! he protested, every fibre of his old frame clinging to the accustomed. Seattle, at seventy! He turned piteous eyes on his son George and his daughter-in-law Nettie. "You're going to make your home with us, Father," they reassured him. He clung to them gratefully. After it was over, Alma went home to her husband and their children.

So now he lived with George and Nettie in the five-room flat on South Park Avenue, just across from Washington Park. And there was no extra pillow on the floor.

Nettie hadn't said he couldn't have the extra pillow. He had told her he used two and she had given him two the first week. But every morning she had found a pillow cast on the floor.

"I thought you used two pillows, Father."

"I do."

"But there's always one on the floor when I make the bed in the morning. You always throw one on the floor. You only sleep on one pillow, really."

"I use two pillows."

But the second week there was one pillow. He tossed and turned a good deal in his bedroom off the kitchen. But he got used to it in time. Not used to it, exactly, but—well——

The bedroom off the kitchen wasn't as menial as it sounds. It was really rather cosy. The five-room flat held living-room, front-bedroom, dining-room, kitchen, and maid's room. The room off the kitchen was intended as a maid's room, but Nettie had no maid. George's business had suffered with the rest. George and Nettie had said, "I wish there was a front room for you, Father. You could have ours and we'd move back here, only this room's too small for twin beds and the dressing-table and the chiffonier." They had meant it—or meant to mean it.

"This is fine," old man Minick had said. "This is good enough for anybody." There was a narrow, white enamel bed and a tiny dresser and a table. Nettie had made gay cretonne covers and spreads and put a little reading-lamp on the table and arranged his things. Ma Minick's picture on the dresser with her mouth sort of pursed to make it look small. It wasn't a recent picture. Nettie and George had had it framed for him as a surprise. They had often urged her to have a picture taken, but she had dreaded it. He needed no photograph of Ma Minick. He had a dozen of them; a gallery of them; thousands of them. Lying on his one pillow he could take them out and look at them one by one as they passed in review, smiling, serious, chiding, praising, there in the dark. He needed no picture on his dresser.

A handsome girl, Nettie, and a good girl. He thought of her as a girl, though she was well past thirty. George and Nettie had married late. This was only the third year of their marriage. Alma, the daughter, had married young, but George had stayed on, unwed, in the old house on Ellis until he was thirty-six and all Ma Minick's friends' daughters had had a try at him in vain. The old people had urged him to marry, but it had been wonderful to have him around the house, just the same. Somebody young around the house. Not that George had stayed around very much. But when he was there you knew he was there. He whistled while dressing. He sang in the bath. He roared down the stairway, "Ma, where's my clean shirts?" The telephone rang for him. Ma Minick prepared special dishes for him. The servant girl said, "Oh, now, Mr. George, look what you've done! Gone and spilled the grease all over my clean kitchen floor!" and wiped it up adoringly while George laughed and gobbled his bit of food filched from pot or frying pan.

They had been a little surprised about Nettie. George was in the bond business and she worked for the same firm. A plump, handsome, eye-glassed woman, with fine fresh colouring, a clear skin that old man Minick called appetising, and a great coil of smooth dark hair. She wore plain tailored things and understood the bond business in a way that might have led you to think her a masculine mind if she hadn't been so feminine, too, in her manner. Old man Minick liked her better than Ma Minick had.

Nettie had called him Pop and joked with him and almost flirted with him in a daughterly sort of way. He liked to squeeze her plump arm and pinch her soft cheek between thumb and finger. She would laugh up at him and pat his shoulder and that shoulder would straighten spryly and he would waggle his head doggishly. "Look out there, George!" the others in the room would say. "Your dad'll cut you out. First thing you know you'll lose your girl, that's all."

Nettie would smile. Her teeth were white and strong and even. Old man Minick would laugh and wink, immensely pleased and flattered. "We understand each other, don't we, Pop?" Nettie would say.

During the first years of their married life Nettie stayed home. She fussed happily about her little flat, gave parties, went to parties, played bridge. She seemed to love the ease, the relaxation, the small luxuries. She and George were very much in love. Before her marriage she had lived in a boarding-house on Michigan Avenue. At the mention of it now she puckered up her face. She didn't attempt to conceal her fondness for these five rooms of hers, so neat, so quiet, so bright, so cosy. Over-stuffed velvet in the living-room, with silk lampshades, and small tables holding books and magazines and little boxes containing cigarettes or hard candies. Very modern. A gate-legged table in the dining-room. Caramel-coloured walnut in the bedroom, rich and dark and smooth. She loved it. An orderly woman. Everything in its place. Before eleven o'clock the little apartment was shining, spotless; cushions plumped, crumbs brushed, vegetables in cold water. The telephone. "Hello! . . . Oh, hello, Bess! Oh, hours ago. . . . Not a thing. . . . Well, if George is willing. . . . I'll call him up and ask him. We haven't seen a show in two weeks. I'll call you back within the next half-hour. . . . No, I haven't done my marketing yet. . . . Yes, and have dinner downtown. Meet at seven."

Into this orderly, smooth-running mechanism was catapulted a bewildered old man. She no longer called him Pop. He never dreamed of squeezing the plump arm or pinching the smooth cheek. She called him Father. Sometimes George's father. Sometimes, when she was telephoning, there came to him— "George's father's living with us now, you know. I can't."

They were very kind to him, Nettie and George. "Now just you sit right down here, Father. What do you want to go poking off into your own room for?"

He remembered that in the last year Nettie had said something about going back to work. There wasn't enough to do around the house to keep her busy. She was sick of afternoon parties. Sew and eat, that's all, and gossip, or play bridge. Besides, look at the money. Business was awful. The two old people had resented this idea as much as George had—more, in fact. They were scandalised.

"Young folks nowadays!" shaking their heads. "Young folks nowadays. What are they thinking of! In my days when you got married you had babies."

George and Nettie had had no babies. At first Nettie had said, "I'm so happy. I just want a chance to rest. I've been working since I was seventeen. I just want to rest first." One year. Two years. Three. And now Pa Minick.

Ma Minick, in the old house on Ellis Avenue, had kept a loose sort of larder; not lavish, but plentiful. They both ate a great deal, as old people are likely to do. Old man Minick, especially, had liked to nibble. A handful of raisins from the box on the shelf. A couple of nuts from the dish on the sideboard. A bit of candy rolled beneath the tongue. At dinner (sometimes, towards the last, even at noon-time) a plate of steaming soup, hot, revivifying, stimulating. Plenty of this and plenty of that. "What's the matter, Jo? You're not eating." But he was, amply. Ma Minick had liked to see him eat too much. She was wrong, of course.

But at Nettie's things were different. Here was a sufficient but stern ménage. So many mouths to feed; just so many lamb chops. Nettie knew about calories and vitamins and mysterious things like that, and talked about them. So many calories in this. So many calories in that. He never was quite clear in his mind about these things said to be lurking in his food. He had always thought of spinach as spinach, chops as chops. But to Nettie they were calories. They lunched together, these two, George was, of course, downtown. For herself Nettie would have one of those feminine pick-up lunches; a dab of apple sauce, a cup of tea, and a slice of cold toast left from breakfast. This she would eat while old man Minick guiltily supped up his cup of warmed-over broth, or his coddled egg. She always pressed upon him any bit of cold meat that was left from the night before, or any remnants of vegetable or spaghetti. Often there was quite a little fleet of saucers and sauce plates grouped about his main plate. Into these he dipped and swooped uncomfortably, and yet with a relish. Sometimes, when he had finished he would look about, furtively.

"What'll you have, Father? Can I get you something?"

"Nothing, Nettie, nothing. I'm doing fine." She had finished the last of her toast and was waiting for him kindly.

Still, this balanced and scientific fare seemed to agree with him. As the winter went on he seemed actually to have regained most of his former hardiness and vigour. A handsome old boy he was, ruddy, hale, with the zest of a juicy old apple, slightly withered but still sappy. It should be mentioned that he had a dimple in his cheek which flashed unexpectedly when he smiled. It gave him a roguish—almost boyish—effect most appealing to the beholder. Especially the feminine beholder. Much of his spoiling at the hands of Ma Minick had doubtless been due to this mere depression of the skin.

Spring was to bring a new and welcome source of enrichment into his life. But these first six months of his residence with George and Nettie were hard. No spoiling there. He missed being made much of. He got kindness, but he needed love. Then, too, he was rather a gabby old man. He liked to hold forth. In the old house on Ellis there had been visiting back and forth between men and women of his own age, and Ma's. At these gatherings he had waxed oratorical or argumentative, and they had heard him, some in agreement, some in disagreement, but always respectfully, whether he prated of real estate or social depravity, prohibition or European exchange.

"Let me tell you, here and now, something's got to be done before you can get a country back on a sound financial basis. Why, take Russia alone, why . . ." Or: "Young people nowadays! They don't know what respect means. I tell you there's got to be a change and there will be, and it's the older generation that's got to bring it about. What do they know of hardship! What do they know of work—real work. Most of 'em's never done a real day's work in their life. All they think of is dancing and gambling and drinking. Look at the way they dress! Look at . . ."

Ad lib.

"That's so," the others would agree. "I was saying only yesterday . . ."

Then, too, until a year or two before, he had taken an active part in business. He had retired, only at the urging of Ma and the children. They said he ought to rest and play and enjoy himself.

Now, as his strength and good spirits gradually returned he began to go downtown, mornings. He would dress, carefully, though a little shakily. He had always shaved himself and he kept this up. All in all, during the day, he occupied the bathroom literally for hours, and this annoyed Nettie to the point of frenzy, though she said nothing. He liked the white cheerfulness of the little tiled room. He puddled about in the water endlessly. Snorted and splashed and puffed and snuffled and blew. He was one of those audible washers who emerge dripping and whose ablutions are distributed impartially over ceilings, walls, and floor.

Nettie, at the closed door: "Father, are you all right?"

Splash! Prrrf! "Yes. Sure. I'm all right."

"Well, I didn't know. You've been in there so long."

He was a neat old man, but there was likely to be a spot or so on his vest or his coat lapel, or his tie. Ma used to remove these from off him, as the occasion demanded, rubbing carefully and scolding a little, making a chiding sound between tongue and tooth indicative of great impatience of his carelessness. He had rather enjoyed these sounds, and this rubbing and scratching on the cloth with the finger-nail and moistened rag. They indicated that someone cared. Cared about the way he looked. Had pride in him. Loved him. Nettie never removed spots. Though infrequently she said, "Father, just leave that suit out, will you? I'll send it to the cleaner's with George's. The man's coming to-morrow morning." He would look down at himself, hastily, and attack a spot here and there with a futile finger-nail.

His morning toilette completed, he would make for the Fifty-first Street L. Seated in the train, he would assume an air of importance and testy haste; glance out of the window; look at his watch. You got the impression of a handsome well-preserved old gentleman on his way downtown to consummate a shrewd business deal. He had been familiar with Chicago's downtown for fifty years and he could remember when State Street was a tree-shaded cottage district. The noise and rush and clangour of the Loop had long been familiar to him. But now he seemed to find the downtown trip arduous, even hazardous. The roar of the elevated trains, the hoarse hoots of the motor horns, the clang of the street cars, the bedlam that is Chicago's downtown district bewildered him, frightened him almost. He would skip across the street like a harried hare, just missing a motor-truck's nose and all unconscious of the stream of invective directed at him by its charioteer. "Heh! Whatcha! . . . Look!"—Sometimes a policeman came to his aid, or attempted to, but he resented his proffered help.

"Say, look here, my lad," he would say to the tall, tired, and not at all burly (standing on one's feet directing traffic at Wabash and Madison for eight hours a day does not make for burliness) policeman, "I've been coming downtown since long before you were born. You don't need to help me. I'm no jay from the country."

He visited the Stock Exchange. This depressed him. Stocks were lower than ever and still going down. His five hundred a year was safe, but the rest seemed doomed for his lifetime, at least. He would drop in at George's office. George's office was pleasantly filled with dapper, neat young men and (surprisingly enough) dapper, slim young women, seated at desks in the big, light-flooded room. At one corner of each desk stood a polished metal placard on a little standard, bearing the name of the desk's occupant: Mr. Owens, Mr. Satterlee, Mr. James, Miss Ranch, Mr. Minick.

"Hello, Father," Mr. Minick would say, looking annoyed. "What's bringing you down?"

"Oh, nothing. Nothing. Just had a little business to tend to over at the Exchange. Thought I'd drop in. How's business?"

"Rotten."

"I should think it was!" old man Minick would agree. "I—should—think—it—was! Hm."

George wished he wouldn't. He couldn't have it, that's all. Old man Minick would stroll over to the desk marked Satterlee, or Owens, or James. These brisk young men would toss an upward glance at him and concentrate again on the sheets and files before them. Old man Minick would stand, balancing from heel to toe and blowing out his breath a little. He looked a bit yellow and granulated and wavering there in the cruel morning light of the big plate glass windows. Or perhaps it was the contrast he presented with these slim, slick young salesmen.

"Well, h'are you to-day, Mr.—uh—Satterlee? What's the good word?"

Mr. Satterlee would not glance up this time. "I'm pretty well. Can't complain."

"Good. Good."

"Anything I can do for you?"

"No—o—o. No. Not a thing. Just dropped in to see my son a minute."

"I see." Not unkindly. Then, as old man Minick still stood there, balancing, Mr. Satterlee would glance up again, frowning a little. "Your son's desk is over there, I believe. Yes."

George and Nettie had a bedtime conference about these visits and Nettie told him gently that the bond house head objected to friends and relatives dropping in. It was against the rules. It had been so when she was employed there. Strictly business. She herself had gone there only once since her marriage.

Well, that was all right. Business was like that nowadays. Rush and grab and no time for anything.

The winter was a hard one, with a record snowfall and intense cold. He stayed indoors for days together. A woman of his own age in like position could have occuped herself usefully and happily. She could have hemmed a sash-curtain; knitted or crocheted; tidied a room; taken a hand with cooking or preparing of food; ripped an old gown; made over a new one; indulged in an occasional afternoon festivity with women of her own years. But for old man Minick there were no small tasks. There was nothing he could do to make his place in the household justifiable. He wasn't even particularly good at those small jobs of hammering, or painting, or general "fixing." He could drive a nail more swiftly, more surely than Nettie. "Now, Father, don't you bother.

I'll do it. Just you go and sit down. Isn't it time for your afternoon nap?''

He waxed a little surly. "Nap! I just got up. I don't want to sleep my life away."

George and Nettie frequently had guests in the evening. They played bridge, or poker, or talked.

"Come in, Father," George would say. "Come in. You all know Dad, don't you, folks?" He would sit down, uncertainly. At first he had attempted to expound, as had been his wont in the old house on Ellis. "I want to say, here and now, that this country's got to . . . ." But they went on, heedless of him. They interrupted or refused, politely, to listen. So he sat in the room, yet no part of it. The young people's talk swirled and eddied all about him. He was utterly lost in it. Now and then Nettie or George would turn to him and with raised voice (he was not at all deaf and prided himself on it) would shout, "It's about this or that, Father. He was saying . . ."

When the group roared with laughter at a sally from one of them he would smile uncertainly but amiably, glancing from one to the other in complete ignorance of what had passed, but not resenting it. He took to sitting more and more in his kitchen bedroom, smoking a comfortable pipe and reading and re-reading the evening paper. During that winter he and Canary, the negro wash-erwoman, become quite good friends. She washed down in the basement once a week but came up to the kitchen for her massive lunch. A walrus-waisted black woman, with a rich, throaty voice, a rolling eye and a kindly heart. He actually waited for her appearance above the laundry stairs.

"Wel, how's Mist' Minick to-day! Ah nev' did see a gemun spry's you ah fo' yo' age. No, suh! Nev' did."

At this rare praise he would straighten his shoulders and waggle his head. "I'm worth any ten of these young sprats to-day." Canary would throw back her head in a loud and companionable guffaw.

Nettie would appear at the kitchen swinging door. "Canary's having her lunch, Father. Don't you want to come into the front room with me? We'll have our lunch in another half-hour."

He followed her obediently enough. Nettie thought of him as a troublesome and rather pathetic child—a child who would never grow up. If she attributed any thoughts to that fine old head they were ambling thoughts bordering, perhaps, on senility. Little did she know how expertly this old one surveyed her and how ruthlessly he passed judgment. She never suspected the thoughts that formed in the active brain.

He knew about women. He had married a woman. He had had children by her. He looked at this woman—his son's wife—moving about her little five-room flat. She had theories about children. You didn't have them except under such and such circumstances. It wasn't fair otherwise. Plenty of money for their education. Well. He and his wife had had three children. Paul, the second, had died at thirteen. A blow, that had been. They had not always planned for the coming of the three but they had always found a way, afterward. You managed somehow, once the little wrinkled red ball had fought its way into the world. You managed. You managed. Look at George. Yet when he was born, thirty-nine years ago, Pa and Ma had been hard put to it.

Sitting there, while Nettie dismissed him as negligible, he saw her clearly, grimly. He looked at her. She was plump, but not too short, with a generous width between the hips; a broad full bosom, but firm; round arms and quick slim legs; a fine sturdy throat. The curve between arm and breast made a graceful, gracious line. . . . Working in a bond office. . . . There was nothing in the Bible about working in a bond office. Here was a woman built for child-bearing.

She thought him senile, negligible.

In March, Nettie had in a sewing-woman for a week. She had her two or three times a year. A hawk-faced woman of about forty-nine, with a blue-bottle figure and a rapacious eye. She sewed in the dining-room, and there was a pleasant hum of machine and snip of scissors and murmur of conversation and rustle of silky stuff; and hot savoury dishes for lunch. She and old man Minick became great friends. She even let him take out bastings. This when Nettie had gone out from two to four, between fittings.

He chuckled and waggled his head. ''I expect to be paid regular assistant's wages for this,'' he said.

''I guess you don't need any wages, Mr. Minick,'' the woman said. ''I guess you're pretty well fixed.''

''Oh, well, I can't complain'' (five hundred a year).

''Complain! I should say not! If I was to complain it'd be different. Work all day to keep myself; and nobody to come home to at night.''

''Widow, ma'am?''

''Since I was twenty. Work, work, that's all I've had. And lonesome. I suppose you don't know what lonesome is.''

''Oh, don't I?'' slipped from him. He had dropped the bastings.

The sewing-woman flashed a look at him from the cold, hard eye. ''Well, maybe you do. I suppose living here like this, with sons and daughters, ain't so grand, for all your money. Now me, I've always managed to keep my own little place that I could call home, to come back to. It's only two rooms, and nothing to rave about, but it's home. Evenings I just cook and fuss around. Nobody to fuss for, but I fuss, anyway. Cooking, that's what I love to do. Plenty of good food, that's what folk need to keep their strength up.'' Nettie's lunch that day had been rather scant.

She was there a week. In Nettie's absence she talked against her. He protested, but weakly. Did she give him egg-noggs? Milk? Hot toddy? Soup? Plenty of good rich gravy and meat and puddings? Well! That's what folks needed when they weren't so young any more. Not that he looked old. My, no! Spryer than many young boys and handsomer than his own son if she did say so.

He fed on it, hungrily. The third day she was flashing meaning glances at him across the luncheon table. The fourth she pressed his foot beneath the table. The fifth, during Nettie's absence, she got up, ostensibly to look for a bit of cloth which she needed for sewing, and, passing him, laid a caressing hand on his shoulder. Laid it there and pressed his shoulder ever so little. He looked up, startled. The glances across the luncheon table had largely passed over his head; the foot beneath the table might have been an accident. But this—this was unmistakable. He stood up, a little shakily. She caught his hand. The hawklike face was close to his.

"You need somebody to love you," she said. "Somebody to do for you, and love you." The hawklike face came nearer. He leaned a little toward it. But between it and his face was Ma Minick's face, plump, patient, quizzical, kindly. His head came back sharply. He threw the woman's hot hand from him.

"Woman!" he cried. "Jezebel!"

The front door slammed. Nettie. The woman flew to her sewing. Old man Minick, shaking, went into his kitchen bedroom.

"Well," said Nettie, depositing her bundles on the dining-room table, "did you finish that faggoting? Why, you haven't done so very much, have you!"

"I ain't feeling so good," said the woman. "That lunch didn't agree with me."

"Why, it was a good plain lunch..I don't see———"

"Oh, it was plain enough, all right."

Next day she did not come to finish her work. Sick, she telephoned. Nettie called it an outrage. She finished the sewing herself, though she hated sewing. Pa Minick said nothing, but there was a light in his eyes. Now and then he chuckled, to Nettie's infinite annoyance, though she said nothing.

"Wanted to marry me!" he said to himself, chuckling. "Wanted to marry me! The old rip!"

At the end of April, Pa Minick discovered Washington Park, and the Club, and his whole life was from that day transformed.

He had taken advantage of the early spring sunshine to take a walk, at Nettie's suggestion.

"Why don't you go into the Park, Father? It's really warm out. And the sun's lovely. Do you good."

He had put on his heaviest shirt, and a muffler, and George's old red sweater with the great white "C" on its front, emblem of George's athletic prowess at the University of Chicago; and over all, his frock coat. He had taken warm mittens and the big cane with the greyhound's-head handle, carved. So equipped, he had ambled uninterestedly over to the Park across the way. And there he had found new life.

New life is old life. For the Park was full of old men. Old men like himself, with greyhound's-head canes, and mufflers, and somebody's sweater worn beneath their greatcoats. They wore arctics, though the weather was fine. The skin of their hands and cheek-bones was glazed and had a tight look though it lay in fine little folds. There were splotches of brown on the back of their hands, and on the temples and foreheads. Their heavy grey or brown socks made comfortable folds above their ankles. From that April morning until winter drew on the Park saw old man Minick daily. Not only daily but by the day. Except for his meals, and a brief hour for his after-luncheon nap, he spent all his time there.

For in the Park old man Minick and all the old men gathered there found a Forum—a safety-valve—a means of expression. It did not take him long to discover that the Park was divided into two distinct sets of old men. There were the old men who lived with their married sons and daughters-in-law or married daughters and sons-in-law. Then there were the old men who lived in the Grant Home for Aged Gentlemen. You saw its fine, red-brick façade through the trees at the edge of the Park.

And the slogan of these first was:

"My son and my daughter, they wouldn't want me to live in any public home. No, siree! They want me right there with them. In their own home. That's the kind of son and daughter I've got!"

The slogan of the second was:

"I wouldn't live with any son or daughter. Independent. That's me. My own boss. Nobody to tell me what I can do and what I can't. Treat you like a child. I'm my own boss! Pay my own good money and get my keep for it."

The first group strangely enough was likely to be spotted of vest and a little frayed as to collar. You saw them going on errands for their daughters-in-law. A loaf of bread. A spool of White No. 100. They took their small grandchildren to the duck-pond and between the two toddlers hand-in-hand—the old and the infirm and the infantile and infirm—it was hard to tell which led which.

The second group was shiny as to shoes, spotless as to mien, dapper as to clothes. They had no small errands. Theirs was a magnificent leisure. And theirs was magnificent conversation. The questions they discussed and settled there in the Park—these old men—were not international merely. They were cosmic in scope.

The War? Peace? Disarmament? China? Free love? Mere conversational bubbles to be tossed in the air and disposed of in a burst of foam. Strong meat for old man Minick who had so long been fed on pap. But he soon got used to it. Between four and five in the afternoon, in a spot known as Under the Willows, the meeting took the form of a club—an open forum. A certain group made of Socialists, Free Thinkers, parlour Anarchists, Bolshevists, had for years drifted there for talk. Old man Minick learned high-sounding phrases. "The Masters . . . democracy . . . toil of the many for the few . . . the ruling class . . . free speech . . . the people . . ."

The strong-minded ones held forth. The weaker ones drifted about on the outskirts, sometimes clinging to the moist and sticky paw of a round-eyed grandchild. Earlier in the day—at eleven o'clock, say—the talk was not so general nor so inclusive. The old men were likely to drift into groups of two or three or four. They sat on sun-bathed benches and their conversation was likely to be rather smutty at times, for all they looked so mild and patriarchal. They paid scant heed to the white-haired old women who like themselves were sunning in the Park. They watched the young women switch by, with appreciative glances at their trim figures and slim ankles. The day of the short skirt was a grand time for them. They chuckled among themselves and made wicked comment. One saw only white-haired, placid, tremulous old men, but their minds still worked with belated masculinity like naughty small boys talking behind the barn.

Old man Minick early achieved a certain leadership in the common talk. He had always liked to hold forth. This last year had been of almost unendurable bottling up. At first he had timidly sought the less assertive ones of his kind. Mild old men who sat in rockers in the pavilion waiting for lunch time. Their conversation irritated him. They remarked on everything that passed before their eyes.

"There's a boat. Fella with a boat."

A silence. Then heavily: "Yeh."

Five minutes.

"Look at those people laying on the grass. Shouldn't think it was warm enough for that. . . . Now they're getting up."

A group of equestrians passed along the bridle path on the opposite side of the lagoon. They made a frieze against the delicate spring greenery. The coats of the women were scarlet, vivid green, arresting, stimulating.

"Riders!"

"Yes."

"Good weather for riding."

A man was fishing nearby. "Good weather for fishing."

"Yes."

"Wonder what time it is, anyway." From a pocket, deep-buried, came forth a great gold blob of a watch. "I've got one minute to eleven."

Old man Minick dragged forth a heavy globe. "Mm. I've got eleven."

"Little fast, I guess."

Old man Minick shook off this conversation impatiently. This wasn't conversation. This was oral death, though he did not put it thus. He joined the other men. They were discussing Spiritualism. He listened, ventured an opinion, was heard respectfully and then combated mercilessly.

He rose to the verbal fight, and won it.

"Let's see," said one of the old men. "You're not living at the Grant Home, are you?"

"No," old man Minick made reply, proudly. "I live with my son and his wife. They wouldn't have it any other way."

"Hm. Like to be independent myself."

"Lonesome, ain't it? Over there?"

"Lonesome! Say, Mr.—what'd you say your name was? Minick? Mine's Hughes—I never was lonesome in my life 'cept for six months when I lived with my daughter and her husband and their five children. Yes, sir. That's what I call lonesome, in an eight-room flat."

George and Nettie said, "It's doing you good, Father, being out in the air so much." His eyes were brighter, his figure straighter, his colour better. It was that day he had held forth so eloquently on the emigration question. He had to read a lot—papers and magazines and one thing and another—to keep up. He devoured all the books and pamphlets about bond issues and national finances brought home by George. In the Park he was considered an authority on bonds and banking. He and a retired real estate man Mowry sometimes debated a single question for weeks. George and Nettie, relieved, thought he ambled to the Park and spent senile hours with his drooling old friends discussing nothing amiably and witlessly. This while he was eating strong meat and drinking strong drink.

Summer sped. Was past. Autumn held a new dread for old man Minick. When winter came where should he go? Where should he go? Not back to the five-room flat all day, and the little back bedroom and nothingness. In his mind there rang a childish old song they used to sing at school. A silly song:

> "Where do all the birdies go?
> *I* know. *I* know.''

But he didn't know. He was terror-stricken. October came and went. With the first of November the Park became impossible, even at noon, and with two overcoats and the sweater. The first frost was a black frost for him. He scanned the heavens daily for rain or snow. There was a cigar store and billiard room on the corner across the boulevard and there he sometimes went, with a few of his Park cronies, to stand behind the players' chairs and watch them at pinochle or rum. But this was a dull business. Besides, the Grant men never came there. They had card rooms of their own.

He turned away from his smoky little den on a drab November day, sick at heart. The winter. He tried to face it, and at what he saw he shrank and was afraid.

He reached the apartment and went around to the rear dutifully. His rubbers were wet and muddy, and Nettie's living-room carpet was a fashionable grey. The back door was unlocked. It was Canary's day downstairs, he remembered. He took off his rubbers in the kitchen and passed into the dining-room. Voices. Nettie had company. Some friends, probably, for tea. He turned to go to his room, but stopped at hearing his own name. Father Minick. Father Minick. Nettie's voice.

"Of course, if it weren't for Father Minick I would have. But how can we as long as he lives with us. There isn't room. And we can't afford a bigger place now, with rents what they are. This way it wouldn't be fair to the child. We've talked it over, George and I. Don't you suppose? But not as long as Father Minick is with us. I don't mean we'd use the maid's room for a—for the—if we had a baby. But I'd have to have someone in to help, then, and we'd have to have that extra room.

He stood there in the dining-room, quiet. Quiet. His body felt queerly remote and numb, but his mind was working frenziedly. Clearly, too, in spite of the frenzy. Death. That was the first thought. Death. It would be easy to die. But he didn't want to die. Strange, but he didn't want to die. He liked life. The Park, the trees, the Club, the talk, the whole show. . . . . Nettie was a good girl

. . . the old must make way for the young. They had the right to be born.
. . . Maybe it was just another excuse.

Almost four years married. Why not three years ago? . . . The right to live.
The right to live. . . .

He turned stealthily, stealthily, and went back into the kitchen, put on his
rubbers, stole out into the darkening November afternoon.

In an hour he was back. He entered at the front door this time, ringing the
bell. He had never had a key. As if he were a child they would not trust him
with one. Nettie's women friends were just leaving. In the air you smelled a
mingling of perfume and tea, and cakes, and powder. He sniffed it, sensitively.

"How do you do, Mr. Minick," they said. "How are you! Well, you certainly look it. And how do you manage these gloomy days?"

He smiled genially, taking off his greatcoat and revealing the red sweater
with the big white "C" on it. "I manage. I manage." He puffed out his chest.
"I'm busy moving."

"Moving!" Nettie's startled eyes flew to his, held them. "Moving, Father?"

"Old folks must make way for the young," he said, gaily. "That's the law
of life. Yes, sir! New ones. New ones."

Nettie's face was scarlet. "Father, what in the world——"

"I signed over at the Grant Home to-day. Move in next week." The women
looked at her, smiling. Old man Minick came over to her and patted her plump
arm. Then he pinched her smooth cheek with a quizzical thumb and forefinger.
Pinched it and shook it ever so little.

"I don't know what you mean," said Nettie, out of breath.

"Yes, you do," said old man Minick, and while his tone was light and jesting there was in his old face something stern, something menacing. "Yes, you
do."

When he entered the Grant Home a group of them were seated about the
fireplace in the main hall. A neat, ruddy, septuagenarian circle. They greeted
him casually, with delicacy of feeling, as if he were merely approaching them
at their bench in the Park.

"Say, Minick, look here. Mowry here says China ought to have been included in the Four-power Treaty. He says——"

Old man Minick cleared his throat. "You take China, now," he said, "with
her vast and practically, you might say, virgin country, why——"

An apple-cheeked maid in a black dress and a white apron stopped before
him. He paused.

"Housekeeper says for me to tell you your room's all ready if you'd like to
look at it now."

"Minute. Minute, my child." He waved her aside with the air of one who
pays five hundred a year for independence and freedom. The girl turned to go.
"Uh—young lady! Young lady!" She looked at him. "Tell the housekeeper
two pillows, please. Two pillows on my bed. Be sure."

"Yes, sir. Two pillows. Yes, sir. I'll be sure."

Grandma

Thyra Samter Winslow

I

Grandma awoke with a start. She gained consciousness with the feeling that something was just about to happen. Then she sank back again on the pillow with a comfortable sigh of remembrance. Of course—this was the day on which she was going travelling.

Even on usual days, Grandma could not lie in bed, idle. So much more reason why she should be up and about, to-day, with so much to do. Her train left at twelve o'clock—she had had her ticket and her berth reservation for over a week, her trunk was all packed, there were just a few necessary articles to put into her bag—but the morning would be busy, as all mornings were at Fred's.

Grandma bathed and dressed hurriedly, her bent, rheumatic fingers grasping each hook and button with a nervous haste. As usual, she was the first one in the bathroom. This morning she was especially glad. For at Fred's, Grandma's second son's house, where she was visiting now, there was only one bathroom and there were eight in the family without her, if you count the two babies. If you didn't get in the bathroom first . . .

Grandma put on her neat house dress, as was her wont. She could change her dress later, and stuff the house dress into her bag. She arranged her thin, grey hair in neat waves around her face—she could smooth that again, too.

From a room at the other end of the house Grandma heard a baby commence to cry. It was Ruthie, Nell's youngest baby, just a year old, one of Grandma's two great-grandchildren. Grandma loved little Ruthie a great deal, a fine baby—still, it did seem good that she wouldn't have to take care of her any more for a long time. Not that Grandma minded work—she had always worked, she liked something to do—but here at Fred's house there were so few moments when she wasn't working. Not that Fred's family were mean to her! Grandma would have been indignant if you had suggested that. Didn't they work as hard as she did, and harder? At seventy-three, Grandma was still strong and capable; no wonder they expected her to do her share and accepted it without comment.

Fred was a good son and a good husband and a good father. Could you expect much more? But Fred never had much of a business head. Here he was, at forty-nine, just about where he had been fifteen years before, book-keeper at the Harper Feed Store, a good enough position when times were better, but, with everything so high, Fred's salary didn't go very far. Still, no use complaining or worrying him about it, it was the best he could do. Fred never had had much ambition or "get up." It was a good thing he had bought the house, years before. It had seemed too big and rambling then. It was just about the right size now, though not so awfully modern—and quite hard to keep clean.

Emma, Fred's wife, was a good woman and a good housekeeper. She wasn't like the average daughter-in-law, either. She never quarrelled with Grandma about things—in fact, she was awfully kind, in her hurried, brusque way. Grandma sometimes wished she weren't so quick about things, and decided— still, when one is as busy as Emma . . .

Emma was nearly Fred's age. They had been married twenty-five years, and she had always been a good wife to him. They had three children, all girls. Grandma had been sorry there couldn't have been a son to help Fred share the burden of supporting the family. But things seemed to be going all right now—a little better than they had been, or so the family seemed to think—and, as long as they were satisfied . . .

Nell, Fred's oldest daughter, had married, four years before, and had gone to housekeeping. But Homer Billingsley, the boy she had married, had been sick for almost a year, so they had given up their little cottage and were living "with the old folks." They had two children now, Freddie and Ruthie, nice good children, too. Grandma liked Homer, Nell's husband, though she was sorry he was so much like Fred in his lack of ambition and power. Now that Homer was able to work again he had his old job at Malton's Hardware Store. There didn't seem much chance of his getting ahead there. Still, he was a good boy and awfully fond of Nell and the children.

Edna, Fred's second daughter, was stenographer at the First National Bank and made fifteen dollars a week. Edna was fine-looking, really the beauty of the family. She paid her board every week, but never had much left over because she bought Alice's clothes, too, and of course being in the bank, she had to look nice herself. Alice, the youngest daughter, was seventeen and in High School. Grandma loved Alice, too. Of course, the child was thoughtless, she could have helped her mother a little more with the housework or Nell with the babies, but Grandma knew that, at seventeen, it's pretty hard to sweep floors or take babies out. After all, Alice was young, and she ought to have a good time.

While she stayed at Fred's house, Grandma did her share of the work. Even this last morning she followed her usual routine.

She hurried to the room where Ruthie lay and soon had her quieted. When Ruthie had her bottle—Grandma has learned all about sterilising, though she hadn't known there was such a thing when she brought up her own children— Grandma set the table, a plate, knife and spoon for each, salt and pepper castors that had been a wedding present to Emma and Fred, a butter dish with an uneven piece of butter in it, a sugar bowl containing rather lumpy sugar and a fluted sugar spoon, a dish of home-made plum preserves. She had the table all set when Emma hurried into the kitchen with a cheery, abrupt "Morning, Ma," and started the coffee.

At half-past seven all but Alice were ready for breakfast. Grandma had got the oatmeal out of the fireless cooker and boiled the eggs for Homer, who was rather delicate and needed eggs for breakfast. When the family sat down to their meal, Grandma put milk and sugar on little Freddie's oatmeal and saw that he ate it—Freddie didn't like oatmeal much.

"Well, Ma," said big Fred, who sat comfortably coatless, "so to-day's the day you go travelling."

"Yes, it is," said Grandma, and smiled.

"You got a good day for it. Let's see, you leave Lexington to-day at noon and get to New York to-morrow at two, don't you?"

"Yes, Fred," said Grandma.

"You know," he went on, munching toast as he talked, "I believe you enjoy travelling, going places. Never saw anything like it. Seems to me a woman your age would want to settle down, quiet. You could stay here all the time if you wanted to, you know that. Got a room all to yourself—more than you get at Mary's—and yet, off you go, after four or five months. Here you've got a good home and all that."

"Well," said Grandma, in her gentle, even tones, "you know you aren't the only child I've got, Fred. There's Albert and Mary."

"Yes," Fred frowned. He disliked even hearing the name of Albert. It was the one thing that made him angry. "But we really want you, honest we do, Ma. Emma and the girls always miss you after you're gone."

"You bet," said Emma.

Grandma smiled. At least at Fred's home she was welcome and helpful. If she were only younger and stronger! At Mary's and Albert's there was a wordless agreement that her visits end, almost mechanically, at the end of four months. Only mere surface invitations of further hospitality were extended "for politeness."

Fred and Homer finished eating and hurried off to business. Alice came down, then, and Grandma served her, bringing in hot coffee and oatmeal, as Emma started to clear away the dishes.

Alice ate rapidly, then kissed Grandma good-bye—she didn't come home at noon—and skipped off. Grandma and her daughter-in-law washed the dishes and, when the dishes were done, they made the beds, one standing on each side, straightening the sheets and pulling up the covers simultaneously.

"Sure will miss you, Ma," said Emma. "Nell's no help at all. Don't blame her. Freddie tagging at her heels and the baby crying."

While Emma straightened up the downstairs rooms, Grandma helped Nell bathe and dress the babies. Then the express-man rang and Grandma hurried to the door, saw that he took her trunk and put the check in her purse. Then Grandma cleaned up the room she had occupied. It was time, then, for Grandma to get ready for her journey. Usually, she helped prepare dinner after these tasks were done, peeling potatoes, setting the table, for at Fred's one ate dinner in the middle of the day.

Grandma put on her travelling dress. It was her best dress, of soft grey silk crêpe, trimmed with a bit of fine cream lace at the throat. Albert had given it to her on her birthday, two years before. Over this she put her best coat of black-ribbed silk, also a gift of Albert. She adjusted her neat bonnet—five years old, but made over every year and you'd never guess it.

Emma and Nell were too busy with dinner and the babies to go to the station with Grandma, but the street-car that passed the corner went right to the station, and Homer and Fred would be there to tell her good-bye. At eleven— Grandma believed in taking plenty of time, you never could tell what might happen on the way to the station—Grandma kissed Emma and Nell and Freddie and Ruthie, giving Ruthie a very tender hug and Freddie a hearty kiss, in spite of much stickiness from the penny lollypop he had been eating. She took her bag and, hurrying as fast as she could—Grandma took little, slow, rheumatic steps—she caught the surface car.

In the railway station Grandma sat down gingerly on one of the long brown benches, carefully pulling her skirts away from suspicious, tobacco-looking spots on the floor, and waited for Fred and Homer and the train.

Fred and Homer came up, together, puffing, just before the train was due. Homer presented Grandma with a half-pound box of candy and Fred gave her a paper bag filled with fruit.

When the train came in, Fred and Homer both assisted Grandma in getting on, took her to her seat and kissed her, loudly, before their hurried exit—the Limited stops for only a minute at Lexington.

Then, as the train moved away, Grandma waved a fluttering good-bye to the two men and sighed again, with happiness. She was travelling!

II

Not consciously, of course, for she never could have admitted such a terrible fact; Grandma looked forward, all year, to her days of travel. Usually, each year contained three trips, each of about the same length, and these days were Grandma's golden milestones. Not that she wasn't happy the rest of the time— of course she was—but this—well, this was different.

At Fred's now—Grandma was happy at Fred's, of course, everyone was friendly and pleasant, though her feet and head and sometimes her back ached at the end of the day. One isn't so young at seventy-three, and younger people are apt to forget how tired seventy-three becomes, after innumerable answerings of the door, step-climbing and dish-washing. Grandma loved being useful, of course, but she did wish that there was a little more leisure, a little time to sit down and rest. If only Fred's and Albert's homes could be combined, in some way!

Grandma had three children. When they were young there had never been much money, but Grandma had tried to do her best for them. They had lived in Lexington then, and the three had been brought up just alike and yet how differently they had turned out! There was Fred, quite poor but happy, still in Lexington, where he was born. Mary had married John Falconer when she was twenty-four and had gone to St. Louis to live, and Albert, the ambitious one of the family, had gone to New York in search of fortune, and had found part of it, at least.

If only Fred and Albert hadn't been so foolish and quarrelled, years ago! But they had. Albert had tried to give Fred advice and Fred had resented it. They had made up the quarrel, but there was nothing that Fred would let Albert do for him, even if Albert had wanted to do something. Fred liked to refer, in scorn, to his elder brother as "that New York millionaire," and say things about being "just as well off if I haven't got his money." But then, Albert probably forgot, most of the time, that he had a younger brother. Outside of a polite inquiry, when Grandma arrived, he never referred to Fred at all. It worried Grandma to think that her children weren't good friends, but she knew she could never do anything to make them feel differently. Years and circumstances had taken them too far apart.

Grandma had no favourite child, unless it was a slight, natural leaning toward her only daughter. She liked Albert and was glad she was on her way to visit him. She just wished that Albert wasn't so—well, so cold. He didn't mean anything, of course. When one is busy all day on the Stock Exchange one hasn't time for other things. And, when one is as rich as Albert, there are so many things to take up one's time. Albert was awfully good to Grandma. She told herself that many times. He asked her if she needed anything, whenever she visited him. He frequently gave her expensive presents. She wouldn't take any more money from him than she had to, and her wants were simple, for that wouldn't have been right, though she let him give her some on her last visit and had given it to Nell for Homer—he had been sick then—without letting Fred find out.

Grandma liked it all right at Albert's. How could there be anything to complain of? At seventy-three, Grandma had learned to make the best of things. Albert was Grandma's oldest child and now he was fifty-two. His ménage consisted of his wife, Florence; their two children, Albert, junior, who, at twenty-four, was being taught the business of Wall Street; their daughter, Arlene, twenty, and six servants.

The Albert Cunninghams lived in a very large apartment on Park Avenue. Mrs. Cunningham was of rather a good New York family. Albert had met her after his first taste of success and had been greatly impressed with her and her antecedents. Even then Albert had learned to look ahead. The family had had some years of social strivings, but now lived rather quietly. Arlene had made her début the year before and now entertained and went out quite a little. Albert, junior, was rather a serious fellow, though he, too, enjoyed the social life that was open to him. Altogether, they were fairly sensible, decent people, a bit snobbish, perhaps, very self-centered, but with no really objectionable features.

The thing that Grandma couldn't understand or enjoy in the Albert Cunninghams' family life was the, to her, great coldness and formality. Grandma's idea of how a family ought to live was the way Fred's family lived, only with more money and more leisure and more pleasure and a servant or two—

friendly, jolly, intimate. At Albert's, the life was strangely lonely and distant. Grandma never felt quite at ease nor at home. She had no definite place in the family life. She had the fear, constantly, that she was doing something wrong, much more so than at Mary's, where her acts were criticised and commented on. No one ever gave Grandma a harsh word at Albert's. Albert, dignified; Florence, courteous, calm; Junior, a young edition of his father; Arlene, gentle, distant, quiet—were all kind to Grandma. But most of the time they unthinkingly ignored her. She didn't fit in, she knew that.

At Albert's, Grandma had her own room and her own bath, as did each member of the family. There was no regular "family breakfast." Albert and Junior breakfasted about nine, going to the office in the closed car. Florence and Arlene breakfasted in their rooms. Grandma had gone to the dining-room for breakfast, on her first visit there, eight years ago, after Grandpa died and her own modest home had been broken up. But Florence decided that it would be more comfortable for Grandma if she breakfasted in her room. So each morning, about nine, Grandma's tray was brought up to her by Florence's own maid, Terry, who asked, each time, "if there is anything I can do?" Grandma rather resented a personal maid. Wasn't she able to bathe and dress herself, even if she was seventy-three? Grandma was always dressed when Terry knocked.

All day there was nothing for Grandma to do at Albert's. She couldn't help at all around the house. She found that out at her first visit. There was no darning or mending to be done—a sewing woman came in regularly to do the things that Terry could not do. Albert didn't care for the home dishes that had once delighted him, and the cook didn't want anyone bothering around the kitchen. Grandma had luncheon at one, with Florence and Arlene, when they were at home, which was seldom enough. In the afternoon, on nice days, Grandma went for a drive, unless the cars were being used. Usually Grandma went alone, getting real pleasure out of the things she saw; sometimes Florence went with her. Florence, too, occasionally took Grandma to teas and receptions and musicales, most of which bored Grandma and at none of which did she feel at home.

Grandma wondered where all of the old ladies were in New York. She seldom saw any. At the theatre, where she was taken once in a while, she would see white-haired old dowagers, carefully marcelled and massaged, in evening gowns with very low-cut bodices. Grandma didn't mean that kind of old lady. She was always looking for comfortable old ladies, with neatly-parted hair, ample old ladies with little rheumatic hands and wrinkles, but she never found them.

Dinner, at Albert's, was at seven. When the family dined alone, at home, the meals were about the same, good things to eat, but everything so cold and distant. It was hard for Grandma to remember just what to do, so that Florence and Arlene wouldn't think she didn't know, though they were always polite and gracious. Grandma was constantly afraid she would spill things when the maid presented the silver dishes to her or that she'd take too large a portion for politeness. Grandma was served first—she couldn't watch to see the way the others did.

When the family was having a real dinner party Grandma found that it was easier for everyone if she had a tray in her room. She really liked that just as well—it was nice, seated at the little table in her room, comfortably unannoyed by manners. About half of the time the Albert Cunninghams did not dine at home—Arlene and Junior went to numerous dinners and even Florence and Albert had frequent engagements. Then Grandma usually dined alone in the big, empty dining-room, a little, lonely figure amid empty chairs, silver and glass. She would have preferred a tray in her room, then, but didn't like to mention it—this arrangement seemed to suit Florence. Grandma's meals were always excellently prepared and served, but eating alone in a big, still room isn't very jolly.

After dinner, Grandma was occasionally included in some social affair, but nearly always she was supposed to sit in the library until about nine or ten and then retire, as the other members of the family·sometimes did when they were at home. The family saw that Grandma was given interesting light fiction and magazines full of stories and current events, but Grandma had never had enough leisure in her youth to find time to learn to enjoy reading. She could read only a short time without falling asleep.

Grandma knitted, too, so she was glad when the fad came back so she could be modern in something. Albert's family approved of knitting, and on the last visit her old fingers had made many pairs of socks and sweaters for charity. Now she was glad to be able to get to knitting—she had had no time for it since she had been there before.

Yes—Albert and his family were awfully nice—of course, they didn't mean anything when they paid no attention to Grandma, when their days went on as serenely undisturbed as if she were not there. They asked her how she felt, nearly every day, a cool "Trust you are well this morning, Mother," and gave her presents. But thinking of the lonely hours in her room, the tiresome evenings, the long, useless, dragged-out days, Grandma wasn't enthusiastic over her visit with Albert.

III

Mary, Mrs. John Falconer, Grandma's youngest child, had always been a bit her favourite. Mary still lived in St. Louis, where she had gone after her marriage. The Falconers had four children, two sons of eighteen and fourteen, two daughters, sixteen and eleven. John Falconer, a lawyer of moderate means, was quite stingy in family matters. Although he had a great deal more money than Fred, the family occupied a much smaller house, though it was modern and in a good neighbourhood, and Grandma had to share the bedroom of the two daughters. Mary's family had an advantage over Fred's in having one maid, who did all of the cooking and washing and some of the cleaning, so there was not so much for Grandma to do. Grandma felt that she should have been very happy with the Falconers. But they were disagreeable people to live with. Grandma tried not to see their faults but it was not easy for her to be contented during her visits there.

The Falconers had the habit of criticism. Nothing was ever just right with them. Mary always told Grandma that if it hadn't been for Grandma's encouragement she would never have married John Falconer—if she had waited she probably could have done much better. John Falconer was a former Lexington boy whom Mary had met when he was visiting his old home. Grandma didn't remember that she had encouraged the match except to tell Mary that John was a nice boy and would probably make a good husband—Mary had been the one who seemed enthusiastic. But somehow, Grandma was blamed whenever John showed disagreeable characteristics.

Mary was dissatisfied with her social position, with the amount of money John gave her to spend, with her children. She spoke slurringly of Albert and "his rich family who are in society." Mary would ask Grandma innumerable questions about the way the Albert Cunninghams lived, copy them when circumstances permitted and later bring the unused bits of information into the conversation, with disagreeable slurs.

"I guess Albert wouldn't call this dinner good enough for him, would he? It's a wonder you are satisfied here, Mamma, without a butler to answer the door or a maid to bring breakfast to your room," or "It's a wonder Albert and Florence wouldn't do something for Irene. I bet she's a lot smarter and better-looking than their stuck-up daughter. But not a thing does he do for her, except send a little box on Christmas—gave Irene a cheap wrist-watch last year—you could buy the same kind right here in St. Louis. He could keep it for all I'd care."

The four Falconer children were badly brought up and noisy. They interrupted each other and all talked at once. At meals they reached across the table for dishes of food. The one maid had had no training and, as she did the cooking, her waitress duties consisted of putting bowls and platters of food on the table. Then John Falconer made a pretence of serving, always, after one or two plates, he'd "pass the things around so you can all help yourselves."

As there was no attempt to show Grandma any special favour—she was never served first, the first plate going to the person in the greatest hurry to get away, frequently Tom the eldest son—usually when the bowl or platter reached Grandma there was little left for her. Grandma didn't mind this, unless the food happened to be a favourite—she had become accustomed to little sacrifices while raising her family. There was always enough bread and butter.

What Grandma did object to at Mary's was the spirit of unrest, the unkindness, the disagreeable taunts of the family, the noise and disorder. Everyone criticised Grandma, calling her attention to the way she held her fork, though their own manners were frequently insufferable. They criticised, too, Grandma's pronunciation of words, idioms of Lexington, and errors in grammar. These were made much of and repeated with laughter. Then, too, if Grandma showed ignorance of any modern appliance or invention, this was thought to be a great joke and was introduced as a tidbit in the table conversation.

Grandma darned all of the stockings at Mary's—there always seemed to be a basketful—and took care of the bedroom in which she slept, relieving the two girls of an unwelcome duty. She straightened the living-room, for Mary hated housework and grumbled about it and the overworked maid never quite got through her round of duties. But Grandma was not too busy at Mary's. She liked having something to do. It was the taunts that made her unhappy, the little barbed things the family said. John Falconer made Grandma feel that she was an actual expense, that the amount of food she ate was a real item in the household budget. Mary came to her with little whines about the relatives—though they lived in other cities and paid little attention to her—about her husband, how stingy he was, how much better she could have done, had she not taken her mother's advice in her marriage, about the children, how much money they spent, how they quarrelled with each other, how disobedient they were. Grandma always went from Mary's home to Fred's, and though she knew the work that awaited her, the tired hours in store, she actually looked forward to the next visit.

IV

So now, Grandma was travelling again. And, as the train covered the miles away from Lexington, Grandma put aside the worries of the visit she had just had, the memories of the unpleasantness of the visit with Mary, the apprehensions of the visit that awaited her. Grandma shed, all at once, all of these things, and emerged, a wonderful, new personality, a dear, happy little old lady, travelling. Grandma became, as she always became, three days of each year, the woman she would have liked to have been, the old lady she sometimes dreamed she was.

First, Grandma rang for the porter. She was well supplied with money, for Albert always sent her a cheque for travelling expenses. She loved feeling independent, a personality. When the porter came, Grandma demanded, in the gentle well-bred tone Florence might have used, that the porter bring her an envelope for her bonnet, a pillow for her head, a stool for her feet. She tipped him generously enough to make him grin his thanks and hurry to her whenever she rang. There were even porters who said, "Yes'm, you travelled on my car before," when they saw Grandma.

From her bag, Grandma took out a small, black, lace cap, with a bit of perky lavender ribbon on it and adjusted it on her thinning hair. At Mary's house they were always telling her how thin her hair looked, the young boy even hinting about old people who ought to wear wigs. Albert had sent her cap in her Christmas box, and, as usual, she had saved it for travelling. Grandma put on, too, a pair of gold-rimmed spectacles. She had needed them for years, but at first a sort of pride in her good eyes had kept her from getting them. Then, at Fred's, she had been too busy; at Albert's no one paid much attention to her needs; at Mary's they had laughed at her near-sightedness without offering a corrective. When she was at Albert's, last year, she had told him, finally, her need of glasses, and the next day Florence had driven her to an oculist. But she felt that she had annoyed and disturbed Florence, that getting glasses for an old lady just wasn't Florence's pattern of things.

Grandma put the cheap candy and the fruit from Fred and Homer into her bag. It had been awfully kind and good of them. She took out her knitting and added row after row, as the minutes passed.

Then Grandma rang for the porter again. But, before he came, she looked at her fellow passengers, as she always looked at them when she travelled. Two seats in front of her sat a tired-looking woman of about forty, with a thin, drawn face. Knitting in hand, Grandma took slow, careful little steps up the train to her.

"How do you do?" said Grandma, with her sweetest smile. "I wonder if you won't have tea with me, keep an old lady company? It seems so—so unsocial, having tea alone."

The woman gasped and looked at Grandma. She saw the well-dressed, comfortable little old lady, with the frill of soft lace at throat and wrists, a tiny black cap on her grey hair, grey knitting in her gnarled hands, a picture-book Grandma for all the world.

"Why, yes, I—that would be delightful," she said.

Grandma led the way back to her own seat. When the porter came she ordered tea and toast and little cakes and sandwiches, "and some of that good orange marmalade you always have on this road."

Grandma hadn't had any lunch but she didn't say so. When the little table was adjusted and the tea things brought in, Grandma poured tea, as if, every day, in her own home, the routine included the serving of tea at a dear little tea-table.

Grandma listened sympathetically to the other woman's story. Grandma knew that each woman who was travelling had a story and would tell it, if encouraged at all, but she wasn't much interested—she had heard so many stories during the past years. Then, when her guest had finished, Grandma talked.

Grandma didn't say much, really. She told about her visits, about her two wonderful sons and her splendid daughter. As Grandma told these things, they, too, emerged into beauty; the journey threw a magic over them as it did over Grandma. The things she told were so real that Grandma believed them, herself, because she wanted to.

"I have three children, so, of course, I spend four months of the year with each of them. Each of them wanted me all the time—they are such good children—so the best way seemed to be to divide the time. I'm on my way to visit my older son now. Maybe, as you've lived in New York, you've heard of him—he has a seat on the Stock Exchange and is a director in so many things—Albert Morrell Cunningham. His wife was a Mornington, and they have two such wonderful children, a boy and a girl. Arlene made her début last year, so you can imagine what a good time she's having and what fun it is to be there with her, she's so popular and pretty. I'll show you her picture later. Each day I'm there, nearly, they do something for me, a drive in the park, theatres and concerts. I really get too gay in the city—it's wonderful.

"Then I go to see Mary, my only daughter, and you know how a mother feels toward a daughter. She is married to a lawyer in St. Louis, and they have four of the dearest children. The oldest, a boy, is eighteen, and the youngest, a girl, is eleven. Quite an ideal family, isn't it? Mary's husband is quite well-to-do, but they live so comfortably and simply, no airs at all. Mary doesn't care a great deal for society, just wrapped up in her husband and children, but she goes with such nice people.

"I've just come from my second son, Fred. And there—perhaps you'd never guess it, people have flattered me so long about looking youthful that I believe them—but I've two great-grandchildren, the older three years old, the younger just a year, the dearest things. Nell, the children's mother and her husband and the children are all living right at home. Fred and his wife won't hear of them going away. They were housekeeping for a while, but the family didn't like it—they are all so devoted to the children. There are two other girls in the family besides Nell and they have a great big old-fashioned home, set way back in a broad lawn, lots of trees and flowers. Yes, it's Fred's own home. It's a good thing he bought such a big one, years ago, he needs it with so many young people. They do have such good times together—and, of course, it's young people who keep us all young, these days."

Then, from her bag, Grandma drew a bundle of photographs. The photographers, from the maker of the shiny products of Lexington to the creator of the soft sepias of Fifth Avenue, had, with their usual skill at disguise, smoothed away the lines of discontent on Mary's face, the bold impudence of her children, had added a little kindness and humanness to Florence and Albert, had made Fred's family look placid, undisturbed and prosperous. The pictures showed Grandma's family to be all she had said of them, even to the dimpled little Ruthie, taken just a few weeks before, on a postcard by a neighbourhood photographer.

It didn't sound like bragging, as Grandma told things. It was just the simple, contented story of an old lady of seventy-three, who spent her days satisfied and serene, travelling from one loving and beloved set of relatives to another.

When tea finished, Grandma allowed the other woman to return to her seat with a gentle nod and a "thank you for keeping an old woman company." Then Grandma knitted and looked at the passengers again. Always, whenever she travelled, out of the set that presented itself, Grandma was able to find those she needed.

A tiny, plump little woman with a too-fat baby was seated just a seat or so back of Grandma, on the left. It was to her that Grandma went now.

"May I hold the baby?" she asked. "I know how tired you must get, holding him all day, on a day like this. I've got two great-grandchildren. Your baby is just about in between them in age, I think. Sometimes, I hold them for just a little while, and I know how heavy babies can be."

Deftly, Grandma took the child in her arms and settled him comfortably.

"When dinner is announced," said Grandma, "you go in and eat. I'll take care of the baby. It will be a rest for you—it is so difficult travelling with a baby—you'll enjoy your dinner more, alone. Sometimes, when we go on picnics with my great-grandchildren . . . ."

Grandma told about the babies, about their mother, about her own grown-up children, whom she visited. She even told little things about their childhood, as mothers tell to mothers, but, always, she came back to the present, telling of her visits, encased in the rose colour of her journey. Not that Grandma told deliberate falsehoods. She didn't claim servants or wealth for Fred, nor jollity for Albert. But each fact she brought forth was broidered with the romance that travel brought to Grandma—the stories all showed Grandma welcome, beloved, happy, made her children kind, considerate, affectionate, successful, capable. Grandma helped her listeners, too, for she spread some of this haze over them. You can't envy, you must enter into the pleasure of it, when an old lady of seventy-three shows you the treasures that a lifetime has handed to her.

Grandma smiled as she sat with the little mother and her baby. And she smiled as she held the heavy, squirming bundle, while the mother ate dinner.

"It's a real pleasure to help you even a little," said Grandma, as the woman came back from the dining-car to claim her baby and thank Grandma.

Grandma washed her face carefully before she went in to her own dinner. She took a clean handkerchief from her bag, dainty, lavender-bordered, the present that Edna, Fred's second daughter, had given her last Christmas. On it she sprinkled a bit of perfume, a gift from Alice, two years before. She smoothed her hair, brushed the dust from her wrist. A new adventure always awaited her in the dining-car.

She walked with stiff little steps the length of the three cars, holding tight to the seats as she passed. And, through the cars, she smiled at the children and to grown-ups, smiles a bit patronising, perhaps, as smiles should be from such a distinguished, contented old lady.

In the diner, Grandma was seated across from a stout, middle-aged man, who was eating an enormous meal. She smiled at him. He couldn't misjudge her—one doesn't flirt that way at seventy-three.

"It's a wonderful day for travelling, isn't it?" she said. "Last time I travelled, four months ago . . . ."

Grandma was telling of her children, of her journeys.

Grandma ordered carefully—a steak, you are really safe about steaks when you travel, a fresh vegetable, a green salad, a bit of pastry, black coffee. Grandma ordered as if the ordering of a dinner were a usual but precious rite. She felt correct, prosperous, a woman of the world. The man across the table, pleased with his meal and moved a bit by Grandma's story of her happy and fortunate life, her devoted children, saw in Grandma the things that made this devotion. He even grew a bit gallant.

"I can see why your children are so good to you, ma'am. It makes me wish I had a grandma or mother like you myself." This during mouthfuls.

Grandma was equal to it.

"Why me, I'm just what my children have made me. Just think of you, making such lovely speeches to an old lady. You're deserving of the best mother a man ever had, I'm sure."

There were more pretty speeches. The man became almost flowery. Grandma actually blushed, before she paid her check, adding her usual generous tip—the stranger had offered to pay, but Grandma wouldn't have that, of course. Then, as Grandma arose, the man opposite rose too, and courteously escorted her through the cars and to her seat, stopping for a moment to talk.

Grandma couldn't knit at night. The motion of the car and the electric lights were not a good combination for her old eyes. She put her knitting into her bag and extracted a deck of cards, flamboyant, with green and gold gift-looking backs. She chose now two young women and a good-looking young man in his early thirties. She approached them all with the same question.

"Wouldn't you like a game of bridge? It seems so lonely, an evening alone, in a sleeper. . . ."

Strangely, all three did play bridge and would like a game. The porter brought a little table again, and they played, rather indifferently, to be sure— Grandma was no expert and one of the young women played even a poorer game than she did—but several hours passed pleasantly. Then, after they stopped playing, Grandma brought the fruit from her bag. Grandma told them about Fred bringing the fruit to her, and as they ate she told, too, of her visits, of her children, her grandchildren, and the two little great-grand ones. The three card-players really seemed interested, so of course the photographs were brought out for a round of approval.

After the guests had gone to their seats, Grandma had her berth made up. She was rather particular about this—she wanted it made with her feet to the engine. Grandma thought this knowing about head and foot gave her a travelled air. Besides, she really didn't like to feel that she was travelling backwards.

In the dressing-room she put on her violet, silk dressing-gown, a gift from Florence three years before, which she kept carefully for travelling, and a frivolous little cap of cream lace, to keep the dust out of her hair while she slept. She spread her ivory travelling articles in their leather case—five years old on her last birthday—before her, and, as she prepared for sleep, talked pleasantly with the woman who happened to come into the dressing-room while she was there.

Grandma slept fairly well for travelling, waking up frequently to pull up the shade and look out on the hurrying landscape, the occasional lights, the little towns. She thought it was mighty pleasant travelling.

She was up at seven and dressed swiftly. A new woman had got on during the night and now occupied the seat opposite Grandma, a well-gowned woman in her late thirties, with a smart, city-like air.

Grandma nodded a pleasant good morning.

"We seem to be making good time," she said.

"Yes, indeed," the woman smiled, "pleasant day for travelling."

With the air of one born traveller to another, Grandma talked a bit, then motioned the woman to sit beside her. The pleasant conversation gave Grandma a warm feeling of well-being. She suggested breakfast, and the two of them went in together, the younger woman steadying Grandma just a bit when the train swayed around a curve.

It was a pleasant breakfast. Grandma ordered three-minute eggs. They were the way she liked eggs best, but she seldom had them. At Albert's it seemed so self-assertive to ask for things like that, special directions and everything—and at Fred's and Mary's!

Grandma and her new friend talked about New York, about plays they had both seen the year before. They discussed food and the cost of living, servants, the usual things that two hardly-acquainted women talk of, when circumstance throws them together. There was nothing condescending in the new acquaintance's attitude. Why should there have been? Grandma was neither an unnecessary member of a cool, indifferent household nor an overworked old woman—she was the ideal Grandma, cultured, clever, kindly. It was no wonder, then, that, after breakfast, the two of them should loiter in Grandma's seat and Grandma should show a few family photographs and dwell, pleasantly, on how fortunate she was in having such splendid sons, such a lovely daughter and such wonders of grandchildren, to say nothing of the two babies.

Then the woman suggested that she and Grandma go to the observation car, and, before long, Grandma was seated in a big chair, knitting again, and glancing at the flying scenery.

All the morning, Grandma's former acquaintances came to talk to her. The thin woman with the sad face offered her some candy. Grandma had a little chat with the plump mother and the baby and held the baby again while his mother ate luncheon. The stout man, reading a magazine, dropped it long enough to come over and ask Grandma how she was feeling and if there was anything he could do for her. Grandma's bridge companions, now well acquainted, with the sudden friendship that travel brings, gathered around Grandma for a chat, laughing at everything. Several others, coming into the car, stopped for a word with Grandma.

Grandma and her latest acquaintance had luncheon together too. Then, after luncheon, Grandma prepared, a whole hour ahead, as she always did, for the end of her journey. She washed off as much of the soot as she could. She took off the little lace cap and replaced it with her decent old bonnet, which had been resting in its bag all this time. She slipped on her black travelling coat over her grey crêpe dress. She took out a clean handkerchief, sprinkling a bit of perfume on it. Before closing her bag, Grandma took out the cheap candy that Homer had brought to the station and gave it, with a gracious smile, to the woman with the baby. It was good to be able to give something—and, besides, what could she do with the candy at Albert's? She didn't care for candy and even the servants would have laughed at it.

Grandma closed her bag then and sat waiting. Her chance acquaintances passed, nodded, smiled and talked. Grandma was a real person of importance, a dear, happy old lady, with a devoted family, spending her life contentedly divided among them. Didn't all these people know about Grandma? Hadn't they heard of her children and her grandchildren and her great-grandchildren? Hadn't they seen their photographs, even? Didn't they know that, after four pleasant months with Fred and his happy, jovial family, she was on her way to visit Albert, rich and prominent and kind?

V

The train drew into the Grand Central Station. Grandma, trembling a little— for the excitement of travelling is apt to make one tremble at seventy-three— allowed the porter to brush her coat, bade farewell to her train acquaintances, followed her bag down the aisle and into the station.

A man in a chauffeur's uniform took Grandma's bag and, addressing Grandma politely, gravely, told her that Mr. and Mrs. Cunningham were sorry, but engagements prevented them from meeting her. They would see her at dinner at seven.

Grandma, with short, unsteady little steps, went out to the waiting car. There was something very near a tear in her eye. After all, travelling has its difficulties when one is seventy-three. The shell of radiance, of smiling independence, of being cared-for, important, loved, fell away. Grandma was just a little tired, lonely old lady again. Another of Grandma's romantic journeys was over.

May and January

Sa'di

Translated from the Persian by James Ross

An old man was telling a story, saying: 'I had married a young virgin, adorned the bridal chamber with flowers, seated myself with her in private, and riveted my heart and eyes upon her. Many a long night I would lie awake, and indulge in pleasantries and jests, in order to remove any coyness on her part, and encourage familiarity. One of those nights I was addressing her, and saying: "Lofty fortune was your friend, and the eye of your prosperity broad awake, when you fell into the society of such an old gentleman as I am, being of mature judgment, well-bred, worldly experienced, inured to the vicissitudes of heat and cold, and practised in the goods and evils of life; who can appreciate the rights of good-fellowship, and fulfil the duties of loving attachment; and is kind and affable, sweet-spoken and cheerful. *I will treat thee with affection, as far as I can, and if thou dealest with me unkindly, I cannot be unkind in return. If, like a parrot, thy food be sugar, I will devote my sweet life for thy nourishment.* And you did not become the victim of a rude, conceited, rash, and headstrong youth, who one moment gratifies his lust, and the next has a fresh object; who every night shifts his abode, and every day changes his mistress. *Young men are lively and handsome, but they keep good faith with nobody. Expect not constancy from nightingales, who will every moment serenade a fresh rose.* Whereas my class of seniors regulate their lives by good breeding and sense, and are not deluded by youthful ignorance. *Court the society of a superior, and make much of the opportunity; for in the company of an equal thy good fortune must decline.'' '*

The old man continued: 'I spoke a great deal in this style, and thought that I had caught her heart in my snare, and made sure of her as my prey; when she suddenly drew a cold sigh from the bottom of a much afflicted bosom, and answered: ''All this speech which you have delivered has not, in the scale of my judgment, the weight of that one sentence which I have heard of my nurse: that it were better to plant a spear in a young maiden's side than to lay her by an old man in bed! *Much contention and strife will arise in that house where the wife shall get up dissatisfied with her husband. Unable to rise without the help of a staff, how can an old man stir the staff of life?'' '*

In short, there being no prospect of concord, they agreed to separate. After the period prescribed by the law, they united her in wedlock with a young man of an ill-tempered and sullen disposition, and in very narrow circumstances, so that she endured much tyranny and violence, penury and hardship; yet she was thus offering up thanksgivings for the Almighty's goodness, and saying: 'Praised be God that I have escaped from such hell-torment, and secured a blessing so permanent. *With all this violence and impetuosity of temper, I bear with thy caprice, because thou art lovely. It were better for me to burn with thee in hell-fire than to dwell in paradise with another. The smell of an onion from the mouth of the lovely is sweeter than a rose in the hand of the ugly.'*

Over the River and Through the Wood

John O'Hara

Mr. Winfield's hat and coat and bag were in the hall of his flat, and when the man downstairs phoned to tell him the car was waiting, he was all ready. He went downstairs and said hello to Robert, the giant Negro chauffeur, and handed Robert the bag, and followed him out to the car. For the first time he knew that he and his granddaughter were not to make the trip alone, for there were two girls with Sheila, and she introduced them: "Grandfather, I'd like to have you meet my friends. This is Helen Wales, and this is Kay Farnsworth. My grandfather, Mr. Winfield." The names meant nothing to Mr. Winfield. What did mean something was that he was going to have to sit on the strapon-tin, or else sit outside with Robert, which was no good. Not that Robert wasn't all right, as chauffeurs go, but Robert was wearing a raccoon coat, and Mr. Winfield had no raccoon coat. So it was sit outside and freeze or sit on the little seat inside.

Apparently it made no difference to Sheila. He got inside, and when he closed the door behind him, she said, "I wonder what's keeping Robert?"

"He's strapping my bag on that thing in the back," said Mr. Winfield. Sheila obviously was not pleased by the delay, but in a minute or two they got under way, and Mr. Winfield rather admired the way Sheila carried on her conversation with her two friends and at the same time routed and rerouted Robert so that they were out of the city in no time. To Mr. Winfield it was pleasant and a little like old times to have the drection and the driving done for you. Not that he ever drove himself any more, but when he hired a car, he always had to tell the driver just where to turn and where to go straight. Sheila knew.

The girls were of an age, and the people they talked about were referred to by first names only. Ted, Bob, Gwen, Jean, Mary, Liz. Listening with some care, Mr. Winfield discovered that school acquaintances and boys whom they knew slightly were mentioned by their last names.

Sitting where he was, he could not watch the girls' faces, but he formed his opinions of the Misses Wales and Farnsworth. Miss Wales supplied every other word when Sheila was talking. She was smallest of the three girls, and the peppy kind. Miss Farnsworth looked out of the window most of the time, and said hardly anything. Mr. Winfield could see more of her face, and he found himself asking, "I wonder if that child really likes anybody." Well, that was one way to be. Make the world show *you*. You could get away with it, too, if you were as attractive as Miss Farnsworth. The miles streamed by and the weather got colder, and Mr. Winfield listened and soon understood that he was not expected to contribute to the conversation.

"We stop here," said Sheila. It was Danbury, and they came to a halt in front of the old hotel. "Wouldn't you like to stop here, Grandfather?" He understood then that his daughter had told Sheila to stop here; obediently and with no dignity he got out. When he returned to the car, the three girls were finishing their cigarettes, and as he climbed back in the car, he noticed how Miss Farnsworth had been looking at him and continued to look at him, almost as though she were making a point of not helping him—although he wanted no help. He wasn't really an *old* man, an *old man*. Sixty-five.

The interior of the car was filled with cigarette smoke, and Miss Farnsworth asked Mr. Winfield if he'd mind opening a window. He opened it. Then Sheila said one window didn't make any difference; open both windows, just long enough to let the smoke get out. "My! That air feels good," said Miss Wales. Then: "But what about you, Mr. Winfield? You're in a terrible draught there." He replied, for the first use of his voice thus far, that he did not mind. And at that moment the girls thought they saw a car belonging to a boy they knew, and they were in Sheffield, just over the Massachusetts line, before Miss Farnsworth realized that the windows were open and creating a terrible draught. She realized it when the robe slipped off her leg, and she asked Mr. Winfield if he would mind closing the window. But he was unable to get the crank started; his hands were so cold there was no strength in them. "We'll be there soon," said Sheila. Nevertheless, she closed the windows, not even acknowledging Mr. Winfield's shamed apologies.

He had to be first out of the car when they arrived at the house in Lenox, and it was then that he regretted having chosen the strapontin. He started to get out of the car, but when his feet touched the ground, the hard-packed frozen cinders of the driveway flew up at him. His knees had no strength in them, and he stayed there on the ground for a second or two, trying to smile it off. Helpful Robert—almost too helpful; Mr. Winfield wasn't that old—jumped out of the car and put his hands in Mr. Winfield's armpits. The girls were frightened, but it seemed to Mr. Winfield that they kept looking toward the library window, as though they were afraid Sheila's mother would be there and blaming them for his fall. If they only knew . . .

"You go on in, Grandfather, if you're sure you're all right," said Sheila. "I have to tell Robert about the bags."

"I'm all right," said Mr. Winfield. He went in, and hung up his coat and hat in the clothes closet under the stairs. A telephone was there, and in front of the telephone a yellow card of numbers frequently called. Mr. Winfield recognized only a few of the names, but he guessed there was an altogether different crowd of people coming up here these days. Fifteen years make a difference, even in a place like Lenox. Yes, it was fifteen years since he had been up here in the summertime. These trips, these annual trips for Thanksgiving, you couldn't tell anything about the character of the place from these trips. You never saw anybody but your own family and, like today, their guests.

He went out to the darkened hall and Ula, the maid, jumped in fright. "Ugh. Oh. It's you, Mr. Winfield. You like to scare me."

"Hello, Ula. Glad to see you're still holding the fort. Where's Mrs. Day?"

"Upstairs, I think . . . Here she is now," said Ula.

His daughter came down the steps; her hand on the banister was all he could see at first. "Is that you, Father? I thought I heard the car."

"Hello, Mary," he said. At the foot of the stairs they went through the travesty of a kiss that both knew so well. He leaned forward so that his head was above her shoulder. To Ula, a good Catholic, it must have looked like the kiss of peace. *"Pax tibi,"* Mr. Winfield felt like saying, but he said, "Where have you—"

"Father! You're freezing!" Mrs. Day tried very hard to keep the vexation out of her tone.

"It was a cold ride," he said. "This time of year. We had snow flurries between Danbury and Sheffield, but the girls enjoyed it."

"You go right upstairs and have a bath, and I'll send up—what would you like? Tea? Chocolate? Coffee?"

He was amused. The obvious thing would be to offer him a drink, and it was so apparent that she was talking fast to avoid that. "I think cocoa would be fine, but you'd better have a real drink for Sheila and her friends."

"Now, why do you take that tone, Father? You could have a drink if you wanted it, but you're on the wagon, aren't you?"

"Still on it. Up there with the driver."

"Well, and besides, liquor doesn't warm you up the same way something hot does. I'll send up some chocolate. I've put you in your old room, of course. You'll have to share the bathroom with one of Sheila's friends, but that's the best I could do. Sheila wasn't even sure she was coming till the very last minute."

"I'll be all right. It sounds like—I didn't bring evening clothes."

"We're not dressing."

He went upstairs. His room, the room itself, was just about the same; but the furniture was rearranged, his favorite chair not where he liked it best, but it was a good house; you could tell it was being lived in, *this year,* today, tomorrow. Little touches, ashtrays, flowers. It seemed young and white, cool with a warm breath, comfortable—and absolutely strange to him and, more especially, he to it. Whatever of the past this house had held, it was gone now. He sat in the chair and lit a cigarette. In a wave, in a lump, in a gust, the old thoughts came to him. Most of the year they were in the back of his mind, but up here Mr. Winfield held a sort of annual review of far-off, but never-out-of-sight regrets. This house, it used to be his until Mary's husband bought it. A good price, and in 1921 he certainly needed the money. He needed everything, and today he had an income from the money he got for this house, and that was about all. He remembered the day Mary's husband came to him and said, "Mr. Winfield, I hate to have to be the one to do this, but Mary—Mary doesn't—well, she thinks you weren't very nice to Mrs. Winfield. I don't know anything about it myself, of course, but that's what Mary thinks. I expected, naturally, I thought you'd come and live with us now that Mrs. Winfield has died, but—well, the point is, I know you've lost a lot of money, and also I happen to know about Mrs. Winfield's will. So I'm prepared to make you a pretty good offer, strictly legitimate based on current values, for the house in Lenox. I'll pay the delinquent taxes myself and give you a hundred and fifty thousand dollars for the house and grounds. That ought to be enough to pay off your debts and give you a fairly decent income. And, uh, I happen to have a friend who knows Mr. Harding quite well. Fact, he sees the President informally one night a week, and I know he'd be only too glad if you were interested . . ."

He remembered how that had tempted him. Harding might have fixed it so he could go to London, where Enid Walter was. But even then it was too late. Enid had gone back to London because he didn't have the guts to divorce his wife, and the reason he wouldn't divorce his wife was that he wanted to "protect" Mary, and Mary's standing, and Mary's husband's standing, and Mary's little daughter's standing; and now he was "protecting" them all over again, by selling his house so that he would not become a family charge—protecting the very same people from the embarrassment of a poor relation. "You can have the house," he told Day. "It's worth that much, but no more, and I'm grateful to you for not offering me more. About a political job, I think I might like to go to California this winter. I have some friends out there I haven't seen in years." He had known that that was exactly what Mary and her husband wanted, so he'd gone.

There was knock on the door. It was Ula with a tray. "Why two cups, Ula?" he said.

"Oh, Di put two cups? So I did. I'm just so used to putting two cups." She had left the door open behind her, and as she arranged the things on the marble-topped table he saw Sheila and the two girls, standing and moving in the hall.

"This is your room, Farnie," said Sheila. "You're down this way, Helen. Remember what I told you, Farnie. Come on, Helen."

"Thank you, Ula," he said. She went out and closed the door, and he stood for a moment, contemplating the chocolate, then poured out a cup and drank it. It made him a little thirsty, but it was good and warming, and Mary was right; it was better than a drink. He poured out another cup and nibbled on a biscuit. He had an idea: Miss Farnsworth might like some. He admired that girl. She had spunk. He bet she knew what she wanted, or seemed to, and no matter how unimportant were the things she wanted, they were the things she wanted, and not someone else. She could damn well thank the Lord, too, that she was young enough to have a whack at whatever she wanted, and not have to wait the way he had. That girl would make up her mind about a man or a fortune or a career, and by God she would attain whatever it was. If she found, as she surely would find, that nothing ever was enough, she'd at least find it out in time; and early disillusionment carried a compensatory philosophical attitude, which in a hard girl like this one would take nothing from her charm. Mr. Winfield felt her charm, and began regarding her as the most interesting person he had met in many dull years. It would be fun to talk to her, to sound her out and see how far she had progressed toward, say, ambition or disillusionment. It would be fun to do, and it would be just plain nice of him, as a former master of this house, to invite her to have a cup of cocoa with him. Good cocoa.

He made his choice between going out in the hall and knocking on her door, and knocking on her door to the bathroom. He decided on the second procedure because he didn't want anyone to see him knocking on her door. So he entered the bathroom and tapped on the door that led to her room. "In a minute," he thought he heard her say. But then he knew he must have been wrong. It sounded more like "Come in." He hated people who knocked on doors and had to be told two or three times to come in, and it would make a bad impression if he started the friendship that way.

He opened the door, and immediately he saw how right he had been in thinking she had said "In a minute." For Miss Farnsworth was standing in the middle of the room, standing there all but nude. Mr. Winfield instantly knew that this was the end of any worthwhile life he had left. There was cold murder in the girl's eyes, and loathing and contempt and the promise of the thought his name forever would evoke. She spoke to him: "Get out of here, you dirty old man."

He returned to his room and his chair. Slowly he took a cigarette out of his case, and did not light it. He did everything slowly. There was all the time in the world, too much of it, for him. He knew it would be hours before he would begin to hate himself. For a while he would just sit there and plan his own terror.

I Never Sang for My Father

Robert Anderson

SYNOPSIS OF SCENES

The time is the present and the past. The places are New York City and a town in Westchester County.

Act One

There are no sets. Lighting is the chief means for setting the stage.
A man comes from the shadows in the rear. He is GENE GARRISON, *age forty. He checks his watch. A* PORTER *passes through with a baggage cart.*

GENE   I wonder if you could help me. (*The* PORTER *stops*) My father and mother are coming in on the Seaboard Express from Florida. I'd like a wheelchair for my mother if I could get one.

PORTER   You have the car number?

GENE   Yes. (*He checks a slip of paper*) One-oh-seven.

PORTER   Due in at three ten. I'll meet you on the platform.

GENE   Thank you. (*The* PORTER *moves away and off.* GENE *comes down and addresses the audience*) Death ends a life, but it does not end a relationship, which struggles on in the survivor's mind toward some final resolution, some clear meaning, which it perhaps never finds. (*He changes the mood*) Pennsylvania Station, New York, a few years ago. My mother and father were returning from Florida. They were both bored in Florida, but they had been going each winter for a number of years. If they didn't go, my father came down with pneumonia and my mother's joints stiffened cruelly with arthritis. My mother read a great deal, liked to play bridge and chatter and laugh gaily with "the girls" . . . make her eyes sparkle in a way she had and pretend that she had not had two operations for cancer, three heart attacks and painful arthritis . . . She used to say, "Old age takes courage." She had it. My father, though he had never been in the service, had the air of a retired brigadier general. He read the newspapers, all editions, presumably to help him make decisions about his investments. He watched Westerns on television and told anyone who would listen the story of his life. I loved my mother . . . I wanted to love my father . . .

(The lights come up on another area of the stage, where the PORTER *is already standing with the wheelchair and baggage cart.* TOM GARRISON *is standing amid the suitcases which have been piled up on the platform. He is a handsome man, almost eighty, erect in his bearing, neat in his dress. He speaks distinctly, and when he is irritated, his voice takes on a hard, harsh edge. At the moment he is irritated, slightly bewildered, on the brink of exasperation)*

TOM   We had four bags. I don't see any of them. We had one in the compartment with us. That can't have been lost.

(He fumes for a moment. As GENE *watches his father for a moment, we can see in his face something of his feelings of tension. On the surface he shows great kindness and consideration for the old man. Underneath there is usually considerable strain)*

GENE   Hello, Dad.

TOM *(Beaming)*   Well, Gene, as I live and breathe. This *is* a surprise.

GENE   I wrote you I'd be here.

TOM   Did you? Well, my mind is like a sieve. *(They have shaken hands and kissed each other on the cheek)* Am I glad to see you! They've lost all our bags.

GENE   I'm sure they're somewhere, Dad.

TOM *(Firmly)*   No. I've looked. It's damnable!

GENE   Well, let's just take it easy. I'll handle it.
(He looks around at the luggage piled on the platform)

TOM   I'm confident we had four bags.

GENE *(Quietly showing the redcap)*   There's one . . . They'll show up. Where's Mother?

TOM   What? . . . Oh, she's still on the train. Wait a minute. Are you sure that's ours?
(*He looks around for bags, fussing and fuming. He shakes his head in exasperation with the world*)

GENE   Yes, Dad. You just relax now.
(TOM *is seized with a fit of coughing*)

TOM (*Is exasperated at the cough*)   Damn cough. You know the wind never stops blowing down there.

GENE   Don't worry about anything now, Dad. We've got a porter, and everything's under control. (TOM *snorts at this idea. The redcap proceeds in a quiet, efficient and amused way to work the luggage*) I brought a wheelchair for Mother.

TOM   Oh. That's very considerate of you.

GENE   I'll go get her.

TOM   I didn't hear you.

GENE (*Raising his voice*)   I said I'll go get Mother.'

TOM   Yes, you do that. I've got to get these damned bags straightened out.
(*His rage and confusion are rising*)

GENE (*To the* PORTER)   There's one. The gray one.

TOM   That's not ours.

GENE (*Patient but irritated*)   Yes, it is, Dad.

TOM   No. Now wait. We don't want to get the wrong bags. Mine is brown.

GENE   The old one was brown, Dad. I got you a new one this year for the trip.

TOM (*Smiling reasonably*)   Now. Gene. I've had the bag in Florida all winter. I should know.

GENE   Dad. Please . . . Please let me handle this.

TOM (*Barks out an order to his son without looking at him*) You go get your mother. I'll take care of the bags.
(GENE*'s mouth thins to a line of annoyance. He points out another bag to the* PORTER, *who is amused.* GENE *moves with the wheelchair to another area of the stage, where his mother,* MARGARET GARRISON, *is sitting.* MARGARET *is waiting patiently. She is seventy-eight, still a pretty woman. She has great spirit and a smile that lights up her whole face. She is a good sport about her problems. When she is put out, she says "darn" and not "damn." She is devoted to her son, but she is not the possessive and smothering mother. She is wearing a white orchid on her mink stole*)

GENE   Hello, Mother.

MARGARET *(Her face lights up)*   Well, Gene. *(She opens her arms, but remains seated. They embrace)* Oh, my, it's good to see you. *(This with real feeling as she holds her son close to her)*

GENE *(When he draws away)*   You look wonderful.

MARGARET   What?

GENE *(Raises his voice slightly. His mother wears a hearing aid)*   You look wonderful.

MARGARET *(Little-girl coy)*   Oh . . . a little rouge . . . This is your Easter orchid. I had them keep it in the icebox in the hotel. This is the fourth time I've worn it.

GENE   You sure get mileage out of those things.

MARGARET *(Raising her voice slightly)*   I say it's the fourth time I've worn it . . . Some of the other ladies had orchids for Easter, but mine was the only white one. *(She knows she is being snobbishly proud and smiles as she pokes at the bow)* I was hoping it would last so you could see it.

GENE   How do you feel?

MARGARET *(Serious, pouting)*   I'm all right, but your father . . . did you see him out there?

GENE   Yes.

MARGARET   He's sick and he won't do anything about it.

GENE   I heard his cough.

MARGARET   It makes me so darned mad. I couldn't get him to see a doctor.

GENE   Why not?

MARGARET   Oh, he's afraid they'd send him a big bill. He says he'll see Mayberry tomorrow . . . But I can't tell you what it's been like. You tell him. Tell him he's got to see a doctor. He's got me sick with worry. *(She starts to cry)*

GENE *(Comforts her)*   I'll get him to a doctor, Mother. Don't you worry.

MARGARET   He makes me so mad. He coughs all night and keeps us both awake. Poor man, he's skin and bone . . . And he's getting so forgetful. This morning he woke up here on the train and he asked me where we were going.

GENE   Well, Mother, he's almost eighty.

MARGARET   Oh, I know. And he's a remarkable man. Stands so straight. Everyone down there always comments on how handsome your father is . . . But I've given up. You get him to a doctor.

GENE   I've got a wheelchair for you, Mother. Save you the long walk up the ramp.

MARGARET   Oh, my precious. What would we ever do without you?

GENE (*He is always embarrassed by these expressions of love and gratitude*)   Oh, you manage pretty well.
(*He helps her up from the chair, and she gives him a big hug as she stands . . . and looks at him*)

MARGARET   Oh, you're a sight for sore eyes.

GENE (*Embarrassed by the intensity*)   It's good to see you.

MARGARET (*She sits in the wheelchair*)   You know, much as we appreciate your coming to meet us . . . I say, much as we appreciate your coming like this, the last thing in the world I'd want to do is take you away from your work.

GENE   You're not, Mother.
(*Father coughs his hacking cough*)

MARGARET   Do you hear that? I'm so worried and so darned mad.
(*They arrive at the platform area*)

TOM   Oh, Gene, this is damnable. They've lost a suitcase. We had four suitcases.

GENE   Let's see, Dad. There are four there.

TOM   Where?

GENE   Under the others. See?

TOM   That's not ours.

GENE   Yes. Your new one.

TOM   Well, I'm certainly glad you're here. My mind's like a sieve. (*Low, to* GENE) It's the confusion and worrying about your mother.

GENE   Well, everything's under control now, Dad, so let's go. We'll take a cab to my apartment, where I've got the car parked, and then I'll drive you out home.

TOM   Your mother can't climb the stairs to your apartment.

GENE   She won't have to. We'll just change from the cab to my car.

TOM   But she might have to use the facilities.

MARGARET   No. No. I'm all right.

TOM (*With a twinkle in his eye . . . the operator*)   You know, if you handle it right, you can get away with parking right out there in front of the station. When I used to come to meet the Senator . . .

GENE   I know, but I'd prefer to do it this way. I'm not very good at that sort of thing.

TOM   Well, all right. You're the boss. It's just that you can get right on the West Side Drive.

GENE   It's easier for me to go up the Major Deegan.

TOM   Rather than the Cross County?

GENE   Yes.

TOM   I don't like to question you, old man, but I'm sure if you clocked it, you'd find it shorter to go up the West Side Drive and—

MARGARET (*Annoyed with him*)   Father, now come on. Gene is handling this.

TOM   All right. All right. Just a suggestion.

GENE   Come on, Dad.

TOM   You go along with your mother. I'll keep an eye on this luggage.

GENE (*Trying to be patient*)   It will be all right.

TOM (*Clenching his teeth and jutting out his jaw, sarcastic*) You don't mind if I want to keep an eye on my luggage, do you? I've traveled a good deal more than you have in my day, old man, and I know what these guys will do if you let them out of your sight. (GENE *is embarrassed. The* PORTER *smiles and starts moving off*) Hey, not so fast there.
(*And he strides after the* PORTER *and the bags.* GENE *moves to the front of the stage again, as the lights dim on the retreating wheelchair and luggage, and on* TOM *and* MARGARET)

GENE   My father's house was in a suburb of New York City, up in Westchester County. It had been a quiet town with elms and chestnut trees, lawns and old sprawling houses with a certain nondescript elegance. My father had been mayor of this town, a long time ago . . . Most of the elms and chestnut trees had gone, and the only elegance left was in the pretentious names of the developments and ugly apartment houses . . . Parkview Meadows Estates . . . only there was no meadow, and no park, and no view except of the neon signs of the chain stores. Some old houses remained, like slightly frowzy dowagers. The lawns were not well kept, and the houses were not painted as often as they should have been, but they remained. My father's house was one of these.
(TOM *and* MARGARET *have now started coming in from the back*)

TOM   Just look at this town.

MARGARET   What, dear?

TOM (*Raises his voice in irritation*)   Do you have that thing turned on?

MARGARET   Yes.

TOM   I said just look at this town.

MARGARET   I know, dear, but time marches on.

TOM   Junky, ugly mess. When we came here . . .

MARGARET   Don't get started on that. You can't play the show over again.

TOM   I can make a comment, can't I?

MARGARET   But you always dwell on the gloomy side. Look at the good things.

TOM   Like what? . . . I'll bet you Murphy didn't bring the battery back for the Buick. I wrote him we'd be home today. (*He heads for the garage*)

MARGARET (*To* GENE)   I don't know what we're going to do about that car. Your father shouldn't be driving any more. But they just keep renewing his license by mail. (*She moves stiffly, looking at her garden and trees and lawn*) I must say, there's no place like home. *Mmmmm.* Just smell the grass.

GENE (*Taking his mother's arm*)   You all right?

MARGARET   It's just my mean old joints getting adjusted. I want to look at my garden. I think I see some crocuses. (*And she moves into the shadows to see her garden*)

TOM (*Coming back*)   Well, he did bring it back.

GENE   Good.

TOM   Can't count on anyone these days. Where's your mother?

GENE   She's walking around her garden.

TOM   What?

GENE   She's walking around her garden.

TOM   You know, Gene, I don't mean to criticize, but I notice you're mumbling a great deal. It's getting very difficult to understand you.

GENE (*Friendly, his hand on his father's shoulder*)   I think you need a hearing aid, Dad.

TOM   I can hear perfectly well if people would only enunciate. "Mr. Garrison, if you would only *E-NUN-CIATE*." Professor Aurelio, night school. Didn't you ever have to take any public speaking?

GENE   No, Dad.

TOM   All your education. Well . . . Where did you say your mother was?

GENE   Walking around her garden.

TOM (*Intense. He has been waiting for someone to say this to*) I tell you, the strain has been awful.

GENE   She looks well.

TOM   I know. But you never know when she might get another of those damned seizures.
(*He looks at the ground and shakes his head at the problem of it all*)

GENE (*Pats his father's shoulder*)   It's rough. I know.

TOM   Well, we'll manage. She's a good soldier. But you know, she eats too fast. The doctor said she must slow down. But not your mother. Incidentally, don't forget she has a birthday coming up.

GENE (*Who knows his mother's birthday and hates being reminded of it each year*)   Yes, I know.

TOM   Before you go, I want to give you some money. Go get something nice for me to give her. Handkerchiefs. You know what she likes.

GENE (*Who has done this every Christmas and birthday for years . . . smiles*)   All right. (TOM *coughs, deep and thick*) We're going to have to get that cough looked into.

TOM   I fully intend to, now I'm home. But I wasn't going to let them get their hands on me down there. If you're a tourist, they just soak you.

GENE   With the problems you've had with pneumonia . . .

TOM   I can take care of myself. Don't worry about me.

GENE   Let's go see if Dr. Mayberry can see you.

TOM   First thing tomorrow.

GENE   Why not make the appointment today?

TOM (*Irked*)   Now, look, I'm perfectly able to take care of myself.

GENE   Mother would feel better if—

TOM (*That smile again*)   Now, Gene, don't you think I have the sense to take care of myself?

GENE (*Smiling, but a little angry*)   Sometimes, no.

TOM (*Considers this, but is mollified by the smile*)   Well, I appreciate your solicitude, old man. Why don't you stay for supper?

GENE   I was planning to take you to Schrafft's.

TOM   Hooray for our side! (GENE *starts out toward the garden*) Oh, Gene. I want to talk to you a minute. We received your four letters from California . . .

GENE   I'm sorry I didn't write more often.

TOM   Well, we *do* look forward to your letters. But this girl, this woman you mentioned several times . . .

GENE   Yes?

TOM   You seemed to see a lot of her.

GENE   Yes. I did.

TOM   Carol's been dead now, what is it? . . .

GENE   About a year.

TOM   And there's no reason why you shouldn't go out with other women. (GENE *just waits*) I was in California with the Senator, and before that. It's a perfectly beautiful place. I can understand your enthusiasm for it. Gorgeous place.

GENE   Yes. I like it a lot.

TOM   But listen, Gene . . . (*He bites his upper lip, and his voice is heavy with emotion*) If you were to go out there, I mean, to live, it would kill your mother. (*He looks at his son with piercing eyes, tears starting. This has been in the nature of a plea and an order.* GENE *says nothing. He is angry at this order, that his father would say such a thing*) God, you know you're her whole life. (GENE *is further embarrassed and troubled by this statement of what he knows to be the truth from his father*) Yes, you are! Oh, she likes your sister. But you . . . are . . . her . . . life!

GENE   Dad, we've always been fond of each other, but—

TOM   Just remember what I said.
(MARGARET *can now be heard reciting to herself, very emotionally*)

MARGARET   "Lovelist of trees, the cherry now / Is hung with bloom along the bough, / And stands about the woodland ride, / Wearing white for Eastertide." (*She opens her eyes*) Oh, Gene, I've just been looking at your garden. Give me a real hug. You haven't given me a real hug yet.
(GENE *hugs her, uncomfortable, but loving and dutiful. It is, after all, a small thing.* MARGARET *looks at him, then kisses him on the lips*) Mmmmmmm. (*She smiles, making a playful thing of it*) Oh, you're a sight for sore eyes.
(TOM *has watched this, and looks significantly at* GENE)

TOM (*Moving off*)   Gene is staying for dinner. We're going to Schrafft's.

MARGARET   Oh. Can you give us all that time?

TOM   He said he would. Now come along. You shouldn't be standing so long. You've had a long trip. (*He exits*)

MARGARET   He worries so about me. I suppose it is a strain, but he makes me nervous reminding me I should be sitting or lying down . . . Oh, well . . . (*She takes* GENE's *arm*) How are you, my precious?

GENE   Fine.

MARGARET   We haven't talked about your trip to California.

GENE   No.

MARGARET (*Raising her voice*)   I say, we haven't talked about your trip.

GENE   We will.

MARGARET (*Low*)   Did you speak to your father about seeing a doctor?

GENE   He promised me tomorrow.

MARGARET   I'll believe it when I see it. He's so darned stubborn. Alice takes after him.

GENE   Oh, I got a piece of it too.

MARGARET (*Her tinkling laugh*)   You? You don't have a stubborn bone in your body.
(*We fade, as they move up and into the shadows*)

Immediately the lights come up on another part of the stage—Schrafft's.

MARY (*A pretty Irish waitress, she is just finishing setting up her table as* TOM *enters*)   Well, good evening, Mr. Garrison. Welcome back.

TOM (*The charmer*)   Greetings and salutations.

MARY   We've missed you.

TOM   It's mutual. Is this your table?

MARY   Yes.

TOM   Is there a draft here? I like to keep Mrs. Garrison out of drafts.
(*He looks around for windows.* MARGARET *and* GENE *come into the area. He is helping her, as she moves slowly and deliberately*)

MARY   Good evening, Mrs. Garrison. Nice to have you back.

TOM   You remember Mary?

MARGARET (*Polite but reserved*)   Yes. Good evening, Mary.

MARY   You're looking well, Mrs. Garrison.

MARGARET (*As* TOM *holds the chair for her*)   But look at him.
(*She nods at* TOM)

MARY   We'll fatten him up.

TOM (*Smiling, flirtatiously*)   Will you do that now? Oh, we've missed you.
We've had a girl down there in Florida, no sense of humor. Couldn't get a
smile out of her.

MARY   Well, we'll have some jokes. Dry martini?

TOM (*A roguish twinkle*)   You twist my arm. Six to one. (*He says this as
though he were being quite a man to drink his martini so dry.* GENE *finds all
this by-play harmless, but uncomfortable*) You remember my son, Gene.

MARY (*Smiles*)   Yes.
(GENE *smiles back*)

TOM   What's your pleasure, Gene . . . Dubonnet?

GENE   I'll have a martini too, please.

TOM   But not six to one.

GENE   Yes. The same.

TOM   Well!

GENE   Mother?

MARGARET   No, nothing. My joints would be stiff as a board.

TOM (*With a twinkle in his eye*)   You said you'd be stiff?

MARGARET   What?

TOM (*Raising his voice*)   You said you'd be stiff?

MARGARET   My joints. My joints.

TOM   Oh, wouldn't want you stiff. (*He thinks he's being very funny, and tries
to share his laugh with* GENE, *who smiles reluctantly.* MARY *exits. To* GENE)
Have I ever shown you this ring?

MARGARET   Oh, Tom, you've shown it to him a hundred times.

TOM (*Ignoring her reminder*)   I never thought I'd wear a diamond ring, but
when the Senator died, I wanted something of his. Last time I had it appraised, they told me it was worth four thousand.

MARGARET   It's his favorite occupation, getting that ring appraised.

TOM (*Again ignoring her*)   Don't let anyone ever tell you it's a yellow diamond. It's a golden diamond. Of course, when I go to see a doctor, I turn it
around.

(*He gives a sly smile. The others look embarrassed*)

MARGARET (*Looking at the menu*)   What are you going to have?

TOM (*Taking out his glasses*)   Now, this is my dinner, understand?

GENE   No. I invited you.

TOM   Uh-uh. You had all the expenses of coming to get us.

GENE   No, it's mine. And order what you want. Don't go reading down the prices first.

TOM (*Smiles at the idea, though he knows he does it*)   What do you mean?

GENE   Whenever I take you out to dinner, you always read down the prices first.

MARGARET   Oh, he does that anyway.

TOM   I do not. But I think it's ridiculous to pay, look, three seventy-five for curried shrimp.

GENE   You like shrimp. Take the shrimp.

TOM   If you'll let me pay for it.

GENE (*Getting annoyed*)   No! Now, come on.

TOM   Look, I appreciate it, Gene, but on what you make . . .

GENE   I can afford it. Now let's not argue.

MARGARET   Tell me, lovey, do you get paid your full salary on your sabbatical?

GENE   No. Fifty percent.

TOM   Well, then, look . . .

MARGARET   Now, Father, he wants to pay. Let him pay. (*They consult their menus*) Incidentally, Tom, you should go over and say hello to Bert Edwards. Gene and I stopped on our way in.

TOM   Why?

MARGARET   While we were gone, he lost his wife.

TOM   Where'd he lose her?

MARGARET   Tom!

TOM   Just trying to get a rise.

MARGARET   And Mrs. Bernard. She looks terrible.

TOM   Always did.

MARGARET   She lost her husband six months ago. She told me, just before we left for Florida, "I hope I go soon."

TOM   Why are you so morbid tonight?

MARGARET   I'm not morbid. They're just there. We really should see them, have them in.

TOM   Phooey! Who needs them?

MARGARET   Oh, Tom! I can't have anyone in. Your father won't play bridge or do anything. He just wants to watch Westerns or tell the story of his life.

TOM   Now, wait a minute.

MARGARET   I can't invite people to come over to watch Westerns or to listen to you go on and on. You embarrass me so. You insist on going into the most gruesome details of your life.

TOM   People seem to be interested.

MARGARET   What?

TOM   Have you got that turned up?

MARGARET   Yes. (*She adjusts the volume*)

TOM   I said they seem to be interested.
(*He tries to take* GENE *in on an exasperated shaking of the head, but* GENE *looks the other way*)

MARGARET   I admit it's a remarkable story, your life. But there are other things to talk about. People want to talk about art or music or books.

TOM   Well, let them.

MARGARET   He keeps going over and over the old times. Other people have had miserable childhoods, and they don't keep going over and over them . . That story of your mother's funeral. And you say I'm morbid.

GENE   What was that? I don't remember that.

MARGARET   Oh, don't get him started.

TOM   And I'd do it again. I was only ten, but I'd do it again. We hadn't seen him in over a year, living, the four of us, in a miserable two-room tenement, and suddenly he shows up weeping and begging, and drunk, as usual. And I shoved him off! (*He almost relives it*) I never saw him again till some years later when he was dying in Bellevue . . . of drink. (*The hatred and anger are held in, but barely*)

MARGARET (*She has been studying the menu*)   What looks good to you?

TOM (*A hard, sharp edge to his voice*)   I have not finished! I went down to see him, to ask him if he wanted anything. He said he wanted an orange. I sent him in a half-dozen oranges. I would have sent more, except I knew he was dying, and there was no point in just giving a lot of oranges to the nurses. The next morning he died.

(*There is a silence for a moment, while* GENE *and* MARGARET *look at the menu, and* TOM *grips and ungrips his hand in memory of his hatred for his father*)

MARGARET (*Gently*)   Look at your menu now, Father. What are you going to eat?

TOM   I don't feel like anything. I have no appetite.
(*He lights a cigarette*)

MARGARET (*To* GENE)   This is the way it's been.

GENE   He'll see a doctor tomorrow. Don't get upset.
(MARY *arrives with the martinis*)

TOM   Your mother wants me to play cards with a lot of women who just want to gossip and chatter about styles. That's why I won't play.

MARGARET   You won't play because you can't follow the play of the cards any more.

TOM   I beg to disagree.

GENE   Please! Don't fight . . . don't fight. (*He's said this in a mock-serious singsong*)

MARGARET   He kept telling everyone how he wouldn't allow his father to come to his mother's funeral.

TOM (*Defensively angry*)   Are you implying that I should have let him?

MARGARET   I'm not saying—

TOM   He'd run out on us when we were kids, and I told him—

MARGARET   I'm not saying you were wrong. You're so defensive about it. I'm saying you're wrong to keep bringing it up.

TOM   You brought it up this time.

MARGARET   Well, I'm sorry. Imagine going around telling everyone he shoved his father off the funeral coach. (*She is consulting the menu*)

TOM   Ah, here we are.

MARY   Six to one. (*She puts the martini in front of him*)

TOM   Damn it. (*He fishes out the lemon peel*)

MARY   But you always ask for lemon peel.

TOM (*Demonstrating*)   Twisted over it, not dumped in it. It's all right. It's all right. (*With an Irish accent*) Well, to your smilin' Irish eyes.

MARY   He hasn't changed, has he?

TOM   What county are you from, did you say?

MARY   Armagh.

TOM   I knew there was something I liked about you. That's where my people came from, County Armagh. (*He drinks*) Do you have any burnt ice cream tonight?

MARY   Ah, you.

TOM (*Smiling*)   No, I mean it. (*To* GENE) They have burnt ice cream here.

MARY   I'll be back.
(*And she exits.* MARGARET *sits embarrassed and piqued by this kind of flirtation which has gone on all their lives*)

TOM (*The sport, to* GENE)   I like to get a rise out of them. If they kid with me, I give them a good tip. If they don't, a straight ten percent. (*He draws a line on the tablecloth to emphasize this. He looks at* MARGARET) What's the matter?

MARGARET   If you want to make a fool of yourself, go right ahead.
(TOM *is angry, hurt and exasperated. He looks at her, and then tries to include* GENE, *to make him share his anger. But* GENE *looks away and to the menu.* TOM *stares at his glass, and his jaw muscles start to work. The scene dims in the Schrafft's area, and* GENE *moves from the table to another side of the stage*)

GENE   We hurried through the last part of our dinner. My father ate only his dessert, burnt almond ice cream. We hurried through to rush home to one of my father's rituals, the television Western. He would sit in front of them hour after hour, falling asleep in one and waking up in the middle of the next one, never knowing the difference. When my father fell in love with a program, it was forever. All during my childhood we ate our dinner to the accompaniment of Lowell Thomas and Amos and Andy. If anyone dared to talk, father would storm away from the table and have his dinner served at the radio . . . I say, we rushed away from Schrafft's. Actually, my father rushed. We just lived down the street. I walked my mother home very slowly, stopping every fifty yards or so.
(MARGARET *has joined* GENE *and taken his arm*)

MARGARET   I don't know how he can sit through hour after hour of those Westerns.

GENE   I think he always wished he'd been a cowboy. "Take 'em out and shoot 'em!"

MARGARET   He won't listen to the things I want to hear. Down in Florida there's only one TV in the lounge, and he rode herd on it. And then he'd fall asleep in three minutes . . . Still, he's a remarkable man.

GENE   Good old Mom.

MARGARET   Well, he is. Not many boys have fathers they could be as proud of.

GENE   I know that, Mom, I'm very . . . proud of him.

MARGARET (*She catches his tone*)   Everything he's done, he's done for his family. (GENE *just looks at her, smiling*) So he didn't dance with me at parties. (*She smiles at* GENE) You took care of that.

GENE   You were just a great dancer, Mother.

MARGARET   I was a terrible dancer. You just couldn't stand seeing me sitting alone at a table at the club while your father was . . .
(*She stops, realizing she's about to make* GENE'*s point*)

GENE   . . . off dancing with various other people, tablehopping or playing poker with the boys in the locker room.

MARGARET   What a shame that children can't see their parents when they're young and courting, and in love. All they see them being is tolerant, sympathetic, forbearing and devoted. All the qualities that are so unimportant to passionate young people.
(TOM *appears*)

TOM   Gene . . . Gene . . . Come watch this one. This is a real shoot-'em-up.

GENE   In a minute, Dad.

MARGARET   Gene, I want to talk to you.

GENE   You should be in bed. You've had a big day.
(*They move to another part of the stage*)

MARGARET   I took another nitro. And I've had something on my mind for a long time now. You remember you gave me that heart-shaped pillow when I was in the hospital once, when you were a boy?
(*She sits on the chaise longue*)

GENE   Yes.

MARGARET   Fidget used to curl up here. (*She indicates the crook in her leg*) And you'd sit over there, and we'd listen to the Metropolitan Opera broadcasts.
(GENE *is made uncomfortable by this attempt to evoke another time, another kind of relationship, but he doesn't show it*)

GENE   Yes. I remember.

MARGARET   You'd dress up in costumes and act in front of that mirror. I remember you were marvelous as D'Artagnan in *The Three Musketeers*. (*For the fun of it, a forty-year-old-man, he assumes the dueling stance, and thrusts at his image in an imaginary mirror.* GENE *sits on a footstool and watches her adjust herself in her chaise. After a moment)* Tell me about California.

GENE (*A little taken by surprise. Here is the subject*)   I loved it.

MARGARET   And the girl, the woman with the children? The doctor? (GENE *doesn't say anything. He frowns, wondering what to say)* You love her too, don't you?

GENE   I think so.

MARGARET   I know when Carol died, you said you'd never marry again. But I hoped you would. I know it's hard, but I think Carol would have wanted you to.

GENE   I don't know.

MARGARET (*Fidgets a moment from embarrassment, then*)   I know it's not a mother's place to pry and talk about these things . . . But I've been worried about you, I mean, you're a man . . . and . . . well . . . sex.

GENE (*Smiles*)   I'm . . . all right.

MARGARET   You mean you've been . . . communicating?

GENE (*With a broad smile*)   Yes. I've been . . . communicating.

MARGARET   You don't mind my talking about that, do you?

GENE (*Amused and a little embarrassed*)   No.

MARGARET   I'll never understand your generation, I guess. I'm glad I didn't have to face all . . . well, all that, in my day. People simply waited. And I'm not so sure we weren't right.

GENE (*Not wanting to go into it*)   Well . . .

MARGARET   Too late for me to worry about that now. Though sometimes I wish I'd known more . . . understood more . . . (*She stops, embarrassed.* GENE *is sad and uncomfortable that his seventy-eight-year-old mother would seem to want to talk to someone at last about her unsatisfactory sex life. The moment passes)* Gene, your sabbatical is over soon, isn't it?

GENE   A few more months.

MARGARET   I think you want to move to California and get a job teaching there and marry this woman.

GENE (*After a moment*)   Yes, I think I do. I wasn't sure while I was there. I suddenly felt I should get away and think. But when I walked into my old apartment, with all Carol's things there . . .

MARGARET   I think it would be the best thing in the world for you to get away, to marry this girl.

GENE (*Touched . . . very simply*)   Thanks.

MARGARET   A new place, a new wife, a new life. I would feel just terrible if you didn't go because of me. There are still planes, trains and telephones, and Alice comes from Chicago once or twice a year and brings the children.

GENE   Thanks, Mother. You've always made things very easy. I think you'll like Peggy.

MARGARET   I'm sure I will. You have good taste in women. And they have good taste when they like you.

GENE   I'm not so sure. I never really knew if I made Carol happy . . . If I did make her happy, I wish she'd let me know it.

MARGARET   I guess a lot of us forget to say thank you until it's too late. (*She takes his hand and smiles at him*) Thank you . . . You have such nice hands. I've always loved your hands . . . You've been so good to me, Gene, so considerate. Perhaps I've let you be too considerate. But it was your nature, and your father just withdrew behind his paper and his investments and his golf. And our interests seem to go together. You liked to sing, and I played the piano, oh, miserably, but I played. (*She strokes his hand*) I tried not to be one of those possessive mothers, Gene. If I did things wrong, I just did the best I knew how.

GENE   You did everything just fine.
(*He pats his mother's hand before he draws his own away*)

MARGARET   And your father has done the best he knew how.

GENE (*With no conviction*)   Yes.
(*This is her old song. She knows that* GENE *knows it's probably true, but he gets no satisfaction from the knowledge*)

MARGARET   Of course you know your father will object to your going away.

GENE   He already has. He said it would kill you.

MARGARET   How sad. Why can't he say it would kill him? He doesn't think it would hold you or mean anything to you. (*She shakes her head*) He dotes on your letters down there. Reads them and rereads them. Tells everyone what a fine relationship he has with you. "My door is always open . . . Anything he wants, he can have . . . We have always had each other's confidence . . ." (GENE *smiles at this and sadly shakes his head*) Well, you go to California. Your father and I can take care of each other. I'll remember where he put his checkbook, and he'll make the beds, which is the only thing I'm really not supposed to do. And, for your information, I have my old-lady's home all picked out. That's what I want, so I won't be a burden to any of you.

GENE   You a burden!

MARGARET (*Wisely*)   Oh, yes! Now don't mention this business to your father tonight. He's not well, and it's been such a nice day. In the next few days I'll talk to him, tell him it's important for you to—

GENE   No, I'll do it.
(*He kisses her on the cheek*)

MARGARET   Good night, my precious.

GENE   Where would you like to celebrate your birthday?

MARGARET   Oh, lovey, you've already given me so much time. Just call me on the phone.

GENE   No . . . We can at least have dinner . . . I'll make some plans.

MARGARET   Gene, if your father gives you money to buy his present for me, please, no more handkerchiefs.

GENE   He always says handkerchiefs.

MARGARET   I know, but I've got dozens and dozens from my past birthdays and Christmases.

GENE   What would you like?

MARGARET   Get me some perfume. You choose the kind, except I don't like lily of the valley, or gardenia.

GENE   You're a hard woman to please . . . Good night . . . You look great.

MARGARET   Oh, a little rouge and lipstick. Thanks for coming to meet us. Tell your father I've gone to bed, and don't let him keep you there to all hours watching television (*Calling after him*) I don't like carnation either.
(GENE *waves back affectionately and moves away, as the lights dim on* MARGARET'*s area.* GENE *moves, then stands and looks at the back of his father's chair as the TV sounds come up, and lights come on in that area.* GENE *moves to his father's chair and gently touches his arm while turning the knob of the TV volume*)

TOM (*Stirring*)   What? . . . What?
(*He comes to slowly, shaking his head and looks at* GENE, *bewildered*)

GENE (*Gently*)   I'm going now, Dad.

TOM   Oh, so soon?

GENE (*Controls his irritation. This has always been his father's response, no matter how long he has been with him*)   Yes. I have to go.

TOM   Where's your mother?

GENE   She's upstairs. She's fine. (TOM *starts to cough*) You see about that in the morning, Dad.

TOM (*Getting up steadying himself*)   I fully intend to. I would have done it down there, but I wasn't going to be charged outrageous prices. (*He glances at the TV screen*) Oh, this is a good one. Why don't you just stay for this show?

GENE (*The anger building*)   No, Dad. I've got to run along.

TOM   Well, all right. We see so little of you.

GENE   I'm up at least once a week, Dad.

TOM   Oh, I'm not complaining. (*But he is*) There just doesn't seem to be any time. And when you are here, your mother's doing all the talking. The way she interrupts. She just doesn't listen. And I say, "Margaret, please." . . . But she goes right on . . . Well, "all's lost, all's spent, when we our desires get without content . . . 'tis better to be that which we destroy, than by destruction dwell with doubtful joy."

GENE (*He is always puzzled by his father's frequent use of this quotation. It never is immediately appropriate, but it indicates such unhappiness that it is sad and touching to him*)   We'll get a chance to talk, Dad.
(*He moves toward the porch*)

TOM   I can't tell you what a comfort it is knowning you are just down in the city. Don't know what we'd do without you. No hat or coat?

GENE   No.

TOM   It's still chilly. You should be careful.

GENE (*Kissing his father on the cheek*)   Good night, Dad. 'I'll call you tomorrow to see if you've gone to the doctor's.

TOM   Well, I may and I may not. I've looked after myself pretty well for almost eighty years. I guess I can judge if I need to see the doctor or not.

GENE (*Angry*)   Look, Dad . . .

TOM   Seventy years ago when I was a snot-nosed kid up in Harlem, a doctor looked at me and said if I were careful, I'd live to be twenty. That's what I think about doctors. Ten dollars to look at your tongue. Phooey! Out! Who needs them?

GENE   Look, Dad, you're worrying Mother to death with that cough.

TOM   All right, all right. I'll go. I'll be a good soldier . . . You're coming up for your mother's birthday, aren't you?

GENE Yes.

TOM And don't forget, Mother's Day is coming up.

GENE Well . . .

TOM Why don't we make reservations at that restaurant in Connecticut where you took us last Mother's Day?

GENE We'll see.

TOM It will be my party. And, Gene, remember what I said about California!

GENE (*Straining to get away from all the encirclements*) Good night, Dad.
(*He moves off*)

TOM Drive carefully. I noticed you were inclined to push it up there a little. (GENE *burns*) Make a full stop going out the driveway, then turn right.

GENE (*Angry, moves further down*) Yes, Dad.

TOM (*Calling after him*) Traffic is terrible out there now. Used to be a quiet little street. Take your first left, and your second right.

GENE (*He has driven this route for many years*) Yes.

TOM The left under the bridge. It's a little tricky down there. (*When he gets no response, he calls*) Gene?

GENE (*In a sudden outburst*) I've driven this road for twenty years, for Christ's sake!
(*He is immediately sorry, and turns away from his father's direction*)

TOM Just trying to be helpful.
(*The lights fade on* TOM *as he goes back into the house.* GENE *is now downstage*)

GENE Take your first left and your second right. Then turn left under the bridge. But do not go as far as California, because it would kill your mother . . . I hated him for that, for sending up warning flares that if I left, it would not be with his blessing, but with a curse . . . as he had banished my sister Alice years ago for marrying a Jew . . . and the scene so terrified me at fourteen, I was sick . . . He knew his man . . . that part of me at least . . . a gentleman who gave way at intersections . . . And yet, when I looked at those two old people, almost totally dependent on me for their happiness . . . This is the way the world ends, all right . . .
(*A phone rings. A light picks out* TOM *holding the phone*)

TOM I was downstairs in the kitchen, and suddenly I heard your mother scream . . . "Tom! Tom!" . . . I ran up the stairs . . . (*He is seized with a fit of coughing*) I ran up the stairs, and there she was stretched out on the

floor of the bedroom . . . "Nitro" . . . "nitro" . . . That's all she could say. You know we have nitroglycerine all over the house.
(*A* NURSE *comes to* TOM *as the lights come up; she leads him into a hospital waiting-room area.* GENE *joins them*)

GENE   Dad.
(*He shakes his hand and kisses him on the cheek*)

TOM   Am I glad to see you! Have you seen your mother?

GENE   Yes. She's sleeping.
(TOM *starts to cough*)

GENE   That doesn't sound any better.

TOM   Well, I've had a shot. After your mother got settled over here, the doctor took me to his office and gave me a shot. I *would* have gone down there in Florida, you know, but . . . well . . . (*Shakes his head*) I just don't know. I was in the kitchen getting breakfast . . . You know I've been getting the breakfasts, when suddenly I heard her scream, "Tom. Tom." I went running up the stairs, and there she was stretched out on the floor. She'd had an attack. "Nitro," she whispered. We've got it all over the house, you know. She'd had attacks before, but I knew at once that this was something more. I gave her the pills and called the doctor . . . "This is an emergency. Come quick." . . . The doctor came, gave her a shot . . . and called the ambulance . . . and here we are. (*He shakes his head, partly in sorrow, but also partly in exasperation that such a thing could happen*) She had a good time in Florida. I don't understand it. She ate too fast, you know. And the doctor had said she should do everything more slowly.

GENE   There's no explaining these things, Dad.

TOM   I suppose I could have seen more of her down there. But she just wanted to play bridge, and I didn't play, because the ladies just chattered all the time about styles and shops . . . And I met some very interesting people. Oh, some of them were bores and just wanted to tell you the story of their life. But there were others. You know, I met a man from Waterbury, Connecticut, used to know Helen Moffett . . . I've told you about Helen Moffett, haven't I? When I was a kid, when the clouds were low and dark, my grandfather'd take me up there sometimes on Sundays . . . a city slum kid in that lovely country . . . And Helen and I . . . oh . . . it never amounted to much. We'd go to church, and then we'd take a walk and sit in a hammock or under an apple tree. I think she liked that. But I didn't have any money, and I couldn't go up there often. Her mother didn't like me . . . "That young man will end up the same way as his father." . . . And that scared her off . . . This man in Florida, I've got his name somewhere . . . (*He fishes out a notebook and starts to go through it*) He said Helen had never married . . . Said she'd been in love as a kid . . . and had never married. (*Tears come to his eyes*) Well, I can't find it. No matter. (GENE *doesn't know what to say. He is touched by this naked and unconscious revelation of an early and deeply meaningful love. But it seems so incongruous under the circumstances*) Some day we might drive out there and look him up . . . Helen's dead now, but it's nice country. I was a kid with nothing . . . living with my grandfather . . . Maybe if she hadn't been so far away . . . Well, that's water over the dam.

GENE (*After a long pause, he touches his father*)   Yes.

TOM (*Just sits for a few moments, then seems to come back to the present, and takes out his watch*)   You know, I'd like to make a suggestion.

GENE   What, Dad?

TOM   If we move right along, we might be able to make the Rotary Club for dinner. (GENE *frowns in bewilderment*) I've been away for three months. They don't like that very much if you're absent too often. They drop you or fine you. How about it?

(*He asks this with a cocked head and a twinkle in his eye*)

GENE   I thought we might eat something around here in the hospital.

TOM   I had lunch in the coffee shop downstairs, and it's terrible. It will only take a little longer. We won't stay for the speeches, though sometimes they're very good, very funny. We'll just say hello to the fellows and get back . . . Your mother's sleeping now. That's what they want her to do.

GENE (*Bewildered by this, but doesn't want to get into an argument*)   Let's drop by and see Mother first.

TOM   They want her to rest. We'd only disturb her.

GENE   All right.

TOM (*As they turn to go, he puts his arm around* GENE's *shoulder*)   I don't know what I'd do without you, old man.
(*As the lights shift, and* TOM *and* GENE *head away, we move to the Rotary gathering, held in the grill room of one of the local country clubs. A piano is heard offstage, playing old-fashioned singing-type songs [badly]. A tinkle of glasses . . . a hum of men talking and laughing. This area is presumably an anteroom with two comfortable leather chairs. A man enters, wearing a large name button and carrying a glass. This is the minister,* REVEREND PELL, *a straightforward, middle-aged man*)

REVEREND PELL   Hello, Tom, good to see you back.

TOM (*His face lights up in a special "greeting the fellows" type grin*)   Hello, Sam.

REVEREND PELL   Did you have a good trip?

TOM   All except for the damned wind down there. *Oooops.* Excuse my French, Sam . . . You know my son, Gene. Reverend Pell.

REVEREND PELL   Yes, of course. Hello, Gene.
(*They shake hands*)

TOM   Gene was a Marine. (GENE *frowns*) You were a Marine, weren't you, Sam?

REVEREND PELL   No. Navy.

TOM   Well, same thing.

REVEREND PELL   Don't say that to a Marine.
(GENE *and* REVEREND PELL *smile*)

TOM   Gene saw the flag go up on Iwo.

GENE (*Embarrassed by all this inappropriate line*)   Let's order a drink, Dad.

TOM   Sam, I've been wanting to talk to you. Now is not the appropriate time, but some bozo has been crowding into our pew at church. You know Margaret and I sit up close because she doesn't hear very well. Well, this guy has been there in our pew. I've given him a pretty sharp look several times, but it doesn't seem to faze him. Now, I don't want to seem unreasonable, but there is a whole church for him to sit in.

REVEREND PELL   Well, we'll see what we can do, Tom.

TOM (*Calling to a bartender*)   A martini, George. Six to one. (*To* GENE) Dubonnet?

GENE   A martini.

TOM   Six to one?

GENE   Yes, Only make mine vodka.

TOM   Vodka? Out! Phooey!

REVEREND PELL   What have you got against vodka, Tom?

TOM   It's Russian, isn't it? However, I don't want to influence you. Make his vodka. Six to one, now! These fellows like to charge you extra for a six to one, and then they don't give you all the gin you've got coming to you.

REVEREND PELL   I hope you don't drink many of those, Tom, six to one.

TOM   My grandmother used to give me, every morning before I went to school, when I was knee-high to a grasshopper . . . she used to give me a jigger of gin with a piece of garlic in it, to keep away colds. I wonder what the teacher thought. Phew. I must have stunk to high heaven . . . She used to put a camphor ball in my necktie too. That was for colds, too, I think . . . But they were good people. They just didn't know any better. That's my grandfather and my grandmother. I lived with them for a while when I was a little shaver, because my father . . . well, that's another story . . . but my grandfather—

REVEREND PELL (*He puts his hand on* TOM's *arm*)   I don't mean to run out on you, Tom, but I was on my way to the little-boy's room. I'll catch up with you later.

TOM   Go ahead. We don't want an accident.

REVEREND PELL (*As he is going, to* GENE)   You got a great dad there. (*And he disappears*)

TOM   I don't really know these fellows any more. (*Indicating people offstage*) All new faces. Most of them are bores. All they want to do is tell you the story of their lives. But sometimes you hear some good jokes . . . Now, here's someone I know. Hello, Marvin.
(MARVIN SCOTT, *a man about sixty-five, enters*)

MARVIN SCOTT   Hello, Tom. Good to see you back.

TOM   You remember my son, Gene.

MARVIN SCOTT   Yes. Hello.

GENE   Hello, Mr. Scott.

MARVIN SCOTT (*To* TOM)   Well, young feller, you're looking great!

TOM   Am I? Well, thank you.

MARVIN SCOTT   How's Margaret?
(TOM *goes very dramatic, pauses for a moment and bites his lip.* MARVIN *looks at* GENE)

GENE   Mother's . . .

TOM   Margaret's in an oxygen tent in the hospital.

MARVIN SCOTT (*Surprised that* TOM *is here, he looks at* GENE, *then at* TOM)   I'm terribly sorry to hear that, Tom.

TOM   Heart.
(*He shakes his head and starts to get emotional*)

GENE (*Embarrassed*)   We're just going to grab a bite and get back. Mother's sleeping, and if we were there, she'd want to talk.

MARVIN SCOTT   I'm sorry to hear that, Tom. When did it happen?

TOM (*Striving for control. His emotion is as much anger that it could happen, and self-pity, as anything else*)   This morning . . . I was in the kitchen, getting something for Margaret, when suddenly I heard her scream . . . "Tom . . . Tom . . ." and I ran upstairs . . . and there she was stretched

out on the bedroom floor . . . "Nitro . . . nitro" . . . she said . . . We have nitroglycerine all over the house, you know . . . since her last two attacks . . . So, I get her the nitro and call the doctor . . . and now she's in an oxygen tent in the hospital . . .
(The bell starts to ring to call them to dinner)

MARVIN SCOTT   Well, I hope everything's all right, Tom.

GENE   Thank you.

TOM   What happened to those martinis? We've got to go into dinner and we haven't gotten them yet.

GENE   We can take them to the table with us.

TOM   I have to drink mine before I eat anything. It brings up the gas. Where the hell are they?
(And he heads off)

MARVIN SCOTT *(To GENE)*   He's quite a fella.
(And they move off as Rotarians start singing to the tune of "Auld Lang Syne," "We're awfully glad you're here," etc.)

    As the lights fade on this group they come up on the hospital bed and MARGARET. *The* NURSE *is sitting there, reading a movie magazine. The oxygen tent has been moved away.* TOM *and* GENE *enter quietly, cautiously. The* NURSE *gets up.* GENE *approaches the bed.*

GENE *(Whispers to the NURSE)*   Anything?

NURSE   The doctor was just here. He said things looked much better.

TOM *(Too loud)*   Hooray for our side.

MARGARET *(Stirs)*   Hm . . . What?
(She looks around)

GENE   Hello, Mother.

MARGARET   Oh, Gene. *(She reaches as though to touch him)* Look where I ended up.

GENE   The doctor says you're better tonight.

MARGARET *(Her eyes flashing)*   You know how this happened, don't you? Why it happened?
(She nods her head in the direction of TOM, who is at the foot of the bed chatting with the NURSE)

GENE *(Quieting)*   Now, Mother. Take it easy. He's seen the doctor. He's had his shot.

MARGARET   Well!

GENE You should be sleeping.

MARGARET That's all I've been doing. (*She takes his hand*) It makes me so mad. I was feeling so well. All the ladies down in Florida said I've never looked so well.

GENE You've had these before, Mother. Easy does it.

MARGARET He's seen the doctor for himself?

GENE Yes. Just a bad cold. He's had a shot.

MARGARET Why wouldn't he have that down there?

GENE Mother, we'll have to go if you talk like this, because you should be resting.

TOM (*Leaving the* NURSE, *cheerful*) Well, how goes it?

MARGARET How do I know?

TOM (*Takes her hand and smiles*) You look better.

MARGARET You know I came without anything. I've still got my stockings on.

TOM (*Kidding. Very gentle*) Well, it all happened pretty quick, my darling.

MARGARET I'll need some things.

TOM Your wish is our command.

GENE I'll write it down. But don't talk too much.

MARGARET Toothbrush . . . some night clothes. I'm still in my slip . . . a hairbrush.

TOM We'll collect some things.

MARGARET (*Joshing*) Oh, you. You wouldn't know what to bring. Gene, you look around.

GENE Yes. Now, take it easy.

MARGARET I hate being seen this way.

TOM We think you look beautiful.

GENE Mother, we're just going to sit here now, because you're talking too much. You're being a bad girl. (MARGARET *makes a childlike face at him, puckering her lips and wrinkling her nose. She reaches out for his hand*) Those are lovely flowers Alice sent. She knows your favorites. I called her. I'll keep in touch with her. She said she'd come on, but I said I didn't think she had to.

MARGARET Did you have any dinner?

TOM   We went to Rotary. Everyone asked for you.

MARGARET   That's nice.
(DR. MAYBERRY *comes into the room, in the shadows of the entrance.* GENE *spots him and goes to him*)

DR. MAYBERRY   Hello, Gene. How are you?

GENE (*Trying to catch him before he enters the room entirely*)   I'd like to—

DR. MAYBERRY (*Pleasant and hearty*)   We can talk right here. She seems to be coming along very well.

GENE   Good.

TOM   That's wonderful news.

DR. MAYBERRY (*Kidding her*)   She's tough. (MARGARET *smiles and makes a face at him*) We won't know the extent of it until we're able to take a car-diogram tomorrow. It was nothing to toss off lightly, but it looks good now.

GENE   Well . . . thank you. (TOM *coughs*) What about that?

DR. MAYBERRY   He'll be all right. Just a deep cough. He'll get another shot tomorrow.

GENE (*Low*)   You don't think we should . . . stay around?

DR. MAYBERRY   I wouldn't say so. And she should rest.

GENE   Thanks, Doctor.
(*They shake hands*)

DR. MAYBERRY   Do I have your number in New York? I'll keep in touch with you. Your dad's a little vague about things. (GENE *jots the number on a slip of paper*) Good night, Mrs. Garrison. I'm going to kick your family out now so that you can get some rest.

MARGARET (*Smiles and makes a small wave of the fingers*)   Take care of Tom.

DR. MAYBERRY   He's going to be fine. (*To* TOM) Drop into the office for another shot tomorrow.

TOM (*Kidding*)   Will you ask that girl of yours to be a little more considerate next time?

DR. MAYBERRY   Oh, you can take it.

TOM   Oh, I'm a good soldier. But, wow!
(*He indicates a sore rump*)

DR. MAYBERRY   Good night.
(*He waves his hand and disappears*)

GENE   We'll run along now, Mother.

(*She reaches her hand out*)

MARGARET My precious.

GENE (*Leans down and kisses her hand*) Good night. Sleep well.

TOM Well, my dearest, remember what we used to say to the children. "When you wake up, may your cheeks be as red as roses and your eyes as bright as diamonds."

MARGARET (*Pouts, half-kidding*) Just you take care of yourself. And get the laundry ready for Annie tomorrow.

TOM (*With a flourish*) Your wish is my command.

MARGARET I put your dirty shirts from Florida in the hamper in the guest bathroom, and my things are—

GENE (*Trying to stop her talking*) We'll find them.

MARGARET (To GENE) Thanks for coming. Don't bother to come tomorrow. Father will keep in touch with you.

GENE We'll see. Good night.
(*He stops at the door for a little wave. She wiggles her fingers in a small motion. The lights dim on the hospital scene as* TOM *and* GENE *move away*)

TOM Well, that's good news.

GENE Yes.

TOM She looks a lot better than when they brought her in here this morning, I can tell you that.

GENE She looked pretty good.

TOM She's a good soldier. Do you remember what she asked us to bring her? My mind is like a sieve.

GENE I'll come along and get the bag ready and round up the laundry.

TOM We should get the laundry ready tonight because Annie arrives at eight sharp, and she starts getting paid the minute she enters the door. But we could leave the bag till morning.

GENE (*Uneasy*) I've got an early appointment at college tomorrow, Dad. I'll have to run along after we have a nightcap.

TOM Oh, I thought you might spend the night.

GENE I . . . uh . . . I've got an early appointment at college tomorrow.

TOM I thought you were on your sabbatical.

GENE I am . . . But I arranged a meeting with someone there, Dad.

TOM   You could stay and still make it.

GENE   It's very early, Dad.

TOM   We've got an alarm. Alarm clocks all over the house.

GENE   I want to change before the appointment . . . Shirt . . .

TOM   I've got plenty of shirts . . . underwear . . . socks . . .

GENE (*More uncomfortable*)   I don't wear your sizes, Dad.

TOM   I could get you up earlier, then. I don't sleep beyond five these days.

GENE (*Tense*)   No, Dad . . . I just . . . No. I'll come by and—

TOM   There may be something good on television . . . Wednesday night. I
think there is . . .

GENE   . . . We'll watch a little television, Dad . . . and have some drinks
. . . But then I'll have to go.

TOM (*After a moment*)   All right, old man.
(GENE *instinctively reaches out to touch his father's arm, to soften the rejection.
They look at each other a moment; then* TOM *drifts off into the dark, as* GENE
moves directly downstage)

GENE   I sat with my father much longer than I meant to . . . Because I knew
I should stay the night. But . . . I couldn't . . . We watched television. He
slept on and off . . . and I went home . . . The next morning, around nine
thirty, my mother died . . .
(GENE *turns and walks upstage, as the lights dim*)

Curtain

Act Two

GENE *and* DR. MAYBERRY *enter from the rear*. GENE *is carrying a small overnight case containing his mother's things.*

GENE   Thank you for all you've done for her over the years. It's been a great
comfort to her, to us all.

DR. MAYBERRY   I was very fond of her.

GENE   She was terribly worried about my father's health. Yesterday she said
to me, "You know what put me here."

DR. MAYBERRY   Well, Gene, I think that's a little too harsh. She's been living
on borrowed time for quite a while, you know.

GENE   Yes . . . Where's Dad?

DR. MAYBERRY   He's gone along to the undertaker's. He wanted to wait for you, but since we couldn't reach you this morning, he went along. We sent your mother's nurse to be with him till you arrived.

GENE   Thank you.

DR. MAYBERRY   He's all right. You know, Gene, old people live with death. He's been prepared for this for years. It may in some way be a relief. He's taken wonderful care of her.

GENE   Yes, he has.

DR. MAYBERRY   Alice will be coming on, I suppose.

GENE   I've called her.

DR. MAYBERRY   He shouldn't be staying in that house alone. (GENE *nods*) Now, you have the suitcase and the envelope with your mother's things.

GENE   Yes. I think she should have her wedding ring.

DR. MAYBERRY   Maybe you ought to check with your father . . .

GENE   No . . . Will you? . . .
(*He hands the ring to* DR. MAYBERRY *and moves away. The lights come up on the undertaker's office.* TOM *and the* NURSE *are there*)

TOM   I find that constant wind down there very annoying. Every year I think it's going to be different, but it isn't. You get a little overheated in the sun, and when you walk out from behind some shelter, it knifes into you.

GENE   (*He has stood looking at his father for a moment. He now comes to him with tenderness, to share the experience*) Dad.

TOM (*Looks up in the middle of his story*)   Oh, Gene.
(*He gets up shakily. They embrace.* GENE *pats him on the back.* TOM *steps away and shakes his head. His mouth contorts, showing emotion and anger that this should have happened. He looks at the floor in moments like this*)

NURSE   We've given him a little sedative.

TOM (*Looks up*)   What?

NURSE   I said we'd given you a little sedative.

TOM (*At once the charmer*)   Oh, yes. This lovely lady has taken wonderful care of me.

GENE (*To the* NURSE)   Thank you.

TOM   It turns out she's been to Florida, very near to where we go.

GENE (*A little surprised at this casual conversation, but playing along*)   Oh, really?

TOM   I was telling her it was too bad we didn't have the pleasure of meeting her down there. But she goes in the summer. Isn't it terribly hot down there in the summer?

NURSE   The trade winds are always blowing.

TOM   Oh, yes, those damnable winds. We wanted this young man to come join us there, but he went to California instead. (*To* GENE) You'll have to come down to Florida sometime. See what lovely girls you'd meet there!

GENE (*Baffled and annoyed by this chatter, but passes it off*)   I will.

TOM   What was your name again? My mind's like a sieve.

NURSE   Halsey.

TOM (*Courtly*)   Miss Halsey . . . My son, Gene.

GENE   How do you do?

TOM   Miss Halsey and I are on rather intimate terms. She . . . uh . . . gave me my shot.

GENE   Good.

TOM (*To the* NURSE)   I had this terrible cough down there. The winds. But I'll be all right. Don't worry about me. If I can get some regular exercise, get over to the club.
(*For a moment they all just sit there. Obviously there is to be no sharing of the experience of the mother's death*)

GENE   I called Alice.

TOM   Oh. Thank you. (*To the* NURSE) Alice was my daughter. She . . . uh . . . lives in Chicago.

NURSE (*Shaking his hand, kindly*)   Good-by, Mr. Garrison.

TOM   Oh, are you going?

NURSE   Yes. Take good care of yourself.

TOM   Oh, well. Thank you very much my dear. You've been very kind.

GENE   Thank you.
(*The* NURSE *exits*)

MARVIN SCOTT (*Entering with some forms and papers*)   Now Tom, all we have to do is—(*He looks up from papers and sees* GENE) Oh, hello, Gene.

GENE   Mr. Scott.

MARVIN SCOTT   I'm terribly sorry.

GENE   Thank you.

MARVIN SCOTT   Now, the burial is to be where, Tom? (*Throughout he is simple, considerate and decent*)

TOM   The upper burial ground. I've got the deed at home in my file cabinet, if I can ever find it. For years I've meant to clean out that file cabinet. But I'll find it.

MARVIN SCOTT (*To* GENE)   Will you see that I get it? At least the number of the plot?

GENE   It's five forty-two.

MARVIN SCOTT   You're sure of that?

GENE   My wife was buried there last year.

TOM (*Suddenly remembering*)   That's right.
(*He reaches out and puts his hand on* GENE's *arm, implying that they have something to share.* GENE *doesn't really want to share his father's kind of emotionalism*)

MARVIN SCOTT (*He has been making notes*)   We'll need some clothes . . . uh . . .

GENE (*Quickly*)   Yes, all right. I'll take care of that.

MARVIN SCOTT   Do you want the casket open or closed while she's resting here?
(*There is a pause*)

GENE   Dad?

TOM   What was that?

GENE   Do you want the casket open or closed?

TOM   Oh . . . open, I think.
(GENE *would have preferred it closed*)

MARVIN SCOTT   Now, an obituary. Perhaps you would like to prepare something, Tom.

TOM   Yes. Well . . . Gene? Gene was very close to his mother.
(MARVIN SCOTT *looks at* GENE)

GENE   Yes, I'll work something up.

MARVIN SCOTT   If you could by this afternoon, so that it would catch the—

TOM   She was my inspiration. When I met her the clouds hung low and dark. I was going to night school, studying shorthand and typing and *elocution* . . . and working in a lumberyard in the daytime . . . wearing a cutaway coat, if you please, someone at the church had given me . . . I was making a home for my brother and sister . . . My mother had died, and my father had deserted us . . . (*He has gone hard on his father . . . and stops a moment*) "He did not know the meaning of the word 'quit.' " They said that some years ago when The Schoolboys of Old Harlem gave me an award. You were there, Gene.

GENE   Yes.

TOM   "Obstructions, yes. But go through them or over them, but never around them." Teddy Roosevelt said that. I took it down in shorthand for practice . . . Early in life I developed a will of iron . . . (*You can feel the iron in the way he says it*) Any young man in this country who has a sound mind and a sound body, who will set himself an objective, can achieve anything he wants, within reason. (*He has said all this firmly, as though lecturing or giving a speech. He now looks at his cigarette*) Ugh . . . Filthy habit. Twenty years ago a doctor told me to give these things up, and I did. But when things pile up . . . Well . . . All's lost, all's spent, when we our desires get without content . . . (*He looks around. There is a pause*)

GENE   I'll write something.

TOM   About what?

GENE   Mother. For an obituary.

TOM   Oh, yes, you do that. He's the lit'ry member of the family. You'll use the church, won't you? Not the chapel. I imagine there'll be hundreds of people there . . . Garden Club . . . Woman's Club . . . Mother's Club.

MARVIN SCOTT   I'm sure that Reverend Pell will use whichever you want. (*He shuffles some papers*) Now, Tom, the only thing that's left is the most difficult. We have to choose a coffin.

TOM   Do we have to do that now?

MARVIN SCOTT   It's easier now, Tom. To get it over with.

TOM (*Firm*)   I want the best. That's one thing. I want the best!

MARVIN SCOTT (*Moves across the stage with* TOM *and* GENE)   There are many kinds.

TOM (*As he takes a few steps, he takes* GENE'*s arm*)   I don't know what I'd do without this young fellow. (*This kind of word-bribery disturbs* GENE. *In the coffin area, overhead lights suddenly come on. Shafts of light in the darkness indicate the coffins.* TOM *clamps his hand to his forehead*) Do I have to look at all these?

MARVIN SCOTT (*Gently*)   It's the only way, Tom. The best way is to just let you wander around alone and look at them. The prices are all marked on the cards inside the caskets.
(*He lifts an imaginary card*)

TOM (*Puts on his glasses to look*)   Nine hundred? For the casket?

MARVIN SCOTT   That includes everything, Tom. All our services, and one car for the mourners. Other cars are extra.

TOM (*To* GENE, *who is standing back*)   Well, we'll have your car, so we shouldn't need another. Anybody else wants to come, let them drive their own car. (*Looks back at the caskets*) Oh, dear . . . Gene! (GENE *comes alongside. He is tender and considerate to the part of his father that is going through a difficult time, though irritated by the part that has always angered him. They walk silently among the caskets for a few moments.* TOM *lifts a price tag and looks at it*) Two thousand! (*He taps an imaginary casket*) What are these made of?

MARVIN SCOTT (*Coming forward*)   They vary, Tom . . . Steel, bronze . . . wood.

TOM   What accounts for the variation in prices?

MARVIN SCOTT   Material . . . workmanship . . . The finish inside. You see, this is all silk.

TOM   I suppose the metal stands up best.

MARVIN SCOTT   Well, yes. (TOM *shakes his head, confused*) Of course the casket does not go directly into the ground. We first sink a concrete outer vault.

TOM   Oh?

MARVIN SCOTT   That prevents seepage, et cetera.

TOM   That's included in the price?

MARVIN SCOTT   Yes.
(TOM *walks on.* GENE *stays in the shadows*)

TOM   How long do any of these stand up?
(GENE *closes his eyes*)

MARVIN SCOTT   It's hard to say, Tom. It depends on the location. Trees, roots, and so on.

TOM   I suppose these metal ones are all welded at the seams?

MARVIN SCOTT   Oh, yes.

TOM   Our plot up there is on a small slope. I suppose that's not so good for wear. I didn't think of that when I bought it . . . And the trees looked so lovely . . . I never thought.

MARVIN SCOTT (*Gently*)   I don't think it makes that much difference, Tom.

TOM (*Moves along, stops*)   For a child?

MARVIN SCOTT   Yes.

TOM (*Shakes his head, moved*)   My mother would have fit in that. She was a little bit of a thing . . . Died when I was ten. (*Tears come to his eyes*) I don't remember much about her funeral except my father . . . He'd run out on us, but he came back when she died . . . and I wouldn't let him come to the cemetery. (*He gets angry all over again . . . then*) Oh, well . . . water over the dam. But this made me think of her . . . a little bit of a thing. (GENE *is touched by his father's memory of his own mother, but still upset at this supermarket type of shopping*) Five hundred. What do you think of this one, Gene? (GENE *comes up*) I like the color of the silk. Did you say that was silk or satin?

MARVIN SCOTT   Silk.

GENE   I don't think it makes much difference, Dad. Whatever you think.

TOM   I mean, they all go into this concrete business. (*He senses some disapproval on* GENE's *part and moves on, then adjusts his glasses*) This one is eight hundred. I don't see the difference. Marvin, what's the difference?

MARVIN SCOTT   It's mostly finish and workmanship. They're both steel.

TOM   I don't like the browns or blacks. Gray seems less somber. Don't you agree, Gene?

GENE   Yes, I do.

TOM   Eight hundred. Is there a tax, Marvin?
(GENE *turns away*)

MARVIN SCOTT   That includes the tax, Tom.

TOM   All right. Let's settle for that, then, and get out of here. (*He shivers*)

MARVIN SCOTT   Fine. (*To* GENE) And you'll send some clothes over?

GENE   Yes. (GENE *bobs his head up and down, annoyed with the details, though* MARVIN *has been considerate and discreet*)

MARVIN SCOTT   I'd estimate that Mrs. Garrison should be . . . that is, if people want to come to pay their respects, about noon tomorrow.

GENE   All right.

MARVIN SCOTT   Would you like to see where Mrs. Garrison will be resting?

GENE (*Definite*)   No, thank you. I think we'll be moving along.

MARVIN SCOTT   I assume your sister Alice will be coming on?

GENE   She arrives this evening. (*He looks around for his father and sees him standing in front of the child's coffin, staring at it. He goes over to his father and takes him gently by the arm*) Shall we go, Dad?

TOM (*Nods his head, far away*)   She was just a little bit of a thing. (*And they start moving out of the room, as the lights dim out*)

As the lights come up again on another part of the stage, ALICE, GENE'*s older sister, is coming on. She is in her early forties, attractive, brisk, realistic, unsentimental.*

ALICE   Shouldn't we be getting home to Dad?

GENE (*Carrying two highballs. He is blowing off steam*)   I suppose so, but I'm not ready to go home yet . . . Let's sit over here, where we can get away from the noise at the bar.

ALICE   You've had quite a day.

GENE   I'm sorry for blowing off, but damn it, Alice, our mother died this morning, and I've wanted to talk about her, but she hasn't been mentioned except as "my inspiration," which is his cue to start the story of his life.

ALICE   I'm sorry you've had to take it all alone.

GENE   Well, I'm glad as hell you're here, and I'm glad of the chance to get out of the house to come to meet you . . . I'm so tired of hearing about "when the clouds hung low and dark" . . . I'm so tired of people coming up to me and saying, "Your dad's a remarkable man." Nobody talks about Mother. Just "He's a remarkable man." Christ, you'd think he died! . . . I want to say to them, "My mother was a remarkable woman . . . You don't know my father. You only know the man in the newspapers. He's a selfish bastard who's lived on the edge of exasperation all his life. You don't know the bite of his sarcasm. The night he banished my sister for marrying a Jew did not get into the papers."

ALICE   *Shhh . . .*

GENE   What a night that was! Mother running from the room sobbing. You shouting at him and storming out, and the two of us, father and son, left to finish dinner, in silence. Afterward I threw up.

ALICE   I shouted and you threw up. That was pretty much the pattern.

GENE   I know I'm being unfair. But I'm in the mood to be unfair. I've wanted to turn to him all day and say, "For Christ's sake, will you for once shut up about your miserable childhood and say something about Mother?" (*A little ashamed of his outburst*) But I can't say that. He's an old man and my father, and his wife has died, and he may be experiencing something, somewhere, I know nothing about. (*He shakes his head for going on like this*) I'm sorry.

ALICE   It's all right.

GENE   No. (*He touches her arm, smiles*) Mother loved your flowers.

ALICE   I've felt guilty about Mother all the way coming here. I should have seen her more, invited her more often, brought the kids more often. Instead I sent flowers.

GENE   I guess that's an inevitable feeling when a person dies. I feel the same way.

ALICE   But you were so good to her. You made her life.

GENE (*He has always hated that phrase. Slowly, quietly*)   A son is not supposed to make his mother's life . . . Oh, I loved Mother. You know that. But to be depended on to make her life . . . Dad says, he boasts, he never knew the meaning of the word "quit." Well, he quit on her all right. And I . . . I was just there. (ALICE *looks at this sudden revelation of his feelings, his resentment that he was left to save his mother from loneliness and unhappiness*) Still, wait till you see him. There's something that comes through . . . the old Tiger. Something that reaches you and makes you want to cry . . . He'll probably be asleep when we get home, in front of the television. And you'll see. The Old Man . . . the Father. But then he wakes up and becomes Tom Garrison, and I'm in trouble . . . Last night he asked me to stay with him, and I didn't . . . I couldn't. I'm ashamed of that now.

ALICE (*Touched by the complexity of* GENE's *feelings, she looks at him a long moment, then*)   Have you called California?

GENE (*Frowns. A problem*)   No. (*He takes a drink, wanting to avoid the subject*)

ALICE   I suppose we have enough problems for the next few days, but . . .

GENE   After?

ALICE   Yes. We'll have to start thinking about Dad, about what we're going to do.

GENE (*Nods his head*)   I don't know. (*They look at each other a moment, then*) Well, let's go home. (*He rises*) Thanks for listening to all this, Alice. You had to pay good money to get someone to listen to you. I appreciate it. (*He smiles*) I thought I wanted to talk to you about Mother, but all I've done is talk about him, just like the others.

ALICE   We'll talk. There'll be time.
(*And they leave. The lights dim out on the bar area and come up on the home area.* TOM *is asleep, his head forward, his glasses on, some legal papers in his lap. Quiet like this, he is a touching picture of old age. The strong face . . . the good but gnarled hands. He is the symbol of* FATHER. *The television is on. As* GENE *and* ALICE *come in, they pause and look. They are impressed by the sad dignity. Finally* GENE *approaches and gently puts his hand on his father's arm, then turns down the television*)

GENE   Dad?

TOM (*Barely stirs*)   Hm?

GENE   Dad?

TOM   Mm? Margaret? (*Coming to a little more and looking up at* GENE) . . . Oh, Gene . . . I must have dozed off.

GENE   Alice is here.

TOM   Alice? . . . What for? (*He is genuinely confused*)

ALICE (*Comes from the shadows*)   Hello, Dad.

TOM (*Looks around, a bit panicky, confused. Then he remembers*)   Oh . . . Oh, yes.
(*He bites his upper lip, and with his gnarled hands grips theirs for a moment of affection and family strength.* ALICE *kisses him on the cheek. They help him from the chair and start putting on his coat. As the lights dim on the home area, they come up on a graveyard area.* TOM, GENE *and* ALICE *and all the people we have met, are gathering as* REVEREND PELL *starts his eulogy*)

REVEREND PELL   Margaret Garrison was a loving 'wife and a kind and generous mother, and a public-spirited member of the community. The many people who were touched by her goodness can attest to the pleasure and joy she brought them through her love of life and her power to communicate this love to others. The many children, now grown . . .

GENE (*Turns from the family group*)   Only a dozen or so people were at my mother's funeral. Most of her friends were dead, or had moved to other cities, or just couldn't make it. Fifteen years earlier the church would have been filled. There were a few men sent from Rotary, a few women from the Garden Club, the Mother's Club, the Woman's Club, and a few members of her bridge club were there . . . The hundreds of children who had listened to her tell stories year after year on Christmas Eve were all gone, or had forgotten . . . Perhaps some of them who were still in the neighborhood looked up from their evening papers to say, "I see Mrs. Garrison died. She was nice . . . Well, she was an old lady." (*He turns to rejoin the family group*)

REVEREND PELL   Earth to earth . . . ashes to ashes . . . dust to dust . . . The Lord giveth and the Lord taketh away . . . Blessed be the name of the Lord . . . Amen.
(TOM *comes to shake hands with* REVEREND PELL. *The others drift about, exchanging nods, and gradually leave during the following*)

TOM   Well, it's a nice place up here.

GENE (*Who has wandered over to look at another grave*)   Yes.

TOM   Your mother and I bought it soon after we were married. She thought it a strange thing to do, but we bought it. (*He looks at the grave* GENE *is looking at*) Now, let's see, that's . . .

GENE   Carol.

TOM   Who?

GENE   Carol. My wife.

TOM   Oh, yes. (*He reaches out a sympathetic hand toward* GENE, *then moves away*) There's room for three more burials up here, as I remember. There . . . there . . . and there. I'm to go there, when the time comes. (*He looks around for a moment*) This plot is in terrible shape . . . I paid three hundred dollars some years ago for perpetual care, and now look at it. Just disgraceful . . . I'm going to talk to that superintendent.

(*And he strides off. The lights change.* ALICE *and* GENE *move into another area, what might be a garden with a bench. For a moment neither says anything.* GENE *lights a cigarette and sits on the grass*)

ALICE   I don't know how you feel, but I'd like to figure out some kind of memorial for Mother . . . Use some of the money she left.

GENE   Yes, definitely.

ALICE   Maybe some shelves of books for the children's library. Christmas books with the stories she liked to tell.

GENE   That's a good idea.
(*There is a long and awkward pause*)

ALICE   Well, Gene, what are we going to do?

GENE (*Frowns*)   Mother always said to put her in an old-people's home. She had one all picked out.

ALICE   Sidney's mother and father saw it coming and arranged to be in one of those cottage colonies for old people.

GENE   Mother and Dad didn't.

ALICE   I think you should go ahead and get married and move to California . . . But . . . I might as well get this off my chest, it would be murder if he came to live with us. In the first place, he wouldn't do it, feeling as he does about Sid, and the kids can't stand how he tells them how to do everything.

GENE   I think you're right. That would never work. (*There is a pause.* GENE *looks out at the garden*) I can't tell you what it does to me as a man . . . to see someone like that . . . a man who was distinguished, remarkable . . . just become a nuisance.

ALICE (*She is disturbed at what her brother may be thinking*)   I know I sound hard, but he's had his life . . . and as long as we can be assured that he's taken care of . . . Oh, I'll feel some guilt, and you, maybe more. But my responsibility is to my husband and my children.

GENE   Yes. That's *your* responsibility.

ALICE   And your responsibility is to yourself . . . to get married again, to get away from memories of Carol and her whole world. Have you called California?

GENE (*Frowns*)   No.

ALICE   If I were the girl you were planning to marry, and you didn't call me to tell me your mother had died . . .

GENE (*Gets up, disturbed*)   I just haven't wanted to go into it all with her.

ALICE (*Understanding, but worried*)   Gene, my friend . . . my brother . . . Get out of here!

GENE   Look, Alice, your situation is quite different. Mine is very complex. You fortunately see things very clearly, but it's not so easy for me. (ALICE *looks at* GENE, *troubled by what his thinking seems to be leading to. After a moment . . . reflective*) We always remember the terrible things about Dad. I've been trying to remember some of the others . . . How much he *did* do for us.

ALICE   I'm doing a lot for my kids. I don't expect them to pay me back at the other end. (GENE *wanders around, thinking, scuffing the grass*) I'm sure we could find a full-time housekeeper. He can afford it.

GENE   He'd never agree.

ALICE   It's that or finding a home. (GENE *frowns*) Sidney's folks like where they are. Also, we might as well face it, his mind's going. Sooner or later, we'll have to think about powers of attorney, perhaps committing him to an institution.

GENE   God, it's all so ugly.

ALICE (*Smiling*)   Yes, my gentle Gene, a lot of life is.

GENE   Now, look, don't go trying to make me out some soft-hearted . . . (*He can't find the word*) I know life is ugly.

ALICE   Yes, I think you know it. You've lived through a great deal of ugliness. But you work like a Trojan to deny it, to make it not so. (*After a moment, not arguing*) He kicked me out. He said he never wanted to see me again. He broke Mother's heart over that for years. He was mean, unloving. He beat the hell out of you when you were a kid . . . You've hated and feared him all your adult life . . .

GENE (*Cutting in*)   Still he's my father, and a man. And what's happening to him appalls me as a man.

ALICE   We have a practical problem here.

GENE   It's not as simple as all that.

ALICE   To me it is. I don't understand this mystical haze you're casting over it. I'm going to talk to him tomorrow, after the session with the lawyer, about a housekeeper. (GENE *reacts but says nothing*) Just let me handle it. He can visit us, and we can take turns coming to visit him. Now, I'll do the dirty work. Only when he turns to you, don't give in.

GENE   I can't tell you how ashamed I feel . . . not to say with open arms, ''Poppa, come live with me . . . I love you, Poppa, and I want to take care of you.'' . . . I need to love him. I've always wanted to love him.
(*He drops his arms and wanders off.* ALICE *watches her brother drift off into the garden as the lights go down in that area. The lights come up in the living room area.* TOM *is seated in his chair, writing.* ALICE *comes into the room. Small packing boxes are grouped around*)

ALICE   How are you coming?

TOM   Oh, Alice, I've written out receipts for you to sign for the jewelry your mother left you. And if you'll sign for the things she left the children.

ALICE   All right.
(*Signs.* GENE *comes into the room carrying a box full of his mother's things. He exchanges a look with* ALICE, *knowing the time has come for the discussion*)

TOM   It may not be necessary, but as executor, I'll be held responsible for these things.

ALICE   Dad, I'd like to talk a little . . . with you . . . about—

TOM   Yes, all right. But first I'd like to read you this letter I've written to Harry Hall . . . He and I used to play golf out in New Jersey . . . He wrote a very nice letter to me about your mother . . . and I've written him as follows . . . It will only take a minute . . . If I can read my own shorthand . . . (*He adjusts his glasses*) ''Dear Harry . . . How thoughtful of you to write me on the occasion of Margaret's death. It was quite a blow. As you know, she was my inspiration, and had been ever since that day fifty-five years ago when I met her . . . when the clouds hung low and dark for me. At that time I was supporting my younger brother and my sister and my aged grandfather in a two-room flat . . . going to work every day in a lumber mill. Providence, which has always guided me, prompted me to take a night course in shorthand and typing, and also prompted me to go to the Underwood Typewriting Company seeking a position as stenographer. They sent me, God be praised, to the office of T. J. Parks . . . and a job that started at five dollars a week, ended in 1929 when I retired, at fifty thousand a year . . .'' That's as far as I've gotten at the moment. (*He looks up for approval*)

GENE   Dad, I don't think financial matters are particularly appropriate in answering a letter of condolence.

TOM   Oh? (*He looks at the letter*) But it's true. You see, it follows. I'm saying she was my inspiration . . . and it seems entirely appropriate to explain that.

GENE   Well, it's your letter, Dad.

TOM (*Looks it over*)   Well . . .

ALICE   Dad, I'm leaving tomorrow . . . and . . .

TOM (*Looking up*)   What?

ALICE   I'm going home tomorrow.

TOM (*Formal*)   Well, Alice, I'm grateful you came. I know it was difficult for you, leaving home. Your mother would have appreciated it. She was very fond of you, Alice.

ALICE   I think we ought to talk over, maybe, what your plans are.

TOM   My plans? I have many letters to answer, and a whole mess in my files and accounts. If the income tax people ever asked me to produce my books . . .

GENE   They're not likely to, Dad. Your income is no longer of that size.

TOM (*With a twinkle in his eye*)   Don't be too sure.

ALICE   I didn't mean exactly that kind of plans. I meant . . . Well, you haven't been well.

TOM (*Belligerent*)   Who said so?

ALICE   Mother was worried to death about—(*She stops*)

TOM   I was under a strain. Your mother's health . . . never knowing when it might happen. Trying to get her to take care of herself, to take it easy. You know, the doctor said if she didn't eat more slowly, this might happen.

ALICE   You plan to keep the house?

TOM   Oh, yes. All my things are here . . . It's a . . . It's a . . . I'll be back on my feet, and my . . . (*Points to his head*) . . . will clear up. Now this strain is over, I'm confident I'll be in shape any day now.

ALICE   I worry, leaving you in this house . . . alone, Dad.

TOM (*Looks around, very alert, defensively*)   I'm perfectly all right. Now don't worry about me . . . either of you. Why, for the last year, since your mother's first attack, I've been getting the breakfast, making the beds, using a dust rag . . . (*He makes quite a performance of this. It is a gallant struggle*)

And the laundress comes in once a week and cleans up for me . . . And Gene here . . . If Gene will keep an eye on me, drop in once or twice a week . . .

ALICE   That's the point.

GENE (*Low*)   Alice!

ALICE   We think you should have a full-time housekeeper, Dad. To live here.

TOM (*Trying to kid it off, but angry*)   Alone here with me? That wouldn't be very proper, would it?

ALICE (*Smiling*)   Nevertheless . . .

TOM   No. Now that's final!

ALICE   Dad, Gene and I would feel a lot better about it, if—

TOM   Look, you don't have to worry about me.

ALICE   Dad, you're forgetting things more and more.

TOM   Who says so?

ALICE   Mother wrote me, and—

TOM   I was under a strain. I just finished telling you. Look, Alice, you can go, leave with a clear mind. I'm all right. (GENE *is touched and moved by his father's effort, his desperate effort to maintain his dignity, his standing as a functioning man*) Of course, I will appreciate Gene's dropping in. But I'm all right.

ALICE   We still would like to get a full-time housekeeper.

TOM (*Bristling*)   What do you mean, you would get? I've hired and fired thousands of people in my day. I don't need anyone *getting* someone for me.

ALICE   Will you do it yourself, then?

TOM   No, I told you. No! (*He gets very angry. His voice sharpens and hardens*) Since I was eight years old I've taken care of myself. What do you two know about it? You were given everything on a platter. At an age when you two were swinging on that tree out there, breaking the branches, I was selling newspapers five hours a day, and at night dancing a jig in saloons for pennies . . . And you're trying to tell me I can't take care of myself . . . If I want a housekeeper, and I don't, I'll hire one . . . I've hired and fired thousands of people in my time. When I was vice-president of Colonial Brass at fifty thousand a year . . . Two thousand people. And you tell me I'm incompetent . . . to hire a housekeeper. And how many people have you hired? (*To* GENE) You teach . . . Well, all right. That's your business, if that's what you want to do. But don't talk to me about hiring and firing.
(*The children are saddened and perhaps a little cowed by this naked outburst,*

the defense of a man who knows that he is slipping, and an angry outburst of hatred and jealousy for his own children. Everyone is quiet for a moment . . . then)

ALICE   Dad, you might fall down.

TOM   Why fall down? There's nothing wrong with my balance.
(GENE *is sick at this gradual attempt to bring to a man's consciousness the awareness that he is finished*)

ALICE   Sometimes, when you get up, you're dizzy.

TOM   Nonsense. (*He gets up abruptly. He makes great effort and stands for a moment, then one foot moves slightly to steady his balance . . . and the children both look away*) Now, I appreciate your concern . . . (*Very fatherly*) But I'm perfectly able to carry on by myself. As I said, with Gene's help from time to time. I imagine we could have dinner every once in a while, couldn't we, Gene . . . once a week or so? Take you up to Rotary. Some of the speakers are quite amusing.
(ALICE *looks at* GENE *to see if he is going to speak up*)

GENE   Sure, Dad.

TOM   Give us some time together at last. Get to know each other.

ALICE (*Quietly but firmly*)   Gene wants to get married.

GENE   Alice!

TOM   What?

ALICE   Gene wants to move to California and get married.

GENE   Alice, shut up.

ALICE (*Almost in tears*)   I can't help it. You've never faced up to him. You'd let him ruin your life.

GENE (*Angry*)   I can take care of my own life.

ALICE   You can't!

TOM (*Loud*)   Children! . . . Children! (*They stop arguing and turn to their father at his command.* TOM *speaks with a note of sarcasm*) I have no desire to interfere with either of your lives. I took care of myself at eight. I can take care of myself at eighty. I have never wanted to be a burden to my children.

GENE   I'm going to hang around, Dad.

TOM   There's no need to.

GENE   I'll move in here at least till you're feeling better. (ALICE *turns away, angry and despairing*)

TOM (*Sarcastically*)   I don't want to ruin your life.

GENE (*Angry now at his father*)   I didn't say that.

TOM   I have long gotten the impression that my only function in this family is to supply the money to—

GENE (*Anguished*)   Dad!

TOM   —to supply the funds for your education, for your—

GENE   Dad, stop it!
(TOM *staggers a little, dizzy.* GENE *goes to his side to steady him.* TOM *breathes heavily in and out in rage. The rage of this man is a terrible thing to see, old as he is. He finally gets some control of himself*)

TOM   As far as I am concerned, this conversation is ended. Alice, we've gotten along very well for some years now without your attention.

GENE (*Protesting, but hating the fight*)   Dad!

ALICE   You sent me away. Don't forget that.

TOM   You chose to lead your own life. Well, we won't keep you now.

GENE   Dad . . .

TOM (*Rage again*)   I was competent to go into the city year after year to earn money for your clothes, your food, the roof over your head. Am I now incompetent? Is that what you're trying to tell me?
(*He looks at* ALICE *with a terrible look. He breathes heavily for a moment or two; then, shaking his head, he turns away from both of them and leaves, disappearing into the shadows*)

GENE (*Angry, troubled*)   For God's sake, Alice!

ALICE   I'm only trying to get a practical matter accomplished.

GENE   You don't have to destroy him in the process.

ALICE   I wasn't discussing his competence. Although that will be a matter for discussion soon.

GENE   Look, Alice, just leave it now, the way it is. Don't say any more.

ALICE   With you staying on.

GENE   Yes. You can go with a clear conscience.

ALICE   My conscience is clear.

GENE   I am doing this because I want to.

ALICE   You're doing it because you can't help yourself.

GENE   Look, when I want to be analyzed, I'll pay for it.

ALICE (*Pleading*)   But I saw you. Didn't you see yourself there, when he started to rage? Didn't you feel yourself pull in? You shrank.

GENE   I shrank at the ugliness of what was happening.

ALICE   You're staying because you can't stand his wrath the day you say, "Dad, I'm leaving." You've never been able to stand up to his anger. He's cowed you.

GENE   Look, Alice . . .

ALICE   He'll call you ungrateful, and you'll believe him. He'll lash out at you with his sarcasm, and that will kill this lovely, necessary image you have of yourself as the good son. Can't you see that?

GENE (*Lashing out*)   What do you want us to do? Shall we get out a white paper? Let it be known that we, Alice and Gene, have done all that we can to make this old man happy in his old age, without inconveniencing ourselves, of course. And he has refused our help. So, if he falls and hits his head and lies there until he rots, it is not our fault. Is that it?

ALICE   You insist on—

GENE (*Running on*)   Haven't you learned on the couch that people do *not* always do what you want them to do? It is sometimes *we* who have to make the adjustments?

ALICE   The difference between us is that I accept the inevitable sadness of this world without an acute sense of personal guilt. You don't. I don't think anyone expects either of us to ruin our lives for an unreasonable old man.

GENE   It's not going to ruin my life.

ALICE   It is.

GENE   A few weeks, a month.

ALICE   Forever!

GENE   Alice, let's not go on discussing it. I know what I am going to do. Maybe I can't explain my reasons to you. I just know I can't do anything else. Maybe there isn't the same thing between a mother and a daughter, but the "old man" in me feels something very deep, wants to extend some kind of mercy to that old man. I never had a father. I ran away from him. He ran away from me. Maybe he's right. Maybe it is time we found each other.

ALICE   Excuse me for saying so, but I find that sentimental crap! I think this is all rationalization to make tolerable a compulsion you have to stay here. You hate the compulsion, so you've dressed it up to look nice.

GENE   How do you know what you're saying isn't a rationalization to cover up a callousness, a selfishness, a coldness in yourself. To make *it* smell nice?

ALICE   What do you think you'll find?

GENE   I don't know.

ALICE   You hope to find love. Couldn't you tell from what he just said what you're going to find? Don't you understand he's got to hate you? He may not think it in his head or feel it in his heart, but you are his enemy! From the moment you were born a boy, you were a threat to this man and his enemy.

GENE   That sounds like the textbooks, Alice.

ALICE   He wants your balls . . . and he's had them! (GENE *stands, starts to leave the room*) I'm sorry. I want to shock you. When has he ever regarded you as a man, an equal, a male? When you were a marine. And that you did for him. Because even back there you were looking for his love. You didn't want to be a marine. "Now, Poppa, will you love me?" And he did. No, not love. But he was proud and grateful because you gave him an extension of himself he could boast about, with his phony set of values. When was he ever proud about the thing *you* do? The things *you* value? When did he ever mention your teaching or your books, except in scorn?

GENE   You don't seem to have felt the absence of a father. But I feel incomplete, deprived. I just do not want to let my father die a stranger to me.

ALICE   You're looking for something that isn't there, Gene. You're looking for a mother's love in a father. Mothers are soft and yielding. Fathers are hard and rough, to teach us the way of the world, which is rough, which is mean, which is selfish and prejudiced.

GENE   All right. That's your definition. And because of what he did to you, you're entitled to it.

ALICE   I've always been grateful to him for what he did. He taught me a marvelous lesson, and has made me able to face a lot. And there has been a lot to face, and I'm grateful as hell to him. Because if I couldn't get the understanding and compassion from a father, who could I expect it from in the world? Who in the world, if not from a father? So I learned, and didn't expect it, and I've found very little, and so I'm grateful to him. I'm grateful as hell to him.

(*The growing intensity ends in tears, and she turns her head*)

GENE (*Looks in pity at the involuntary revelation of her true feeling. He moves to her and touches her*)   I'll stay, Alice . . . for a while, at least . . . for whatever reasons. Let's not argue any more.

ALICE   And Peggy?

GENE   She'll be coming in a week or two, we'll see.

ALICE   Don't lose her, Gene. Maybe I'm still fouled up on myself, but I think I've spoken near the truth about you.

GENE   I keep wondering why I haven't called her, or wanted to call her. Why I seem so much closer to Carol at the moment.

ALICE (*Gently, tentatively*)   The image . . . of the eternally bereaved husband . . . forgive me . . . the dutiful son . . . They're very appealing and seductive . . . But they're not living. (GENE *just stands, looking at her, thinking about what she has said.* ALICE *kisses him on the cheek*) Good night, Gene.

GENE (*His hands on her shoulders*)   Good night.

ALICE (*She suddenly puts her head tight against his shoulder and holds him*)   Suddenly I miss Mother so. (*She sobs. He just holds her and strokes her back*)

GENE   Yes. (*And he holds her, comforting her, as the lights dim*)

After a few moments of darkness the lights come up on TOM *in his bedroom in pajamas and bathrobe, kneeling by his bed, praying. On his bed is a small top drawer of a bureau, filled with mementos.* GENE *comes in. He stands in the shadows and watches his father at his prayers.* GENE *does not pray any more, and he has always been touched by the sight of his father praying.* TOM *gets up and starts to untie his bathrobe.*

GENE   You ready to be tucked in?

TOM (*Smiling*)   Yes. (*Loosening his robe*) Look at the weight I've lost.

GENE (*Troubled at the emaciated body, which is pathetic. The face is ruddy and strong, the body that of an old man*)   Since when?

TOM   Oh, I don't know.

GENE (*Tapping his father's stomach*)   Well, you had quite a little pot there, Dad.

TOM (*Smiling*)   Did I?

GENE   Yes.

TOM   But look, all through here, through my chest.

GENE   Well, we'll put some back on you. You've been eating pretty well this last week.

TOM (*Looking at his own chest*)   You know, I never had hair on my chest. I don't understand it. You have hair on your chest. I just didn't have any. Well, I'm confident if I could get some exercise . . . Do you remember when I used to get you up in the morning, and we'd go down and do calisthenics to the radio?

GENE (*Smiling*)   Yes.

TOM (*Stands very straight, swings his arms*)   One-two-three-four . . . One-two-three-four . . .

GENE   Hey, take it easy.

TOM   I used to swing the Indian clubs every day at lunchtime. I gave you a set once, didn't I?

GENE   I think so.

TOM   We'll have to dig them out. (*Starts bending exercises*) One-two-three-four . . . one-two-three-four.

GENE   Why don't you wait till morning for that?

TOM   Remember when we used to put on the gloves and spar down on the side porch? . . . I don't think you ever liked it very much. (*He crouches in boxing position*) The manly art of self-defense . . . Gentleman Jim Corbett . . . Now it's something else again . . . Oh, well, things to worry about. But I intend to get over to the club, play some golf, sit around and swap stories with the boys. Too bad you never took up golf. Alice could have played a good game of golf. But she had a temper. Inherited it from your mother's father. Irascible old bastard, if you'll pardon my French. (*He fishes in the bureau drawer on the bed*) I was looking through my bureau drawer . . . I don't know, just going over things . . . Did you ever see this?
(*He takes out a small revolver*)

GENE   Yes.

TOM   Never had occasion to use it. Oh, I took it out West one winter when we went to Arizona instead of Florida. Shot at rattlesnakes in a rock pile. (*Takes pot shots*) I don't have a permit for this any more. (*Starts putting it back in its box*) I suppose they wouldn't give me one. I don't know anyone up there any more. When I was Mayor, cops on every corner would wave . . . "Hello, Mr. Garrison . . . 'Morning, Mr. Garrison." Now, one of the young whippersnappers gave me a ticket, just before we left for Florida. Said I'd passed a full-stop sign. That's what *he* said. First ticket I had in forty or more years of driving, so keep this quiet. (*He takes out a packet of photographs wrapped in tissue paper*) Pictures . . . I think you've seen most of them . . . The family.

GENE (*Very tentatively*)   You know, Dad, I've never seen a picture of your father. (TOM *looks at him a long time. Then finally, with his hatred showing on his face, he unwraps another tissue and hands over a small picture.* GENE *looks at it a long moment*) He's just a boy.

TOM   That was taken about the time he was married.

GENE   I'd always thought of him as . . . the way you talked about him . . . as . . .
(GENE *is obviously touched by the picture*)

TOM   Oh, he was a fine-looking man before he started to drink. Big, square, high color. But he became my mortal enemy . . . Did I ever show you that? (*He takes out a small piece of paper*) Careful . . . When I set up a home for my brother and sister, one day we were all out, and he came around and ripped up all my sister's clothes and shoes. Drunk, of course. A few days later he came around to apologize and ask for some money, and I threw him out . . . The next day he left this note . . . "You are welcome to your burden."

GENE   And you kept it?

TOM   Yes. I never saw him again until many years later he was dying, in Bellevue, and someone got word to me, and I went down and asked him if he wanted anything. He said he'd like some fruit. So I sent him in a few oranges. He died the next day.

GENE   There must have been something there to love, to understand.

TOM   In my father? (*Shakes his head "no." Then he shows* GENE *another card*) Do you remember this? (*He reads*) "To the best dad in the world on Father's Day." That was in . . . (*Turns over and reads the notation*) 1946 . . . Yes. (*Emotional*) I appreciate that, Gene. That's a lovely tribute. I think I have all your Father's Day cards here. You know, your mother used to talk of you children as her jewels. Maybe because my interests were different, I've always said you were my dividends . . . You know, I didn't want children, coming from the background I did . . . and we didn't have Alice for a long time. But your mother finally persuaded me. She said they would be a comfort in our old age. And you are, Gene.

GENE (*Touched, but embarrassed and uncomfortable*)   Well . . .

TOM (*Fishes in the drawer and brings out a sheet of paper*)   A program of yours from college . . . some glee club concert . . . I've got everything but the kitchen stove in here. (*Looks over the program*) Do you still sing?

GENE (*Smiling*)   Not in years.

TOM   That's too bad. You had a good voice. But we can't do everything . . . I remember your mother would sit at the piano, hour after hour, and I'd be up here at my desk, and I'd hear you singing.

GENE   You always asked me to sing "When I Grow Too Old to Dream."

TOM   Did I? . . . I don't remember your ever singing that . . . You always seemed to be just finishing when I came into the room . . . (*Looks at* GENE) Did you used to sing that for me?

GENE (*Not a joke any more*)   No . . . But you always asked me to sing it for you.

TOM   Oh . . . (*Puts the program away*) Well, I enjoyed sitting up here and listening. (*He pokes around in his box and takes something out . . . in tissue paper. He unwraps a picture carefully*) And that's my mother.

GENE (*Gently*)   Yes. I've seen that, Dad. It's lovely.

TOM   She was twenty-five when that was taken. She died the next year . . . I carried it in my wallet for years . . . And then I felt I was wearing it out. So I put it away . . . Just a little bit of a thing . . . (*He starts to cry, and the deep, deep, sobs finally come and his emaciated body is wracked by them. It is a terrible, almost soundless sobbing.* GENE *comes to his father and puts his arms around him and holds him. After moments*) I didn't think it would be this way . . . I always thought I'd go first. (*He sobs again, gasping for air.* GENE *continues to hold him, inevitably moved and touched by this genuine suffering. Finally,* TOM *gets a stern grip on himself*) I'm sorry . . . (*Tries to shake it off*) It just comes over me . . . It'll pass . . . I'll get a hold of myself.

GENE   Don't try, Dad . . . Believe me, it's best.

TOM (*Angry with himself*)   No . . . It's just that . . . I'll be all right. (*He turns and blows his nose*)

GENE   It's rough, Dad . . . It's bound to be rough.

TOM (*Shakes his head to snap out of it*)   It'll pass . . . it'll pass . . . (*Starts to wrap up the picture of his mother*)

GENE   Can I help you put these things away, Dad?

TOM   No . . . No . . . I can . . . (*He seems to be looking for something he can't find*) Well, if you would. (GENE *helps him wrap the pictures*) I don't know what we'd do without you . . .

(*And together they put the things back in the box. As they do so,* GENE *is deeply moved with feelings of tenderness for his father. After a few moments he starts, with great consideration*)

GENE   Dad?

TOM   Yes?

GENE (*Carefully*)   You remember . . . I wrote you about California . . . and Peggy?

TOM   What?

GENE   The girl . . . in California.

TOM (*On guard*)   Oh, yes.

GENE (*Putting it carefully, and slowly*)   I'm thinking very seriously, Dad . . . of going out there . . . to marry . . . and to live. (TOM *straightens up a little*) Now, I know this is your home, where you're used to . . . But I'd

like you to come out there with me, Dad . . . It's lovely out there, as you
said, and we could find an apartment for you, near us.
(*This is the most loving gesture* GENE *has made to his father in his life*)

TOM (*Thinks for a moment, then looks at* GENE *with a smile*)   You know, I'd
like to make a suggestion . . . Why don't you all come live here?

GENE (*Explaining calmly*)   Peggy has a practice out there.

TOM   A what?

GENE   She's a doctor. I told you. And children with schools and friends.

TOM   We have a big house here. You always liked this house. It's wonderful
for children. You used to play baseball out back, and there's that basketball
thing.

GENE   Dad, I'd like to get away from this part of the country for a while. It's
been rough here ever since Carol died. It would be good for you too, getting
away.

TOM   Your mother would be very happy to have the house full of children
again. I won't be around long, and then it would be all yours.

GENE   That's very kind of you, Dad. But I don't think that would work. Besides her work and the children, all Peggy's family is out there.

TOM   Your family is here.

GENE   Yes, I know.

TOM   Just me, of course.

GENE   You see, the children's father is out there, and they're very fond of
him and see him a lot.

TOM   Divorced?

GENE   Yes.

TOM   You know, Gene, I'm only saying this for your own good, but you
went out there very soon after Carol's death, and you were exhausted from
her long illness, and well, naturally, very susceptible . . . I was wondering
if you've really waited long enough to know your own mind.

GENE   I know my own mind.

TOM   I mean, taking on another man's children. You know, children are far
from the blessing they're supposed to be . . . And then there's the whole
matter of discipline, of keeping them in line. You may rule them with a rod
of iron, but if this father—

GENE (*Cutting in*)   I happen to love Peggy.

TOM (*Looks at* GENE *a long moment*)   Did you mention this business of California to your mother?

GENE (*Gets the point, but keeps level*)   She mentioned it to me, and told me to go ahead, with her blessings.

TOM   She would say that, of course . . . But I warned you.

GENE (*Turns away*)   For God's sake—

TOM (*Giving up, angry*)   All right, go ahead. I can manage . . . (*His sarcasm*) Send me a Christmas card . . . if you remember.

GENE (*Enraged*)   Dad!

TOM   What?

GENE   I've asked you to come with me!

TOM   And I've told you I'm not going.

GENE   I understand that, but not this "send me a Christmas card, if you remember."

TOM   I'm very sorry if I offended you. Your mother always said I mustn't raise my voice to you. (*Suddenly hard and vicious*) Did you want me to make it easy for you the way your mother did? Well, I won't. If you want to go, go!

GENE   God damn it . . .

TOM (*Running on*)   I've always known it would come to this when your mother was gone. I was tolerated around this house because I paid the bills and—

GENE   Shut up!

TOM (*Coming at him*)   Don't you—

GENE (*Shouting*)   Shut up! I asked you to come with me. What do you want? What the hell do you want? If I lived here the rest of my life, it wouldn't be enough for you. I've tried, God damn it, I've tried to be the dutiful son, to maintain the image of the good son . . . Commanded into your presence on every conceivable occasion . . . Easter, Christmas, birthdays, Thanksgiving . . . Even that Thanksgiving when Carol was dying, and I was staying with her in the hospital. "We miss you so. Our day is nothing without you. Couldn't you come up for an hour or two after you leave Carol?" You had no regard for what was really going on . . . My wife was dying!

TOM   Is it so terrible to want to see your own son?

GENE   It is terrible to want to possess him . . . entirely and completely!

TOM (*Coldly . . . after a moment*)   There will be some papers to sign for your mother's estate. Be sure you leave an address with my lawyer . . .

GENE (*Cutting in*)   Dad!

TOM (*Cutting, with no self-pity*)   From tonight on, you can consider me dead. (*Turns on him in a rage of resentment*) I gave you everything. Since I was a snot-nosed kid I've worked my fingers to the bone. You've had everything and I had nothing. I put a roof over your head, clothes on your back—

GENE   Food on the table.

TOM   —things I never had.

GENE   I know!

TOM   You ungrateful bastard!

GENE (*Seizes him, almost as though he would hit him*)   What do you want for gratitude? Nothing, nothing would be enough. You have resented everything you ever gave me. The orphan boy in you has resented everything. I'm sorry as hell about your miserable childhood. When I was a kid, and you told me those stories, I used to go up to my room at night and cry. But there is nothing I can do about it . . . and it does not excuse everything . . . I *am* grateful to you. I also admire you and respect you, and stand in awe of what you have done with your life. I will never be able to touch it. (TOM *looks at him with contempt*) But it does not make me love you. And I wanted to love you. (TOM *snorts his disbelief*) You hated your father. I saw what it did to you. I did not want to hate you.

TOM   I don't care what you feel about me.

GENE   I do! (*He moves away from his father*) I came so close to loving you tonight . . . I'd never felt so open to you. You don't know what it cost me to ask you to come with me . . . when I have never been able to sit in a room alone with you . . . Did you really think your door was always open to me?

TOM   It was not my fault if you never came in.

GENE (*Starts to move out*)   Good-by, Dad. I'll arrange for someone to come in.

TOM (*Shouting*)   I don't want anyone to come in! I can take care of myself! I have always had to take care of myself. Who needs you? Out! . . . I have lived each day of my life so that I could look any man in the eye and tell him to *go to hell!*
(*This last, wildly at* GENE. *The lights dim out quickly, except for a lingering light on* GENE)

GENE (*After a few moments*)   That night I left my father's house forever . . .
I took the first right and the second left . . . and this time I went as far as
California . . . Peggy and I visited him once or twice . . . and then he
came to California to visit us, and had a fever and swollen ankles, and we
put him in a hospital, and he never left . . . The reason we gave, and which
he could accept, for not leaving . . . the swollen ankles. But the real reason
. . . the arteries were hardening, and he gradually over several years slipped
into complete and speechless senility . . . with all his life centered in his
burning eyes. (*A* NURSE *wheels in* TOM, *dressed in a heavy, warm bathrobe,
and wearing a white linen golf cap to protect his head from drafts. The*
NURSE *withdraws into the shadows*) When I would visit him, and we would sit
and look at each other, his eyes would mist over and his nostrils would pinch
with emotion . . . But I never could learn what the emotion was . . . anger
. . . or love . . . or regret . . . One day, sitting in his wheelchair and staring without comprehension at television . . . he died . . . alone . . . without even an orange in his hand. (*The light fades on* TOM) Death ends a life
. . . but it does not end a relationship, which struggles on in the survivor's
mind . . . toward some resolution, which it never finds. Alice said I would
not accept the sadness of the world . . . What did it matter if I never loved
him, or if he never loved me? . . . Perhaps she was right . . . But, still,
when I hear the word "father" . . . (*He cannot express it . . . there is still
the longing, the emotion. He looks around . . . out . . . as though he
would finally be able to express it, but he can only say . . .*) It matters.
(*He turns and walks slowly away, into the shadows . . . as the lights dim*)

Curtain

The Name

Aharon Megged

Translated from the Hebrew by Minna Givton

Grandfather Zisskind lived in a little house in a southern suburb of the town.
About once a month, on a Saturday afternoon, his granddaughter Raya and her
young husband Yehuda would go and pay him a visit.

Raya would give three cautious knocks on the door (an agreed signal between herself and her grandfather ever since her childhood, when he had lived
in their house together with the whole family) and they would wait for the door
to be opened. "Now he's getting up," Raya would whisper to Yehuda, her
face glowing, when the sound of her grandfather's slippers was heard from

within, shuffling across the room. Another moment, and the key would be turned and the door opened.

"Come in," he would say somewhat absently, still buttoning up his trousers, with the rheum of sleep in his eyes. Although it was very hot he wore a yellow winter vest with long sleeves, from which his wrists stuck out—white, thin, delicate as a girl's, as was his bare neck with its taut skin.

After Raya and Yehuda had sat down at the table, which was covered with a white cloth showing signs of the meal he had eaten alone—crumbs from the Sabbath loaf, a plate with meat leavings, a glass containing some grape pips, a number of jars and so on—he would smooth the crumpled pillows, spread a cover over the narrow bed and tidy up. It was a small room, and its obvious disorder aroused pity for the old man's helplessness in running his home. In the corner was a shelf with two sooty kerosene burners, a kettle and two or three saucepans, and next to it a basin containing plates, knives and forks. In another corner was a stand holding books with thick leather bindings, leaning and lying on each other. Some of his clothes hung over the backs of the chairs. An ancient walnut cupboard with an empty buffet stood exactly opposite the door. On the wall hung a clock which had long since stopped.

"We ought to make Grandfather a present of a clock," Raya would say to Yehuda as she surveyed the room and her glance lighted on the clock; but every time the matter slipped her memory. She loved her grandfather, with his pointed white silky beard, his tranquil face from which a kind of holy radiance emanated, his quiet, soft voice which seemed to have been made only for uttering words of sublime wisdom. She also respected him for his pride, which had led him to move out of her mother's house and live by himself, accepting the hardship and trouble and the affliction of loneliness in his old age. There had been a bitter quarrel between him and his daughter. After Raya's father had died, the house had lost its grandeur and shed the trappings of wealth. Some of the antique furniture which they had retained—along with some crystalware and jewels, the dim lustre of memories from the days of plenty in their native city—had been sold, and Rachel, Raya's mother, had been compelled to support the home by working as a dentist's nurse. Grandfather Zisskind, who had been supported by the family ever since he came to the country, wished to hand over to his daughter his small capital, which was deposited in a bank. She was not willing to accept it. She was stubborn and proud like him. Then, after a prolonged quarrel and several weeks of not speaking to each other, he took some of the things in his room and the broken clock and went to live alone. That had been about four years ago. Now Rachel would come to him once or twice a week, bringing with her a bag full of provisions, to clean the room and cook some meals for him. He was no longer interested in expenses and did not even ask about them, as though they were of no more concern to him.

"And now . . . what can I offer you?" Grandfather Zisskind would ask when he considered the room ready to receive guests. "There's no need to offer us anything, Grandfather; we didn't come for that," Raya would answer crossly.

But protests were of no avail. Her grandfather would take out a jar of fermenting preserves and put it on the table, then grapes and plums, biscuits and two glasses of strong tea, forcing them to eat. Raya would taste a little of this and that just to please the old man, while Yehuda, for whom all these visits were unavoidable torment, the very sight of the dishes arousing his disgust, would secretly indicate to her by pulling a sour face that he just couldn't touch the preserves. She would smile at him placatingly, stroking his knee. But Grandfather insisted, so he would have to taste at least a teaspoonful of the sweet and nauseating stuff.

Afterwards Grandfather would ask about all kinds of things. Raya did her best to make the conversation pleasant, in order to relieve Yehuda's boredom. Finally would come what Yehuda dreaded most of all and on account of which he had resolved more than once to refrain from these visits. Grandfather Zisskind would rise, take his chair and place it next to the wall, get up on it carefully, holding on to the back so as not to fall, open the clock and take out a cloth bag with a black cord tied round it. Then he would shut the clock, get off the chair, put it back in its place, sit down on it, undo the cord, take out of the cloth wrapping a bundle of sheets of paper, lay them in front of Yehuda and say:

"I would like you to read this."

"Grandfather," Raya would rush to Yehuda's rescue, "but he's already read it at least ten times. . . ."

But Grandfather Zisskind would pretend not to hear and would not reply, so Yehuda was compelled each time to read there and then that same essay, spread over eight, long sheets in a large, somewhat shaky handwriting, which he almost knew by heart. It was a lament for Grandfather's native town in the Ukraine which had been destroyed by the Germans, and all its Jews slaughtered. When he had finished, Grandfather would take the sheets out of his hand, fold them, sigh and say:

"And nothing of all this is left. Dust and ashes. Not even a tombstone to bear witness. Imagine, a community of twenty thousand Jews not even one survived to tell how it happened . . . Not a trace."

Then out of the same cloth bag, which contained various letters and envelopes, he would draw a photograph of his grandson Mendele, who had been twelve years old when he was killed; the only son of his son Ossip, chief engineer in a large chemical factory. He would show it to Yehuda and say:

"He was a genius. Just imagine, when he was only eleven he had already finished his studies at the Conservatory, won a scholarship from the Government and was considered an outstanding violinist. A genius! Look at that forehead. . . ." And after he had put the photograph back he would sigh and repeat "Not a trace."

A strained silence of commiseration would descend on Raya and Yehuda, who had already heard these same things many times over and no longer felt anything when they were repeated. And as he wound the cord round the bag the old man would muse: "And Ossip was also a prodigy. As a boy he knew

Hebrew well, and could recite Bialik's poems by heart. He studied by himself. He read endlessly, Gnessin, Frug, Bershadsky . . . You didn't know Bershadsky; he was a good writer . . . He had a warm heart, Ossip had. He didn't mix in politics, he wasn't even a Zionist, but even when they promoted him there he didn't forget that he was a Jew . . . He called his son Mendele, of all names, after his dead brother, even though it was surely not easy to have a name like that among the Russians . . . Yes, he had a warm Jewish heart . . .''

He would turn to Yehuda as he spoke, since in Raya he always saw the child who used to sit on his knee listening to his stories, and for him she had never grown up, while he regarded Yehuda as an educated man who could understand someone else, especially inasmuch as Yehuda held a government job.

Raya remembered how the change had come about in her grandfather. When the war was over he was still sustained by uncertainty and hoped for some news of his son, for it was known that very many had succeeded in escaping eastwards. Wearily he would visit all those who had once lived in his town, but none of them had received any sign of life from relatives. Nevertheless he continued to hope, for Ossip's important position might have helped to save him. Then Raya came home one evening and saw him sitting on the floor with a rent in his jacket. In the house they spoke in whispers, and her mother's eyes were red with weeping. She, too, had wept at Grandfather's sorrow, at the sight of his stricken face, at the oppressive quiet in the rooms. For many weeks afterwards it was as if he had imposed silence on himself. He would sit at his table from morning to night, reading and re-reading old letters, studying family photographs by the hour as he brought them close to his shortsighted eyes, or leaning backwards on his chair, motionless, his hand touching the edge of the table and his eyes staring through the window in front of him, into the distance, as if he had turned to stone. He was no longer the same talkative, wise and humorous grandfather who interested himself in the house, asked what his granddaughter was doing, instructed her, tested her knowledge, proving boastfully like a child that he knew more than her teachers. Now he seemed to cut himself off from the world and entrench himself in his thoughts and his memories, which none of the household could penetrate. Later, a strange perversity had taken hold of him which it was hard to tolerate. He would insist that his meals be served at his table, apart, that no one should enter his room without knocking at the door, or close the shutters of his window against the sun. When any one disobeyed these prohibitions he would flare up and quarrel violently with his daughter. At times it seemed that he hated her.

When Raya's father died, Grandfather Zisskind did not show any signs of grief, and did not even console his daughter. But when the days of mourning were past it was as if he had been restored to new life, and he emerged from his silence. Yet he did not speak of his son-in-law, nor of his son Ossip, but only of his grandson Mendele. Often during the day he would mention the boy by name as if he were alive, and speak of him familiarly, although he had seen him only in photographs—as though deliberating aloud and turning the matter over, he would talk of how Mendele ought to be brought up. It was hardest of all when he started criticizing his son and his son's wife for not having foreseen the impending disaster, for not having rushed the boy away to a safe place, not having hidden him with non-Jews, not having tried to get him to the Land of Israel in good time. There was no logic in what he said; this would so infuriate Rachel that she would burst out with, "Oh, do stop! Stop it! I'll go out of my mind with your foolish nonsense!" She would rise from her seat in anger, withdraw to her room, and afterwards, when she had calmed down, would say to Raya, "Sclerosis, apparently. Loss of memory. He no longer knows what he's talking about."

One day—Raya would never forget this—she and her mother saw that Grandfather was wearing his best suit, the black one, and under it a gleaming white shirt; his shoes were polished, and he had a hat on. He had not worn these clothes for many months, and the family was dismayed to see him. They thought that he had lost his mind. "What holiday is it today?" her mother asked. "Really, don't you know?" asked her grandfather. "Today is Mendele's birthday!" Her mother burst out crying. She too began to cry and ran out of the house.

After that, Grandfather Zisskind went to live alone. His mind, apparently, had become settled, except that he would frequently forget things which had occurred a day or two before, though he clearly remembered, down to the smallest detail, things which had happened in his town and to his family more than thirty years ago. Raya would go and visit him, at first with her mother and, after her marriage, with Yehuda. What bothered them was that they were compelled to listen to his talk about Mendele his grandson, and to read that same lament for his native town which had been destroyed.

Whenever Rachel happened to come there during their visit, she would scold Grandfather rudely. "Stop bothering them with your masterpiece," she would say, and herself remove the papers from the table and put them back in their bag. "If you want them to keep on visiting you, don't talk to them about the dead. Talk about the living. They're young people and they have no mind for such things." And as they left his room together she would say, turning to Yehuda in order to placate him, "Don't be surprised at him. Grandfather's already old. Over seventy. Loss of memory."

When Raya was seven months pregnant, Grandfather Zisskind had in his absent-mindedness not yet noticed it. But Rachel could no longer refrain from letting him share her joy and hope, and told him that a great-grandchild would soon be born to him. One evening the door of Raya and Yehuda's flat opened, and Grandfather himself stood on the threshold in his holiday clothes, just as on the day of Mendele's birthday. This was the first time he had visited them at home, and Raya was so surprised that she hugged and kissed him as she had not done since she was a child. His face shone, his eyes sparkled with the same intelligent and mischievous light they had in those far-off days before the calamity. When he entered he walked briskly through the rooms, giving his opinion on the furniture and its arrangement, and joking about everything around him. He was so pleasant that Raya and Yehuda could not stop laughing all the time he was speaking. He gave no indication that he knew what was about to take place, and for the first time in many months he did not mention Mendele.

"Ah, you naughty children," he said, "is this how you treat Grandfather? Why didn't you tell me you had such a nice place?"

"How many times have I invited you here, Grandfather?" asked Raya.

"Invited me? You ought to have *brought* me here, dragged me by force!"

"I wanted to do that too, but you refused."

"Well, I thought that you lived in some dark den, and I have a den of my own. Never mind, I forgive you."

And when he took leave of them he said:

"Don't bother to come to me. Now that I know where you're to be found and what a palace you have, I'll come to you . . . if you don't throw me out, that is."

Some days later, when Rachel came to their home and they told her about Grandfather's amazing visit, she was not surprised:

"Ah, you don't know what he's been contemplating during all these days, ever since I told him that you're about to have a child . . . He has one wish— that if it's a son, it should be named . . . after his grandson."

"Mendele?" exclaimed Raya, and involuntarily burst into laughter. Yehuda smiled as one smiles at the fond fancies of the old.

"Of course, I told him to put that out of his head," said Rachel, "but you know how obstinate he is. It's some obsession and he won't think of giving it up. Not only that, but he's sure that you'll willingly agree to it, and especially you, Yehuda."

Yehuda shrugged his shoulders. "Crazy. The child would be unhappy all his life."

"But he's not capable of understanding that," said Rachel, and a note of apprehension crept into her voice.

Raya's face grew solemn. "We have already decided on the name," she said. "If it's a girl she'll be called Osnath, and if it's a boy—Ehud."

Rachel did not like either.

The matter of the name became almost the sole topic of conversation between Rachel and the young couple when she visited them, and it infused gloom into the air of expectancy which filled the house.

Rachel, midway between the generations, was of two minds about the matter. When she spoke to her father she would scold and contradict him, flinging at him all the arguments she had heard from Raya and Yehuda as though they were her own, but when she spoke to the children she sought to induce them to meet his wishes, and would bring down their anger on herself. As time went on, the question of a name, to which in the beginning she had attached little importance, became a kind of mystery, concealing something preordained, fearful, and pregnant with life and death. The fate of the child itself seemed in doubt. In her innermost heart she prayed that Raya would give birth to a daughter.

"Actually, what's so bad about the name Mendele?" she asked her daughter. "It's a Jewish name like any other."

"What are you talking about, Mother"—Raya rebelled against the thought—"a Ghetto name, ugly, horrible! I wouldn't even be capable of letting it cross my lips. Do you want me to hate my child?"

"Oh, you won't hate your child. At any rate, not because of the name . . ."

"I should hate him. It's as if you'd told me that my child would be born with a hump! And anyway—why should I? What for?"

"You have to do it for Grandfather's sake," Rachel said quietly, although she knew that she was not speaking the whole truth.

"You know, Mother, that I am ready to do anything for Grandfather," said Raya. "I love him, but I am not ready to sacrifice my child's happiness on account of some superstition of his. What sense is there in it?"

Rachel could not explain the "sense in it" rationally, but in her heart she rebelled against her daughter's logic which had always been hers too and now seemed very superficial, a symptom of the frivolity afflicting the younger generation. Her old father now appeared to her like an ancient tree whose deep roots suck up the mysterious essence of existence, of which neither her daughter nor she herself knew anything. Had it not been for this argument about the name, she would certainly never have got to meditating on the transmigration of souls and the eternity of life. At night she would wake up covered in cold sweat. Hazily, she recalled frightful scenes of bodies of naked children, beaten and trampled under the jackboots of soldiers, and an awful sense of guilt oppressed her spirit.

Then Rachel came with a proposal for a compromise: that the child should be named Menachem. A Hebrew name, she said; an Israeli one, by all standards. Many children bore it, and it occurred to nobody to make fun of them. Even Grandfather had agreed to it after much urging.

Raya refused to listen.

"We have chosen a name, Mother," she said, "which we both like, and we won't change it for another. Menachem is a name which reeks of old age, a name which for me is connected with sad memories and people I don't like. Menachem you could call only a boy who is short, weak and not good-looking. Let's not talk about it any more, Mother."

Rachel was silent. She almost despaired of convincing them. At last she said:

"And you are ready to take the responsibility of going against Grandfather's wishes?"

Raya's eyes opened wide, and fear was reflected in them:

"Why do you make such a fateful thing of it? You frighten me!" she said, and burst into tears. She began to fear for her offspring as one fears the evil eye.

"And perhaps there *is* something fateful in it . . . ." whispered Rachel without raising her eyes. She flinched at her own words.

"What is it?" insisted Raya, with a frightened look at her mother.

"I don't know . . . ." she said. "Perhaps all the same we are bound to retain the names of the dead . . . in order to leave a remembrance of them . . . ." She was not sure herself whether there was any truth in what she said or whether it was merely a stupid belief, but her father's faith was before her, stronger than her own doubts and her daughter's simple and understandable opposition.

"But I don't always want to remember all those dreadful things, Mother. It's impossible that this memory should always hang about this house and that the poor child should bear it!"

Rachel understood. She, too, heard such a cry within her as she listened to her father talking, sunk in memories of the past. As if to herself, she said in a whisper:

"I don't know . . . at times it seems to me that it's not Grandfather who's suffering from loss of memory, but ourselves. All of us."

About two weeks before the birth was due, Grandfather Zisskind appeared in Raya and Yehuda's home for the second time. His face was yellow, angry, and the light had faded from his eyes. He greeted them, but did not favor Raya with so much as a glance, as if he had pronounced a ban upon the sinner. Turning to Yehuda he said, "I wish to speak to you."

They went into the inner room. Grandfather sat down on the chair and placed the palm of his hand on the edge of the table, as was his wont, and Yehuda sat, lower than he, on the bed.

"Rachel has told me that you don't want to call the child by my grandchild's name," he said.

"Yes . . . ." said Yehuda diffidently.

"Perhaps you'll explain to me why?" he asked.

"We . . . ." stammered Yehuda, who found it difficult to face the piercing gaze of the old man. "The name simply doesn't appeal to us."

Grandfather was silent. Then he said, "I understand that Mendele doesn't appeal to you. Not a Hebrew name. Granted! But Menachem—what's wrong with Menachem?" It was obvious that he was controlling his feelings with difficulty.

"It's not . . . ." Yehuda knew that there was no use explaining; they were two generations apart in their ideas. "It's not an Israeli name . . . it's from the *Golah*."

"*Golah*," repeated Grandfather. He shook with rage, but somehow he maintained his self-control. Quietly he added, "We all come from the *Golah*. I, and Raya's father and mother. Your father and mother. All of us."

"Yes . . . ." said Yehuda. He resented the fact that he was being dragged into an argument which was distasteful to him, particularly with this old man whose mind was already not quite clear. Only out of respect did he restrain himself from shouting: That's that, and it's done with! . . . "Yes, but we were born in this country," he said aloud; "that's different."

Grandfather Zisskind looked at him contemptuously. Before him he saw a wretched boor, an empty vessel.

"You, that is to say, think that there's something new here," he said, "that everything that was there is past and gone. Dead, without sequel. That you are starting everything anew."

"I didn't say that. I only said that we were born in this country. . . ."

"You were born here. Very nice . . ." said Grandfather Zisskind with rising emotion. "So what of it? What's so remarkable about that? In what way are you superior to those who were born *there?* Are you cleverer than they? More cultured? Are you greater than they in Torah or good deeds? Is your blood redder than theirs?" Grandfather Zisskind looked as if he could wring Yehuda's neck.

"I didn't say that either, I said that *here* it's different. . . ."

Grandfather Zisskind's patience with idle words was exhausted.

"You good-for-nothing!" he burst out in his rage. "What do you know about what was there? What do you know of the *people* that were there? The communities? The cities? What do you know of the *life* they had there?"

"Yes," said Yehuda, his spirit crushed, "but we no longer have any ties with it."

"You have no ties with it?" Grandfather Zisskind bent towards him. His lips quivered in fury. "With what . . . with what *do* you have ties?"

"We have . . . with this country," said Yehuda and gave an involuntary smile.

"Fool!" Grandfather Zisskind shot at him. "Do you think that people come to a desert and make themselves a nation, eh? That you are the first of some new race? That you're not the son of your father? Not the grandson of your grandfather? Do you want to forget them? Are you ashamed of them for having had a hundred times more culture and education than you have? Why . . . why, everything here"—he included everything around him in the sweep of his arm—"is no more than a puddle of tapwater against the big sea that was there! What have you here? A mixed multitude! Seventy languages! Seventy distinct groups! Customs? A way of life? Why, every home here is a nation in itself, with its own customs and its own names! And with this you have ties, you say . . ."

Yehuda lowered his eyes and was silent.

"I'll tell you what ties are," said Grandfather Zisskind calmly. "Ties are remembrance! Do you understand? The Russian is linked to his people because he remembers his ancestors. He is called Ivan, his father was called Ivan and his grandfather was called Ivan, back to the first generation. And no Russian has said: From today onwards I shall not be called Ivan because my fathers and my fathers' fathers were called that; I am the first of a new Russian nation which has nothing at all to do with the Ivans. Do you understand?"

"But what has that got to do with it?" Yehuda protested impatiently. Grandfather Zisskind shook his head at him.

"And you—you're ashamed to give your son the name Mendele lest it remind you that there were Jews who were called by that name. You believe that his name should be wiped off the face of the earth. That not a trace of it should remain . . ." He paused, heaved a deep sigh and said:

"O children, children, you don't know what you're doing . . . You're finishing off the work which the enemies of Israel began. They took the bodies away from the world, and you—the name and the memory . . . No continuation, no evidence, no memorial and no name. Not a trace . . ."

And with that he rose, took his stick and with long strides went towards the door and left.

The new-born child was a boy and he was named Ehud, and when he was about a month old, Raya and Yehuda took him in the carriage to Grandfather's house.

Raya gave three cautious knocks on the door; and when she heard a rustle inside she could also hear the beating of her anxious heart. Since the birth of the child Grandfather had not visited them even once. "I'm terribly excited," she whispered to Yehuda with tears in her eyes. Yehuda rocked the carriage and did not reply. He was now indifferent to what the old man might say or do.

The door opened, and on the threshold stood Grandfather Zisskind, his face weary and wrinkled. He seemed to have aged. His eyes were sticky with sleep, and for a moment it seemed as if he did not see the callers.

"Good Sabbath, Grandfather," said Raya with great feeling. It seemed to her now that she loved him more than ever.

Grandfather looked at them as if surprised, and then said absently, "Come in, come in."

"We've brought the baby with us!" said Raya, her fact shining, and her glance traveled from Grandfather to the infant sleeping in the carriage.

"Come in, come in," repeated Grandfather Zisskind in a tired voice. "Sit down," he said as he removed his clothes from the chairs and turned to tidy the disordered bedclothes.

Yehuda stood the carriage by the wall and whispered to Raya, "It's stifling for him here." Raya opened the window wide.

"You haven't seen our baby yet, Grandfather!" she said with a sad smile.

"Sit down, sit down," said Grandfather, shuffling over to the shelf, from which he took the jar of preserves and the biscuit tin, putting them on the table.

"There's no need, Grandfather, really there's no need for it. We didn't come for that," said Raya.

"Only a little something. I have nothing to offer you today. . . ." said Grandfather in a dull, broken voice. He took the kettle off the kerosene burner and poured out two glasses of tea which he placed before them. Then he too sat down, and said "Drink, drink," and softly tapped his fingers on the table.

"I haven't seen your Mother for several days now," he said at last.

"She's busy . . ." said Raya in a low voice, without raising her eyes to him. "She helps me a lot with the baby. . . ."

Grandfather Zisskind looked at his pale, knotted and veined hands lying helplessly on the table; then he stretched out one of them and said to Raya, "Why don't you drink? The tea will get cold."

Raya drew up to the table and sipped the tea.

"And you—what are you doing now?" he asked Yehuda.

"Working as usual," said Yehuda, and added with a laugh, "I play with the baby when there's time."

Grandfather again looked down at his hands, the long thin fingers of which shook with the palsy of old age.

"Take some of the preserves," he said to Yehuda, indicating the jar with a shaking finger. "It's very good." Yehuda dipped the spoon in the jar and put it to his mouth.

There was a deep silence. It seemed to last a very long time. Grandfather Zisskind's fingers gave little quivers on the white tablecloth. It was hot in the room, and the buzzing of a fly could be heard.

Suddenly the baby burst out crying, and Raya started from her seat and hastened to quiet him. She rocked the carriage and crooned, "Quiet, child, quiet, quiet . . ." Even after he had quieted down she went on rocking the carriage back and forth.

Grandfather Zisskind raised his head and said to Yehuda in a whisper:

"You think it was impossible to save him . . . it was possible. They had many friends. Ossip himself wrote to me about it. The manager of the factory had a high opinion of him. The whole town knew them and loved them. . . . How is it they didn't think of it . . . ?" he said, touching his forehead with the palm of his hand. "After all, they knew that the Germans were approaching . . . It was still possible to do something . . ." He stopped a moment and then added, "Imagine that a boy of eleven had already finished his studies at the Conservatory—wild beasts!" He suddenly opened eyes filled with terror. "Wild beasts! To take little children and put them into wagons and deport them . . ."

When Raya returned and sat down at the table, he stopped and became silent; and only a heavy sigh escaped from deep within him.

Again there was a prolonged silence, and as it grew heavier Raya felt the oppressive weight on her bosom increasing till it could no longer be contained. Grandfather sat at the table tapping his thin fingers, and alongside the wall the infant lay in his carriage; it was as if a chasm gaped between a world which was passing and a world that was born. It was no longer a single line to the fourth generation. The aged father did not recognize the great-grandchild whose life would be no memorial.

Grandfather Zisskind got up, took his chair and pulled it up to the clock. He climbed on to it to take out his documents.

Raya could no longer stand the oppressive atmosphere.

"Let's go," she said to Yehuda in a choked voice.

"Yes, we must go," said Yehuda, and rose from his seat. "We have to go," he said loudly as he turned to the old man.

Grandfather Zisskind held the key of the clock for a moment more, then he let his hand fall, grasped the back of the chair and got down.

"You have to go. . . ." he said with a tortured grimace. He spread his arms out helplessly and accompanied them to the doorway.

When the door had closed behind them the tears flowed from Raya's eyes. She bent over the carriage and pressed her lips to the baby's chest. At that moment it seemed to her that he was in need of pity and of great love, as though he were alone, an orphan in the world.

Search for a Future

Arthur Miller

I read where a great writer, just before he died, was having dinner in a restaurant, and said, "It all tastes the same." Maybe I am dying. But I feel good.

I was pasting on my beard. My mind was going back through the mirror to all the other beards, and I counted this as number nine in my life. I used to like beard parts when I was younger because they made me look mature and more sure of myself. But I don't like them as much now that I'm older. No matter how I try I can't help acting philosophical on stage with a beard, and in this part I'm a loud farmer.

That night I looked at my makeup jars, the sponge, the towel, the eye pencil, and I had a strong feeling all of a sudden. That it had always been the same jars, the same sponge, the same towel stained with pink pancake exactly like this one, that I had not gotten up from this dressing table for thirty-five years, and that I had spent my whole life motionless, twenty minutes before curtain. That everything tasted the same. Actually I feel I am optimistic. But for quite a lengthened-out minute there I felt that I had never done anything but make myself up for a role I never got to play. Part of it is, I suppose, that all dressing rooms are the same. The other part is that I have been waiting to hear that my father has died. I don't mean that I think of him all the time, but quite often when I hear a telephone ring, I think: There it is, they are going to tell me the news.

The stage-door man came in. I thought he was going to announce ten minutes to curtain, but instead he said that somebody was asking to see me. People never visit before a show. I thought it might be somebody from the nursing home. I felt frightened. But I wanted to know immediately, and the stage-door man hurried out to bring in my visitor.

I have never married, although I have been engaged several times. But always to a Gentile girl, and I didn't want to break my mother's heart. I have since learned that I was too attached to her, but I don't feel sure about that. I love nothing more than children, family life. But at the last minute a certain idea would always come to me and stick in my brain, the idea that this marriage was not absolutely necessary. It gave me a false heart, and I never went ahead with it. There are many times when I wish I had been born in Europe, in my father's village where they arranged marriages and you never even saw the bride's face under the veil until after the ceremony. I would have been a faithful husband and a good father, I think. It's a mystery. I miss the wife and children I have never had.

I was surprised to see a boy of twenty-two or -three walk in. He was short, with curly hair and a pink complexion that made him look as though he never had to shave. He had a sweet expression, a twinkle in his eye. "I just wanted to remind you about midnight," he said.

About midnight? What about midnight? I was completely lost. For a minute there I even thought: My father has died and I have forgotten about it and there is some kind of procedure or a ceremony at midnight.

"The meeting," he said.

Then I remembered. I had agreed to sit on the platform at a meeting called "Broadway for Peace." My dresser's nephew, a musician twenty-one years old, had just had his eyes shot out in Vietnam somewhere, and I was sick about it. I still haven't seen my dresser, Roy Delcampo; he doesn't even call me up since it happened. I know he'll show up one of these nights, but so far there is no sign of him. To tell the truth, I do not know who is right about this war, but I know that nobody is going to remember ten years from now what it was all for—just as I know that I have had forty-three shows, forty-three openings, but who can even remember the casts, the exact kind of battles we had in production, let alone the review or even most of the titles? I know it all kept me alive, but it is even hard to remember the kind of actor I had wanted to be. It wasn't this kind, is all I know.

Suddenly I was a little nervous about this meeting. I have always respected actors with convictions, the people in the old days who were Leftists, and so on. Whatever people might say, those guys and girls had wonderful friendships. But I never felt it was really necessary for me to put my name on anything political; I never felt it would make any difference if I put down my name or if I didn't.

I looked at this boy and he looked at me, and I could see once again how my generation used to see things when I was his age. This meeting was more than a meeting; it was to stop the world from ending. Which I didn't believe, but for him it wasn't all the same. For him—and I could see he was an actor—every experience was some kind of new beginning. I could see that he still remembered every single thing that had ever happened to him, that he was on his way up, up.

Actually, I was quite frightened about the meeting, but I couldn't bear to say to him that it was not going to make any difference whether or not I appeared. So we shook hands, and he even grasped my arm as though we were in league, or even to indicate that he felt especially good that an older man was going to be with them. Something of that kind.

When he turned around and walked out, I saw that the seat of his overcoat was worn; it was a much lighter color than the rest of the coat. An actor notices such things. It means that he sits a lot in his overcoat, and on rough places. Like the steps in front of the Forty-second Street library, or even park benches, or some of the broken chairs in producers' outer offices. And here he is, this boy, spending his time with meetings. I thought to myself, I cannot imagine anything I would sit and wait for, and I wished I had something like that. I ended up a little glad that I was going to be at the meeting. Exactly why, I don't know.

I think I acted better that night, not that anyone else would notice, but I found myself really looking at my fellow actors as though I had never seen them before. Suddenly it was remarkable to me, the whole idea of a play, of being able to forget everything else so that we were really angry up there, or really laughing, or really drinking the cider we were supposed to drink, which is actually tea, and coughing as though it were bitter. Toward the end of Act Two some man got up from the third row and walked out. I usually feel upset about a walkout, but this night it went through my mind that it was his role to walk out, that the whole audience was acting too. After all, the whole idea of so many people sitting together, facing in the same direction, not talking, is a kind of acting.

Even the President gets made up now for his TV talks. Everybody every morning gets into costume. As we were taking the curtain calls, I thought: Maybe I never got married because it would make my life real; it would rip me off the stage somehow.

The next morning I went to visit my father at the nursing home. I had been there only four or five days before, but I felt pulled. So I went.

It was a very windy day in October, a clear blue sky over New York. My father always liked strong wind and cold weather. He would put up his coat collar and say, "Ahhh," and even as a little boy I imitated the way he exhaled and enjoyed facing into a cold wind. He would look down at me and laugh, "This is not a hot day, boy."

The old man is in a cage. But the bars are so close to his face he cannot see them, so he keeps moving, a step this way and a step that way. And finally he knows, for the hundredth time every day, that he is not free.

But he does not know why. He feels someone knows, and whoever it is means him harm. Something is going to happen. Someone is keeping him here for a long temporarily, as you might say.

The room is freshly painted and smells it. A light blue color over many coats of paint, so that the shiny surface is lumpy. A string hangs from the middle of the ceiling with a fluorescent plastic tassel on the end of it. His head strikes it whenever he moves about the room. In the dark at night he lies on his bed and goes to sleep with the bluish glow of this tassel on his retina. In the afternoons he can pull the string and make the ceiling light go on. He has never been at ease with machinery, so when he pulls the string he looks up at the ceiling fixture, a little surprised that the light went on. Sometimes after his head has hit the tassel he scratches the spot lightly as though a fly had sat on his skin. The word "stroke" is very right, like a touch on the brain, just enough.

The nursing home is an old, converted apartment house, but an extremely narrow one. The corridors on each floor are hardly wider than a man. You come in and on the right is an office where a fat woman is always looking into a thick registry book. On the left is a slow elevator. A zoo smell is always in the air as soon as you walk into the building, and it gets thicker upstairs. But it is not a filthy smell. It is like earth, humid but not diseased. At my first visit I was repelled by it, as by sewage. But after a while, if you allow yourself to breathe in deeply, you realize it is the odor of earth and you respect it.

Up one flight is my father's floor. There is always a mattress or springs standing on edge in the corridor; someone has been moved out or died. Rooms open off the corridor, most of them occupied by old women. They sit motionlessly facing their beds, some asleep in their chairs. There is no sound in the place; they are all dozing like thin, white-haired birds which do not thrive in captivity. All their eyes seem blue.

The old man's room is the last one on the corridor. Opposite his door is a widened space where the nurses have a desk. They do not look up when I open his door. Nobody is going to steal anything here or do any harm. Everyone is so old that there cannot be an emergency.

He is usually asleep on his bed, whatever time I come. I am already twenty years older than he was at my birth. I am an older man than the one I looked up at during the windy walks. My hair is gray at the sides. Mother has been dead a long, long time. All of his brothers and sisters are dead; everyone he knew and played cards with. I have also lost many friends. It turns out that he is not really too much older than I am, than I am becoming.

I stood there looking down at him and recalled the meeting the night before. About fifteen others were sitting on a row of chairs on the stage. The chairman introduced us by turn. For some reason, when I stood up there seemed to be heavier applause, probably because it was the first time I had ever come out for such a thing, and also because I have been quite a hit in this current play, and they knew my face. But when I stood up and the applause continued, the chairman waved for me to come up to the microphone. I was frightened that the newspapers would pick up what I might say, and I had no idea what to say. So I came to the microphone. There was a really good silence. The theater was packed. They said that people were jammed up outside trying to get in. I bent over to the microphone and heard my own voice saying, "Someone went blind that I knew." Then I realized that I did not actually know the boy who had been blinded, and I stopped. I realized that it sounded crazy. I realized that I was frightened; that some day there might be investigations and I could be blamed for being at such a meeting. I said; "I wish the war would stop. I don't understand this war." Then I went back to my chair.

There was terrific applause. I didn't understand why I wondered what I had really said that made them so enthusiastic. It was like an opening night when a line you never had thought about very much gets a big reaction. But I felt happy, and I didn't know why. Maybe it was only the applause, which I didn't understand either, but I felt a happiness, and I thought suddenly that it had been a terrible, terrible mistake not to have gotten married.

"Pop?" I said softly, so as not to shock him. He opened his eyes and raised his head, blinking at me. He always smiles now when he is awakened, and the lower part of his long face pulls down at his eyes to open them wider. It isn't clear whether or not he knows who you are as he smiles at you. I always slip in my identification before I say anything. "I'm Harry," I say, but I make it sound casual, as though I am saying it only because he hasn't got his glasses on. His fingers dance nervously along his lower lip. He is touching himself, I think, because he is no longer certain what is real and what is dream, when people he is not sure he knows suddenly appear and disappear every day.

He immediately insists on getting out of bed. He is fully dressed under the blankets, sometimes even with his shoes on. But today he has only socks. "My slippers."

I get his slippers from the metal closet and help him into them. He stands on the floor tucking in his shirt, saying, "And uh . . . and uh," as though a conversation has been going on. There are no immense emotions here, but deep currents without light. He is bent a little, and stiff-kneed, and plucks at his clothes to be sure everything is on. He is very interested that someone is here but he knows that nothing, absolutely nothing, will come of it. But he wants to lengthen it out anyway, just in case something might happen to free him. He is afraid the end of the visit will suddenly be announced, so he tries to be quick about everything. He says, "Sit down, sit down," not only to make you comfortable but to stall off the end. Then he sits in the one armchair, the fire escape and a patch of city sky behind him, and I sit on the edge of the bed facing him.

"I hear you went for a walk today with the nurse?"

"Ya. Awd the river. Doom days deen unden, but this here's a beautiful day. Some day."

"Yes. It's a beautiful day," I repeat so that he'll know I understand what he is talking about, although it doesn't make much difference to him. Some things he says, though, he is very anxious should be understood, and then it all gets terrible. But I am not sure he knows he is mostly incomprehensible.

He wanders his arm vaguely toward the night table. "My glasses" I open the drawer and hand him one of the two pairs he keeps in there.

"Are these the ones?"

He puts on the wobbly frames which his incapable hands have bent out of shape. The lenses are coated with his fingerprints. "Ya," he says, blinking around. Then he says, "No," and roots around in the drawer. I give him the other pair, and he takes off the first pair, opens the second, and puts the first ones on again and looks at me.

I realize as he is looking at me that he feels friendship between us, and that he is glad to see me, but that he is not sure who I am. "I'm Harry," I say.

He smiles. He is still a big man, even though he is very thin now. His head is massive, and his teeth are good and strong, and there is some kind of force lying in pieces inside of him, the force of a man who has not at all settled for this kind of room and this kind of life. For him, as for me and everybody else, it is all some kind of mistake. He has a future. I suppose I still go to see him for that reason.

I never realized before that his ears stick out, that they face front. I think I was always so busy looking into his eyes that I never really saw his ears. Because there is nothing more to listen to from him or to fear, I have time to look at his body now.

His left leg is quite bowed out, more than I ever realized. His hands are very slender and even artistic. His feet are long and narrow. He has strangely high, almost Slavic, cheekbones which I never noticed when his face was fuller. The top of his head is flatter, and the back of his neck. It was less than five years ago that I first realized he was an old man, an aged man. I happened to meet him walking on Broadway one afternoon and I had to walk very slowly beside him. A little breeze in his face made his eyes tear. But I felt then that it was not something very sad; I felt that after all he had lived a long time.

But this day I felt a difference about him. He had not given up his future. In fact, he was reaching toward his future even more energetically than I was toward mine. He really wanted something.

"Linnen, I ah gedda hew orthing. Very important."

"You want something?"

"No-no. I ah gedda hew orthing."

He waited for me to reply. "I don't understand what you're saying, but keep talking, maybe I'll understand."

He reached over toward the door and tested that it was shut. Now, as he spoke, he kept glancing with widened eyes toward the door as though interlopers who meant him no good were out in the corridor. Then he shook his head angrily. "I never in my life. Never."

"What's the matter?"

"Hew maug lee me ounigh."

"They won't let you out?"

He nodded, scandalized, angry. "Hew maug lee me ounigh."

"But you went out with the nurse, didn't you?"

"Lennen. Hew linnen?" He was impatient.

"Yes, Pop, I'm listening. What do you want?"

Something politic came over him as he prepared to speak again, something calculating. He was positioning himself for a deal. His lips, without sound, flicked in and out like a chimpanzee's as he practiced an important message.

Then he crossed his legs and leaned over the arm of the chair toward me.

"Naw gen my money."

"Your money?"

"Naw gen. Yesterday she said sure. Today, naw gen."

"The lady downstairs?"

"Ya."

"She asked you for money?"

"Naw gen my money."

"She wouldn't give you your money?"

He nodded. "Naw gen. Fifty thousand dollars."

"You asked her for fifty thousand dollars?"

"For my money gen."

He was leaning toward me crosslegged, just as I had seen him do with businessmen, that same way of talking in a hotel lobby or in a Pullman, a rather handsome posture and full of grace. Of course, he had no fifty thousand dollars; he had nothing anymore, but I did not realize at the time what he really had in his mind even though he was telling it to me clearly.

"Well, you don't need money here, Pop."

He gave me a suspicious look with a little wise smile; I, too, was not on his side. "Linnen."

"I'm listening."

"I could go home," he said with sudden clarity. He had no home either. His wife was dead eight years now, and even his hotel room had been given up. "I wouldn't even talk," he said.

"It's better for you here, Pop."

"Better!" He looked at me with open anger.

"You need nursing," I explained. He listened with no attention, his eyes glancing at the door, while I explained how much better off he was here than at home. But his anger passed. Then he said, "I could live." I nodded. "I could live," he repeated.

Now came the silence, which is always the worst part. I could find nothing further to say, and he no longer had a way to enlist my help. Or maybe he was expecting me to start packing his things and getting him out. All we had in the room was his low-burning pleasure that someone was here with him, even though he did not know for sure who it was, excepting that it was someone familiar; and for me there was only the knowledge that he had this pleasure.

He would look at me now and then with various expressions. Once it would be with narrowed eyes, an estimating look, as though he were about to speak some searching sentence. Then he would blink ahead again and test his lips. After a few moments he would look at me, this time with the promise of his warm, open smile, then once again drift into a stare.

Finally he raised his finger as though to draw my attention, a stranger's attention, and tilting back his head as though recalling, he said, "Did you St. Louis?"

"Yes, I'm back now. I was there and now I'm back." I had been in St. Louis with a show nine or ten years ago. One of his factories had been in St. Louis forty years ago.

He broke into a pleased smile. He loved cities. He had enjoyed entering them and leaving them, being well served in hotels. He had loved recalling buildings that had been demolished, the marvelous ups and downs of enterprises and business careers. I knew what he was smiling at. He had once brought me a toy bus from St. Louis, with a whole band on top which moved its arms when the bus moved, and inside it was a phonograph record which played "The Stars and Stripes Forever." He had come home just as I had gotten up from my nap. In his arms were gift boxes—this bus, and I remember a long pair of beige kid gloves for my mother. He always brought fresh air into the house with him—the wind, his pink face, and his reedy laugh.

"Well, I have to go now, Pop."

"Ya, ya."

He stood up, hiking his pants up where his belly used to be, plucking at his brown sweater to keep it properly placed on his shoulders. He hurried to stand, and even enjoyed the good-bye, thinking I had important work to do—appointments, the world's business—with which no one had a right to interfere. We shook hands. I opened the door, and he insisted on escorting me to the elevator. "This way, this way," he said in a proprietary manner as though he could not help being in charge. He walked ahead of me, bent, heavily favoring his bowed left leg, down the narrow corridor, his face very much averted from the open rooms where the old ladies sat motionless.

Outside, the wind was even faster than before, but the sky was turning gray. I had some time so I walked for a while, thinking of him turning back and re-entering his room, lying down on the bed, probably exhausted, and the plastic thing on the light string swaying overhead.

It was fine to walk without a limp. I resolved again to stop smoking. I have wide hands and feet. I am not at all built like him. I crossed from Riverside Drive to the Park and caught a bus to Harlem, where I was born. But as soon as I got out I knew I had lost the feeling I had started with, and it was impossible to feel what I had felt there in my youth forty years ago.

There was only one moment that held me: I found myself facing a dry-cleaning store which had once been one of the best restaurants in New York. On Sundays the old man would take my mother and me for dinner. There had been a balcony where a baker in a tall white hat baked fresh rolls, and whenever a customer entered, the baker would look down and put in a fresh batch. I could smell the rolls through the odor of benzine on Lenox Avenue. I could see the manager who always sat down with us while we ate. He had some disease, I suppose, because the right side of his face was swollen out like a balloon, but he always wore a hard wing collar and a white tie, and never seemed sick. A Negro with a moustache was looking through the store window at me. For a moment I had the urge to go and tell him what I remembered, to describe this avenue when no garbage cans were on the street, when the Daimlers and

Minervas and Locomobiles had cruised by, and the cop on the corner threw back the ball when it got through the outfield on 114th Street. I did not go into the store, nor even toward our house. Any claim I had to anything had lapsed. I went downtown instead and sat in my dressing room, trying to read.

I was just opening my pancake can when I thought of something which I still don't altogether understand: that the old man is the only one who is not an actor. I am, the President is, and the chairman of the protest meeting is, even though his convictions are very sincere; but on the platform the other night I could tell, probably because I am an actor, that he was listening to his modulations, that he was doing what he was doing because he had told himself to do it. But he is not desperate enough, not like the old man is desperate. The old man does not know enough to listen to his own voice or to ask himself what he ought to do; he just speaks from his heart, and he has even lost his hold on the language, so all that is left is the sound, you might say, of his gut. The old man is not acting.

I wondered about the young, pink-cheeked boy who had come to remind me about the meeting—if he also was acting. Maybe in his case, with the draft grabbing for him, it was real. I started pasting on my beard and I thought again of my not being married. It was like all this agitation now, like everything I see and know about: It was a lack of some necessity. Nobody seems to *have* to do anything, and the ones who say they *do* have to, who say that something is absolutely necessary for them, may only be the best actors. Because that is what a really good actor does: He manages to make his feelings necessary, so that suddenly there is no longer the slightest choice for him. He has to scream or die, laugh or die, cry real tears or die. And at the same time he knows that he is not going to die, and this thought makes him happy while he is screaming or crying, and it may be what makes the audience happy to cry too.

I was just taking off my clothes in my bedroom that night when the telephone rang. And it frightened me, as it usually does these days. It really was the fat woman in the nursing home this time. The old man had escaped. It seems he had slipped out not long after I had left, and here it was nearly two in the morning and the police had a missing-persons alarm out but there was no sign of him yet. The worst thing was that he had gone out without his overcoat, and it was raining and blowing like hell. There was nothing more to be done now, as long as the police had an eye out for him, but I couldn't go back to sleep. I couldn't help feeling proud of him and hoping they would never find him, that he would just disappear. I have always admired his willfulness, his blind push toward what he has to have. I have admired his not being an actor, I suppose, and he was not acting tonight, not out there in that rain and wind. I couldn't sleep, but there was nothing I could do. The clock was inching up to three by this time. I got dressed and went out.

I had only walked a block when I felt my socks getting wet, so I stepped into a doorway, trying to think what to do. It was somehow strange that both of us were walking around in the same rain. But who was he looking for? Or what? I half didn't want to find him. In fact, for moments I had visions of him crossing the river to the west, just getting the hell out of here, out of the world. But how would he talk to anybody? Would he know enough to get onto a bus? Did he have any money? Naturally, I ended up being worried about him, and after a while I saw a taxi and got in.

I joke with cab drivers but I never *talk* with them, but this time I had to explain myself for wanting to cruise around. I told the driver that I was looking for my father. Cab drivers never seem to believe anything, but he believed me; it seemed perfectly natural to him. Maybe it happens quite often like this. I don't even remember what the cab driver looked like, even whether he was white or Negro. I remember the rain pouring over the windshield and the side windows because I was trying to see through them. It was getting on toward half-past four by the time I got home again, and the rain was coming down stiff. I went into my bedroom and undressed and lay down and looked toward my window, which was running with water. I felt as though the whole city was crying.

They found him next morning at about ten o'clock, and the police called me. They had already returned him to the nursing home, so I hurried up there. The rain was over and once again the sky was clear, a good, sharp, sunny October day. He was asleep on his bed, wrapped in his flannel robe. A bandage was plastered over his nose, and he seemed to have a black eye coming on. His knuckles were scraped and had been painted with Merthiolate. He badly needed a shave. I went downstairs and talked with the fat woman in the office. She was wary and cautious because they can probably be sued, but I finally got the story out of her. He had been found in Harlem. He had gone into a luncheonette and ordered some food, but the counterman had probably realized that he was not quite right and asked for the money in advance. The old man had a dollar but would not pay in advance, and they went looking for a cop to take care of him. When he realized they were looking for a cop he got up and tried to leave, and stumbled and fell on his face.

I went up again and sat in the armchair, waiting for him to wake up. But after a while one of the nurses came in and said they had given him a sedative which would keep him under for several hours. When I left just before my show, he was sitting in the armchair, eating some chicken. He looked up at me very surprised and again felt his lips with rapid fingers. I smiled at him. "I'm Harry," I said.

He looked at me without much recognition, only knowing that there was something of a past between us. I sat on the bed and watched him eat. I talked at length about the good day we were having, and how hard it had rained last night. I kept wishing and wishing that even for one split second he would look at me clearly and laugh. Just one shrewd laugh between us to celebrate his outing. But he sat there eating, glancing at me with a little warmth and a little suspicion, and finally I grinned and said, "I hear you went for a walk last night."

He stopped eating and looked at me with surprise. He shook his head. "No. Oh, no."

"Don't you remember the rain?"

"The rain?"

"You went to Harlem, Pa. Were you going home?"

A new attention crossed his eyes, and a sharpened interest. "I en home raro." He spoke the sounds with an attempt to convince me. He had one finger raised.

"You're going home tomorrow?"

"Ya."

Then he glanced toward the closed door and returned to the chicken.

Every night, sitting here putting on my beard, I keep expecting a telephone call or a visitor, a stranger, and I feel I am about to be afraid.

He was trying to reach home, where ages ago he had entered so many times carrying presents. He has a future which they will never be able to rip away from him. He will close his eyes for the last time thinking of it. He does not have to teach himself or remind himself of it. As long as he can actually walk they are going to have trouble with him, keeping him from going where he wants to go and has to go.

I'm not sure how to go about it, but I have a terrific desire to live differently. Maybe it is even possible to find something honorable about acting, some way of putting my soul back into my body. I think my father is like a man in love, or at least the organism inside him is. For moments, just for moments, he makes me feel as I used to when I started, when I thought that being a great actor was like making some kind of a gift to the people.

Sixteen

Jessamyn West

Winter

The steam from the kettle had condensed on the cold window and was running down the glass in tearlike trickles. Outside in the orchard the man from the smudge company was refilling the pots with oil. The greasy smell from last night's burning was still in the air. Mr. Delahanty gazed out at the bleak darkening orange grove; Mrs. Delahanty watched her husband eat, nibbling up to the edges of the toast then stacking the crusts about his tea cup in a neat fence-like arrangement.

"We'll have to call Cress," Mr. Delahanty said, finally. "Your father's likely not to last out the night. She's his only grandchild. She ought to be here."

Mrs. Delahanty pressed her hands to the bones above her eyes. "Cress isn't going to like being called away from college," she said.

"We'll have to call her anyway. It's the only thing to do." Mr. Delahanty swirled the last of his tea around in his cup so as not to miss any sugar.

"Father's liable to lapse into unconsciousness any time," Mrs. Delahanty argued. "Cress'll hate coming and Father won't know whether she's here or not. Why not let her stay at Woolman?"

Neither wanted, in the midst of their sorrow for the good man whose life was ending, to enter into any discussion of Cress. What was the matter with Cress? What had happened to her since she went away to college? She, who had been open and loving? And who now lived inside a world so absolutely fitted to her own size and shape that she felt any intrusion, even that of the death of her own grandfather, to be an unmerited invasion of her privacy. Black magic could not have changed her more quickly and unpleasantly and nothing except magic, it seemed, would give them back their lost daughter.

Mr. Delahanty pushed back his cup and saucer. "Her place is here, Gertrude. I'm going to call her long distance now. She's a bright girl and it's not going to hurt her to miss a few days from classes. What's the dormitory number?"

"I know it as well as our number," Mrs. Delahanty said. "But at the minute it's gone. It's a sign of my reluctance, I suppose. Wait a minute and I'll look it up."

Mr. Delahanty squeezed out from behind the table. "Don't bother, I can get it."

Mrs. Delahanty watched her husband, his usually square shoulders sagging with weariness, wipe a clear place on the steamy windowpane with his napkin. Some of the green twilight appeared to seep into the warm dingy little kitchen. "I can't ever remember having to smudge before in February. I expect you're right," he added as he went toward the phone. "Cress isn't going to like it."

Cress didn't like it. It was February, the rains had been late and the world was burning with a green fire; a green smoke rolled down the hills and burst shoulder-high in the cover crops that filled the spaces between the trees in the orange orchards. There had been rain earlier in the day and drops still hung from the grass blades, sickle-shaped with their weight. Cress, walking across the campus with Edwin, squatted to look into one of these crystal globes.

"Green from the grass and red from the sun," she told him. "The whole world right there in one raindrop."

"As Blake observed earlier about a grain of sand," said Edwin.

"O.K., show off," Cress told him. "You know it—but I saw it." She took his hand and he pulled her up, swinging her in a semi-circle in front of him. "Down there in the grass the world winked at me."

"Don't be precious, Cress," Edwin said.

"I will," Cress said, "just to tease you. I love to tease you, Edwin."

"Why?" Edwin asked.

"Because you love to have me," Cress said confidently, taking his hand. Being older suited Edwin. She remembered when she had liked him in spite of his looks; but now spindly had become spare, and the dark shadow of his beard—Edwin had to shave every day while other boys were still just fuzzy—lay under his pale skin; and the opinions, which had once been so embarrassingly unlike anyone else's, were now celebrated at Woolman as being "Edwinian." Yes, Edwin had changed since that day when she had knocked his tooth out trying to rescue him from the mush pot. And had she changed? Did she also look better to Edwin, almost slender now and the freckles not noticeable except at the height of summer? And with her new-found ability for light talk? They were passing beneath the eucalyptus trees and the silver drops, falling as the wind shook the leaves, stung her face, feeling at once both cool and burning. Meadow larks in the fields which edged the campus sang in the quiet way they have after the rain has stopped.

"Oh Edwin," Cress said, "no one in the world loves the meadow lark's song the way I do!"

"It's not a competition," Edwin said, "you against the world in an 'I-love-meadow-larks' contest. Take it easy, kid. Love em as much as in you lieth, and let it go at that."

"No," she said. "I'm determined to overdo it. Listen," she exclaimed, as two birds sang together. "Not grieving, nor amorous, nor lost. Nothing to read into it. Simply music. Like Mozart. Complete. Finished. Oh it is rain to listening ears." She glanced at Edwin to see how he took this rhetoric. He took it calmly. She let go his hand and capered amidst the fallen eucalyptus leaves.

"The gardener thinks you've got St. Vitus' dance," Edwin said.

Old Boat Swain, the college gardener whose name was really Swain, was leaning on his hoe, watching her hopping and strutting. She didn't give a hoot about him or what he thought.

"He's old," she told Edwin. "He doesn't exist." She felt less akin to him than to a bird or toad.

There were lights already burning in the dorm windows. Cress could see Ardis and Nina still at their tables, finishing their Ovid or looking up a final logarithm. But between five and six most of the girls stopped trying to remember which form of the sonnet Milton had used or when the Congress of Vienna had met, and dressed for dinner. They got out of their sweaters and jackets and into their soft bright dresses. She knew just what she was going to wear when she came downstairs at six to meet Edwin—green silk like the merman's wife. They were going to the Poinsettia for dinner, escaping salmon-wiggle night in the college dining room.

"At six," she told him, "I'll fly down the stairs to meet you like a green wave."

"See you in thirty minutes," Edwin said, leaving her at the dorm steps.

The minute she opened the door, she began to hear the dorm sounds and smell the dorm smells—the hiss and rush of the showers, the thud of the iron, a voice singing, "Dear old Woolman we love so well," the slap of bare feet down the hall, the telephone ringing.

And the smells! Elizabeth Arden and Cashmere Bouquet frothing in the showers; talcum powder falling like snow; *Intoxication* and *Love Me* and *Devon Violet;* rubber-soled sneakers, too, and gym T-shirts still wet with sweat after basketball practice, and the smell of the hot iron on damp wool.

But while she was still listening and smelling, Edith shouted from the top of the stairs, "Long distance for you, Cress. Make it snappy."

Cress took the stairs three at a time, picked up the dangling receiver, pressed it to her ear.

"Tenant calling Crescent Delahanty," the operator said. It was her father: "Grandfather is dying, Cress. Catch the 7:30 home. I'll meet you at the depot."

"What's the matter—Cressie?" Edith asked.

"I have to catch the 7:30 Pacific Electric. Grandfather's dying."

"Oh poor Cress," Edith cried and pressed her arm about her.

Cress scarcely heard her. Why were they calling her home to watch Grandpa die, she thought, angrily and rebelliously. An old man, past eighty. He'd never been truly alive for her, never more than a rough, hot hand, a scraggly mustache that repelled her when he kissed her, an old fellow who gathered what he called "likely-looking" stones and kept them washed and polished, to turn over and admire. It was silly and unfair to make so much of his dying.

But before she could say a word, Edith was telling the girls. They were crowding about her. "Don't cry," they said. "We'll pack for you. Be brave, darling Cress. Remember your grandfather has had a long happy life. He wouldn't want you to cry."

"Brave Cress—brave Cress," they said. "Just frozen."

She wasn't frozen. She was determined. She was not going to go. It did not make sense. She went downstairs to meet Edwin as she had planned, in her green silk, ready for dinner at the Poinsettia. The girls had told him.

"Are you wearing that home?" he asked.

"I'm not going home," she said. "It's silly and useless. I can't help Grandfather. It's just a convention. What *good* can I do him, sitting there at home?"

"He might do you some good," Edwin said. "Had you thought about that?"

"Why, Edwin!" Cress said. "Why, Edwin!" She had the girls tamed, eating out of her hand, and here was Edwin who loved her—he said so, anyway—cold and disapproving. Looking at herself through Edwin's eyes, she hesitated.

"Go on," Edwin said. "Get what you need and I'll drive you to the station."

She packed her overnight bag and went with him; there didn't seem—once she'd had Edwin's view of herself—anything else to do. But once on the train her resentment returned. The Pacific Electric was hot and smelled of metal and dusty plush. It clicked past a rickety Mexican settlement, through La Habra and Brea, where the pool hall signs swung in the night wind off the ocean. An old man in a spotted corduroy jacket, and his wife, with her hair straggling through the holes in her broken net, sat in front of her.

Neat, thought Cress, anyone can be neat, if he wants to.

Her father, bareheaded, but in his big sheepskin jacket, met her at the depot. It was after nine, cold and raw.

"This is a sorry time, Cress," he said. He put her suitcase in the back of the car and climbed into the driver's seat without opening the door for her.

Cress got in, wrapped her coat tightly about herself. The sky was clear, the wind had died down.

"I don't see any sense in my having to come home," she said at last. "What good can I do Grandpa? If he's dying, how can I help?"

"I was afraid that was the way you might feel about it. So was your mother."

"Oh Mother," Cress burst out. "Recently she's always trying to put me . . ."

Her father cut her off. "That'll be about enough, Cress. Your place is at home and you're coming home and keeping your mouth shut, whatever you think. I don't know what's happened to you recently. If college does this to you, you'd better stay home permanently."

There was nothing more said until they turned up the palm-lined driveway that led to the house. "Here we are," Mr. Delahanty told her.

Mrs. Delahanty met them at the door, tired and haggard in her Indian design bathrobe.

"Cress," she said, "Grandfather's conscious now. I told him you were coming and he's anxious to see you. You'd better go in right away—this might be the last time he'd know you."

Cress was standing by the fireplace holding first one foot then the other toward the fire. "Oh Mother, what am I to say?" she asked. "What can I say? Or does Grandfather just want to see me?"

Her father shook his head as if with pain. "Aren't you sorry your grandfather's dying, Cress? Haven't you any pity in your heart? Don't you understand what death means?"

"He's an old man," Cress said obstinately. "It's what we must expect when we grow old." Though she, of course, would never grow old.

"Warm your hands, Cress," her mother said. "Grandfather's throat bothers him and it eases him to have it rubbed. I'll give you the ointment and you can rub it in. You won't need to say anything."

Cress slid out of her coat and went across the hall with her mother to her grandfather's room. His thin old body was hardly visible beneath the covers; his head, with its gray skin and sunken eyes, lay upon the pillow as if bodiless. The night light frosted his white hair, but made black caverns of his closed eyes.

"Father," Mrs. Delahanty said. "Father." But the old man didn't move. There was nothing except the occasional hoarse rasp of an indrawn breath to show that he was alive.

Mrs. Delahanty pulled the cane-bottomed chair a little closer to the bed. "Sit here," she said to Cress, "and rub this into his throat and chest." She opened her father's nightshirt so that an inch or two of bony grizzled chest was bared. "He says that this rubbing relieves him, even if he's asleep or too tired to speak. Rub it in with a slow steady movement." She went out to the living room leaving the door a little ajar.

Cress sat down on the chair and put two squeamish fingers into the jar of gray ointment; but she could see far more sense to this than to any talking or being talked to. If they had brought her home from school because she was needed in helping to care for Grandpa, that she could understand—but not simply to be present at his death. What had death to do with her?

She leaned over him, rubbing, but with eyes shut, dipping her fingers often into the gray grease. The rhythm of the rubbing, the warmth and closeness of the room, after the cold drive, had almost put her to sleep when the old man startled her by lifting a shaking hand to the bunch of yellow violets Edith had pinned to the shoulder of her dress before she left Woolman. She opened her eyes suddenly at his touch, but the old man said nothing, only stroked the violets awkwardly with a trembling forefinger.

Cress unpinned the violets and put them in his hand.

"There, Grandpa," she said, "there. They're for you."

The old man's voice was a harsh and faltering whisper and to hear what he said Cress had to lean very close.

"I used to—pick them—on Reservoir Hill. I was always sorry to—plow them up. Still—so sweet. Thanks," he said, "to bring them. To remember. You're like her. Your grandmother," he added after a pause. He closed his eyes, holding the bouquet against his face, letting the wilting blossoms spray across one cheek like a pulled-up sheet of flowering earth. He said one more word, not her name but her grandmother's.

The dikes about Cress's heart broke. "Oh Grandpa, I love you," she said. He heard her. He knew what she said, his fingers returned the pressure of her hand. "You were always so good to me. You were young and you loved flowers." Then she said what was her great discovery. "And you still do. You still love yellow violets, Grandpa, just like me."

At the sound of her controlled crying, Mr. and Mrs. Delahanty came to the door. "What's the matter, Cress?"

Cress turned, lifted a hand toward them. "Why didn't you tell me?" she demanded. And when they didn't answer, she said, "Edwin knew."

Then she dropped her head on to her grandfather's outstretched hand and said something, evidently to him, which neither her father nor her mother understood.

"It's just the same."

Part Two

Disappointment, The Life Review, and Unresolved Conflicts

OPTIONS FOR SIGNIFICANT BEHAVIORAL AND ROLE CHANGE ARE OPEN TO THE individual early in life and, in a development that has occurred only within the past decade or two, through the years of middle age. Resolving the mid-life crisis (described in connection with the story ''Search for a Future'' in Part 1) involves change in at least some of the dimensions of a person's life. Change occurs in attitudes toward and perceptions of one's life; occupation or some aspect of it (for example, change from administrative work to teaching within the same school system); marriage—either the style of marriage or the spouse; appearance; hobbies; political views; and so on. In the past decade or two, the potential for self-initiated extensive change through the middle years has been considerable.

It is still difficult, however, for adults to achieve voluntary and significant change in the later years of adulthood. Some individuals do of course change, but this is not as widespread as in the preceding decades of the life cycle. One is much more locked into one's roles and one's psyche in old age, both from the point of view of society and from the point of view of the individual. Occupational change is difficult when it involves moving from one job or type of job to another. While considerable change occurs with retirement, much of it is involuntary. Researchers Lenore A. Epstein and Janet H. Murray reported an exception to this in that they found some shifting into new occupations among men sixty-two and over who had been clerks and sales workers and who after partial retirement bought and ran their own small businesses.[1] Other occupations are less amenable to this flexibility. Owning one's own business is a natural and consistent change from sales work that probably involves a repertoire of fantasy[2] over the preceding years that prepares the individual for the change.

Marriage, too, tends to be more stable after the male mid-life crisis and the female empty-nest periods. The lower divorce rate in old age could mean several things: high marital satisfaction; the illness of one spouse and the feeling of involvement, empathy, love, obligation, or worry of the other; tolerance, sameness, and continuity (the partners are used to each other); the feeling that one is fortunate to have a spouse at all later in life; or the lack of alternatives. Major change in this role has more to do with the death of one spouse rather than a voluntary dissolution of the marriage. For a variety of reasons, then, voluntary change is difficult to achieve with increasing age.

The difficulty of voluntarily initiating change in later life conflicts with the tendency of some elderly to reminisce about their lives and, in the course of their reminiscing, to experience a strong wish to change the past as well as the present and future direction of their lives. These individuals experience keen

[1] Lenore A. Epstein and Janet H. Murray, ''Employment and Retirement,'' in Neugarten, *Middle Age and Aging,* pp. 354–56.

[2] *repertoire of fantasy:* a stock or supply of daydreams and products of the imagination that involve wish-fulfillment.

regrets about the past, regrets about what they might have done or did do or neglected to do or neglected to be. They wish that they could go back and redo
certain things, live differently in some important ways, recognize problems
sooner and do something about them rather than vacillate as they had done, be
more in tune with themselves earlier so as to avoid some of the problems, had
some of the opportunities when they were young that their sons and daughters
and grandchildren have had; and so on. These elderly persons realize, however,
that it is too late to correct problems, and this realization can cause depression
with its attendant diminution of memory.

Erik Erikson referred to this crisis as ego integrity versus despair.[3] It involves either acceptance of the person's one and only life cycle as he or she has
lived it—an *attitude* of acceptance rather than acceptance of each detail—or
rejection, bitterness, and a wish to have the chance to do things differently.
These are what I call the "if onlys": "If only I had been born rich, handsome
or beautiful, of a different race, tall or short, had had children, had changed my
occupation or specific job when I'd had the chance, had married someone different, had not been orphaned or rejected (like Tom in "I Never Sang For My
Father," in Part 1), had been born to different parents, had lived in a different
place rather than in the place I did live in, had not made that particular mistake,
had lived in a different period of history," and so on. In later life, for many
persons, it is too late to do anything about these disappointments and about
one's attitudes toward life. The regrets, reliving, and redoing become much of
the content of conversation for some elderly persons; this is what is repeated
frequently. At every opportunity, Grandfather Zisskind in "The Name," for
example, relives and repeats his "if onlys" about his grandson who had been
killed. Many elderly persons verbally repeat stories or descriptions of events or
experiences in the unconscious hope of changing them. Sometimes the wish to
change some significant aspect of one's life is so strong that it results in continual, sometimes consecutive, repetitions.

One thing that is apparent to younger people who have either been exposed
to this problem personally—by knowing an older person who repeats stories
and underlying ideas, or through studying gerontology—is that since change is
much easier to accomplish when one is young or middle-aged, one should *deliberately* change what one is dissatisfied with while one can. One should not
merely wait for it to go away or for something else to happen. Some disappointed elderly, with their complaining or their critical cutting down of others
or their verbal repetition, are living proof that "something" will not happen.

Psychiatrist Robert N. Butler has written about "the life review," the *normal* process in which a person reminisces about his or her life—reviewing it,
sorting our loose ends, making sense of them, integrating them into personality, and attempting to work through some of the conflicts.[4] This process results

---

[3] Erik H. Erikson, *Childhood and Society,* pp. 231–33.

[4] Robert N. Butler, "The Life Review: An Interpretation of Reminiscence in the Aged," in
Neugarten, *Middle Age and Aging,* pp. 486–96.

in some minor reorganization of personality. It is a normal and necessary process because one continually wants and needs to understand oneself and what one's life is about. Children very often review the main points of their earlier lives (such as where they were born, events surrounding their birth, a previous neighborhood they have lived in, a particular trip, and so on). It is probably a process that is continuous in life but more noticeable in and more frequently practiced by the elderly. Also, there is a much greater need to make sense of one's life as one increasingly realizes that one's life will end sometime in the near future. Persons who work with the elderly often encourage them to write or speak their autobiographies as a way of helping the process of reflecting, sorting and organizing, and understanding.

The classic story "The Death of Ivan Ilych" by Leo Tolstoy (1828–1910), published in 1886, illustrates the recognition, as the main character reviews his life, of a serious unresolved conflict which, once recognized, it is too late to resolve—too late, because it is only while he is dying that he becomes aware of it. It is then too late to change the course of his life, too late to experience what he has missed, too late to regain the sense of joy he experienced as a child. As he becomes increasingly ill, he despairs that he had not brought himself happiness while he was healthy.

As a young man he merely accepted foreclosure of his identity, rather than identity achievement, by automatically following in his father's footsteps.[5] His one-dimensional identity has been limited to concerns about achievement in the social system: concerns having to do with success, prestige, promotions, money, power, and approval from superiors and peers.[6] He has done only what was proper and avoided anything unpleasant. His roles are all there is in his adult life until he becomes seriously ill, and then he sees them, and his behavior in them, as deceptive, empty, and fraudulent. He begins to find himself while he lies dying and is brutally honest with himself. As he realizes what has happened in his life, he becomes increasingly despairing, for it is too late to change. He grows bitter and angry with his wife and daughter whom he blames for the direction of his life and death and who also remind him of his dishonesty. However, as he reflects on the meaning of his life, he experiences emotions long dormant and, to the extent that he becomes more sensitive to his inner feelings, he changes and grows. This change is not sufficient to satisfy him, however, and he feels angry about his wasted life.

As he lies dying, he experiences a number of feelings that he did not know he cared about. He wants to be pitied, touched, caressed, kissed, held, and loved. He develops a sensitivity to and acceptance of certain of his feelings that

[5] James E. Marcia, "Development and Validation of Ego-Identity Status," in *Adolescent Behavior and Society: A Book of Readings*, ed. Rolf E. Muuss, 3rd ed. (New York: Random House, 1975), pp. 279–91. Foreclosure refers to automatic, unquestioning commitment, usually to parents' goals and values, without a crisis, without confusion, and without considering alternatives.

[6] Though the story was published in 1886, Ivan Ilych is similar to the contemporary other-directed character that David Riesman thought many Americans had become. Both reflect the same bourgeois values (David Riesman, *The Lonely Crowd*, New York: Doubleday, 1955).

he did not previously recognize, especially weakness and fear. He continues to maintain a hard outer shell, however, and remains unable to express his human feelings to anyone except his servant and, slightly, to his son. Only Gerasim and his son pity him. His relationship with his wife becomes increasingly tense. When she goes to see him, she should be silent and hold his hand; instead, she tries to make conversation. This irritates him and creates greater distance between them. She of course has not shared his inner meditation and dissatisfaction—that has only occurred since he became ill. Since she is not ill, she continues the life-style that they enjoyed before. Nothing has changed for her. That others close to him cannot share his experiences—both reflections and pain—makes him feel increasingly lonely.

A further contribution to his sense of despair is the denial of death by most people around him, including the doctors. Ivan Ilych is aware of his reality and he feels isolated, especially when those close to him refuse to recognize or care about that reality. Psychiatrist Elisabeth Kübler-Ross has found that the person who is dying generally knows the truth and would feel more comfortable if others, including family members and doctors, didn't try to fool him or her at so important a time.[7] Deception reduces dying to a mundane level with everything else, reduces its importance, its reality, when they deny it.

"The Jilting of Granny Weatherall" by Katherine Anne Porter (born 1894), published initially in 1930, has to do with an unresolved conflict that the main character has not faced, has tried to forget; and it, instead, emerges to bother her as she lies dying. She has not worked through her angry feelings of having been rejected on her wedding day by George, who jilted her, and, quite possibly, by the death of her husband John.

This gem of a story illustrates the importance of dealing with emotional pain when it occurs rather than carrying the burden with one to the end. Granny Weatherall should have attempted to deal with her anger, hurt, and resentment toward George some sixty years before, when the pain occurred, instead of allowing it to simmer inside. Had she come to terms with the anger then, she would have more fully enjoyed what she found subsequently: John and their children. With that marriage, she acquired the name and the capacity to "weather all"—with the one exception of the earlier rejection.

With John's death, she became tough, self-reliant, competent, and independent in bringing up the children by herself and in running the farm. She is in control of everything in her life except that one experience in the past. This strong old woman—defiant, assertive, spirited, lively to the end—continues to be annoyed that someone has done something to her that she has not controlled. She has tried to repress her feelings about it, but her anger surfaces at a crucial time. This strong, self-reliant woman, who controls everything in her life—including her own death—could not control that one experience. She is unable to achieve the sense of peace and acceptance that Kübler-Ross believes is important to the dying person.

---

[7] Elisabeth Kübler-Ross, *On Death and Dying* (New York: Macmillan, 1969).

The "if onlys" are most clearly seen in the biting story by Lusin (also spelled Lu Hsün, pen name of Chou Shu-jen, 1881–1936), "The Widow" (or "The New Year's Sacrifice"), written in 1924. They form the total content of Sister Hsiang-lin's conversations after the wolf kills her son; they are limited to her single obsession, her one "if only," her verbal attempt to redo that event. So great is her burden of anguish, guilt, remorse, and self-pity that, according to the story, it causes her to age rapidly. She slows down considerably after having been a diligent, rapid, thorough, energetic, and cheerful worker. Slowing down is characteristic of the normal aging process called senescence; however, she slows much sooner than normal. All of the changes we observe in her occur between the ages of twenty-six and forty; hence the aging processes, both normal and atypical, are speeded up by her experiences of remorse and rejection. Her hair turns white; she seems confused; she continually repeats the one story that is so painful to her and that she cannot deal with; she becomes forgetful, emotionally numb, listless, and without hope.

The author, Lusin, felt that it was the oppressive and rigid traditional Chinese society that aged Hsiang-lin and killed her.[8] That society frowned on the remarriage of a widow. In the story, it condemns her because she does not fight hard enough to prevent her remarriage. It does not condemn her mother-in-law, who, as a financial investment, has bought her as a wife for her child-son ten years earlier, because this was a conventional and accepted practice (which provided the family with additional workers, since daughters-in-law lived and worked in the homes of the in-laws and were totally subservient to them). It does not condemn her mother-in-law when she places Hsiang-lin in a bind by selling her later to finance the marriage of her younger son—a bind because a widow, no matter what her age when her husband died, morally was not supposed to remarry (while widowers were expected to, in order to bring another wife-worker into the household). Instead, only Hsiang-lin is condemned and, regardless of what a pitiable and forlorn creature she becomes, at no point is sympathy and forgiveness offered her. Rather, she is repeatedly rejected, both by the rigidly moral Neo-Confucian Uncle Four and his wife, Aunt Four, and by the folk Buddhism of Liu Ma (who suggests buying an expiatory threshold in the local temple to substitute for her body, so that as people walk over it and trample on it, her sins will be wiped away).

Out of her guilt, despair, and remorse, she repeats her story endlessly. She is obsessed by the loss she thinks she has caused; through repetition perhaps she can take it back and redo the whole situation, giving it a different ending. She is totally broken and defeated, both by the loss of her own child and by the rejection from those around her. She is made to feel guilty because she has broken the moral code. Moreover, so improper and impure is a twice-married widow, especially this miserable and unlucky one, that Uncle Four is afraid the ancestors will not accept the ritual sacrifices if she has any part in preparing

---

[8] William A. Lyell, Jr., *Lu Hsün's Vision of Reality* (Berkeley: Univ. of California Press, 1976), pp. 141–44, 177–79.

them. Hence she is excluded and isolated from all of the family preparations and festivities, which of course further demoralizes her. Finally she dies, and even for this she is criticized because she dies during the New Year's festivities, which could bring the family bad luck for the coming year. In this structured and controlling society, the series of events traps her, and she is unable to change the direction of her life.

The final selection in this section is from the powerful *Spoon River Anthology,* published in 1915, by Edgar Lee Masters (1868–1950). Abel Melveny, one of the citizens buried in a cemetery in a small midwestern town, reviews and sums up his life. Self-awareness, unfortunately, comes to him too late, and he regrets that he has wasted his life.

The Death of Ivan Ilych

Leo Tolstoy

Translated from the Russian by Louise and Aylmer Maude

I

During an interval in the Melvinski trial in the large building of the Law Courts, the members and public prosecutor met in Ivan Egorovich Shebek's private room, where the conversation turned on the celebrated Krasovski case. Fëdor Vasilievich warmly maintained that it was not subject to their jurisdiction, Ivan Egorovich maintained the contrary, while Peter Ivanovich, not having entered into the discussion at the start, took no part in it but looked through the *Gazette* which had just been handed in.

"Gentlemen," he said, "Ivan Ilych has died!"

"You don't say so!"

"Here, read it yourself," replied Peter Ivanovich, handing Fëdor Vasilievich the paper still damp from the press. Surrounded by a black border were the words: "Praskovya Fëdorovna Golovina, with profound sorrow, informs relatives and friends of the demise of her beloved husband Ivan Ilych Golovin, Member of the Court of Justice, which occurred on February the 4th of this year 1882. The funeral will take place on Friday at one o'clock in the afternoon."

Ivan Ilych had been a colleague of the gentlemen present and was liked by them all. He had been ill for some weeks with an illness said to be incurable. His post had been kept open for him, but there had been conjectures that in the case of his death Alexeev might receive his appointment, and that either Vinnikov or Shtabel would succeed Alexeev. So on receiving the news of Ivan Ilych's death the first thought of each of the gentlemen in that private room was of the changes and promotions it might occasion among themselves or their acquaintances.

"I shall be sure to get Shtabel's place or Vinnikov's," thought Fëdor Vasilievich. "I was promised that long ago, and the promotion means an extra eight hundred rubles a year for me beside the allowance."

"Now I must apply for my brother-in-law's transfer from Kaluga," thought Peter Ivanovich. "My wife will be very glad, and then she won't be able to say that I never do anything for her relations."

"I thought he would never leave his bed again," said Peter Ivanovich aloud. "It's very sad."

"But what really was the matter with him?"

"The doctors couldn't say—at least they could, but each of them said something different. When last I saw him I thought he was getting better."

"And I haven't been to see him since the holidays. I always meant to go."

"Had he any property?"

"I think his wife had a little—but something quite trifling."

"We shall have to go to see her, but they live so terribly far away."

"Far away from you, you mean. Everything's far away from your place."

"You see, he never can forgive my living on the other side of the river," said Peter Ivanovich, smiling at Shebek. Then, still talking of the distances between different parts of the city, they returned to the Court.

Besides considerations as to the possible transfers and promotions likely to result from Ivan Ilych's death, the mere fact of the death of a near acquaintance aroused, as usual, in all who heard of it the complacent feeling that, "it is he who is dead and not I."

Each one thought or felt, "Well, he's dead but I'm alive!" But the more intimate of Ivan Ilych's acquaintances, his so-called friends, could not help thinking also that they would now have to fulfil the very tiresome demands of propriety by attending the funeral service and paying a visit of condolence to the widow.

Fëdor Vasilievich and Peter Ivanovich had been his nearest acquaintances. Peter Ivanovich had studied law with Ivan Ilych and had considered himself to be under obligations to him.

Having told his wife at dinner-time of Ivan Ilych's death and of his conjecture that it might be possible to get her brother transferred to their circuit, Peter Ivanovich sacrificed his usual nap, put on his evening clothes, and drove to Ivan Ilych's house.

At the entrance stood a carriage and two cabs. Leaning against the wall in the hall downstairs near the cloak-stand was a coffin-lid covered with cloth of gold, ornamented with gold cord and tassels, that had been polished up with metal powder. Two ladies in black were taking off their fur cloaks. Peter Ivanovich recognized one of them as Ivan Ilych's sister, but the other was a stranger to him. His colleague Schwartz was just coming downstairs, but on seeing Peter Ivanovich enter he stopped and winked at him, as if to say: "Ivan Ilych has made a mess of things—not like you and me."

Schwartz's face with his Piccadilly whiskers and his slim figure in evening dress, had as usual an air of elegant solemnity which contrasted with the playfulness of his character and had a special piquancy here, or so it seemed to Peter Ivanovich.

Peter Ivanovich allowed the ladies to precede him and slowly followed them upstairs. Schwartz did not come down but remained where he was, and Peter Ivanovich understood that he wanted to arrange where they should play bridge that evening. The ladies went upstairs to the widow's room, and Schwartz with seriously compressed lips but a playful look in his eyes, indicated by a twist of his eyebrows the room to the right where the body lay.

Peter Ivanovich, like everyone else on such occasions, entered feeling uncertain what he would have to do. All he knew was that at such times it is always safe to cross oneself. But he was not quite sure whether one should make obeisances while doing so. He therefore adopted a middle course. On entering the room he began crossing himself and made a slight movement resembling a bow. At the same time, as far as the motion of his head and arm allowed, he surveyed the room. Two young men—apparently nephews, one of whom was a high-school pupil—were leaving the room, crossing themselves as they did so. An old woman was standing motionless, and a lady with strangely arched eyebrows was saying something to her in a whisper. A vigorous, resolute Church Reader, in a frock-coat, was reading something in a loud voice with an expression that precluded any contradiction. The butler's assistant, Gerasim, stepping lightly in front of Peter Ivanovich, was strewing something on the floor. Noticing this, Peter Ivanovich was immediately aware of a faint odour of a decomposing body.

The last time he had called on Ivan Ilych, Peter Ivanovich had seen Gerasim in the study. Ivan Ilych had been particularly fond of him and he was performing the duty of a sick nurse.

Peter Ivanovich continued to make the sign of the cross slightly inclining his head in an intermediate direction between the coffin, the Reader, and the icons on the table in a corner of the room. Afterwards, when it seemed to him that this movement of his arm in crossing himself had gone on too long, he stopped and began to look at the corpse.

The dead man lay, as dead men always lie, in a specially heavy way, his rigid limbs sunk in the soft cushions of the coffin, with the head forever bowed on the pillow. His yellow waxen brow with bald patches over his sunken temples was thrust up in the way peculiar to the dead, the protruding nose seeming to press on the upper lip. He was much changed and had grown even thinner since Peter Ivanovich had last seen him, but, as is always the case with the dead, his face was handsomer and above all more dignified than when he was alive. The expression on the face said that what was necessary had been accomplished, and accomplished rightly. Besides this there was in that expression a reproach and a warning to the living. This warning seemed to Peter Ivanovich out of place, or at least not applicable to him. He felt a certain discomfort and so he hurriedly crossed himself once more and turned and went out of the door—too hurriedly and too regardless of propriety, as he himself was aware.

Schwartz was waiting for him in the adjoining room with legs spread wide apart and both hands toying with his top-hat behind his back. The mere sight of that playful, well-groomed, and elegant figure refreshed Peter Ivanovich. He felt that Schwartz was above all these happenings and would not surrender to any depressing influences. His very look said that this incident of a church service for Ivan Ilych could not be sufficient reason for infringing the order of the session—in other words, that it would certainly not prevent his unwrapping a new pack of cards and shuffling them that evening while a footman placed four fresh candles on the table: in fact, that there was no reason for supposing that this incident would hinder their spending the evening agreeably. Indeed he said this in a whisper as Peter Ivanovich passed him, proposing that they should

meet for a game at Fëdor Vasilievich's. But apparently Peter Ivanovich was not
destined to play bridge that evening. Praskovya Fëdorovna (a short, fat woman
who despite all efforts to the contrary had continued to broaden steadily from
her shoulders downwards and who had the same extraordinary arched eyebrows
as the lady who had been standing by the coffin), dressed all in black, her head
covered with lace, came out of her own room with some other ladies, conducted them to the room where the dead body lay, and said: "The service will
begin immediately. Please go in."

Schwartz, making an indefinite bow, stood still, evidently neither accepting
nor declining this invitation. Praskovya Fëdorovna, recognizing Peter Ivanovich, sighed, went close to him, took his hand, and said: "I know you were a
true friend to Ivan Ilych . . ." and looked at him awaiting some suitable
response. And Peter Ivanovich knew that, just as it had been the right thing to
cross himself in that room, so what he had to do here was to press her hand,
sigh, and say, "Believe me. . . ." So he did all this and as he did it felt that
the desired result had been achieved: that both he and she were touched.

"Come with me. I want to speak to you before it begins," said the widow.
"Give me your arm."

Peter Ivanovich gave her his arm and they went to the inner rooms, passing
Schwartz, who winked at Peter Ivanovich compassionately.

"That does for our bridge! Don't object if we find another player. Perhaps
you can cut in when you do escape," said his playful look.

Peter Ivanovich sighed still more deeply and despondently, and Praskovya
Fëdorovna pressed his arm gratefully. When they reached the drawing-room,
upholstered in pink cretonne and lighted by a dim lamp, they sat down at the
table—she on a sofa and Peter Ivanovich on a low pouffe, the springs of which
yielded spasmodically under his weight. Praskovya Fëdorovna had been on the
point of warning him to take another seat, but felt that such a warning was out
of keeping with her present condition and so changed her mind. As he sat down
on the pouffe Peter Ivanovich recalled how Ivan Ilych had arranged this room
and had consulted him regarding this pink cretonne with green leaves. The
whole room was full of furniture and knick-knacks, and on her way to the sofa
the lace of the widow's black shawl caught on the carved edge of the table.
Peter Ivanovich rose to detach it, and the springs of the pouffe, relieved of his
weight, rose also and gave him a push. The widow began detaching her shawl
herself, and Peter Ivanovich again sat down, suppressing the rebellious springs
of the pouffe under him. But the widow had not quite freed herself and Peter
Ivanovich got up again, and again the pouffe rebelled and even creaked. When
this was all over she took out a clean cambric handkerchief and began to weep.
The episode with the shawl and the struggle with the pouffe had cooled Peter
Ivanovich's emotions and he sat there with a sullen look on his face. This
awkward situation was interrupted by Sokolov, Ivan Ilych's butler, who came
to report that the plot in the cemetery that Praskovya Fëdorovna had chosen
would cost two hundred rubles. She stopped weeping and, looking at Peter

Ivanovich with the air of a victim, remarked in French that it was very hard for her. Peter Ivanovich made a silent gesture signifying his full conviction that it must indeed be so.

"Please smoke," she said in a magnanimous yet crushed voice, and turned to discuss with Sokolov the price of the plot for the grave.

Peter Ivanovich while lighting his cigarette heard her inquiring very circumstantially into the prices of different plots in the cemetery and finally decide which she would take. When that was done she gave instructions about engaging the choir. Sokolov then left the room.

"I look after everything myself," she told Peter Ivanovich, shifting the albums that lay on the table; and noticing that the table was endangered by his cigarette-ash, she immediately passed him an ash-tray, saying as she did so: "I consider it an affectation to say that my grief prevents my attending to practical affairs. On the contrary, if anything can—I won't say console me, but—distract me, it is seeing to everything concerning him." She again took out her handkerchief as if preparing to cry, but suddenly, as if mastering her feeling, she shook herself and began to speak calmly. "But there is something I want to talk to you about."

Peter Ivanovich bowed, keeping control of the springs of the pouffe, which immediately began quivering under him.

"He suffered terribly the last few days."

"Did he?" said Peter Ivanovich.

"Oh, terribly! He screamed unceasingly, not for minutes but for hours. For the last three days he screamed incessantly. It was unendurable. I cannot understand how I bore it; you could hear him three rooms off, what I have suffered!"

"Is it possible that he was conscious all that time?" asked Peter Ivanovich.

"Yes," she whispered. "To the last moment. He took leave of us a quarter of an hour before he died, and asked us to take Volodya away."

The thought of the sufferings of this man he had known so intimately, first as a merry little boy, then as a school-mate, and later as a grown-up colleague, suddenly struck Peter Ivanovich with horror, despite an unpleasant consciousness of his own and this woman's dissimulation. He again saw that brow, and that nose pressing down on the lip, and felt afraid for himself.

"Three days of frightful suffering and then death! Why, that might suddenly, at any time, happen to me," he thought, and for a moment felt terrified. But—he did not himself know how—the customary reflection at once occurred to him that this had happened to Ivan Ilych and not to him, and that it should not and could not happen to him, and to think that it could would be yielding to depression which he ought not to do, as Schwartz's expression plainly showed. After which reflection Peter Ivanovich felt reassured, and began to ask with interest about the details of Ivan Ilych's death, as though death was an accident natural to Ivan Ilych but certainly not to himself.

After many details of the really dreadful physical sufferings Ivan Ilych had endured (which details he learnt only from the effect those sufferings had produced on Praskovya Fëdorovna's nerves) the widow apparently found it necessary to get to business.

"Oh, Peter Ivanovich, how hard it is! How terribly, terribly hard!" and she again began to weep.

Peter Ivanovich sighed and waited for her to finish blowing her nose. When she had done so he said, "Believe me . . ." and she again began talking and brought out what was evidently her chief concern with him—namely, to question him as to how she could obtain a grant of money from the government on the occasion of her husband's death. She made it appear that she was asking Peter Ivanovich's advice about her pension, but he soon saw that she already knew about that to the minutest detail, more even than he did himself. She knew how much could be got out of the government in consequence of her husband's death, but wanted to find out whether she could not possibly extract something more. Peter Ivanovich tried to think of some means of doing so, but after reflecting for a while and, out of propriety, condemning the government for its niggardliness, he said he thought that nothing more could be got. Then she sighed and evidently began to devise means of getting rid of her visitor. Noticing this, he put out his cigarette, rose, pressed her hand, and went out into the anteroom.

In the dining-room where the clock stood that Ivan Ilych had liked so much and had bought at an antique shop, Peter Ivanovich met a priest and a few acquaintances who had come to attend the service, and he recognized Ivan Ilych's daughter, a handsome young woman. She was in black and her slim figure appeared slimmer than ever. She had a gloomy, determined, almost angry expression, and bowed to Peter Ivanovich as though he were in some way to blame. Behind her, with the same offended look, stood a wealthy young man, an examining magistrate, whom Peter Ivanovich also knew and who was her fiancé, as he had heard. He bowed mournfully to them and was about to pass into the death-chamber, when from under the stairs appeared the figure of Ivan Ilych's schoolboy son, who was extremely like his father. He seemed a little like Ivan Ilych, such as Peter Ivanovich remembered when they studied law together. His tear-stained eyes had in them the look that is seen in the eyes of boys thirteen or fourteen who are not pure-minded. When he saw Peter Ivanovich he scowled morosely and shamefacedly. Peter Ivanovich nodded to him and entered the death-chamber. The service began: candles, groans, incense, tears, and sobs. Peter Ivanovich stood looking gloomily down at his feet. He did not look once at the dead man, did not yield to any depressing influence, and was one of the first to leave the room. There was no one in the anteroom, but Gerasim darted out of the dead man's room, rummaged with his strong hands among the fur coats to find Peter Ivanovich's and helped him on with it.

"Well, friend Gerasim," said Peter Ivanovich, so as to say something. "It's a sad affair, isn't it?"

"It's God's will. We shall all come to it some day," said Gerasim, displaying his teeth—the even, white teeth of a healthy peasant—and, like a man in the thick of urgent work, he briskly opened the front door, called the coach-man, helped Peter Ivanovich into the sledge, and sprang back to the porch as if in readiness for what he had to do next.

Peter Ivanovich found the fresh air particularly pleasant after the smell of in-cense, the dead body, and carbolic acid.

"Where to, sir?" asked the coachman.

"It's not too late even now. . . . I'll call round on Fëdor Vasilievich."

He accordingly drove there and found them just finishing the first rubber, so that it was quite convenient for him to cut in.

II

Ivan Ilych's life had been most simple and most ordinary and therefore most terrible.

He had been a member of the Court of Justice, and died at the age of forty-five. His father had been an official who after serving in various ministries and departments in Petersburg had made the sort of career which brings men to positions from which by reason of their long service they cannot be dismissed, though they are obviously unfit to hold any responsible position, and for whom therefore posts are especially created, which though fictitious carry salaries of from six to ten thousand rubles that are not fictitious, and in receipt of which they live on to a great age.

Such was the Privy Councillor and superfluous member of various superflu-ous institutions, Ilya Epimovich Golovin.

He had three sons, of whom Ivan Ilych was second. The eldest son was fol-lowing in his father's footsteps only in another department, and was already approaching that stage in the service at which a similar sinecure would be reached. The third son was a failure. He had ruined his prospects in a number of positions and was now serving in the railway department. His father and brothers, and still more their wives, not merely disliked meeting him, but avoided remembering his existence unless compelled to do so. His sister had married Baron Greff, a Petersburg official of her father's type. Ivan Ilych was *le phénix de la famille* as people said. He was neither as cold and formal as his elder brother nor as wild as the younger, but was a happy mean between them—an intelligent, polished, lively and agreeable man. He had studied with his younger brother at the School of Law, but the latter had failed to complete the course and was expelled when he was in the fifth class. Ivan Ilych finished the course well. Even when he was at the School of Law he was just what he remained for the rest of his life: a capable, cheerful, good-natured, and sociable man, though strict in the fulfilment of what he considered to be his duty: and he considered his duty to be what was so considered by those in authority. Neither as a boy nor as a man was he a toady, but from early youth was by nature at-tracted to people of high station as a fly is drawn to the light, assimilating their ways and views of life and establishing friendly relations with them. All the en-thusiasms of childhood and youth passed without leaving much trace on him;

he succumbed to sensuality, to vanity, and latterly among the highest classes to liberalism, but always within limits which his instinct unfailingly indicated to him as correct.

At school he had done things which had formerly seemed to him very horrid and made him feel disgusted with himself when he did them; but when later on he saw that such actions were done by people of good position and that they did not regard them as wrong, he was able not exactly to regard them as right, but to forget about them entirely or not be at all troubled at remembering them.

Having graduated from the School of Law and qualified for the tenth rank of the civil service, and having received money from his father for his equipment, Ivan Ilych ordered himself clothes at Scharmer's, the fashionable tailor, hung a medallion inscribed *respice finem* * on his watch-chain, took leave of his professor and the prince who was patron of the school, had a farewell dinner with his comrades at Donon's first-class restaurant, and with his new and fashionable portmanteau, linen, clothes, shaving and other toilet appliances, and a travelling rug, all purchased at the best shops, he set off for one of the provinces where, through his father's influence, he had been attached to the Governor as an official for special service.

In the province Ivan Ilych soon arranged as easy and agreeable a position for himself as he had had at the School of Law. He performed his official tasks, made his career, and at the same time amused himself pleasantly and decorously. Occasionally he paid official visits to country districts, where he behaved with dignity both to his superiors and inferiors, and performed the duties entrusted to him, which related chiefly to the sectarians, with an exactness and incorruptible honesty of which he could not but feel proud.

In official matters, despite his youth and taste for frivolous gaiety, he was exceedingly reserved, punctilious, and even severe; but in society he was often amusing and witty, and always good-natured, correct in his manner, and *bon enfant*,** as the governor and his wife—with whom he was like one of the family—used to say of him.

In the province he had an affair with a lady who made advances to the elegant young lawyer, and there was also a milliner; and there were carousals with aides-de-camp who visited the district, and after-supper visits to a certain outlying street of doubtful reputation; and there was too some obsequiousness to his chief and even to his chief's wife, but all this was done with such a tone of good breeding that no hard names could be applied to it. It all came under the heading of the French saying: *"Il faut que jeunesse se passe."* † It was all done with clean hands, in clean linen, with French phrases, and above all among people of the best society and consequently with the approval of people of rank.

So Ivan Ilych served for five years and then came a change in his official life. The new and reformed judicial institutions were introduced, and new men

---

* *respice finem:* look to the end
** *bon enfant:* a good child
† *Il faut . . . passe:* You're only young once

were needed. Ivan Ilych became such a new man. He was offered the post of examining magistrate, and he accepted it though the post was in another province and obliged him to give up the connexions he had formed and to make new ones. His friends met to give him a send-off; they had a group-photograph taken and presented him with a silver cigarette-case, and he set off to his new post.

As examining magistrate Ivan Ilych was just as *comme il faut* and decorous a man, inspiring general respect and capable of separating his official duties from his private life, as he had been when acting as an official on special service. His duties now as examining magistrate were far more interesting and attractive than before. In his former position it had been pleasant to wear an undress uniform made by Scharmer, and to pass through the crowd of petitioners and officials who were timorously awaiting an audience with the governor, and who envied him as with free and easy gait he went straight into his chief's private room to have a cup of tea and a cigarette with him. But not many people had then been directly dependent on him—only police officials and the sectarians when he went on special missions—and he liked to treat them politely, almost as comrades, as if he were letting them feel that he who had the power to crush them was treating them in this simple, friendly way. There were then but few such people. But now, as an examining magistrate, Ivan Ilych felt that everyone without exception, even the most important and self-satisfied, was in his power, and that he need only write a few words on a sheet of paper with a certain heading, and this or that important, self-satisfied person would be brought before him in the role of an accused person or a witness, and if he did not choose to allow him to sit down, would have to stand before him and answer his questions. Ivan Ilych never abused his power; he tried on the contrary to soften its expression, but the consciousness of it and of the possibility of softening its effect, supplied the chief interest and attraction of his office. In his work itself, especially in his examinations, he very soon acquired a method of eliminating all considerations irrelevant to the legal aspect of the case, and reducing even the most complicated case to a form in which it would be presented on paper only in its externals, completely excluding his personal opinion of the matter, while above all observing every prescribed formality. The work was new and Ivan Ilych was one of the first men to apply the new Code of 1864.

On taking up the post of examining magistrate in a new town, he made new acquaintances and connexions, placed himself on a new footing, and assumed a somewhat different tone. He took up an attitude of rather dignified aloofness towards the provincial authorities, but picked out the best circle of legal gentlemen and wealthy gentry living in the town and assumed a tone of slight dissatisfaction with the government, of moderate liberalism, and of enlightened citizenship. At the same time, without at all altering the elegance of his toilet, he ceased shaving his chin and allowed his beard to grow as it pleased.

Ivan Ilych settled down very pleasantly in this new town. The society there, which inclined towards opposition to the Governor, was friendly, his salary was larger, and he began to play *vint*, which he found added not a little to the pleasure of life, for he had a capacity for cards, played good-humouredly, and calculated rapidly and astutely, so that he usually won.

After living there for two years he met his future wife, Praskovya Fëdorovna Mikhel, who was the most attractive, clever, and brilliant girl of the set in which he moved, and among other amusements and relaxations from his labours as examining magistrate, Ivan Ilych established light and playful relations with her.

While he had been an official on special service he had been accustomed to dance, but now as an examining magistrate it was exceptional for him to do so. If he danced now, he did it as if to show that though he served under the reformed order of things, and had reached the fifth official rank, yet when it came to dancing he could do it better than most people. So at the end of an evening he sometimes danced with Praskovya Fëdorovna, and it was chiefly during these dances that he captivated her. She fell in love with him. Ivan Ilych had at first no definite intention of marrying, but when the girl fell in love with him he said to himself: "Really, why shouldn't I marry?"

Praskovya Fëdorovna came of a good family, was not bad looking, and had some little property. Ivan Ilych might have aspired to a more brilliant match, but even this was good. He had his salary, and she, he hoped, would have an equal income. She was well connected, and was a sweet, pretty, and thoroughly correct young woman. To say that Ivan Ilych married because he fell in love with Praskovya Fëdorovna and found that she sympathized with his views of life would be as incorrect as to say that he married because his social circle approved of the match. He was swayed by both these considerations: the marriage gave him personal satisfaction, and at the same time it was considered the right thing by the most highly placed of his associates.

So Ivan Ilych got married.

The preparations for marriage and the beginning of married life, with its conjugal caresses, the new furniture, new crockery, and new linen, were very pleasant until his wife became pregnant—so that Ivan Ilych had begun to think that marriage would not impair the easy, agreeable, gay and always decorous character of his life, approved by society and regarded by himself as natural, but would even improve it. But from the first months of his wife's pregnancy, something new, unpleasant, depressing, and unseemly, and from which there was no way of escape, unexpectedly showed itself.

His wife, without any reason—*de gaieté de coeur* * as Ivan Ilych expressed it to himself—began to disturb the pleasure and propriety of their life. She began to be jealous without any cause, expected him to devote his whole attention to her, found fault with everything, and made coarse and ill-mannered scenes.

At first Ivan Ilych hoped to escape from the unpleasantness of this state of affairs by the same easy and decorous relation to life that had served him heretofore: he tried to ignore his wife's disagreeable moods, continued to live in his

---

* *de gaieté de coeur:* out of sheer wantonness

usual easy and pleasant way, invited friends to his house for a game of cards, and also tried going out to his club or spending his evenings with friends. But one day his wife began upbraiding him so vigorously, using such coarse words, and continued to abuse him every time he did not fulfill her demands, so resolutely and with such evident determination not to give way till he submitted—that is, till he stayed at home and was bored just as she was—that he became alarmed. He now realized that matrimony—at any rate with Praskovya Fëdorovna—was not always conducive to the pleasures and amenities of life, but on the contrary often infringed both comfort and propriety, and that he must therefore entrench himself against such infringement. And Ivan Ilych began to seek for means of doing so. His official duties were the one thing that imposed upon Praskovya Fëdorovna, and by means of his official work and the duties attached to it he began struggling with his wife to secure his own independence.

With the birth of their child, the attempts to feed it and the various failures in doing so, and with the real and imaginary illnesses of mother and child, in which Ivan Ilych's sympathy was demanded but about which he understood nothing, the need for securing for himself an existence outside his family life became still more imperative.

As his wife grew more irritable and exacting and Ivan Ilych transferred the centre of gravity of his life more and more to his official work, so did he grow to like his work better and became more ambitious than before.

Very soon, within a year of his wedding, Ivan Ilych had realized that marriage, though it may add some comforts to life, is in fact a very intricate and difficult affair towards which in order to perform one's duty, that is, to lead a decorous life approved of by society, one must adopt a definite attitude just as toward one's official duties.

And Ivan Ilych evolved such an attitude towards married life. He only required of it those conveniences—dinner at home, housewife, and bed—which it could give him, and above all that propriety of external forms required by public opinion. For the rest he looked for light-hearted pleasure and propriety, and was very thankful when he found them, but if he met with antagonism and querulousness he at once retired into his separate fenced-off world of official duties, where he found satisfaction.

Ivan Ilych was esteemed a good official, and after three years was made Assistant Public Prosecutor. His new duties, their importance, the possibility of indicting and imprisoning anyone he chose, the publicity his speeches received, and the success he had in all these things, made his work still more attractive.

More children came. His wife became more and more querulous and ill-tempered, but the attitude Ivan Ilych had adopted towards his home life rendered him almost impervious to her grumbling.

After seven years' service in that town he was transferred to another province as Public Prosecutor. They moved, but were short of money and his wife did not like the place they moved to. Though the salary was higher the cost of living was greater, besides which two of their children died and family life became still more unpleasant for him.

Praskovya Fëdorovna blamed her husband for every inconvenience they encountered in their new home. Most of the conversations between husband and wife, especially as to the children's education, led to topics which recalled former disputes, and those disputes were apt to flare up again at any moment. There remained only those rare periods of amorousness which still came to them at times but did not last long. These were islets at which they anchored for a while and then again set out upon that ocean of veiled hostility which showed itself in their aloofness from one another. This aloofness might have grieved Ivan Ilych had he considered that it ought not to exist, but he now regarded the position as normal, and even made it the goal at which he aimed in family life. His aim was to free himself more and more from those unpleasantnesses and to give them a semblance of harmlessness and propriety. He attained this by spending less and less time with his family, and when obliged to be at home he tried to safeguard his position by the presence of outsiders. The chief thing however was that he had his official duties. The whole interest of his life now centred in the official world and that interest absorbed him. The consciousness of his power, being able to ruin anybody he wished to ruin, the importance, even the external dignity of his entry into court, or meetings with his subordinates, his success with superiors and inferiors, and above all his masterly handling of cases, of which he was conscious—all this gave him pleasure and filled his life, together with chats with his colleagues, dinners, and bridge. So that on the whole Ivan Ilych's life continued to flow as he considered it should do—pleasantly and properly.

So things continued for another seven years. His eldest daughter was already sixteen, another child had died, and only one son was left, a schoolboy and a subject of dissension. Ivan Ilych wanted to put him in the School of Law, but to spite him Praskovya Fëdorovna entered him at the High School. The daughter had been educated at home and had turned out well: the boy did not learn badly either.

III

So Ivan Ilych lived for seventeen years after his marriage. He was already a Public Prosecutor of long standing, and had declined several proposed transfers while awaiting a more desirable post, when an unanticipated and unpleasant occurrence quite upset the peaceful course of his life. He was expecting to be offered the post of presiding judge in a University town, but Happe somehow came to the front and obtained the appointment instead. Ivan Ilych became irritable, reproached Happe, and quarrelled both with him and with his immediate superiors—who became colder to him and again passed him over when other appointments were made.

This was in 1880, the hardest year of Ivan Ilych's life. It was then that it became evident on the one hand that his salary was insufficient for them to live on, and on the other that he had been forgotten, and not only this, but that what was for him the greatest and most cruel injustice appeared to others a quite ordinary occurrence. Even his father did not consider it his duty to help him. Ivan Ilych felt himself abandoned by everyone, and that they regarded his position with a salary of 3,500 rubles as quite normal and even fortunate. He alone knew that with the consciousness of the injustices done him, with his wife's incessant nagging, and with the debts he had contracted by living beyond his means, his position was far from normal.

In order to save money that summer he obtained leave of absence and went with his wife to live in the country at her brother's place.

In the country, without his work, he experienced *ennui* for the first time in his life, and not only *ennui* but intolerable depression, and he decided that it was impossible to go on living like that, and that it was necessary to take energetic measures.

Having passed a sleepless night pacing up and down the veranda, he decided to go to Petersburg and bestir himself, in order to punish those who had failed to appreciate him and to get transferred to another ministry.

Next day, despite many protests from his wife and her brother, he started for Petersburg with the sole subject of obtaining a post with a salary of five thousand rubles a year. He was no longer bent on any particular department, or tendency, or kind of activity. All he now wanted was an appointment to another post with a salary of five thousand rubles, either in administration, in the banks, with the railways, in one of the Empress Marya's Institutions, or even in the customs—but it had to carry with it a salary of five thousand rubles and be in a ministry other than that in which they had failed to appreciate him.

And this quest of Ivan Ilych's was crowned with remarkable and unexpected success. At Kursk an acquaintance of his, F. I. Ilyin, got into the first-class carriage, sat down beside Ivan Ilych, and told him of a telegram just received by the Governor of Kursk announcing that a change was about to take place in the ministry: Peter Ivanovich was to be superseded by Ivan Semënovich.

The proposed change, apart from its significance for Russia, had a special significance for Ivan Ilych, because by bringing forward a new man, Peter Petrovich, and consequently his friend Zachar Ivanovich, it was highly favourable for Ivan Ilych, since Zachar Ivanovich was a friend and colleague of his.

In Moscow this news was confirmed, and on reaching Petersburg Ivan Ilych found Zachar Ivanovich and received a definite promise of an appointment in his former department of Justice.

A week later he telegraphed to his wife: "Zachar in Miller's place. I shall receive appointment on presentation of report."

Thanks to this change of personnel, Ivan Ilych had unexpectedly obtained an appointment in his former ministry which placed him two stages above his former colleagues besides giving him five thousand rubles salary and three thousand five hundred rubles for expenses connected with his removal. All his ill humour towards his former enemies and the whole department vanished, and Ivan Ilych was completely happy.

He returned to the country more cheerful and contented than he had been for a long time. Praskovya Fëdorovna also cheered up and a truce was arranged between them. Ivan Ilych told of how he had been fêted by everybody in Petersburg, how all those who had been his enemies were put to shame and now fawned on him, how envious they were of his appointment, and how much everybody in Petersburg had liked him.

Praskovya Fëdorovna listened to all this and appeared to believe it. She did not contradict anything, but only made plans for their life in the town to which they were going. Ivan Ilych saw with delight that these plans were his plans, that he and his wife agreed, and that, after a stumble, his life was regaining its due and natural character of pleasant lightheartedness and decorum.

Ivan Ilych had come back for a short time only, for he had to take up his new duties on the 10th of September. Moreover, he needed time to settle into the new place, to move all his belongings from the province, and to buy and order many additional things: in a word, to make such arrangements as he had resolved on, which were almost exactly what Praskovya Fëdorovna too had decided on.

Now that everything had happened so fortunately, and that he and his wife were at one in their aims and moreover saw so little of one another, they got on together better than they had done since the first years of marriage. Ivan Ilych had thought of taking his family away with him at once, but the insistence of his wife's brother and her sister-in-law, who had suddenly become particularly amiable and friendly to him and his family, induced him to depart alone.

So he departed, and the cheerful state of mind induced by his success and by the harmony between his wife and himself, the one intensifying the other, did not leave him. He found a delightful house, just the thing both he and his wife had dreamt of. Spacious, lofty reception rooms in the old style, a convenient and dignified study, rooms for his wife and daughter, a study for his son—it might have been specially built for them. Ivan Ilych himself superintended the arrangements, chose the wallpapers, supplemented the furniture (preferably with antiques which he considered particularly *comme il faut*), and supervised the upholstering. Everything progressed and progressed and approached the ideal he had set himself: even when things were only half completed they exceeded his expectations. He saw what a refined and elegant character, free from vulgarity, it would all have when it was ready. On falling asleep he pictured to himself how the reception-room would look. Looking at the yet unfinished drawing-room he could see the fireplace, the screen, the what-not, the little chairs dotted here and there, the dishes and plates on the walls, and the bronzes, as they would be when everything was in place. He was pleased by the thought of how his wife and daughter, who shared his taste in this matter, would be impressed by it. They were certainly not expecting as much. He had been particularly successful in finding, and buying cheaply, antiques which gave a particularly aristocratic character to the whole place. But in his letters he intentionally understated everything in order to be able to surprise them. All this so absorbed him that his new duties—though he liked his official work—

interested him less than he had expected. Sometimes he even had moments of absent-mindedness during the Court Sessions, and would consider whether he should have straight or curved cornices for his curtains. He was so interested in it all that he often did things himself, rearranging the furniture, or rehanging the curtains. Once when mounting a step-ladder to show the upholsterer, who did not understand, how he wanted the hangings draped, he made a false step and slipped, but being a strong and agile man he clung on and only knocked his side against the knob of the window frame. The bruised place was painful but the pain soon passed, and he felt particularly bright and well just then. He wrote: "I feel fifteen years younger." He thought he would have everything ready by September, but it dragged on till mid-October. But the result was charming not only in his eyes but to everyone who saw it.

In reality it was just what is usually seen in the houses of people of moderate means who want to appear rich, and therefore succeed only in resembling others like themselves: there were damasks, dark wood, plants, rugs, and dull and polished bronzes—all the things people of a certain class have in order to resemble other people of that class. His house was so like the others that it would never have been noticed, but to him it all seemed to be quite exceptional. He was very happy when he met his family at the station and brought them to the newly furnished house all lit up, where a footman in a white tie opened the door into the hall decorated with plants, and when they went on into the drawing-room and the study uttering exclamations of delight. He conducted them everywhere, drank in their praises eagerly, and beamed with pleasure. At tea that evening, when Praskovya Fëdorovna among other things asked him about his fall, he laughed and showed them how he had gone flying and frightened the upholsterer.

"It's a good thing I'm a bit of an athlete. Another man might have been killed, but I merely knocked myself, just here; it hurts when touched, but it's passing off already—it's only a bruise."

So they began living in their new home—in which, as always happens, when they got thoroughly settled in they found they were just one room short—and with the increased income, which as always was just a little (some five hundred rubles) too little, but it was all very nice.

Things went particularly well at first, before everything was finally arranged and while something had still to be done: this thing bought, that thing ordered, another thing moved, and something else adjusted. Though there were some disputes between husband and wife, they were both so well satisfied and had so much to do that it all passed off without any serious quarrels. When nothing was left to arrange it became rather dull and something seemed to be lacking, but they were then making acquaintances, forming habits, and life was growing fuller.

Ivan Ilych spent his mornings at the law court and came home to dinner, and at first he was generally in a good humour, though he occasionally became irritable just on account of his house. (Every spot on the tablecloth or the upholstery, and every broken window-blind string, irritated him. He had devoted so much trouble to arranging it all that every disturbance of it distressed him.) But on the whole his life ran its course as he believed life should do: easily, pleasantly, and decorously.

He got up at nine, drank his coffee, read the paper, and then put on his undress uniform and went to the law courts. There the harness in which he worked had already been stretched to fit him and he donned it without a hitch: petitioners, inquiries at the chancery, the chancery itself, and the sittings public and administrative. In all this the thing was to exclude everything fresh and vital, which always disturbs the regular course of official business, and to admit only official relations with people, and then only on official grounds. A man would come, for instance, wanting some information. Ivan Ilych, as one in whose sphere the matter did not lie, would have nothing to do with him: but if the man had some business with him in his official capacity, something that could be expressed on officially stamped paper, he would do everything, positively everything he could within the limits of such relations, and in doing so would maintain the semblance of friendly human relations, that is, would observe the courtesies of life. As soon as the official relations ended, so did everything else. Ivan Ilych possessed this capacity to separate his real life from the official side of affairs and not mix the two, in the highest degree, and by long practice and natural aptitude had brought it to such a pitch that sometimes, in the manner of a virtuoso, he would even allow himself to let the human and official relations mingle. He let himself do this just because he felt that he could at any time he chose resume the strictly official attitude again and drop the human relation. And he did it all easily, pleasantly, correctly, and even artistically. In the intervals between the sessions he smoked, drank tea, chatted a little about politics, a little about general topics, a little about cards, but most of all about official appointments. Tired, but with the feelings of a virtuoso—one of the first violins who has played his part in an orchestra with precision—he would return home to find that his wife and daughter had been out paying calls, or had a visitor, and that his son had been to school, had done his homework with his tutor, and was duly learning what is taught at High Schools. Everything was as it should be. After dinner, if they had no visitors, Ivan Ilych sometimes read a book that was being much discussed at the time, and in the evening settled down to work, that is, read official papers, compared the depositions of witnesses, and noted paragraphs of the Code applying to them. This was neither dull nor amusing. It was dull when he might have been playing bridge, but if no bridge was available it was at any rate better than doing nothing or sitting with his wife. Ivan Ilych's chief pleasure was giving little dinners to which he invited men and women of good social position, and just as his drawing-room resembled all other drawing-rooms so did his enjoyable little parties resemble all other such parties.

Once they even gave a dance. Ivan Ilych enjoyed it and everything went off well, except that it led to a violent quarrel with his wife about the cakes and sweets. Praskovya Fëdorovna had made her own plans, but Ivan Ilych insisted on getting everything from an expensive confectioner and ordered too many cakes, and the quarrel occurred because some of those cakes were left over and the confectioner's bill came to forty-five rubles. It was a great and disagreeable quarrel. Praskovya Fëdorovna called him "a fool and an imbecile," and he clutched at his head and made angry allusions to divorce.

But the dance itself had been enjoyable. The best people were there, and Ivan Ilych had danced with Princess Trufonova, a sister of the distinguished founder of the Society "Bear my Burden."

The pleasures connected with his work were pleasures of ambition; his social pleasures were those of vanity; but Ivan Ilych's greatest pleasure was playing bridge. He acknowledged that whatever disagreeable incident happened in his life, the pleasure that beamed like a ray of light above everything else was to sit down to bridge with good players, not noisy partners, and of course to four-handed bridge (with five players it was annoying to have to stand out, though one pretended not to mind), to play a clever and serious game (when the cards allowed it) and then to have supper and drink a glass of wine. After a game of bridge, especially if he had won a little (to win a large sum was unpleasant), Ivan Ilych went to bed in specially good humour.

So they lived. They formed a circle of acquaintances among the best people and were visited by people of importance and by young folk. In their views as to their acquaintances, husband, wife and daughter were entirely agreed, and tacitly and unanimously kept at arm's length and shook off the shabby friends and relations who, with much show of affection, gushed into the drawing-room with its Japanese plates on the walls. Soon these shabby friends ceased to obtrude themselves and only the best people remained in the Golovins' set.

Young men made up to Lisa, and Petrishchev, and examining magistrate and Dmitri Ivanovich Petrishchev's son and sole heir, began to be so attentive to her that Ivan Ilych had already spoken to Praskovya Fëdorovna about it, and considered whether they should not arrange a party for them, or get up some private theatricals.

So they lived, and all went well without change, and life flowed pleasantly.

IV

They were all in good health. It could not be called ill health if Ivan Ilych sometimes said that he had a queer taste in his mouth and felt some discomfort in his left side.

But this discomfort increased and, though not exactly painful, grew into a sense of pressure in his side accompanied by ill humour. And his irritability became worse and worse and began to mar the agreeable, easy, and correct life that had established itself in the Golovin family. Quarrels between husband and wife became more and more frequent, and soon the ease and amenity disappeared and even the decorum was barely maintained. Scenes again became frequent, and very few of those islets remained on which husband and wife could meet without an explosion. Praskovya Fëdorovna now had good reason to say that her husband's temper was trying. With characteristic exaggeration she said he had always had a dreadful temper, and that it had needed all her good nature to put up with it for twenty years. It was true that now the quarrels were started by him. His bursts of temper always came just before dinner, often just as he began to eat his soup. Sometimes he noticed that a plate or dish was chipped, or the food was not right, or his son put his elbow on the table, or his daughter's hair was not done as he liked it, and for all this he blamed Prasko- vya Fëdorovna. At first she retorted and said disagreeable things to him, but once or twice he fell into such a rage at the beginning of dinner that she realized it was due to some physical derangement brought on by taking food, and so she restrained herself and did not answer, but only hurried to get the dinner over. She regarded this self-restraint as highly praiseworthy. Having come to the conclusion that her husband had a dreadful temper and made her life miserable, she began to feel sorry for herself, and the more she pitied her- self the more she hated her husband. She began to wish he would die; yet she did not want him to die because then his salary would cease. And this irritated her against him still more. She considered herself dreadfully unhappy just because not even his death could save her, and though she concealed her exas- peration, that hidden exasperation of hers increased his irritation also.

After one scene in which Ivan Ilych had been particularly unfair and after which he had said in explanation that he certainly was irritable but that it was due to his not being well, she said that if he was ill it should be attended to, and insisted on his going to see a celebrated doctor.

He went. Everything took place as he had expected and as it always does. There was the usual waiting and the important air assumed by the doctor, with which he was so familiar (resembling that which he himself assumed in court), and the sounding and listening, and the questions which called for answers that were foregone conclusions and were evidently unnecessary, and the look of im- portance which implied that "if only you put yourself in our hands we will ar- range everything—we know indubitably how it has to be done, always in the same way for everybody alike." It was all just as it was in the law courts. The doctor put on just the same air towards him as he himself put on towards an ac- cused person.

The doctor said that so-and-so indicated that there was so-and-so inside the patient, but if the investigation of so-and-so did not confirm this, then he must assume that and that. If he assumed that and that, then . . . and so on. To Ivan Ilych only one question was important: was his case serious or not? But the doctor ignored that inappropriate question. From his point of view it was not the one under consideration, the real question was to decide between a floating kidney, chronic catarrh, or appendicitis. It was not a question of Ivan Ilych's life or death, but one between a floating kidney and appendicitis. And that question the doctor solved brilliantly, as it seemed to Ivan Ilych, in favour of the appendix, with the reservation that should an examination of the urine give fresh indications the matter would be reconsidered. All this was just what Ivan Ilych had himself brilliantly accomplished a thousand times in dealing with men on trial. The doctor summed up just as brilliantly, looking over his spectacles triumphantly and even gaily at the accused. From the doctor's summing up Ivan Ilych concluded that things were bad, but that for the doctor, and perhaps for everybody else, it was a matter of indifference, though for him it was bad. And this conclusion struck him painfully, arousing in him a great feeling of pity for himself and of bitterness towards the doctor's indifference to a matter of such importance.

He said nothing of this, but rose, placed the doctor's fee on the table, and remarked with a sigh: "We sick people probably often put inappropriate questions. But tell me, in general, is this complaint dangerous, or not? . . ."

The doctor looked at him sternly over his spectacles with one eye, as if to say: "Prisoner, if you will not keep to the questions put to you, I shall be obliged to have you removed from the court."

"I have already told you what I consider necessary and proper. The analysis may show something more." And the doctor bowed.

Ivan Ilych went out slowly, seated himself disconsolately in his sledge, and drove home. All the way home he was going over what the doctor had said, trying to translate those complicated, obscure, scientific phrases into plain language and find in them an answer to the question: "Is my condition bad: Is it very bad? Or is there as yet nothing much wrong?" And it seemed to him that the meaning of what the doctor had said was that it was very bad. Everything in the streets seemed depressing. The cabmen, the houses, the passers-by, and the shops, were dismal. His ache, this dull gnawing ache that never ceased for a moment, seemed to have acquired a new and more serious significance from the doctor's dubious remarks. Ivan Ilych now watched it with a new and oppressive feeling.

He reached home and began to tell his wife about it. She listened, but in the middle of his account his daughter came in with her hat on, ready to go out with her mother. She sat down reluctantly to listen to this tedious story, but could not stand it long, and her mother too did not hear him to the end.

"Well, I am very glad," she said. "Mind now to take your medicine regularly. Give me the prescription and I'll send Gerasim to the chemist's." And she went to get ready to go out.

While she was in the room Ivan Ilych had hardly taken time to breathe, but he sighed deeply when she left it.

"Well," he thought, "perhaps it isn't so bad after all."

He began taking his medicine and following the doctor's directions, which had been altered after the examination of the urine. But then it happened that there was a contradiction between the indications drawn from the examination of the urine and the symptoms that showed themselves. It turned out that what was happening differed from what the doctor had told him, and that he had either forgotten, or blundered or hidden something from him. He could not, however, be blamed for that, and Ivan Ilych still obeyed his orders implicitly and at first derived some comfort from doing so.

From the time of his visit to the doctor, Ivan Ilych's chief occupation was the exact fulfilment of the doctor's instructions regarding hygiene and the taking of medicine, and the observation of his pain and his excretions. His chief interests came to be people's ailments and people's health. When sickness, deaths, or recoveries were mentioned in his presence, especially when the illness resembled his own, he listened with agitation which he tried to hide, asked questions, and applied what he heard to his own case.

The pain did not grow less, but Ivan Ilych made efforts to force himself to think that he was better. And he could do this so long as nothing agitated him. But as soon as he had any unpleasantness with his wife, or a lack of success in his official work, or held bad cards at bridge, he was at once acutely sensible of his disease. He had formerly borne such mischances, hoping soon to adjust what was wrong, to master it and attain success, or make a grand slam. But now every mischance upset him and plunged him into despair. He would say to himself: "There now, just as I was beginning to get better and the medicine had begun to take effect, comes this accursed misfortune, or unpleasantness . . . ." And he was furious with the mishap, or with the people who were causing the unpleasantness and killing him, for he felt that this fury was killing him but could not restrain it. One would have thought that it should have been clear to him that this exasperation with circumstances and people aggravated his illness, and that he ought therefore to ignore unpleasant occurrences. But he drew the very opposite conclusion: he said that he needed peace, and he watched for everything that might disturb it and became irritable at the slightest infringement of it. His condition was rendered worse by the fact that he read medical books and consulted doctors. The progress of his disease was so gradual that he could deceive himself when comparing one day with another—the difference was so slight. But when he consulted the doctors it seemed to him that he was getting worse, and even very rapidly. Yet despite this he was continually consulting them.

That month he went to see another celebrity, who told him almost the same as the first had done but put his questions rather differently, and the interview with this celebrity only increased Ivan Ilych's doubts and fears. A friend of a friend of his, a very good doctor, diagnosed his illness again quite differently from the others, and though he predicted recovery, his questions and suppositions bewildered Ivan Ilych still more and increased his doubts. A homoeopathist diagnosed the disease in yet another way, and prescribed medicine which Ivan Ilych took secretly for a week. But after a week, not feeling any improvement and having lost confidence both in the former doctor's treatment and in this one's, he became still more despondent. One day a lady acquaintance mentioned a cure effected by a wonder-working icon. Ivan Ilych caught himself listening attentively and beginning to believe that it had occurred. This incident alarmed him. "Has my mind really weakened to such an extent?" he asked himself. "Nonsense! It's all rubbish. I mustn't give way to nervous fears but having chosen a doctor must keep strictly to his treatment. That is what I will do. Now it's all settled. I won't think about it, but will follow the treatment seriously till summer, and then we shall see. From now there must be no more of this wavering!" This was easy to say but impossible to carry out. The pain in his side oppressed him and seemed to grow worse and more incessant, while the taste in his mouth grew stranger and stranger. It seemed to him that his breath had a disgusting smell, and he was conscious of a loss of appetite and strength. There was no deceiving himself: something terrible, new, and more important than anything before in his life, was taking place within him of which he alone was aware. Those about him did not understand or would not understand it, but thought everything in the world was going on as usual. That tormented Ivan Ilych more than anything. He saw that his household, especially his wife and daughter who were in a perfect whirl of visiting, did not understand anything of it and were annoyed that he was so depressed and so exacting, as if he were to blame for it. Though they tried to disguise it he saw that he was an obstacle in their path, and that his wife had adopted a definite line in regard to his illness and kept to it regardless of anything he said or did. Her attitude was this: "You know," she would say to her friends, "Ivan Ilych can't do as other people do, and keep to the treatment prescribed for him. One day he'll take his drops and keep strictly to his diet and go to bed in good time, but the next day unless I watch him he'll suddenly forget his medicine, eat sturgeon—which is forbidden—and sit up playing cards till one o'clock in the morning."

"Oh, come, when was that?" Ivan Ilych would ask in vexation. "Only once at Peter Ivanovich's."

"And yesterday with Shebek."

"Well, even if I hadn't stayed up, this pain would have kept me awake."

"Be that as it may you'll never get well like that, but will always make us wretched."

Praskovya Fëdorovna's attitude to Ivan Ilych's illness, as she expressed it both to others and to him, was that it was his own fault and was another of the annoyances he caused her. Ivan Ilych felt that this opinion escaped her involuntarily—but that did not make it easier for him.

At the law courts too, Ivan Ilych noticed, or thought he noticed, a strange attitude towards himself. It sometimes seemed to him that people were watching him inquisitively as a man whose place might soon be vacant. Then again, his friends would suddenly begin to chaff him in a friendly way about his low spirits, as if the awful, horrible, and unheard-of thing that was going on within him, incessantly gnawing at him and irresistibly drawing him away, was a very agreeable subject for jests. Schwartz in particular irritated him by his jocularity, vivacity, and *savoir-faire,* which reminded him of what he himself had been ten years ago.

Friends came to make up a set and they sat down to cards. They dealt, bending the new cards to soften them, and he sorted the diamonds in his hand and found he had seven. His partner said "No trumps" and supported him with two diamonds. What more could be wished for? It ought to be jolly and lively. They would make a grand slam. But suddenly Ivan Ilych was conscious of that gnawing pain, that taste in his mouth, and it seemed ridiculous that in such circumstances he should be pleased to make a grand slam.

He looked at his partner, Mikhail Mikhaylovich, who rapped the table with his strong hand and instead of snatching up the tricks pushed the cards courteously and indulgently towards Ivan Ilych that he might have the pleasure of gathering them up without the trouble of stretching out his hand for them. "Does he think I am too weak to stretch out my arm?" thought Ivan Ilych, and forgetting what he was doing he over-trumped his partner, missing the grand slam by three tricks. And what was most awful of all was that he saw how upset Mikhail Mikhaylovich was about it but did not himself care. And it was dreadful to realize why he did not care.

They all saw that he was suffering, and said: "We can stop if you are tired. Take a rest." Lie down? No, he was not at all tired, and he finished the rubber. All were gloomy and silent. Ivan Ilych felt that he had diffused this gloom over them and could not dispel it. They had supper and went away, and Ivan Ilych was left alone with the consciousness that his life was poisoned and was poisoning the lives of others, and that this poison did not weaken but penetrated more and more deeply into his whole being.

With this consciousness, and with physical pain besides that terror, he must go to bed, often to lie awake the greater part of the night. Next morning he had to get up again, dress, go the law courts, speak, and write; or if he did not go out, spend at home those twenty-four hours a day each of which was a torture. And he had to live thus all alone on the brink of an abyss, with no one who understood or pitied him.

V

So one month passed and then another. Just before the New Year his brother-in-law came to town and stayed at their house. Ivan Ilych was at the law courts and Praskovya Fëdorovna had gone shopping. When Ivan Ilych came home and entered his study he found his brother-in-law there—a healthy, florid man—unpacking his portmanteau himself. He raised his head on hearing Ivan Ilych's footsteps and looked up at him for a moment without a word. That stare told Ivan Ilych everything. His brother-in-law opened his mouth to utter an exclamation of surprise but checked himself, and that action confirmed it all.

"I have changed, eh?"

"Yes, there is a change."

And after that, try as he would to get his brother-in-law to return to the subject of his looks, the latter would say nothing about it. Praskovya Fëdorovna came home and her brother went out to her. Ivan Ilych locked the door and began to examine himself in the glass, first full face, then in profile. He took up a portrait of himself taken with his wife, and compared it with what he saw in the glass. The change in him was immense. Then be bared his arms to the elbow, looked at them, drew the sleeves down again, sat down on an ottoman, and grew blacker than night.

"No, no, this won't do!" he said to himself, and jumped up, went to the table, took up some law papers and began to read them, but could not continue.

He unlocked the door and went into the reception-room. The door leading to the drawing-room was shut. He approached it on tiptoe and listened.

"No, you are exaggerating!" Praskovya Fëdorovna was saying.

"Exaggerating! Don't you see it? Why, he's a dead man! Look at his eyes—there's no light in them. But what is it that is wrong with him?"

"No one knows. Nikolaevich said something, but I don't know what. And Leshchetitsky said quite the contrary . . . ."

Ivan Ilych walked away, went to his own room, lay down, and began musing: "The kidney, a floating kidney." He recalled all the doctors had told him of how it detached itself and swayed about. And by an effort of imagination he tried to catch that kidney and arrest it and support it. So little was needed for this, it seemed to him. "No, I'll go see Peter Ivanovich again." He rang, ordered the carriage, and got ready to go.

"Where are you going, Jean?" asked his wife, with a specially sad and exceptionally kind look.

This exceptionally kind look irritated him. He looked morosely at her.

"I must go to see Peter Ivanovich."

He went to see Peter Ivanovich, and together they went to see his friend, the doctor. He was in, and Ivan Ilych had a long talk with him.

Reviewing the anatomical and physiological details of what in the doctor's opinion was going on inside him, he understood it all.

There was something, a small thing, in the vermiform appendix. It might all come right. Only stimulate the energy of one organ and check the activity of another, then absorption would take place and everything would come right. He got home rather late for dinner, ate his dinner, conversed cheerfully, but could not for a long time bring himself to go back to work in his room. At last, however, he went to his study and did what was necessary, but the consciousness that he had put something aside—an important, intimate matter which he would revert to when his work was done—never left him. When he had finished his work he remembered that this intimate matter was the thought of his vermiform appendix. But he did not give himself up to it, and went to the drawing-room for tea. There were callers there, including the examining magistrate who was a desirable match for his daughter, and they were conversing, playing the piano, and singing. Ivan Ilych, as Praskovya Fëdorovna remarked, spent that evening more cheerfully than usual, but he never for a moment forgot that he had postponed the important matter of the appendix. At eleven o'clock he said goodnight and went to his bedroom. Since his illness he had slept alone in a small room next to his study. He undressed and took up a novel by Zola, but instead of reading it fell into thought, and in his imagination that desired improvement in the vermiform appendix occurred. There was the absorption and evacuation and the re-establishment of normal activity. "Yes, that's it!" he said to himself. "One need only assist nature, that's all." He remembered his medicine, rose, took it, and lay down on his back watching for the beneficent action of the medicine and for it to lessen the pain. "I need only take it regularly and avoid all injurious influences. I am already feeling better, much better." He began touching his side: it was not painful to the touch. "There, I really don't feel it. It's much better already." He put out the light and turned on his side . . . "The appendix is getting better, absorption is occurring." Suddenly he felt the old, familiar, dull, gnawing pain, stubborn and serious. There was the same familiar loathsome taste in his mouth. His heart sank and he felt dazed. "My God! My God!" he muttered. "Again, again! and it will never cease." And suddenly the matter presented itself in a quite different aspect. "Vermiform appendix! Kidney!" he said to himself. "It's not a question of appendix or kidney, but of life and . . . death. Yes, life was there and now it is going, going and I cannot stop it. Yes. Why deceive myself? Isn't it obvious to everyone but me that I'm dying, and that it's only a question of weeks, days . . . it may happen this moment. There was light and now there is darkness. I was here and now I'm going there! Where?" A chill came over him, his breathing ceased, and he felt only the throbbing of his heart.

"When I am not, what will there be? There will be nothing. Then where shall I be when I am no more? Can this be dying? No, I don't want to!" He jumped up and tried to light the candle, felt for it with trembling hands, dropped candle and candlestick on the floor, and fell back on his pillow.

"What's the use? It makes no difference," he said to himself, staring with wide-open eyes into the darkness. "Death. Yes, death. And none of them know or wish to know it, and they have no pity for me. Now they are playing." (He heard through the door the distant sound of a song and its accompaniment.) "It's all the same to them, but they will die too! Fools! I first, and they later, but it will be the same for them. And now they are merry . . . the beasts!"

Anger choked him and he was agonizingly, unbearably, miserable. "It is impossible that all men have been doomed to suffer this awful horror!" He raised himself.

"Something must be wrong. I must calm myself—must think it all over from the beginning." And he again began thinking. "Yes, the beginning of my illness: I knocked my side, but I was quite well that day and the next. It hurt a little, then rather more. I saw the doctor, then followed despondency and anguish, more doctors, and I drew nearer to the abyss. My strength grew less and I kept coming nearer and nearer, and now I have wasted away and there is no light in my eyes. I think of the appendix—but this is death! I think of mending the appendix, and all the while here is death! Can it really be death?" Again terror seized him and he gasped for breath. He leant down and began feeling for the matches, pressing with his elbow on the stand beside the bed. It was in the way and hurt him, he grew furious with it, pressed on it still harder, and upset it. Breathless and in despair he fell on his back, expecting death to come immediately.

Meanwhile the visitors were leaving. Praskovya Fëdorovna was seeing them off. She heard something fall and came in.

"What has happened?"

"Nothing. I knocked it over accidentally."

She went out and returned with a candle. He lay there panting heavily, like a man who has run a thousand yards, and stared upwards at her with a fixed look.

"What is it, Jean?"

"No . . . o . . . thing. I upset it." ("Why speak of it? She won't understand," he thought.)

And in truth she did not understand. She picked up the stand, lit his candle, and hurried away to see another visitor off. When she came back he still lay on his back, looking upwards.

"What is it? Do you feel worse?"

"Yes."

She shook her head and sat down.

"Do you know, Jean, I think we must ask Leshchetitsky to come and see you here."

This meant calling in the famous specialist, regardless of expense. He smiled malignantly and said "No." She remained a little longer and then went up to him and kissed his forehead.

While she was kissing him he hated her from the bottom of his soul and with difficulty refrained from pushing her away.

"Good-night. Please God you'll sleep."

"Yes."

VI

Ivan Ilych saw that he was dying, and he was in continual despair.

In the depth of his heart he knew he was dying, but not only was he not accustomed to the thought, he simply did not and could not grasp it.

The syllogism he had learnt from Kiezewetter's Logic: "Caius is a man, men are mortal, therefore Caius is mortal," had always seemed to him correct as applied to Caius, but certainly not as applied to himself. That Caius—man in the abstract—was mortal, was perfectly correct, but he was not Caius, not an abstract man, but a creature quite, quite separate from all others. He had been little Vanya, with a mamma and a papa, with Mitya and Volodya, with the toys, a coachman and a nurse, afterwards with Katenka and with all the joys, griefs, and delights of childhood, boyhood, and youth. What did Caius know of the smell of that striped leather ball Vanya had been so fond of? Had Caius kissed his mother's hand like that, and did the silk of her dress rustle so for Caius? Had he rioted like that at school when the pastry was bad? Had Caius been in love like that? Could Caius preside at a session as he did? "Caius really was mortal, and it was right for him to die; but for me, little Vanya, Ivan Ilych, with all my thoughts and emotions, it's altogether a different matter. It cannot be that I ought to die. That would be too terrible."

Such was his feeling.

"If I had to die like Caius, I should have known it was so. An inner voice would have told me so, but there was nothing of the sort in me and I and all my friends felt that our case was quite different from that of Caius. And now here it is!'' he said to himself. "It can't be. It's impossible! But here it is. How is this? How is one to understand it?''

He could not understand it, and tried to drive this false, incorrect, morbid thought away and to replace it by other proper and healthy thoughts. But that thought, and not the thought only but the reality itself, seemed to come and confront him.

And to replace that thought he called up a succession of others, hoping to find in them some support. He tried to get back into the former current of thoughts that had once screened the thought of death from him. But strange to say, all that had formerly shut off, hidden, and destroyed, his consciousness of death, no longer had that effect. Ivan Ilych now spent most of his time in attempting to re-establish that old current. He would say to himself: "I will take up my duties again—after all I used to live by them.'' And banishing all doubts he would go to the law courts, enter into conversation with his colleagues, and sit carelessly as was his wont, scanning the crowd with a thoughtful look and leaning both his emaciated arms on the arms of his oak chair; bending over as usual to a colleague and drawing his papers nearer he would interchange whispers with him, and then suddenly raising his eyes and sitting erect would pronounce certain words and open the proceedings. But suddenly in the midst of those proceedings the pain in his side, regardless of the stage the proceedings had reached, would begin its own gnawing work. Ivan Ilych would turn his attention to it and try to drive the thoughts of it away, but without success. *It* would come and stand before him and look at him, and he would be petrified and the light would die out of his eyes, and he would again begin asking himself whether *It* alone was true. And his colleagues and subordinates would see with surprise and distress that he, the brilliant and subtle judge, was becoming confused and making mistakes. He would shake himself, try to pull himself together, manage somehow to bring the sitting to a close, and return home with the sorrowful consciousness that his judicial labours could not as formerly hide from him what he wanted them to hide, and could not deliver him from *It*. And what was worst of all was that *It* drew his attention to itself not in order to take some action but only that he should look at *It,* look it straight in the face: look at it without doing anything, suffer inexpressibly.

And to save himself from this condition Ivan Ilych looked for consolations— new screens—and new screens were found and for a while seemed to save him, but then they immediately fell to pieces or rather became transparent, as if *It* penetrated them and nothing could veil *It*.

In these latter days he would go into the drawing-room he had arranged— that drawing-room where he had fallen and for the sake of which (how bitterly ridiculous it seemed) he had sacrificed his life—for he knew that his illness originated with that knock. He would enter and see that something had scratched the polished table. He would look for the cause of this and find that it was the bronze ornamentation of an album, that had got bent. He would take up the expensive album which he had lovingly arranged, and feel vexed with his daughter and her friends for their untidiness—for the album was torn here and

there and some of the photographs turned upside down. He would put it carefully in order and bend the ornamentation back into position. Then it would
occur to him to place all those things in another corner of the room, near the
plants. He would call the footman, but his daughter or wife would come to help
him. They would not agree, and his wife would contradict him, and he would
dispute and grow angry. But that was all right, for then he did not think about
It. It was invisible.

But then, when he was moving something himself, his wife would say: "Let
the servants do it. You will hurt yourself again." And suddenly *It* would flash
through the screen and he would see it. It was just a flash, and he hoped it
would disappear, but he would, involuntarily pay attention to his side. "It sits
there as before, gnawing just the same!" And he could no longer forget *It*, but
could distinctly see it looking at him from behind the flowers. "What is it all
for?"

"It really is so! I lost my life over the curtain as I might have done when
storming a fort. Is that possible? How terrible and how stupid. It can't be true!
It can't, but it is."

He would go to his study, lie down, and again be alone with *It:* face to face
with *It*. And nothing could be done with *It* except to look at it and shudder.

VII

How it happened it is impossible to say because it came about step by step,
unnoticed, but in the third month of Ivan Ilych's illness, his wife, his daughter,
his son, his acquaintances, the doctors, the servants, and above all he himself,
were aware that the whole interest he had for other people was whether he
would soon vacate his place, and at last release the living from the discomfort
caused by his presence and he himself released from his sufferings.

He slept less and less. He was given opium and hypodermic injections of
morphine, but this did not relieve him. The dull depression he experienced in a
somnolent condition at first gave him a little relief, but only as something new,
afterwards it became as distressing as the pain itself or even more so.

Special foods were prepared for him by the doctors' orders, but all those
foods became increasingly distasteful and disgusting to him.

For his excretions also special arrangements had to be made, and this was a
torment to him every time—a torment from the uncleanliness, the un-
seemliness, and the smell, and from knowing that another person had to take
part in it.

But just through this most unpleasant matter, Ivan Ilych obtained comfort.
Gerasim, the butler's young assistant, always came in to carry the things out.
Gerasim was a clean, fresh peasant lad, grown stout on town food and always
cheerful and bright. At first the sight of him, in his clean Russian peasant costume, engaged in that disgusting task embarrassed Ivan Ilych.

Once when he got up from the commode too weak to draw up his trousers, he dropped into a soft armchair and looked with horror at his bare, enfeebled thighs with the muscles so sharply marked on them.

Gerasim with a firm light tread, his heavy boots emitting a pleasant smell of tar and fresh winter air, came in wearing a clean Hessian apron, the sleeves of his print shirt tucked up over his strong bare young arms; and refraining from looking at his sick master out of consideration for his feelings, and restraining the joy of life that beamed from his face, he went up to the commode.

"Gerasim!" said Ivan Ilych in a weak voice.

Gerasim started, evidently afraid he might have committed some blunder, and with a rapid movement turned his fresh, kind, simple young face which just showed the first downy signs of a beard.

"Yes, sir?"

"That must be very unpleasant for you. You must forgive me. I am helpless."

"Oh, why, sir," and Gerasim's eyes beamed and he showed his glistening white teeth, "what's a little trouble? It's a case of illness with you, sir."

And his deft strong hands did their accustomed task, and he went out of the room stepping lightly. Five minutes later he as lightly returned.

Ivan Ilych was still sitting in the same position in the armchair.

"Gerasim," he said when the latter had replaced the freshly-washed utensil. "Please come here and help me." Gerasim went up to him. "Lift me up. It is hard for me to get up, and I have sent Dmitri away."

Gerasim went up to him, grasped his master with his strong arms deftly but gently, in the same way that he stepped—lifted him, supported him with one hand, and with the other drew up his trousers and would have set him down again, but Ivan Ilych asked to be led to the sofa. Gerasim, without an effort and without apparent pressure, led him, almost lifting him, to the sofa and placed him on it.

"Thank you. How easily and well you do it all!"

Gerasim smiled again and turned to leave the room. But Ivan Ilych felt his presence such a comfort that he did not want to let him go.

"One thing more, please move up that chair. No, the other one—under my feet. It is easier for me when my feet are raised."

Gerasim brought the chair, set it down gently in place, and raised Ivan Ilych's legs on to it. It seemed to Ivan Ilych that he felt better while Gerasim was holding up his legs.

"It's better when my legs are higher," he said. "Place that cushion under them."

Gerasim did so. He again lifted the legs and placed them, and again Ivan Ilych felt better while Gerasim held his legs. When he set them down Ivan Ilych fancied he felt worse.

"Gerasim," he said. "Are you busy now?"

"Not at all, sir," said Gerasim, who had learnt from the townfolk how to speak gentlefolk.

"What have you still to do?"

"What have I to do? I've done everything except chopping the logs for to-morrow."

"Then hold my legs up a bit higher, can you?"

"Of course I can. Why not?" And Gerasim raised his master's legs higher and Ivan Ilych thought that in that position he did not feel any pain at all.

"And how about the logs?"

"Don't trouble about that, sir. There's plenty of time."

Ivan Ilych told Gerasim to sit down and hold his legs, and began to talk to him. And strange to say it seemed to him that he felt better while Gerasim held his legs up.

After that Ivan Ilych would sometimes call Gerasim and get him to hold his legs on his shoulders, and he liked talking to him. Gerasim did it all easily, willingly, simply, and with a good nature that touched Ivan Ilych. Health, strength, and vitality in other people were offensive to him, but Gerasim's strength and vitality did not mortify but soothed him.

What tormented Ivan Ilych most was the deception, the lie, which for some reason they all accepted, that he was not dying but was simply ill, and that he only need keep quiet and undergo a treatment and then something very good would result. He however knew that do what they would nothing would come of it, only still more agonizing suffering and death. This deception tortured him—their not wishing to admit what they all knew and what he knew, but wanting to lie to him concerning his terrible condition, and wishing and forcing him to participate in that lie. Those lies—lies enacted over him on the eve of his death and destined to degrade this awful, solemn act to the level of their visitings, their curtains, their sturgeon for dinner—were a terrible agony for Ivan Ilych. And strangely enough, many times when they were going through their antics over him he had been within a hairbreadth of calling out to them: "Stop lying! You know and I know that I am dying. Then at least stop lying about it!" But he had never had the spirit to do it. The awful, terrible act of his dying was, he could see, reduced by those about him to the level of a casual, unpleasant, and almost indecorous incident (as if someone entered a drawing-room diffusing an unpleasant odour) and this was done by that very decorum which he had served all his life long. He saw that no one felt for him, because no one even wished to grasp his position. Only Gerasim recognized it and pitied him. And so Ivan Ilych felt at ease only with him. He felt comforted when Gerasim supported his legs (sometimes all night long) and refused to go to bed saying: "Don't you worry, Ivan Ilych. I'll get sleep enough later on," or when he suddenly became familiar and exclaimed: "If you weren't sick it would be another matter, but as it is, why should I grudge a little trouble?" Gerasim alone did not lie; everything showed that he alone understood the facts of the case and did not consider it necessary to disguise them, but simply felt sorry for his emaciated and enfeebled master. Once when Ivan Ilych was sending him away he even said straight out: "We shall all of us die, so why should I grudge a little trouble?''—expressing the fact that he did not think his work burdensome, because he was doing it for a dying man and hoped someone would do the same for him when his time came.

Apart from this lying, or because of it, what most tormented Ivan Ilych was that no one pitied him as he wished to be pitied. At certain moments after prolonged suffering he wished most of all (though he would have been ashamed to confess it) for someone to pity him as a sick child is pitied. He longed to be petted and comforted. He knew he was an important functionary, that he had a beard turning grey, and that therefore what he longed for was impossible, but still he longed for it. And in Gerasim's attitude towards him there was something akin to what he wished for, and so that attitude comforted him. Ivan Ilych wanted to weep, wanted to be petted and cried over, and then his colleague Shebek would come, and instead of weeping and being petted, Ivan Ilych would assume a serious, severe, and profound air, and by force of habit would express his opinion on a decision of the Court of Cassation and would stubbornly insist on that view. This falsity around him and within him did more than anything else to poison his last days.

VIII

It was morning. He knew it was morning because Gerasim had gone, and Peter the footman had come and put out the candles, drawn back one of the curtains, and begun quietly to tidy up. Whether it was morning or evening, Friday or Sunday, made no difference, it was all just the same: the gnawing, unmitigated, agonizing pain, never ceasing for an instant, the consciousness of life inexorably waning but not yet extinguished, the approach of that ever dreaded and hateful Death which was the only reality, and always the same falsity. What were days, weeks, hours, in such a case?

"Will you have some tea, sir?"

"He wants things to be regular, and wishes the gentlefolk to drink tea in the morning," thought Ivan Ilych, and only said "No."

"Wouldn't you like to move onto the sofa, sir?"

"He wants to tidy up the room, and I'm in the way. I am uncleanliness and disorder," he thought, and said only:

"No, leave me alone."

The man went on bustling about. Ivan Ilych stretched out his hand. Peter came up, ready to help.

"What is it, sir?"

"My watch."

Peter took the watch which was close at hand and gave it to his master.

"Half-past eight. Are they up?"

"No, sir, except Vladimir Ivanich" (the son) "who has gone to school. Praskovya Fëdorovna ordered me to wake her if you asked for her. Shall I do so?"

"No, there's no need to." "Perhaps I'd better have some tea," he thought, and added aloud: "Yes, bring me some tea."

Peter went to the door, but Ivan Ilych dreaded being left alone. "How can I keep him here? Oh yes, my medicine." "Peter, give me my medicine." "Why not? Perhaps it may do me some good." He took a spoonful and swallowed it. "No, it won't help. It's all tomfoolery, all deception," he decided as soon as he became aware of the familiar, sickly, hopeless taste. "No, I can't believe in it any longer. But the pain, why this pain? If it would only cease just for a moment!" And he moaned. Peter turned towards him. "It's all right. Go and fetch me some tea."

Peter went out. Left alone Ivan Ilych groaned not so much with pain, terrible though that was, as from mental anguish. Always and for ever the same, always these endless days and nights. If only it would come quicker! If only *what* would come quicker? Death, darkness? . . . No, no! Anything rather than death!

When Peter returned with the tea on a tray, Ivan Ilych stared at him for a time in perplexity, not realizing who and what he was. Peter was disconcerted by that look and his embarrassment brought Ivan Ilych to himself.

"Oh, tea! All right, put it down. Only help me to wash and put on a clean shirt."

And Ivan Ilych began to wash. With pauses for rest, he washed his hands and then his face, cleaned his teeth, brushed his hair, and looked in the glass. He was terrified by what he saw, especially the limp way in which his hair clung to his pallid forehead.

While his shirt was being changed he knew that he would be still more frightened at the sight of his body, so he avoided looking at it. Finally he was ready. He drew on a dressing-gown, wrapped himself in a plaid, and sat down in the armchair to take his tea. For a moment he felt refreshed, but as soon as he began to drink the tea he was again aware of the same taste, and the pain also returned. He finished it with an effort, and then lay down stretching out his legs, and dismissed Peter.

Always the same. Now a spark of hope flashes up, then a sea of despair ranges, and always pain; always pain, always despair, and always the same. When alone he had a dreadful and distressing desire to call someone, but he knew beforehand that with others present it would be still worse. "Another dose of morphine—to lose consciousness. I will tell him, the doctor, that he must think of something else. It's impossible, impossible to go on like this."

An hour and another pass like that. But now there is a ring at the door bell. Perhaps it's the doctor? It is. He comes in fresh, hearty, plump, and cheerful, with that look on his face that seems to say: "There now, you're in a panic about something, but we'll arrange it all for you directly!" The doctor knows this expression is out of place here, but he has put it on once for all and can't take it off—like a man who has put on a frock-coat in the morning to pay a round of calls.

The doctor rubs his hands vigorously and reassuringly.

"Brr! How cold it is! There's such a sharp frost; just let me warm myself!" he says, as if it were only a matter of waiting till he was warm, and then he would put everything right.

"Well now, how are you?"

Ivan Ilych feels that the doctor would like to say: "Well, how are your affairs?" but that even he feels that this would not do, and says instead: "What sort of a night have you had?"

Ivan Ilych looks at him as much as to say: "Are you really never ashamed of lying?" But the doctor does not wish to understand this question, and Ivan Ilych says: "Just as terrible as ever. The pain never leaves me and never subsides. If only something . . ."

"Yes, you sick people are always like that . . . There, now I think I am warm enough. Even Praskovya Fëdorovna, who is so particular, could find no fault with my temperature. Well, now I can say good-morning," and the doctor presses his patient's hand.

Then, dropping his former playfulness, he begins with a most serious face to examine the patient, feeling his pulse and taking his temperature, and then begins the sounding and auscultation.

Ivan Ilych knows quite well and definitely that all this is nonsense and pure deception, but when the doctor, getting down on his knee, leans over him, putting the ear first higher then lower, and performs various gymnastic movements over them with a significant expression on his face, Ivan Ilych submits to it all as he used to submit to the speeches of the lawyers, though he knew very well they were all lying and why they were lying.

The doctor, kneeling on the sofa, is still sounding him when Praskovya Fëdorovna's silk dress rustles at the door and she is heard scolding Peter for not having let her know of the doctor's arrival.

She comes in, kisses her husband, and at once proceeds to prove that she has been up a long time already, and only owing to a misunderstanding failed to be there when the doctor arrived.

Ivan Ilych looks at her, scans her all over, sets against her the whiteness and plumpness and cleanness of her hands and neck, the gloss of her hair, and the sparkle of her vivacious eyes. He hates her with his whole soul. And the thrill of hatred he feels for her makes him suffer from her touch.

Her attitude towards him and his disease is still the same. Just as the doctor had adopted a certain relation to his patient which he could not abandon, so had she formed one towards him—that he was not doing something he ought to do and was himself to blame, and that she reproached him lovingly for this—and she could not now change that attitude.

"You see he doesn't listen to me and doesn't take his medicine at the proper time. And above all he lies in a position that is no doubt bad for him—with his legs up."

She described how he made Gerasim hold his legs up.

The doctor smiled with a contemptuous affability that said: "What's to be done? These sick people do have foolish fancies of that kind, but we must forgive them.''

When the examination was over the doctor looked at his watch, and then Praskovya Fëdorovna announced to Ivan Ilych that it was of course as he pleased, but she had sent today for a celebrated specialist who would examine him and have a consultation with Michael Danilovich (their regular doctor).

''Please don't raise any objections. I am doing this for my own sake,'' she said ironically, letting it be felt that she was doing this all for his sake and only said this to leave him no right to refuse. He remained silent, knitting his brows. He felt that he was so surrounded and involved in a mesh of falsity that it was hard to unravel anything.

Everything she did for him was entirely for her own sake, and she told him she was doing for herself what she actually was doing for herself, as if that was so incredible that he must understand the opposite.

At half-past eleven the celebrated specialist arrived. Again the sounding began and the significant conversations in his presence and in another room about the kidneys and the appendix, and the questions and answers, with such an air of importance that again, instead of the real question of life and death which now alone confronted him, the question arose of the kidney and appendix which were not behaving as they ought to and would now be attacked by Michael Danilovich and the specialist and forced to mend their ways.

The celebrated specialist took leave of him with a serious though not hopeless look, and in reply to the timid question Ivan Ilych, with eyes glistening with fear and hope, put to him as to whether there was a chance of recovery, said that he could not vouch for it but there was a possibility. The look of hope with which Ivan Ilych watched the doctor out was so pathetic that Praskovya Fëdorovna, seeing it, even wept as she left the room to hand the doctor his fee.

The gleam of hope kindled by the doctor's encouragement did not last long. The same room, the same pictures, curtains, wall-paper, medicine bottles, were all there, and the same aching suffering body, and Ivan Ilych began to moan. They gave him a subcutaneous injection and he sank into oblivion.'

It was twilight when he came to. They brought him his dinner and he swallowed some beef tea with difficulty, and then everything was the same again and night was coming on.

After dinner, at seven o'clock, Praskovya Fëdorovna came into the room in evening dress, her full bosom pushed up by her corset, and with traces of powder on her face. She had reminded him in the morning that they were going to the theatre. Sarah Bernhardt was visiting the town and they had a box, which he had insisted on their taking. Now he had forgotten about it and her toilet offended him, but he concealed his vexation when he remembered that he had himself insisted on their securing a box and going because it would be an instructive and aesthetic pleasure for the children.

Praskovya Fëdorovna came in, self-satisfied but yet with a rather guilty air. She sat down and asked how he was, but, as he saw, only for the sake of asking and not in order to learn about it, knowing that there was nothing to learn—

and then went on to what she really wanted to say: that she would not on any account have gone but that the box had been taken and Helen and their daughter were going, as well as Petrishchev (the examining magistrate, their daughter's fiancé) and that it was out of the question to let them go alone; but that she would have much preferred to sit with him for a while; and he must be sure to follow the doctor's orders while she was away.

"Oh, and Fëdor Petrovich" (the fiancé) "would like to come in. May he? and Lisa?"

"All right."

Their daughter came in in full evening dress, her fresh young flesh exposed (making a show of that very flesh which in his own case caused so much suffering), strong, healthy, evidently in love, and impatient with illness, suffering, and death, because they interfered with her happiness.

Fëdor Petrovich came in too, in evening dress, his hair curled *à la Capoul,* a tight stiff collar round his long sinewy neck, an enormous white shirt-front and narrow black trousers tightly stretched over his strong thighs. He had one white glove tightly drawn on, and was holding his opera hat in his hand.

Following him the schoolboy crept in unnoticed, in a new uniform, poor little fellow, and wearing gloves. Terribly dark shadows showed under his eyes, the meaning of which Ivan Ilych knew well.

His son had always seemed pathetic to him, and now it was dreadful to see the boy's frightened look of pity. It seemed to Ivan Ilych that Vasya was the only one besides Gerasim who understood and pitied him.

They all sat down and again asked how he was. A silence followed. Lisa asked her mother about the opera-glasses, and there was an altercation between mother and daughter as to who had taken them and where they had been put. This occasioned some unpleasantness.

Fëdor Petrovich inquired of Ivan Ilych whether he had ever seen Sarah Bernhardt. Ivan Ilych did not at first catch the question, but then replied: "No, have you seen her before?"

"Yes, in *Adrienne Lecouvreur.*"

Praskovya Fëdorovna mentioned some rôles in which Sarah Bernhardt was particularly good. Her daughter disagreed. Conversation sprang up as to the elegance and realism of her acting—the sort of conversation that is always repeated and is always the same.

In the midst of the conversation Fëdor Petrovich glanced at Ivan Ilych and became silent. Ivan Ilych was staring with glittering eyes straight before him, evidently indignant with them. This had to be rectified, but it was impossible to do so. The silence had to be broken, but for a time no one dared to break it and they all became afraid that the conventional deception would suddenly become obvious and the truth become plain to all. Lisa was the first to pluck up courage and break the silence, but by trying to hide what everybody was feeling, she betrayed it.

"Well, if we are going it's time to start," she said, looked at her watch, a present from her father, and with a faint and significant smile at Fëdor Petrovich relating to something known only to them. She got up with a rustle of her dress.

They all rose, said good-night, and went away.

When they had gone it seemed to Ivan Ilych that he felt better; the falsity had gone with them. But the pain remained—that same pain and that same fear that made everything monotonously alike, nothing harder and nothing easier. Everything was worse.

Again minute followed minute and hour followed hour. Everything remained the same and there was no cessation. And the inevitable end of it all became more and more terrible.

"Yes, send Gerasim here," he replied to a question Peter asked.

IX

His wife returned late at night. She came in on tiptoe, but he heard her, opened his eyes, and made haste to close them again. She wished to send Gerasim away and to sit with him herself, but he opened his eyes and said: "No, go away."

"Are you in great pain?"

"Always the same."

"Take some opium."

He agreed and took some. She went away.

Till about three in the morning he was in a state of stupefied misery. It seemed to him that he and his pain were being thrust into a narrow, deep black sack, but though they were pushed further and further in they could not be pushed to the bottom. And this, terrible enough in itself, was accompanied by suffering. He struggled but yet cooperated. And suddenly he broke through, fell, and regained consciousness. Gerasim was sitting at the foot of the bed dozing quietly, while he himself lay with his emaciated stockinged legs resting on Gerasim's shoulders; the same shaded candle was there and the same unceasing pain.

"Go away, Gerasim," he whispered.

"It's all right, sir. I'll stay a while."

"No. Go away."

He removed his legs from Gerasim's shoulders, turned sideways onto his arm, and felt sorry for himself. He only waited till Gerasim had gone into the next room and then restrained himself no longer but wept like a child. He wept on account of his helplessness, his terrible loneliness, the cruelty of man, the cruelty of God, and the absence of God.

"Why hast Thou done all this? Why hast Thou brought me here? Why, why dost Thou torment me so terribly?"

He did not expect an answer and yet wept because there was no answer and could be none. The pain grew more acute, but he did not stir and did not call. He said to himself: "Go on! Strike me! But what is it for? What have I done to Thee? What is it for?"

Then he grew quiet and not only ceased weeping but even held his breath and became all attention. It was as though he were listening not to an audible voice but to the voice of his soul, to the current of thoughts arising within him.

"What is it you want?" was the first clear conception of expression in words, that he heard.

"What do you want? What do you want?" he repeated to himself.

"What do I want? To live and not to suffer," he answered.

And again he listened with such concentrated attention that even his pain did not distract him.

"To live? How?" asked his inner voice.

"Why, to live as I used to—well and pleasantly."

"As you lived before, well and pleasantly?" the voice repeated.

And in imagination he began to recall the best moments of his pleasant life. But strange to say none of those best moments of his pleasant life now seemed at all what they had then seemed—none of them except the first recollections of childhood. There, in childhood, there had been something really pleasant with which it would be possible to live if it could return. But the child who had experienced that happiness existed no longer, it was like a reminiscence of somebody else.

As soon as the period began which had produced the present Ivan Ilych, all that had then seemed joys now melted before his sight and turned into something trivial and often nasty.

And the further he departed from childhood and the nearer he came to the present the more worthless and doubtful were the joys. This began with the School of Law. A little that was really good was still found there—there was light-heartedness, friendship, and hope. But in the upper classes there had already been fewer of such good moments. Then during the first years of his official career, when he was in the service of the Governor, some pleasant moments again occurred: they were the memories of love for a woman. Then all became confused and there was still less of what was good; later on again there was still less that was good, and the further he went the less there was. His marriage, a mere accident, then the disenchantment that followed it, his wife's bad breath and the sensuality and hypocrisy: then that deadly official life and those preoccupations about money, a year of it, and two, and ten, and twenty, and always the same thing. And the longer it lasted the more deadly it became. "It is as if I had been going downhill while I imagined I was going up. And that is really what it was. I was going up in public opinion, but to the same extent life was ebbing away from me. And now it is all done and there is only death."

"Then what does it mean? Why? It can't be that life is so senseless and horrible. But if it really has been so horrible and senseless, why must I die and die in agony? There is something wrong!"

"Maybe I did not live as I ought to have done," it suddenly occurred to him. "But how could that be, when I did everything properly?" he replied, and immediately dismissed from his mind this, the sole solution of all the riddles of life and death, as something quite impossible.

"Then what do you want now? To live? Live how? Live as you lived in the law courts when the usher proclaimed 'The judge is coming!' The judge is coming, the judge!" he repeated to himself. "Here he is, the judge. But I am not guilty!" he exclaimed angrily. "What is it for?" And he ceased crying, but turning his face to the wall continued to ponder on the same question: Why, and for what purpose, is there all this horror? But however much he pondered he found no answer. And whenever the thought occurred to him, as it often did, that it all resulted from his not having lived as he ought to have done, he at once recalled the correctness of his whole life and dismissed so strange an idea.

X

Another fortnight passed. Ivan Ilych now no longer left his sofa. He would not lie in bed but lay on the sofa, facing the wall nearly all the time. He suffered ever the same unceasing agonies and in his loneliness pondered always on the same insoluble question: "What is this? Can it be that it is Death?" And the inner voice answered: "Yes, it is Death."

"Why these sufferings?" And the voice answered, "For no reason—they just are so." Beyond and besides this there was nothing.

From the very beginning of his illness, ever since he had first been to see the doctor, Ivan Ilych's life had been divided between two contrary and alternating moods: now it was despair and the expectation of this uncomprehended and terrible death, and now hope and an intently interested observation of the functioning of his organs. Now before his eyes there was only a kidney or an intestine that temporarily evaded its duty, and now only that incomprehensible and dreadful death from which it was impossible to escape.

These two states of mind had alternated from the very beginning of his illness, but the further it progressed the more doubtful and fantastic became the conception of the kidney, and the more real the sense of impending death.

He had but to call to mind what he had been three months before and what he was now, to call to mind with what regularity he had been going downhill, for every possibility of hope to be shattered.

Latterly during that loneliness in which he found himself as he lay facing the back of the sofa, a loneliness in the midst of a populous town and surrounded by numerous acquaintances and relations but that yet could not have been more complete anywhere—either at the bottom of the sea or under the earth—during that terrible loneliness Ivan Ilych had lived only in memories of the past. Pictures of his past rose before him one after another. They always began with what was nearest in time and then went back to what was the most remote—to his childhood—and rested there. If he thought of the stewed prunes that had been offered him that day, his mind went back to the raw shrivelled French plums of his childhood, their peculiar flavour and the flow of saliva when he sucked their stones, and along with the memory of that taste came a whole series of memories of those days: his nurse, his brother, and their toys. "No, I mustn't think of that . . . It is too painful," Ivan Ilych said to himself, and brought himself back to the present—to the button on the back of the sofa and the creases in its morocco. "Morocco is expensive, but it does not wear well: there had been a quarrel about it. It was a different kind of quarrel and a different kind of morocco that time when we tore father's portfolio and were punished, and Mamma brought us some tarts . . ." And again his thoughts dwelt on his childhood, and again it was painful and he tried to banish them and fix his mind on something else.

Then again together with that chain of memories another series passed through his mind—of how his illness had progressed and grown worse. There also the further back he looked the more life there had been. There had been more of what was good in life and more of life itself. The two merged together. "Just as the pain went on getting worse and worse, so my life grew worse and worse," he thought. "There is one bright spot there at the back, at the beginning of life, and afterwards all becomes blacker and blacker and proceeds more and more rapidly—in inverse ratio to the square of the distance from death," thought Ivan Ilych. And the example of a stone falling downwards with increasing velocity entered his mind. Life, a series of increasing sufferings, flies further and further towards its end—the most terrible suffering. "I am flying . . ." He shuddered, shifted himself, and tried to resist, but was already aware that resistance was impossible, and again with eyes weary of gazing but unable to cease seeing what was before them, he stared at the back of the sofa and waited—awaiting that dreadful fall and shock and destruction.

"Resistance is impossible!" he said to himself. "If I could only understand what it is all for! But that too is impossible. An explanation would be possible if it could be said that I have not lived as I ought to. But it is impossible to say that," and he remembered all the legality, correctitude, and propriety of his life. "That at any rate can certainly not be admitted," he thought, and his lips smiled ironically as if someone could see that smile and be taken in by it. "There is no explanation! Agony, death . . . What for?"

XI

Another two weeks went by in this way and during that fortnight an event occurred that Ivan Ilych and his wife had desired. Petrishchev formally proposed. It happened in the evening. The next day Praskovya Fëdorovna came into her husband's room considering how best to inform him of it, but that very night there had been a fresh change for the worse in his condition. She found him lying on the sofa but in a different position. He lay on his back, groaning and staring fixedly in front of him.

She began to remind him of his medicines, but he turned his eyes towards her with such a look that she did not finish what she was saying; so great an animosity, to her in particular, did that look express.

"For Christ's sake let me die in peace!" he said.

She would have gone away, but just then their daughter came in and went up to say good morning. He looked at her as he had done at his wife, and in reply to her inquiry about his health said dryly that he would soon free them all of himself. They were both silent and after sitting with him for a while went away.

"Is it our fault?" Lisa said to her mother. "It's as if we were to blame! I am sorry for papa, but why should we be tortured?"

The doctor came at his usual time. Ivan Ilych answered "Yes" and "No," never taking his angry eyes from him, and at last said: "You know you can do nothing for me, so leave me alone."

"We can ease your sufferings."

"You can't even do that. Let me be."

The doctor went into the drawing-room and told Praskovya Fëdorovna that the case was very serious and that the only resource left was opium to allay her husband's sufferings, which must be terrible.

It was true, as the doctor said, that Ivan Ilych's physical sufferings were terrible, but worse than the physical sufferings were his mental sufferings, which were his chief torture.

His mental sufferings were due to the fact that that night, as he looked at Gerasim's sleepy, good-natured face with its prominent cheek-bones, the question suddenly occurred to him: "What if my whole life has really been wrong?"

It occurred to him that what had appeared perfectly impossible before, namely that he had not spent his life as he should have done, might after all be true. It occurred to him that his scarcely perceptible attempts to struggle against what was considered good by the most highly placed people, those scarcely noticeable impulses which he had immediately suppressed, might have been the real thing, and all the rest false. And his professional duties and the whole arrangement of his life and of his family, and all his social and official interests, might all have been false. He tried to defend all those things to himself and suddenly felt the weakness of what he was defending. There was nothing to defend.

"But if that is so," he said to himself, "and I am leaving this life with the consciousness that I have lost all that was given me and it is impossible to rectify it—what then?"

He lay on his back and began to pass his life in review in quite a new way. In the morning when he saw first his footman, then his wife, then his daughter, and then the doctor, their every word and movement confirmed to him the awful truth that had been revealed to him during the night. In them he saw himself—all that for which he had lived—and saw clearly that it was not real at all, but a terrible and huge deception which had hidden both life and death. This consciousness intensified his physical suffering tenfold. He groaned and tossed about, and pulled at his clothing which choked and stifled him. And he hated them on that account.

He was given a large dose of opium and became unconscious, but at noon his sufferings began again. He drove everybody away and tossed from side to side.

His wife came to him and said:

"Jean, my dear, do this for me. It can't do any harm and often helps. Healthy people often do it."

He opened his eyes wide.

"What? Take communion? Why? It's unnecessary! However . . ."

She began to cry.

"Yes, do, my dear. I'll send for our priest. He is such a nice man."

"All right. Very well," he muttered.

When the priest came and heard his confession, Ivan Ilych was softened and seemed to feel a relief from his doubts and consequently from his sufferings, and for a moment there came a ray of hope. He again began to think of the vermiform appendix and the possibility of correcting it. He received the sacrament with tears in his eyes.

When they laid him down again afterwards he felt a moment's ease, and the hope that he might live awoke in him again. He began to think of the operation that had been suggested to him. "To live! I want to live!" he said to himself.

His wife came to congratulate him after his communion, and when uttering the usual conventional words she added:

"You feel better, don't you?"

Without looking at her he said "Yes."

Her dress, her figure, the expression of her face, the tone of her voice, all revealed the same thing. "This is wrong, it is not as it should be. All you have lived for and still live for is falsehood and deception, hiding life and death from you." And as soon as he admitted that thought, his hatred and his agonizing physical suffering again sprang up, and with that suffering a consciousness of the unavoidable, approaching end. And to this was added a new sensation of grinding shooting pain and feeling of suffocation.

The expression of his face when he uttered that "yes" was dreadful. Having uttered it, he looked her straight in the eyes, turned on his face with a rapidity extraordinary in his weak state and shouted:

"Go away! Go away and leave me alone!"

XII

From that moment the screaming began that continued for three days, and was so terrible that one could not hear it through two closed doors without horror. At the moment he answered his wife he realized that he was lost, that there was no return, that the end had come, the very end, and his doubts were still unsolved and remained doubts.

"Oh! Oh! Oh!" he cried in various intonations. He had begun by screaming "I won't!" and continued screaming on the letter *O*.

For three whole days, during which time did not exist for him, he struggled in that black sack into which he was being thrust by an invisible, resistless force. He struggled as a man condemned to death struggles in the hands of the executioner, knowing that he cannot save himself. And every moment he felt that despite all his efforts he was drawing nearer and nearer to what terrified him. He felt that his agony was due to his being thrust into that black hole and still more to his not being able to get right into it. He was hindered from getting into it by his conviction that his life had been a good one. That very justification of his life held him fast and prevented his moving forward, and it caused him most torment of all.

Suddenly some force struck him in the chest and side, making it still harder to breathe, and he fell through the hole and there at the bottom was a light. What had happened to him was like the sensation one sometimes experiences in a railway carriage when one thinks one is going backwards while one is really going forwards and suddenly becomes aware of the real direction.

"Yes, it was all not the right thing," he said to himself, "but that's no matter. It can be done. But what *is* the right thing?" he asked himself, and suddenly grew quiet.

This occurred at the end of the third day, two hours before his death. Just then his schoolboy son had crept softly in and gone up to the bedside. The dying man was still screaming and waving his arms. His hand fell on the boy's head, and the boy caught it, pressed it to his lips, and began to cry.

At that very moment Ivan Ilych fell through and caught sight of the light, and it was revealed to him that though his life had not been what it should have been, this could still be rectified. He asked himself, "What *is* the right thing?" and grew still, listening. Then he felt that someone was kissing his hand. He opened his eyes, looked at his son, and felt sorry for him. His wife came up to him and he glanced at her. She was gazing at him openmouthed, with undried tears on her nose and cheek and a despairing look on her face. He felt sorry for her too.

"Yes, I am making them wretched," he thought. "They are sorry, but it will be better for them when I die." He wished to say this but had not the strength to utter it. "Besides, why speak? I must act," he thought. With a look at his wife he indicated his son and said: "Take him away . . . sorry for him . . . sorry for you too . . ." He tried to add, "forgive me," but said "forgo" and waved his hand, knowing that He whose understanding mattered would understand.

And suddenly it grew clear to him that what had been oppressing him and would not leave him was dropping away at once from two sides, from ten sides, and from all sides. He was sorry for them, he must act so as not to hurt them and free himself from these sufferings. "How good and how simple!" he thought. "And the pain?" he asked himself. "What has become of it? Where are you, pain?"

He turned his attention to it.

"Yes, here it is. Well, what of it? Let the pain be."

"And death . . . where is it?"

He sought his former accustomed fear of death and did not find it. "Where is it? What death?" There was no fear because there was no death.

In place of death there was light.

"So that's what it is!" he suddenly exclaimed aloud. "What joy!"

To him all this happened in a single instant, and the meaning of that instant did not change. For those present his agony continued for another two hours. Something rattled in his throat, his emaciated body twitched, then the gasping and rattle became less and less frequent.

"It is finished!" said someone near him.

He heard these words and repeated them in his soul.

"Death is finished," he said to himself. "It is no more!"

He drew in a breath, stopped in the midst of a sigh, stretched out, and died.

The Jilting of
Granny Weatherall

Katherine Anne Porter

She flicked her wrist neatly out of Doctor Harry's pudgy careful fingers and pulled the sheet up to her chin. The brat ought to be in knee breeches. Doctoring around the country with spectacles on his nose! "Get along now, take your schoolbooks and go. There's nothing wrong with me."

Doctor Harry spread a warm paw like a cushion on her forehead where the forked green vein danced and made her eyelids twitch. "Now, now, be a good girl, and we'll have you up in no time."

"That's no way to speak to a woman nearly eighty years old just because she's down. I'd have you respect your elders, young man."

"Well, Missy, excuse me." Doctor Harry patted her cheek. "But I've got to warn you, haven't I? You're a marvel, but you must be careful or you're going to be good and sorry."

"Don't tell me what I'm going to be. I'm on my feet now, morally speaking. It's Cornelia. I had to go to bed to get rid of her."

Her bones felt loose, and floated around in her skin, and Doctor Harry floated like a balloon around the foot of the bed. He floated and pulled down his waistcoat and swung his glasses on a cord. "Well, stay where you are, it certainly can't hurt you."

"Get along and doctor your sick," said Granny Weatherall. "Leave a well woman alone. I'll call for you when I want you. . . . Where were you forty years ago when I pulled through milk-leg and double pneumonia? You weren't even born. Don't let Cornelia lead you on,'' she shouted, because Doctor Harry appeared to float up to the ceiling and out. "I pay my own bills, and I don't throw my money away on nonsense!''

She meant to wave good-by, but it was too much trouble. Her eyes closed of themselves, it was like a dark curtain drawn around the bed. The pillow rose and floated under her, pleasant as a hammock in a light wind. She listened to the leaves rustling outside the window. No, somebody was swishing newspapers: no, Cornelia and Doctor Harry were whispering together. She leaped broad awake, thinking they whispered in her ear.

"She was never like this, *never* like this!'' "Well, what can we expect?'' "Yes, eighty years old. . . .''

Well, and what if she was? She still had ears. It was like Cornelia to whisper around doors. She always kept things secret in such a public way. She was always being tactful and kind. Cornelia was dutiful; that was the trouble with her. Dutiful and good: "So good and dutiful,'' said Granny, "that I'd like to spank her.'' She saw herself spanking Cornelia and making a fine job of it.

"What'd you say, Mother?''

Granny felt her face tying up in hard knots.

"Can't a body think, I'd like to know?''

"I thought you might want something.''

"I do. I want a lot of things. First off, go away and don't whisper.''

She lay and drowsed, hoping in her sleep that the children would keep out and let her rest a minute. It had been a long day. Not that she was tired. It was always pleasant to snatch a minute now and then. There was always so much to be done, let me see: tomorrow.

Tomorrow was far away and there was nothing to trouble about. Things were finished somehow when the time came; thank God there was always a little margin over for peace: Then a person could spread out the plan of life and tuck in the edges orderly. It was good to have everything clean and folded away, with the hair brushes and tonic bottles sitting straight on the white embroidered linen: the day started without fuss and the pantry shelves laid out with rows of jelly glasses and brown jugs and white stone-china jars with blue whirligigs and words painted on them: coffee, tea, sugar, ginger, cinnamon, allspice: and the bronze clock with the lion on top nicely dusted off. The dust that lion could collect in twenty-four hours! The box in the attic with all those letters tied up, well, she'd have to go through that tomorrow. All those letters—George's letters and John's letters and her letters to them both—lying around for the children to find afterwards made her uneasy. Yes, that would be tomorrow's business. No use to let them know how silly she had been once.

While she was rummaging around she found death in her mind and it felt clammy and unfamiliar. She had spent so much time preparing for death there was no need for bringing it up again. Let it take care of itself now. When she was sixty she had felt very old, finished, and went around making farewell trips to see her children and grandchildren, with a secret in her mind: This is the very last of your mother, children! Then she made her will and came down with a long fever. That was all just a notion like a lot of other things, but it was lucky too, for she had once for all got over the idea of dying for a long time. Now she couldn't be worried. She hoped she had better sense now. Her father had lived to be one hundred and two years old and had drunk a noggin of strong hot toddy on his last birthday. He told the reporters it was his daily habit, and he owed his long life to that. He had made quite a scandal and was very pleased about it. She believed she'd just plague Cornelia a little.

"Cornelia! Cornelia!" No footsteps, but a sudden hand on her cheek. "Bless you, where have you been?"

"Here, Mother."

"Well, Cornelia, I want a noggin of hot toddy."

"Are you cold, darling?"

"I'm chilly, Cornelia. Lying in bed stops the circulation. I must have told you that a thousand times."

Well, she could just hear Cornelia telling her husband that Mother was getting a little childish and they'd have to humor her. The thing that most annoyed her was that Cornelia thought she was deaf, dumb, and blind. Little hasty glances and tiny gestures tossed around her and over her head saying, "Don't cross her, let her have her way, she's eighty years old," and she sitting there as if she lived in a thin glass cage. Sometimes Granny almost made up her mind to pack up and move back to her own house where nobody could remind her every minute that she was old. Wait, wait, Cornelia, till your own children whisper behind your back!

In her day she had kept a better house and had got more work done. She wasn't too old yet for Lydia to be driving eighty miles for advice when one of the children jumped the track, and Jimmy still dropped in and talked things over: "Now, Mammy, you've a good business head, I want to know what you think of this? . . ." Old. Cornelia couldn't change the furniture around without asking. Little things, little things! They had been so sweet when they were little. Granny wished the old days were back again with the children young and everything to be done over. It had been a hard pull, but not too much for her. When she thought of all the food she had cooked, and all the clothes she had cut and sewed, and all the gardens she had made—well, the children showed it. There they were, made out of her, and they couldn't get away from that. Sometimes she wanted to see John again and point to them and say, Well, I didn't do so badly, did I? But that would have to wait. That was for tomorrow. She used to think of him as a man, but now all the children were older than their father, and he would be a child beside her if she saw him now. It seemed strange and there was something wrong in the idea. Why, he couldn't possibly recognize her. She had fenced in a hundred acres once, digging the post holes herself and clamping the wires with just a negro boy to help. That changed a woman. John would be looking for a young woman with the peaked Spanish comb in her hair and the painted fan. Digging post holes changed a woman. Riding country roads in the winter when women had their babies was another thing: sitting up nights with sick horses and sick negroes and sick children and hardly ever losing one. John, I hardly ever lost one of them! John would see that in a minute, that would be something he could understand, she wouldn't have to explain anything!

It made her feel like rolling up her sleeves and putting the whole place to rights again. No matter if Cornelia was determined to be everywhere at once, there were a great many things left undone on this place. She would start to-morrow and do them. It was good to be strong enough for everything, even if all you made melted and changed and slipped under your hands, so that by the time you finished you almost forgot what you were working for. What was it I set out to do? she asked herself intently, but she could not remember. A fog rose over the valley, she saw it marching across the creek swallowing the trees and moving up the hill like an army of ghosts. Soon it would be at the near edge of the orchard, and then it was time to go in and light the lamps. Come in, children, don't stay out in the night air.

Lighting the lamps had been beautiful. The children huddled up to her and breathed like little calves waiting at the bars in the twilight. Their eyes fol-lowed the match and watched the flame rise and settle in a blue curve, then they moved away from her. The lamp was lit, they didn't have to be scared and hang on to mother any more. Never, never, never more. God, for all my life I thank Thee. Without Thee, my God, I could never have done it. Hail, Mary, full of grace.

I want you to pick all the fruit this year and see that nothing is wasted. There's always someone who can use it. Don't let good things rot for want of using. You waste life when you waste good food. Don't let things get lost. It's bitter to lose things. Now, don't let me get to thinking, not when I am tired and taking a little nap before supper. . . .

The pillow rose about her shoulders and pressed against her heart and the memory was being squeezed out of it: oh, push down the pillow, somebody: it would smother her if she tried to hold it. Such a fresh breeze blowing and such a green day with no threats in it. But he had not come, just the same. What does a woman do when she has put on the white veil and set out the white cake for a man and he doesn't come? She tried to remember. No, I swear he never harmed me but in that. He never harmed me but in that . . . and what if he did? There was the day, the day, but a whirl of dark smoke rose and covered it, crept up and over into the bright field where everything was planted so care-fully in orderly rows. That was hell, she knew hell when she saw it. For sixty years she had prayed against remembering him and against losing her soul in the deep pit of hell, and now the two things were mingled in one and the thought of him was a smoky cloud from hell that moved and crept in her head when she had just got rid of Doctor Harry and was trying to rest a minute. Wounded vanity, Ellen, said a sharp voice in the top of her mind. Don't let your wounded vanity get the upper hand of you. Plenty of girls get jilted. You were jilted, weren't you? Then stand up to it. Her eyelids wavered and let in streamers of blue-gray light like tissue paper over her eyes. She must get up and pull the shades down or she'd never sleep. She was in bed again and the shades were not down. How could that happen? Better turn over, hide from the light, sleeping in the light gave you nightmares. "Mother, how do you feel now?" and a stinging wetness on her forehead. But I don't like having my face washed in cold water!

Hapsy? George? Lydia? Jimmy? No, Cornelia, and her features were swollen and full of little puddles. "They're coming, darling, they'll all be here soon." Go wash your face, child, you look funny.

Instead of obeying, Cornelia knelt down and put her head on the pillow. She seemed to be talking but there was no sound. "Well, are you tongue-tied? Whose birthday is it? Are you going to give a party?"

Cornelia's mouth moved urgently in strange shapes. "Don't do that, you bother me, daughter."

"Oh, no, Mother. Oh, no. . . ."

Nonsense. It was strange about children. They disputed your every word. "No what, Cornelia?"

"Here's Doctor Harry."

"I won't see that boy again. He just left five minutes ago."

"That was this morning, Mother. It's night now. Here's the nurse."

"This is Doctor Harry, Mrs. Weatherall. I never saw you look so young and happy!"

"Ah, I'll never be young again—but I'd be happy if they'd let me lie in peace and get rested."

She thought she spoke up loudly, but no one answered. A warm weight on her forehead, a warm bracelet on her wrist, and a breeze went on whispering, trying to tell her something. A shuffle of leaves in the everlasting hand of God, He blew on them and they danced and rattled. "Mother, don't mind, we're going to give you a little hypodermic." "Look here, daughter, how do ants get in this bed? I saw sugar ants yesterday." Did you send for Hapsy too?

It was Hapsy she really wanted. She had to go a long way back through a great many rooms to find Hapsy standing with a baby on her arm. She seemed to herself to be Hapsy also, and the baby on Hapsy's arm was Hapsy and himself and herself, all at once, and there was no surprise in the meeting. Then Hapsy melted from within and turned flimsy as gray gauze and the baby was a gauzy shadow, and Hapsy came up close and said, "I thought you'd never come," and looked at her very searchingly and said, "You haven't changed a bit!" They leaned forward to kiss, when Cornelia began whispering from a long way off, "Oh, is there anything you want to tell me? Is there anything I can do for you?"

Yes, she had changed her mind after sixty years and she would like to see George. I want you to find George. Find him and be sure to tell him I forgot him. I want him to know I had my husband just the same and my children and my house like any other woman. A good house too and a good husband that I loved and fine children out of him. Better than I hoped for even. Tell him I was given back everything he took away and more. Oh, no, oh, God, no, there was something else besides the house and the man and the children. Oh, surely they were not all? What was it? Something not given back. . . . Her breath crowded down under her ribs and grew into a monstrous frightening shape with cutting edges; it bored up into her head, and the agony was unbelievable: Yes, John, get the Doctor now, no more talk, my time has come.

When this one was born it should be the last. The last. It should have been born first, for it was the one she had truly wanted. Everything came in good time. Nothing left out, left over. She was strong, in three days she would be as well as ever. Better. A woman needed milk in her to have her full health.

"Mother, do you hear me?"

"I've been telling you—"

"Mother, Father Connolly's here."

"I went to Holy Communion only last week. Tell him I'm not so sinful as all that."

"Father just wants to speak to you."

He could speak as much as he pleased. It was like him to drop in and inquire about her soul as if it were a teething baby, and then stay on for a cup of tea and a round of cards and gossip. He always had a funny story of some sort, usually about an Irishman who made his little mistakes and confessed them, and the point lay in some absurd thing he would blurt out in the confessional showing his struggles between native piety and original sin. Granny felt easy about her soul. Cornelia, where are your manners? Give Father Connolly a chair. She had her secret comfortable understanding with a few favorite saints who cleared a straight road to God for her. All as surely signed and sealed as the papers for the new Forty Acres. Forever . . . heirs and assigns forever. Since the day the wedding cake was not cut, but thrown out and wasted. The whole bottom dropped out of the world, and there she was blind and sweating with nothing under her feet and the walls falling away. His hand had caught her under the breast, she had not fallen, there was the freshly polished floor with the green rug on it, just as before. He had cursed like a sailor's parrot and said, "I'll kill him for you." Don't lay a hand on him, for my sake leave something to God. "Now, Ellen, you must believe what I tell you. . . ."

So there was nothing, nothing to worry about any more, except sometimes in the night one of the children screamed in a nightmare, and they both hustled out shaking and hunting for the matches and calling, "There, wait a minute, here we are!" John, get the doctor now, Hapsy's time has come. But there was Hapsy standing by the bed in a white cap. "Cornelia, tell Hapsy to take off her cap. I can't see her plain."

Her eyes opened very wide and the room stood out like a picture she had seen somewhere. Dark colors with the shadows rising towards the ceiling in long angles. The tall black dresser gleamed with nothing on it but John's picture, enlarged from a little one, with John's eyes very black when they should have been blue. You never saw him, so how do you know how he looked? But the man insisted the copy was perfect, it was very rich and handsome. For a picture, yes, but it's not my husband. The table by the bed had a linen cover and a candle and a crucifix. The light was blue from Cornelia's silk lampshades. No sort of light at all, just frippery. You had to live forty years with kerosene lamps to appreciate honest electricity. She felt very strong and she saw Doctor Harry with a rosy nimbus around him.

"You look like a saint, Doctor Harry, and I vow that's as near as you'll ever come to it."

"She's saying something."

"I heard you, Cornelia. What's all this carrying-on?"

"Father Connolly's saying—"

Cornelia's voice staggered and bumped like a cart in a bad road. It rounded corners and turned back again and arrived nowhere. Granny stepped up in the cart very lightly and reached for the reins, but a man sat beside her and she knew him by his hands, driving the cart. She did not look in his face, for she knew without seeing, but looked instead down the road where the trees leaned over and bowed to each other and a thousand birds were singing a Mass. She felt like singing too, but she put her hand in the bosom of her dress and pulled out a rosary, and Father Connolly murmured Latin in a very solemn voice and tickled her feet. My God, will you stop that nonsense? I'm a married woman. What if he did run away and leave me to face the priest by myself? I found another a whole world better. I wouldn't have exchanged my husband for anybody except St. Michael himself, and you may tell him that for me with a thank you in the bargain.

Light flashed on her closed eyelids, and a deep roaring shook her. Cornelia, is that lightning? I hear thunder. There's going to be a storm. Close all the windows. Call the children in. . . . "Mother, here we are, all of us." "Is that you, Hapsy?" "Oh, no, I'm Lydia. We drove as fast as we could." Their faces drifted above her, drifted away. The rosary fell out of her hands and Lydia put it back. Jimmy tried to help, their hands fumbled together, and Granny closed two fingers around Jimmy's thumb. Beads wouldn't do, it must be something alive. She was so amazed her thoughts ran round and round. So, my dear Lord, this is my death and I wasn't even thinking about it. My children have come to see me die. But I can't, it's not time. Oh, I always hated surprises. I wanted to give Cornelia the amethyst set—Cornelia, you're to have the amethyst set, but Hapsy's to wear it when she wants, and, Doctor Harry, do shut up. Nobody sent for you. Oh, my dear Lord, do wait a minute. I meant to do something about the Forty Acres, Jimmy doesn't need it and Lydia will later on, with that worthless husband of hers. I meant to finish the altar cloth and send six bottles of wine to Sister Borgia for her dyspepsia. I want to send six bottles of wine to Sister Borgia, Father Connolly, now don't let me forget.

Cornelia's voice made short turns and tilted over and crashed. "Oh, Mother, oh, Mother, oh, Mother. . . ."

"I'm not going, Cornelia. I'm taken by surprise. I can't go."

You'll see Hapsy again. What about her? "I thought you'd never come." Granny made a long journey outward, looking for Hapsy. What if I don't find her? What then? Her heart sank down and down, there was no bottom to death, she couldn't come to the end of it. The blue light from Cornelia's lampshade drew into a tiny point in the center of her brain, it flickered and winked like an eye, quietly it fluttered and dwindled. Granny lay curled down within herself, amazed and watchful, staring at the point of light that was herself; her body was now only a deeper mass of shadow in an endless darkness and this darkness would curl around the light and swallow it up. God, give a sign!

For the second time there was no sign. Again no bridegroom and the priest in the house. She could not remember any other sorrow because this grief wiped them all away. Oh, no, there's nothing more cruel than this—I'll never forgive it. She stretched herself with a deep breath and blew out the light.

The Widow

Lusin

Translated from the Chinese by Chi-Chen Wang

The year-end according to the old calendar is, after all, more like what a year-end should be, for the holiday spirit is not only reflected in the life of the people, but seems to pervade the atmosphere itself. Frequent flashes light up the heavy, gray evening clouds, followed by the crisp report of firecrackers set off in honor of the Kitchen God. Those fired in the immediate neighborhood explode, of course, with a louder noise, and before the deafening sound has ceased ringing in one's ears, the air is filled with the acrid aroma of sulphuric smoke. On such an evening I returned for a visit to my native village, Luchen. As we no longer had a house there, I stayed with His Honor Lu the Fourth. He was my kin—my Uncle Four, as he was one generation above me—and a very moral and righteous old graduate. He had not changed much since my previous visit; he had grown a little older, but he did not yet have a beard. After we had exchanged greetings, he remarked that I was stouter, and immediately thereafter launched into a tirade against the reform movement. I knew, however, that his tirade was not directed against me but against the ancient reformers of the nineties, such as K'ang Yu-wei. In any case we could not be said to understand each other, and I was left alone in the study shortly afterwards.

I got up very late the next day. After the midday meal I went out to call on friends and relatives. On the third day I did the same thing. None of them had changed much, they were merely a little older. All were busy with the preparations for the Invocation of Blessings, the most solemn and elaborate ceremony of the year, at which they offered the most generous sacrifices to the God of Blessings and prayed for good luck for the coming year. Chickens and ducks were killed and pork was bought at the butcher's. Carefully washed by women (whose hands and arms—some adorned with silver bracelets—became red from long immersions in the water), and then boiled and studded with chopsticks, they were offered with candles and incense in the early hour of the fifth watch. Only the male members of the family participated in the ceremony, which was always concluded with firecrackers. Every year it was like this in families that could afford it, and so it was this year.

The overcast sky grew darker and darker, and in the afternoon it began to snow. The dancing snowflakes, as large as plum flowers, the smoke from burning incense and from the chimneys, and the bustle of the people all gave Luchen a festive air. When I returned to Uncle Four's stody, the rooftops were white, making the room lighter than usual at that hour. I could make out very clearly the large shou (longevity) character on a scroll hung on the wall, a rubbing based on what was supposed to be the actual handwriting of the Taoist immortal Ch'en T'uan. One of the side scrolls had come off and lay loosely rolled up on the long table against the wall; the one still hanging on the wall expressed the sentiment "Peace comes with understanding." I strolled over to the desk by the window and looked over the books. There were only a few odd volumes of the K'ang Hsi Dictionary and an annotated edition of the *Analects*.

I decided that I must leave the next day, whatever happened. What had depressed me most was a meeting with Sister Hsiang-lin the day before. I encountered her in the afternoon as I was returning home along the riverbank after visiting some friends in the eastern part of the village, and by the direction of her vacant stare I knew that she was heading for me. Of the people that I had seen at Luchen on this visit no one had changed as much as she. Her gray hair of five years ago had turned entirely white; she was not at all like a woman of only forty. Her face was intolerably drawn and thin; it had lost its sad and sorrowful aspect and was now as expressionless as if carved of wood. Only an occasional movement of her eyes indicated that she was still a living creature. She held in one hand a bamboo basket containing a chipped and empty bowl; with the other hand, she supported herself with a bamboo stick, a little split at the lower end. She had evidently become a beggar.

I stopped, expecting her to ask for money.

"Have you come back?" she asked.

"Yes."

"I am very glad. You are a scholar, and you have been to the outside world and learned of many things. I want to ask you about something." Her lusterless eyes suddenly lighted up as she advanced a few steps towards me, lowered her voice, and said in a very earnest and confidential manner, "It is this: is there another life after this one?"

I was taken aback by the unexpectedness of the question; the wild look in her eyes, which were fixed on mine, gave me a creepy sensation on my back and made me feel more uncomfortable than I used to at school when an examination was sprung upon us, with the teacher watching vigilantly by our side. I had never concerned myself with the afterlife. How was I to answer her now? Most people here believe in the survival of the soul, I thought rapidly as I considered an answer, but this woman seemed to have her doubts. Perhaps it was a matter of hope with her, the hope that there was an afterlife and that the afterlife would be a better one than this. Why should I add to the unhappiness of this miserable woman? For her sake I had better say that there was another life after this one.

"Maybe there is . . . I think," I said haltingly and without conviction.

"Then there would also be a hell?"

"Oh! Hell?" I was again taken unawares and so I temporized, "Hell?—It would seem logical . . . though it may not necessarily exist . . . but who cares about such things?"

"Then we will meet members of our family after death?"

"Er, er, do we meet them?" I then realized that I was still a very ignorant man and that no amount of temporizing and cogitation would enable me to stand the test of three questions. I became less and less sure of myself and wished to recant all that I had said. "That . . . but really, I cannot say. I cannot really say whether souls survive or not."

Before she could ask any more questions, I fled back to Uncle Four's house very much agitated in spirit. I told myself that my answer to her questions might lead to something unfortunate and that I should be held responsible for what might happen. She probably felt lonely and unhappy at a time when others were celebrating; but was that all, or had she formed a definite plan of action? Then I laughed at myself for taking such a trivial incident so seriously, for pondering upon it and analyzing it. The psychologist would undoubtedly call such a morbid interest or fear pathological. Besides, had I not explicitly said "I cannot really say," thus annulling all my answers and relieving myself of all responsibility?

"I cannot really say" is a very useful sentence. Inexperienced youths are often rash enough to give answers to the difficult problems of life and prescribe remedies for others, and thus lay themselves open to blame when things go wrong. If, however, they qualify their statements by concluding them with "I cannot really say," they will assure themselves of a safe and happy life. I then realized the indispensability of this sentence, indispensable even when one is talking with a beggarwoman.

But my uneasiness persisted; I kept recalling the meeting with a presentiment of evil. On this dark, heavy, snowy afternoon in that dreary study my uneasiness became stronger. I felt I had better go away and spend a day at the county seat. I recalled Fu-hsing-lou's excellent shark's fin cooked in clear broth at only a dollar a plate, and wondered if the price had gone up. Although my friends of former days had scattered hither and yon, I must not fail to feast upon this delicacy, even if I had to eat by myself. Whatever happens, I must leave this place tomorrow, I repeated to myself.

Because I have often seen things happen which I had hoped would not happen, which I had told myself might not necessarily happen, but which had a way of happening just the same, I was very much afraid that it would be so on this occasion. And surely something did happen, for towards evening I overheard a discussion going on in the inner courtyard. Presently it stopped, and after a silence I distinguished the voice of Uncle Four.

"Of course a *thing like that* would choose of all times a time like this."

"I was first puzzled and then felt uncomfortable, for the remark sounded as if it might have something to do with me. I looked out the door but did not see anyone that I could ask. Not until the hired man came in to replenish my tea toward suppertime did I have an opportunity to make inquiries.

"With whom was His Honor Four angry a little while ago?" I asked.

"Who else but Sister Hsiang-lin?" he answered very simply.

"Sister Hsiang-lin? What did she do?" I hurriedly pursued.

"She died."

"Died?" My heart sank and I almost jumped. My face must have changed color. But the man did not raise his head and so did not notice it. I calmed myself and continued:

"When did she die?"

"When? Last night or early this morning. I can't really say."

"What did she die of?"

"What did she die of? Why, what else would it be if not poverty?" the man answered in a matter of course way and went out without ever raising his head to look at me.

My terror was transient, for I realized that, since that which was to come to pass had come to pass, there was no longer need for me to worry about my responsibility. Gradually I regained my composure; a sense of regret and disquiet only occasionally intruded. Supper was served, with Uncle Four keeping me company. I wanted to find out more about Sister Hsiang-lin, but I knew that though he had read that "Ghosts and spirits are only the manifestations of the two cardinal principles of nature," he was still subject to many taboos; that such topics as sickness and death should be carefully avoided at a time when New Year blessings were about to be asked; and that if I must satisfy my curiosity, I should resort to some well-considered euphemism. As I unfortunately knew no such euphemisms, I withheld the question I was several times on the point of asking. From the look of displeasure on his face I began to imagine it quite possible that he considered me a "thing like that" for coming to bother him at such a time; thereupon I hastened to set him at ease and told him that I was going to leave Luchen the following day. He did not show much warmth in urging me to stay. Thus we dragged through supper.

Winter days are short at best, and, with snow falling, night soon enveloped the village. Everyone was busy by the lamplight, but outdoors it was quiet and still. Falling upon a thick mattress of snow, the flakes seemed to swish-swish, making one feel all the more lonely and depressed. Sitting alone under the yellow light of the vegetable-oil lamp, I thought of the fate of the poor, forlorn woman who had been cast into the garbage dump like a discarded toy. Hitherto she had continued to remind people of her miserable existence in the garbage dump, much to the surprise and wonder of those who have reason to find life worth living. Now she had at last been swept away clean by the Unpredictable.

Whether souls continue to exist or not I do not know, but I did know that at least one who had no reason to find life worth living was at last no longer living and that those who looked upon her as an eyesore no longer had to look at her. It was a good thing, whether looked at from her point of view or from that of others. As I listened to the swish-swashing of the snowflakes outside and pondered along this line of thought I began to take comfort and to feel better.

And I began to put together the fragments that I had heard about her until her story became a fairly coherent whole.

Sister Hsiang-lin was not a native of Luchen. One year in the early part of winter they needed a new maid at Uncle Four's and the middlewoman, old Mrs. Wei, had brought her. She wore a black skirt, a blue, lined coat and a light blue vest, and her hair was tied with white strings as a sign of mourning. She was about twenty-six years old, of a dark yellow complexion, with a faint suggestion of color in her cheeks. Old Mrs. Wei called her Sister Hsiang-lin, said that she was a neighbor of her mother's and that as her husband had recently died she had come out to seek employment. Uncle Four frowned and Aunt Four guessed the cause; he did not like the idea of widows. But the woman had regular features and large, strong hands and feet. She was quiet and docile and it appeared that she would make an industrious and faithful servant. Aunt Four kept her in spite of Uncle Four's frown. During the trial period she worked all day as though unhappy without employment. She was strong and could do everything that a man could do. On the third day they decided to keep her, at a monthly wage of 500 *cash*.

Everyone called her Sister Hsiang-lin; no one asked her surname, but since the middlewoman was from Weichiashan and said that she was a neighbor of her mother's, her name was probably Wei. She was not talkative and spoke only in answer to questions, and that rather briefly. Not until after some ten days did it gradually become known that she had at home a stern mother-in-law, a brother-in-law about ten years old and able to go out to gather fuel, and that her husband who had died in the spring was ten years younger than she and also made his living by cutting firewood. This was all that was known about her.

The days went by quickly and she showed no signs of losing her initial industry; she never complained about her fare or spared her strength. People all talked about the woman help in the house of His Honor Lu who was more capable and industrious than a man. At the year-end she did all the cleaning, sweeping, and killed the chickens and ducks and cooked them; it was actually not necessary to hire temporary help. She seemed happy too; her face grew fuller and traces of smiles appeared around the corners of her mouth.

But shortly after the New Year she returned one day, pale and agitated, from washing rice at the river; she said she had seen a man who looked like an elder cousin-in-law loitering in the distance on the opposite bank, and she feared he was watching her. Aunt Four questioned her but could get no more out of her.

When he heard of this incident, Uncle Four knitted his brows and said, "I do not like it. I am afraid that she ran away from home."

As a matter of fact, she had come away without her mother-in-law's permission, and it was not long before this supposition proved to be true.

About ten days later, when the incident had been almost forgotten, old Mrs. Wei suddenly appeared with a woman about thirty years old, whom she introduced as Sister Hsiang-lin's mother-in-law. Though dressed like a woman from the hill villages, she was self-composed and capable of speech. She apologized for her intrusion and said that she had come to take her daughter-in-law home to help with the spring chores, as only she and her young son were at home.

"What else can we do since her mother-in-law wants her back?" Uncle Four said.

Therefore, her wages, which amounted to 1,750 *cash* and of which she had not spent a penny, were handed over to the mother-in-law. The woman took Sister Hsiang-lin's clothes, expressed her thanks, and went away.

Sister Hsiang-lin was not present during this transaction and it did not occur to Aunt and Uncle Four to summon her. It was not until toward noon when she began to feel hungry that Aunt Four suddenly remembered that Sister Hsiang-lin had gone out to wash rice and wondered what had happened to her.

"Aiya! Where is the rice?" she exclaimed. "Did not Sister Hsiang-lin go out to wash the rice?"

She began searching for the washing basket, first in the kitchen, then in the courtyard, then in the bedroom, but there was no trace of it. Uncle Four looked outside the gate but did not see it either, and it was not until he went to the river that he saw the basket resting peacefully on the bank, a head of green vegetable beside it.

Then he learned from eyewitnesses what had happened. A covered boat had been moored in the river all morning, but no one paid any attention to it at the time. When Sister Hsiang-lin came out to wash rice, two men that looked like people from the hills jumped out, seized her as she bent over her task and dragged her into the boat. Sister Hsiang-lin uttered a few cries but was soon silent, probably because she was gagged. Then two women embarked, one a stranger and the other old Mrs. Wei. Some thought that they did see Sister Hsiang-lin lying bound on the bottom of the boat.

"The rascals! But . . . ," Uncle Four said.

That day Aunt Four cooked the midday dinner herself, while her son Niu-erh tended the fire.

Old Mrs. Wei returned after the midday dinner.

"What do you mean by your outrageous behavior? And you have the audacity to come back to see us!" Aunt Four said vehemently over the dishwashing. "You brought her here yourself, and then you conspire with them to kidnap her, causing such a scandal. What will people say? Do you want to make a laughingstock of us?"

"Aiya, aiya! I was duped, really, and I have come back to explain. She came to me and asked me to find a place for her. How was I to know that her mother-in-law knew nothing of it? I beg your forgiveness. It was all my fault, old and weak woman that I am. I should have been more careful. Fortunately, your house has been noted for its generosity and I know you would not return measure for measure with people like us. I shall most certainly find you a good maid to atone for myself."

Thus the episode was closed and shortly afterwards forgotten.

Only Aunt Four, who had difficulty in finding a satisfactory servant, sometimes mentioned Sister Hsiang-lin, whose successors either were lazy or complained of their food, or both. "I wonder what has become of her," Aunt Four would say, hoping that she might come back again. By the beginning of the following year she gave up this hope.

Toward the end of the first month, however, old Mrs. Wei came to offer her New Year's greetings. She was slightly intoxicated with wine and said that she had been late in coming because she had visited her mother at Weichiashan for a few days. The conversation naturally turned to Sister Hsiang-lin.

"That one. She has entered her lucky years," old Mrs. Wei said with pleasure. "When her mother-in-law came to get her, she was already promised to Huo Lao-lui of Huochiatsun and so a few days after her return she was put into a wedding-sedan and carried away."

"Aiya! what a mother-in-law!" Aunt Four said, surprised.

"Aiya! you talk exactly like a lady of a great family. Among us poor people in the hills this is nothing. She has a younger brother-in-law who had to get married. If they did not marry her off where were they to get the money for his wedding? Her mother-in-law was a capable and clever one. She knew how to go about things. She married her off into the hills. In the village, she would not have gotten much for Sister Hsiang-lin, but because there are not many who will marry into the hills, she got 80,000 *cash*. Now her second son is married. She spent only 50,000 and had a clear profit of over 10,000 after expenses. See what a good stroke of business that was?"

"But how could Sister Hsiang-lin ever consent to such a thing?"

"What is there to consent or not to consent? Any bride will make a scene; but all one has to do is bind her up, stuff her into the sedan, carry her to the groom's house, put the bridal hat on her, assist her through the ceremony, put her into the bridal chamber, shut the door—and leave the rest to the groom. But Sister Hsiang-lin was different and unusually difficult. People said it was probably because she had worked in the house of a scholar that she acted differently from the common people. *Tai-tai,* we have seen all sorts of them, these 'again' women; we have seen the kind that weep and cry, the kind that attempt suicide, and the kind that spoil the wedding ceremony by upsetting and breaking things. But Sister Hsiang-lin was worse than any of these. I was told that she bellowed and cursed all the way, so that she had lost her voice when she reached the Huo village. Dragging her out of the sedan, three men were not enough to hold her through the ceremony. Once they loosed their hold on her for a moment, and—*Amitofo*—she dashed her head against the corner of the wedding table, and gave herself a big gash. The blood flowed so freely that two handfuls of incense ash and a bandage could not stop it. She continued to curse after she had been dragged into the wedding chamber and shut in with her man. Aiya-ya, I never . . .'' she shook her head, lowered her eyes and was silent for a moment.

"And later?" Aunt Four asked.

"It was said that she did not get up all the next day," she answered, raising her eyes.

"And after that?"

"Well, she got up eventually and by the end of the year she gave birth to a boy. Someone happened to visit the Huo village while I was at my mother's and said on his return that he had seen the mother and the child and that they were both healthy and plump. There is no mother-in-law above her and her man is strong and a willing worker. They have their own house. Ai-ai, she has entered her lucky years.''

After that Aunt Four no longer mentioned Sister Hsiang-lin.

But in the fall of one year—it must have been two years after the news of Sister Hsiang-lin's good luck was brought by Mrs. Wei—she reappeared in the courtyard of Uncle Four's house. She put on the table a round basket in the form of a water chestnut and outside under the eaves she left her bundle of bedding. She wore, as on her first visit, white hairstrings, black skirt, blue, lined coat, light blue vest, and her skin was dark yellow as before, but without any trace of color in her cheeks. Instead, traces of tears could be observed around her eyes, which were not as alive as before. Old Mrs. Wei again accompanied her and made this recital to Aunt Four:

"This is truly what is called 'Heaven has unpredictable storms.' Her man was a strong and sturdy one. Who would ever have thought that he would die of influenza? He had gotten well, but he ate a bowl of cold rice and it came back again. Fortunately she had her son and she was capable, could cut firewood, pick tea, and raise silkworms. She was managing all right. Who would ever have thought that her child would be carried off by a wolf? Spring was nearing its end and yet a wolf appeared in the village. Who would have thought of such a thing? Now she is alone. Her elder brother-in-law took possession of her house and put her out. She is now at the end of her road and has no other way except to appeal to her old mistress. Now she has no entanglements and as *tai-tai* happens to be in need of a new maid I have brought her. I think as she is familiar with things here she would be much better than a strange hand.''

"I was a fool, really," Sister Hsiang-lin raised her lusterless eyes and said. "I knew that the wild beasts came down to the village to seek food when they couldn't find anything in the hills during the snow season, but I did not know they would come down in the spring. I got up early and opened the door. I gave a basket of beans to our Ah Mao and told him to sit on the gate sill and peel them. He was an obedient child and did everything I told him. He went out and I went behind the house to cut wood and wash rice. After putting the rice in the pot, I wanted to put the beans over it to steam. I called Ah Mao but he did not answer. I went out and looked. I saw beans spilled all over the ground but could not see our Ah Mao. He never went out to play at the neighbors' but I went and looked for him. I did not find him. I was frightened and asked people to go out and search for him. In the afternoon they found one of his shoes in the bramble. They all said that there was no hope, that the wolf must have got him. They went into the bush and sure enough they found him lying in the grass, all his insides gone, his hand still holding on tightly to the handle of the basket . . .'' She broke off sobbing.

Aunt Four hesitated at first, but her eyes reddened after hearing the story. Then she told Sister Hsiang-lin to take the basket and bundle to the maid's room. Old Mrs. Wei sighed with relief, and Sister Hsiang-lin seemed to feel better than when she arrived. As she was familiar with the house, she went and set her things in order without being directed, and thenceforward she again became a maidservant at Luchen.

And everybody called her Sister Hsiang-lin as before.

But this time her fortune had changed considerably. Two or three days later her employers realized that her hands were not as clever and efficient as formerly, her memory failed, her deathlike face never showed the shadow of a smile. Aunt Four could not conceal her displeasure. Uncle Four had frowned as usual when she came, but made no protest as he knew how difficult it was to find a satisfactory servant; he only cautioned Aunt Four, saying that though such people were a pitiable lot, yet she was after all a bane against morality, and that it was all right for her to help in ordinary tasks but she must not touch anything in connection with the ancestral sacrifices. These Aunt Four must prepare herself, else they would be unclean and the ancestors would not touch them.

Preparation of the ancestral sacrifices was the most important event in Uncle Four's house and Sister Hsiang-lin used to be busiest at such a time. Now she had nothing to do. When the table was placed in the center of the' hall with a curtain in front of it, she started to arrange the wine cups and chopsticks as she used to do.

"Sister Hsiang-lin, please leave those things alone. I will arrange them," Aunt Four hastened to say.

She drew back her hands in embarrassment and then went to get the candlesticks.

"Sister Hsiang-lin, leave that alone. I'll get it," Aunt Four again said hastily. After hovering around for a little while, Sister Hsiang-lin withdrew in bewilderment. The only thing she was permitted to do that day was to tend the fire in the kitchen.

People in the village still called her Sister Hsiang-lin, but the tone of their voices was different; they still talked with her, but they were scornful of her. She did not seem to notice the change; she only stared vacantly and recited the story that she could not forget, night or day—

"I was a fool, really . . .'' Her tears would flow and her voice grow tremulous.

It was a very effective story; men would stop smiling and walk away in confusion; women not only seemed to forgive her and to banish the look of scorn on their faces, but shed tears with her. Some older women, not having heard her own recital, would come to her and listen to her until her voice broke, when they would let fall the tears that had been gradually accumulating in their eyes, heave some sighs and go away satisfied. She was their chief topic of conversation.

Sister Hsiang-lin continued to repeat her story and often attracted three or five listeners. But the story soon became familiar to everyone, and after a while even the kindest and most patient of old ladies ceased to shed any tears. Still later almost everyone in the village could recite her story, and was bored by it.

"I was really a fool, really," she would begin.

"Yes, you knew that wild beasts came down to the village to seek food only when they cannot find anything in the hills," people would thus stop her and walk away.

She would stand gaping and staring for a while and then walk away, a little embarrassed. Still, she tried to bring up the story of Ah Mao by some ruse—a basket, beans, or some other children. For instance, if she saw a child two or three years old, she would say, "Ai-ai, if our Ah Mao were alive he would be as big as that . . ."

The children were afraid of her and of the look in her eyes, and they would tug at their mothers' coats and urge them to go away. And thus Sister Hsiang-lin would be left alone to wander off by herself. Soon people caught on to her new trick; they would forestall her when there were children around by saying, "Sister Hsiang-lin, if your Ah Mao were alive, would he not be as big as that?"

She might not have realized that her sorrow, after having been carefully chewed and relished for so long, had now become insipid dregs, only fit to spit out; but she was able to sense the indifference and the sarcasm in the question and to realize that there was no need of her answering it.

The New Year festivities last a long time in Luchen and begin to occupy people after the twentieth of the last month of the year. At Uncle Four's house they had to hire a temporary man helper, but the work was too much for him and another woman was hired. But she, Liu-ma, was a devout vegetarian and would not kill the chickens and ducks; she only washed dishes. Sister Hsiang-lin had nothing to do but tend the fire. She sat and watched Liu-ma wash the dishes. A light snow was falling outside.

"Ai-ai, I was really a fool," Sister Hsiang-lin soliloquized after looking at the sky, sighing.

"Sister Hsiang-lin, there you go again," Liu-ma looked at her impatiently. "Let me ask you, did you not get your scar when you dashed your head against the table that time?"

"Mmm," she answered evasively.

"Let me ask you, why did you finally give in?"

"I?"

"Yes, you. I think you must have been willing. Otherwise . . ."

"Ah, ah, but you do not know how strong he was."

"I do not believe it. I do not believe that a strong woman like you could not resist him. You must have finally become willing though you now blame it on his strength."

"Ah-ah you . . . you should have tried to resist him yourself," she said with a smile.

Liu-ma laughed, her wrinkled face shriveling up like a peach stone; her tiny dry eyes shifted from the scar on Sister Hsiang-lin's forehead to the latter's eyes, discomforting her and causing her to gather up her smile and turn her eyes to look at the snowflakes.

"Sister Hsiang-lin, you have miscalculated badly," Liu-ma said mysteriously. "You should have resisted to the end, or dashed your head until you were dead. That would have been the thing to do. But now? You lived with your second man only two years and got for it a monstrous evil name. Just think, when you get to the lower world, those two ghost husbands will fight over you. Whom would they give you to? The Great King Yenlo could only have you sawed in two and divided between them . . ."

Sister Hsiang-lin was terrified: this was something that she had not heard about in the hills.

"I think you should atone for your crime while there is still time. Donate a doorsill to the T'u-ti temple as your effigy, so that you might be trampled upon by a thousand men's feet and straddled over by ten thousand men's legs as atonement for your great sin. Then you may escape the tortures in store for you."

Sister Hsiang-lin did not say anything then, but she must have been deeply affected. The next day she got up with black rings around her eyes. After breakfast she went to the T'u-ti temple on the western edge of the village to donate the doorsill. At first the keeper would not accept the gift, but her tears and entreaties finally prevailed and he accepted the offer at the price of 12,000 *cash*.

She had not spoken with anyone for a long time, for she had become an avoided object because of the tiresome story about her Ah Mao; nevertheless, after her conversation with Liu-ma—which seemed to have been broadcast immediately—people began to take a new interest in her and would try to coax her to talk. As to the subject, it was naturally a new one, centering upon the scar on her forehead.

"Sister Hsiang-lin, let me ask you, why did you finally give in?" one would say.

"Ai, too bad you broke your head for nothing," another would echo, looking at her scar.

From their faces and voices she gathered that they were making fun of her; she only stared vacantly and said nothing, later she did not even turn her head. She tightened her mouth and went about her duties—sweeping, washing vegetables and rice, running errands, bearing the scar of her shame. In about a year, she got all the wages that Aunt Four had kept for her, changed them into twelve Mexican dollars, asked for leave to go to the western edge of the village. She soon returned and told Aunt Four that she had donated her doorsill at the T'u-ti temple. She appeared to be in better spirits than she had been for a long time and her eyes showed signs of life.

She worked unusually hard at the ancestral sacrifices at the winter solstice. After watching Aunt Four fill the dishes with the sacrificial things and Ah Niu place the table in the center of the hall, she went confidently to get the wine cups and chopsticks. "Don't you bother, Sister Hsiang-lin!" Aunt Four said in a panicky voice.

She withdrew her hands as if from a hot iron, her face black and pale like burnt coal. She did not try to get the candlesticks. She only stood as if lost, and did not go away until Uncle Four came in to light the incense sticks and dismissed her. This time the change in her was extraordinary. Not only were her eyes sunken the next day, but her wits seemed to have left her entirely. She became terribly afraid, not only of the night and dark corners, but also of people, including her own employers. She would sneak about, trembling like a mouse that had ventured out of its hole in daylight; or she would sit abstractedly like a wooden idol. In less than half a year, her hair became gray, her memory grew worse and worse, until she sometimes forgot to go out to wash rice in the river.

"What is the matter with Sister Hsiang-lin? We should not have kept her in the first place," Aunt Four would say sometimes, in her hearing, as a warning to her.

But she continued in the same condition, and showed no signs of recovering her wits. They began to think of sending her away, to tell her to go back to old Mrs. Wei. When I was still living at Luchen they used to talk of sending her away, but they only talked about it; from what I saw on this visit, it was evident that they did finally carry out their threat. But whether she became a beggar immediately after leaving Uncle Four's house, or whether she first went to old Mrs. Wei and then became a beggar, I could not say.

I was awakened by loud explosions of firecrackers close by. As I blinked at the yellow lamp flame about the size of a bean I heard the crackling of a string of firecrackers—the New Year's ceremony was on at Uncle Four's and I knew that it must be about the fifth watch. With half-shut eyes I heard dreamily the continued crackling in the distance; it seemed to form a thick cloud of festive sounds in the sky, mingling with the snowflakes and enveloping the entire village. In the arms of this festive sound, I felt carefree and comfortable, and the fears and melancholy I had felt all the previous day and the first part of the night were swept away by this atmosphere of joy and blessedness. I fancied that the gods and sages of heaven above and earth below, drunk and satiated with incense and sacrifices of wine and meat, were reeling unsteadily in the sky, ready to confer unlimited blessings upon the inhabitants of Luchen.

Abel Melveny

Edgar Lee Masters

I bought every kind of machine that's known—
Grinders, shellers, planters, mowers,
Mills and rakes and ploughs and threshers—
And all of them stood in the rain and sun,
Getting rusted, warped and battered,
For I had no sheds to store them in,
And no use for most of them.
And toward the last, when I thought it over,
There by my window, growing clearer
About myself, as my pulse slowed down,
And looked at one of the mills I bought—
Which I didn't have the slightest need of,
As things turned out, and I never ran—
A fine machine, once brightly varnished,
And eager to do its work,
Now with its paint washed off—
I saw myself as a good machine
That Life had never used.

Part Three

Old Age
as Wisdom
and Peace

BY THE TIME AN INDIVIDUAL REACHES OLD AGE—VARIOUSLY DEFINED IN terms of age, experience, and health—she or he is generally in touch with his or her own feelings and thoughts. As a result of this greater wholeness, she or he is able to see and define situations much more clearly and sensitively and feel more comfortable and relaxed. The personality confusions, identity problems, and self-consciousness of youth are long gone; the struggles, daily problems, and elusive goals of middle age have been handled and more or less dealt with, so that by the time an individual reaches later adulthood, there ought to be a sense of relaxation and oneness within the self. The individual might act on the environment and relate to other persons in a variety of ways, but always in ways that are consistent with the total self. The individual in later adulthood, in short, is more likely to be in harmony within.

Not all older people are in harmony, of course, as we have seen earlier. Some are bitter and angry about some aspect of their lives or their lives as a whole and are unable to relax within themselves. Some are just beginning to realize, in their later years, what they really wanted in life and that it is too late to achieve it. Also, some fortunate individuals are able to achieve a sense of inner harmony long before later life. But for many individuals, harmony and inner peace occur for the first time, if at all, in later adulthood. As a result, older people are less likely than those at other ages to do things that are out of character.

Plato viewed old age from a slightly different point of view: he thought that old age brought profound repose or rest and freedom from love and other intense passions. He thought that passions are a burden in earlier years in that they interfere with the individual's capacity for reflection, clear thinking, and comprehension of ideas. Passions or emotions, according to Plato, interfere with the young person's ability to reason clearly and consistently because the young person frequently becomes excited, enthusiastic, or exuberant about the content of the discussion and thereby loses the objectivity and distance necessary to clear thinking. One can think logically in old age, if one is capable of rational thought, in large part because one is finally free of the passions that are a burden in earlier years.

Either of these changes—the inner harmony and wholeness within or the freedom from passion that is necessary to logical thinking—can result in the characteristic called wisdom. The individual is able to see himself and life clearly and simply, without pretense and dishonesty, which gives depth to his thoughts. That individual appreciates life more and does not want to waste time with deceit and false appearances.

If earlier life is a search for elusive identity clarification and self-acceptance, old age can bring acceptance of whatever circumstances exist, because self-acceptance is higher in older persons than in younger persons (although it is often a self-acceptance based on habit rather than on self-examination and self-understanding). Because of greater self-acceptance, one can make the best of a bad situation. This often requires that the individual change his perception of life as the circumstances change, as in "Ilyas" by Leo Tolstoy (1828–1910), written in 1885.

Some individuals who were to suffer Ilyas's fall from wealth might become bitter about their losses and might dwell on their failures, their hardships, and their "come-down." Further, this kind of bitter elderly person would be jealous of the young because young people have a future which they do not have; would condemn the young as unappreciative; and would be irritated by the happiness and playfulness of the young, calling them spoiled. Such people would also condemn their middle-aged offspring, thinking that only they themselves have suffered. The relationships between generations would likely be filled with conflict and verbal abuse. This pattern is, unfortunately, common in the United States.

For Ilyas and his wife, however, old age brings contentment, reflection, and rational assessment. They achieve the qualities of wisdom and inner peace as they disengage from the heavy responsibility of owning much property and accept a simpler life without worries. One cannot imagine that they would be jealous of the young, for they totally accept the particular circumstances of their own lives and are completely content within those circumstances. They have the ability, the willingness, to find acceptance and peace in old age rather than condemn their lives. Thus "Ilyas" illustrates one of the truths of old age: at that point it is too late to live life over or change circumstances in order to live it differently, but one *can* change one's perceptions, reinterpret one's life and therein find peace, fulfillment, and acceptance.

One might say that they had rationalized the failures in their lives. So be it. It brought them peace rather than bitterness.

Of further interest in this story is the fact that it is the woman who is assertive in expressing the sense that they have jointly made of their lives. Even though she has to stay behind the curtain, she is not at all timid. As we have noted in other selections, older women often become much more assertive than they were earlier in their lives. They are much more likely to express their opinions and to function as independent individuals. Ilyas's wife speaks for both of them, saying that they both found inner peace and serenity once they disengaged from their heavy responsibilities, which, while appealing to others, had become burdensome to them. It is she who provides the rationale for their happiness.

Acceptance of life in old age is also the statement of Tom Beatty in *Spoon River Anthology*, though expressed in much more assertive and colorful language. He, too, expresses the idea that it does not do any good, at least at the age of seventy, to protest life and how one has lived. Sara Teasdale (1884–1933), in "Wisdom," adds the point that it is necessary to compromise rather than to continue to demand perfection, and that this is what is meant by wisdom. It is not likely to be achieved, however, by the young, who are impatient.

In a Japanese Horatio Alger story—one about the elderly rather than the young—we find the assumption that it is never too late to change, though in this case one changes when one has wealth. "The Story of the Old Man who Made Withered Trees to Blossom," is a traditional Japanese folk tale in which virtue and goodness are recognized and rewarded and evil is punished. It also contains the obvious point that is sometimes unrecognized: in some basic ways, old people are just like everyone else—particularly in that some are bad and some are good.

A simple statement of acceptance and integrity about his life is made by Walter Savage Landor (1775–1864) in his well-known poem, "On His Seventy-Fifth Birthday."

A story in the first section of this anthology, "Grandma," illustrates the sensitivity, insight, and understanding that one frequently finds among the elderly. Grandma understands each of her offspring, their family styles, her place in the lives of each, and the shortcomings of each. So does "Old Man Minick," who sizes up the situation and figures out how to improve his own life. In both of these stories, the elderly individual accepts himself or herself and is able to modify the situation without destroying the relationships. Each situation involves compromise as well as self-acceptance.

A person can be content to sit in quiet solitude in old age, alone and at peace with memories, as in "Twilight" by A. Mary Robinson (1857–1944). She says that at this time of life it is enjoyable to be alone at twilight, while this was boring to her when she was young. Many younger persons do not understand this and think that something is wrong if the older person is not doing or talking; but, instead, the person is remembering, thinking, being.

"Terminus," written in 1866 by Ralph Waldo Emerson (1803–1882), expresses the theme of disengagement. As we age and physically decline, we gradually withdraw from the active and ambitious life, condensing our pleasures and enjoying what remains.

Peace and serenity can be found once one disengages from lust for love, greed, profit, and fame, as expressed in "On Being Sixty" by Po Chü-i (772–846). Then one can enjoy the basics of life as long as one remains in good health. Again, one can easily find peace, serenity, and happiness in simple pleasures. Just like Tolstoy's Ilyas, one finds the real pleasures of life in the natural, the uncomplicated, and the nonmaterial areas. With increasing age, one leaves behind the worldly pleasures which in the past, to Tolstoy and Po Chü-i, have interfered with one's enjoyment of the simpler pleasures.

The contrast between the struggle of the early years of youth and the peace and serenity of old age is very clearly expressed in "Promise of Peace" by Robinson Jeffers (1887–1962). However, the ultimate peace is death.

The "Seven Poems on Aging" by Yüan Mei (1716–1798) contain a number of relevant themes. There is the fact of aging that occurs casually and without public notice, unlike other events. There is the reluctance to age, even in a culture (traditional Chinese) that gave high prestige to the aged. As in the poem, "Twilight," there is the feeling that time passes quickly as one ages, which makes the remaining time much more precious than when one was young. As in some of the other poems and the story of Ilyas, Yüan Mei affirms that one comes to appreciate the simpler and more basic (and less costly) pleasures. The pleasures of old age are not the wild, dramatic, and adventurous pleasures of youth; rather, they are simple, easily attainable, natural, quiet pleasures. Earlier, one might take them for granted; later, they become much more meaningful as one settles down and finds peace and contentment within.

Yüan Mei suggests that our intellectual capabilities remain alive as we age, even though we might not think so. Our ability to think, to be creative, and to be productive with words continues and does not diminish with age. This observation is totally consistent with the research findings of gerontologists.

The capacity for deep and sustained sleep does decline (again, this is consistent with current research findings), one is awakened more easily than previously, is more inclined to rise early, and to feel less refreshed on rising. These changes, having to do with changes in the sleep cycle that are not well understood at the present time, often result in the need for "cat-naps" during the day.

There is a quality of gentleness, inner peace, and acceptance in this series of seven poems. Life is precious and to be lived and cherished. Unlike Tom Garrison in "I Never Sang For My Father," for example, Yüan Mei is able to approach each day as though it were a treasure and a special event. He is glad for each day, serene and yet sensitive to the chances for the enjoyment of observable nature.

The 1863 poem "Rabbi Ben Ezra" by Robert Browning (1812–1889), the first two or three lines of which are often quoted in gerontological and journalistic reports, asserts the desirability of growing old. *The Norton Anthology of English Literature,* Third Edition, offers this note to the poem: "Stanzas 20 and 21 affirm that in age we can more readily think independently than in youth. Maturity enables us to ignore the pressure of having to conform to the thinking of the crowd of small-minded people." [1]

---

[1] *The Norton Anthology of English Literature,* 3rd edition (New York: W. W. Norton, 1974), Vol. II, p. 1202.

Ilyas

Leo Tolstoy

Translated from the Russian by Nathan Haskell Dole

There lived in the government of Ufa a Bashfir by the name of Ilyas. When his father died, Ilyas was left by no means rich, but the year before his father had got him a wife, and at that time Ilyas's possessions consisted of seven mares, two cows, and a score of sheep. Now Ilyas was a good manager, and he began to gain; from morning till night he and his wife worked; he got up earlier than any one else, and went to bed later than any one else, and each year he kept getting richer.

Thus Ilyas toiled for thirty-five years, and he made a great fortune. He had two hundred head of horse, a hundred and fifty head of horned cattle, and twelve hundred sheep. The servants pastured the flocks and herds; and the maidservants milked the mares and cows, and made kumys, butter, and cheese.

Ilyas had plenty of everything, and every one round about envied Ilyas's life. Men said:—

"Lucky man, Ilyas. He has plenty of everything; he doesn't need to die."

Fine people began to get acquainted with Ilyas, and associated with him. And guests came to visit him from far and near. And Ilyas received them all, and gave them all food and drink. Whoever came had kumys; all had tea, chowder, and mutton. As soon as guests came, he would immediately have a ram or two killed; and if many came, they would have a mare also killed.

Ilyas had two sons and a daughter. He married off his sons, and got his daughter a husband. When Ilyas was poor, his sons worked with him, and they themselves pastured the flocks and herds; but as they became rich, the sons began to get spoiled, and one took to drinking.

One, the elder, was killed in a brawl; and the other, the younger, got a proud wife; and this son began to be disobedient to his father, and Ilyas was compelled to banish him.

Ilyas banished him, but gave him a house and cattle; and Ilyas's wealth was diminished. And soon after this a distemper fell upon Ilyas's sheep, and many perished. Then there came a year of famine; the hay did not ripen; many cattle died during the winter. Then the Kirgiz carried off his best horses, and Ilyas's property was still further diminished.

Ilyas began to fall lower and lower. And his strength was less than it had been. And at the age of seventy years, Ilyas had come to such a pass that he began to sell out his furs, his carpets, saddles, and kibitkas; and then he had to dispose of his last cattle, and Ilyas came to nothing.

He himself did not realize how he had nothing left; but he and his wife were obliged, in their old age, to hire out as servants. All Ilyas's possessions consisted of the clothes on his body, his shuba, a hat, shoes, and slippers—yes, and his wife, Sham-Shemagi, now an old woman. His banished son had gone to a far-off land, and his daughter died. And then there was no one to help the old people.

Their neighbor, Muhamedshah, felt sorry for the old people. Muhamedshah himself was neither poor nor rich, but lived in medium circumstances; and he was a good man.

He remembered Ilyas's hospitality, and pitied him, and said to Ilyas:—

"Come, Ilyas," says he, "and live with me—you and your old woman. In summer you can work for me in the garden, and in winter take care of the cattle; and Sham-Shemagi may milk the mares, and make kumys. I will feed and clothe you both; and whatever you need, tell me; I will give it."

Ilyas thanked his neighbor, and he and his wife began to live with Muhamedshah as servants. At first it came hard to them, but afterward they got used to it; and the old people went on living and working as much as their strength permitted.

The khozyaïn found it profitable to keep such people, because they had been masters themselves, and knew how to keep things orderly, and were not lazy, and worked according to their strength; only Muhamedshah felt sorry to see how people of such high station should have fallen to such a low condition.

Once it came to pass that some guests, some kinsmen from a distance, came to visit Muhamedshah; a Mulla came with them.

Muhamedshah gave orders to have a ram caught and killed. Ilyas dressed the ram, cooked it, and served it to the guests. The guests ate the mutton, drank some tea, and took some kumys.

While the guests were sitting with the khozyaïn on down pillows, on carpets, and were drinking kumys out of cups, and chatting, Ilyas had finished his chores, and was passing in front of the door.

Muhamedshah saw him, and asked a guest:—

"Did you see that old man who went by the door?"

"I saw him," said the guest; "but what is there remarkable about him?"

"This is remarkable—he was once our richest man. His name is Ilyas; maybe you have heard of him?"

"Certainly I have," said the guest. "I never saw him before, but his fame has been widespread."

"Now he has nothing at all left, and lives out at service with me; he and his old woman milk the cows."

The guest was amazed, clucked with his tongue, shook his head, and said:—

"Yes, this shows how fortune turns round like a wheel; he who is on top gets to the bottom. Well, I suppose the old man feels pretty bad about it?"

"Who can tell about him? He lives quietly, peacefully; works well."

The guest said:—

"May I have a talk with him? I should like to ask him about his life."

"Well, you can," says the khozyaïn, and shouts toward the kibitka, "Babaï, come in; bring some kumys, and call your old woman."

So Ilyas came with his wife. He greeted the guests and his master, repeated a prayer, and squatted down by the door. But his wife went behind the curtain, and sat with her mistress.

Ilyas was given a cup of kumys. Ilyas wished the health of the guests and of his master, bowed, sipped a little, and set it down.

"Well, dyedushka," says the guest, "I suppose you feel rather blue looking at us, to remember your past life,—how you used to be in luck, and how now your life is spent in sorrow?"

And Ilyas smiled and said:—

"If I told you about my fortune and misfortune, you would not believe me. Better ask my wife. She is a woman,—what's in her heart's on her tongue also. She will tell you the whole truth about this matter."

And the guest spoke to her behind the curtain: "Well, now, babushka, tell us what you think about your former luck, and your present misfortune."

And Sham-Shemagi spoke from behind the curtain:—

"This is what I think about it: my old man and I have lived fifty years. We sought for happiness, and did not find it; and now here it is two years since we lost everything, and have been living out at service; and we have found real happiness, and ask for nothing better."

The guests were amazed; and the khozyaïn was amazed, and even rose from his seat, lifted the curtain to look at the old woman; and the old woman was standing, with folded arms. She smiled as she looked at her old man, and the old man smiled back.

The old woman went on:—

"I am speaking the truth, not jesting. We sought for happiness for half a century, and as long as we were rich we did not find it; but now that we have nothing left, and have to go out to service, we have found such happiness that we ask for nothing better."

"But wherein consists your happiness now?"

"Well, in this: while we were rich, my old man and' I never had an hour's rest. We never had time to talk, nor to think about our souls, nor to pray to God. There was nothing for us but care. When we had guests, it was a bother how to treat them, what to give them, so that they might not talk ill about us. Then, when guests went away, we had to look after our work-people; they would have to rest, they would have to be furnished with enough to eat, and we would have to see to it that nothing that was ours got lost. So we sinned. Then, again, there was worry lest the wolf should kill a colt or a calf, or lest thieves should drive off our horses. We would lie down to sleep, but could not sleep for fear the sheep should trample the lambs. We would go out, and we would walk in the night; and at last, when we would get ourselves calmed down, then, again, there would be anxiety about getting food for the winter. Besides this, my old man and I never agreed. He would say we must do so, and I would say we must do *so;* and we would begin to quarrel; so we sinned. So we lived in worry and care, in worry and care, and never knew the happiness of life."

"Well, and now?"

"Now, when my old man and I get up in the morning, we always have a talk, in love and sympathy, we have nothing to quarrel about, nothing to worry about; our only care is to serve our khozyaïn. We work according to our strength, we work willingly, so that our khozyaïn may not lose, but gain. When we come in, we have dinner, we have supper, we have kumys. If it is cold, we have our kizyak to warm us, and a sheepskin shuba. And we have time to talk and think about our souls, and to pray to God. For fifty years we sought for happiness, and only now we have found it!''

The guests began to laugh.

But Ilyas said:—

"Don't laugh, brothers; this thing is no jest, but human life. And the old woman and I were foolish when we wept over the loss of our property, but now God has revealed the truth to us; and it is not for our own consolation, but for your good, that we reveal it to you.''

And the Mulla said:—

"This is a wise saying, and Ilyas has told the exact truth; and this is written also in the Scriptures.''

And the guests ceased laughing, and were lost in thought.

Tom Beatty

Edgar Lee Masters

I was a lawyer like Harmon Whitney
Or Kinsey Keene or Garrison Standard,
For I tried the rights of property,
Although by lamp-light, for thirty years,
In that poker room in the opera house.
And I say to you that Life's a gambler
Head and shoulders above us all.
No mayor alive can close the house.
And if you lose, you can squeal as you will;
You'll not get back your money.
He makes the percentage hard to conquer;
He stacks the cards to catch your weakness
And not to meet your strength.
And he gives you seventy years to play:
For if you cannot win in seventy
You cannot win at all.
So, if you lose, get out of the room—
Get out of the room when your time is up.
It's mean to sit and fumble the cards,
And curse your losses, leaden-eyed,
Whining to try and try.

Wisdom

Sara Teasdale

When I have ceased to break my wings
Against the faultiness of things.
And learned that compromises wait
Behind each hardly opened gate,
When I can look Life in the eyes,
Grown calm and very coldly wise,
Life will have given me the Truth,
And taken in exchange—my youth.

The Story of the Old Man Who Made Withered Trees to Blossom

A Japanese Folk Tale

Translated by A. B. Mitford

In the old, old days, there lived an honest man with his wife, who had a favourite dog, which they used to feed with fish and tidbits from their own kitchen. One day, as the old folks went out to work in their garden, the dog went with them, and began playing about. All of a sudden, the dog stopped short, and began to bark, "Bow, wow, wow!" wagging his tail violently. The old people thought that there must be something nice to eat under the ground, so they brought a spade and began digging, when, lo and behold! the place was full of gold pieces and silver, and all sorts of precious things, which had been buried there. So they gathered the treasure together, and, after giving alms to the poor, bought themselves rice-fields and corn-fields, and became wealthy people.

Now, in the next house there dwelt a covetous and stingy old man and woman, who, when they heard what had happened, came and borrowed the dog, and, having taken him home, prepared a great feast for him, and said—

"If you please, Mr. Dog, we should be much obliged to you if you would show us a place with plenty of money in it."

215

The dog, however, who up to that time had received nothing but cuffs and kicks from his hosts, would not eat any of the dainties which they set before him; so the old people began to get cross, and, putting a rope round the dog's neck, led him out into the garden. But it was all in vain; let them lead him where they might, not a sound would the dog utter: he had no "bow-wow" for them. At last, however, the dog stopped at a certain spot, and began to sniff: so, thinking that this must surely be the lucky place, they dug, and found nothing but a quantity of dirt and nasty offal, over which they had to hold their noses. Furious at being disappointed, the wicked old couple seized the dog, and killed him.

When the good old man saw that the dog, whom he had lent, did not come home, he went next door to ask what had become of him; and the wicked old man answered that he had killed the dog, and buried him at the root of a pine-tree; so the good old fellow, with a heavy heart, went to the spot, and, having set out a tray with delicate food, burnt incense, and adorned the grave with flowers, as he shed tears over his lost pet.

But there was more good luck in store yet for the old people—the reward of their honesty and virtue. How do you think that happened, my children? It is very wrong to be cruel to dogs and cats.

That night, when the good old man was fast asleep in bed, the dog appeared to him, and, after thanking him for all his kindness, said—

"Cause the pine-tree, under which I am buried, to be cut down and made into a mortar, and use it, thinking of it as if it were myself."

The old man did as the dog had told him to do, and made a mortar out of the wood of the pine-tree; but when he ground his rice in it, each grain of rice was turned into some rich treasure. When the wicked old couple saw this, they came to borrow the mortar; but no sooner did they try to use it, than all their rice was turned into filth; so, in a fit of rage, they broke up the mortar and burned it. But the good old man, little suspecting that his precious mortar had been broken and burnt, wondered why his neighbours did not bring it back to him.

One night the dog appeared to him again in a dream, and told him what had happened, adding that if he would take the ashes of the burnt mortar and sprinkle them on withered trees, the trees would revive, and suddenly put out flowers. After saying this the dream vanished, and the old man, who heard for the first time of the loss of his mortar, ran off weeping to the neighbours' house, and begged them, at any rate, to give him back the ashes of his treasure. Having obtained these, he returned home, and made a trial of their virtues upon a withered cherry-tree, which, upon being touched by the ashes, immediately began to sprout and blossom. When he saw this wonderful effect, he put the ashes into a basket, and went about the country, announcing himself as an old man who had the power of bringing dead trees to life again.

A certain prince, hearing of this, and thinking it a mighty strange thing, sent for the old fellow, who showed his power by causing all the withered plum and cherry-trees to shoot out and put forth flowers. So the prince gave him a rich reward of pieces of silk and cloth and other presents, and sent him home rejoicing.

So soon as the neighbours heard of this they collected all the ashes that remained, and, having put them in a basket, the wicked old man went out into the castle town, and gave out that he was the old man who had the power of reviving dead trees, and causing them to flower. He had not to wait long before he was called into the prince's palace, and ordered to exhibit his power. But when he climbed up into a withered tree and began to scatter the ashes, not a bud nor a flower appeared; but the ashes all flew into the prince's eyes and mouth, blinding and choking him. When the prince's retainers saw this, they seized the old man, and beat him almost to death, so that he crawled off home in a very sorry plight. When he and his wife found out what a trap they had fallen into, they stormed and scolded, and put themselves into a passion; but that did no good at all.

The good old man and woman, so soon as they heard of their neighbours' distress, sent for them, and, after reproving them for their greed and cruelty, gave them a share of their own riches, which, by repeated strokes of luck, had now increased to a goodly sum. So the wicked old people mended their ways, and led good and virtuous lives ever after.

On His Seventy-Fifth Birthday

Walter Savage Landor

I strove with none, for none was worth my strife;
　　Nature I loved, and next to Nature, Art;
I warmed both hands before the fire of life,
　　It sinks, and I am ready to depart.

Twilight

A. Mary F. Robinson

When I was young the twilight seemed too long.
How often on the western window-seat
    I leaned my book against the misty pane
    And spelled the last enchanting lines again,
The while my mother hummed an ancient song,
Or sighed a little and said: "The hour is sweet!"
When I, rebellious, clamored for the light.

But now I love the soft approach of night,
    And now with folded hands I sit and dream
    While all too fleet the hours of twilight seem;
And thus I know that I am growing old.

O granaries of Age! O manifold
And royal harvest of the common years!
There are in all thy treasure-house no ways
But lead by soft descent and gradual slope
To memories more exquisite than hope.
Thine is the Iris born of olden tears,
And thrice more happy are the happy days
That live divinely in the lingering rays.

Terminus

Ralph Waldo Emerson

It is time to be old,
To take in sail:—
The god of bounds,
Who sets to seas a shore,
Came to me in his fatal rounds,
And said: "No more!
No farther shoot
Thy broad ambitious branches, and thy root.
Fancy departs: no more invent;
Contract thy firmament
To compass of a tent.
There's not enough for this and that,
Make thy option which of two;
Economize the failing river,
Not the less revere the Giver,
Leave the many and hold the few.
Timely wise accept the terms,
Soften the fall with wary foot;
A little while
Still plan and smile,
And,—fault of novel germs,—
Mature the unfallen fruit.
Curse, if thou wilt, thy sires,
Bad husbands of their fires,
Who, when they gave thee breath,
Failed to bequeath
The needful sinew stark as once,
The Baresark marrow to thy bones,
But left a legacy of ebbing veins,
Inconstant heat and nerveless reins,—
Amid the Muses, left thee deaf and dumb,
Amid the Gladiators, halt and numb."

As the bird trims her to the gale,
I trim myself to the storm of time,
I man the rudder, reef the sail,
Obey the voice at eve obeyed at prime:
"Lowly faithful, banish fear,
Right onward drive unharmed;
The port, well worth the cruise, is near,
And every wave is charmed."

On Being Sixty

Po Chü-i

Translated from the Chinese by Arthur Waley

Between thirty and forty, one is distracted by the Five Lusts;
Between seventy and eighty, one is a prey to a hundred diseases.
But from fifty to sixty one is free from all ills;
Calm and still—the heart enjoys rest.
I have put behind me Love and Greed; I have done with Profit and Fame;
I am still short of illness and decay and far from decrepit age.
Strength of limb I still possess to seek the rivers and hills;
Still my heart has spirit enough to listen to flutes and strings.
At leisure I open new wine and taste several cups;
Drunken I recall old poems and sing a whole volume.
Meng-te has asked for a poem and herewith I exhort him
Not to complain of three-score, ''the time of obedient ears.''

Promise of Peace

Robinson Jeffers

The heads of strong old age are beautiful
Beyond all grace of youth. They have strange quiet,
Integrity, health, soundness, to the full
They've dealt with life and been attempered by it.
A young man must not sleep; his years are war
Civil and foreign but the former's worse;
But the old can breathe in safety now that they are
Forgetting what youth meant, the being perverse,
Running the fool's gauntlet and being cut
By the whips of the five senses. As for me,
If I should wish to live long it were but
To trade those fevers for tranquillity,
Thinking though that's entire and sweet in the grave
How shall the dead taste the deep treasure they have?

Seven Poems on Aging

Yüan Mei

Translated from the Chinese by Arthur Waley

I

For the present I am happy to wield a feather fan
While I cross the river, singing the *A-t'ung*.
To drink my health there are no companions or guests;
To row me on, plenty of hands at the oars.
Wave on wave the gray waters flow;
Gust on gust, the breeze from the distant hills.
There is no one to point at the misty waves and say,
"Out in the offing is an old man of fifty."

II

On this night year after year I have listened eagerly,
Never missing a single sound of the crackers till dawn came.
But this year on New Year's Eve I cannot bring myself to listen,
Knowing that when the cock crows I shall enter my sixtieth year.
The mighty din of the celebrations has already died away;
If a little time is still left, it is only a last scrap
But the cock, as though feeling for my plight, is slow to open its mouth,
And I that write this am still a man of fifty-nine!

III

If at seventy I still plant trees,
Lookers-on, do not laugh at my folly.
It is true of course that no one lives forever;
But nothing is gained by knowing so in advance.

IV

When one is old, one treasures every minute;
A single day is precious as a whole year.
And how seldom, even in a whole year,
Does a true rapture of the senses come one's way!
Man is born to get pleasure where he can;
How he sets about it depends on how he is made.
All that matters is to find out in good time,
Each for himself, which things he really enjoys.
I was born with many strong cravings;
Now that I am old they are gradually slipping away.
There are only left two or three things
That still delight me as they did in former days—
To spread out a book beside a bamboo stream,
To run my fingers along an ancient jade,
To climb a hill with a stout stick in my hand,
To drink wine in the presence of lovely flowers,
Talk of books—why they please or fail to please—
Or of ghosts and marvels, no matter how far-fetched.
These are excesses in which, should he feel inclined,
A man of seventy-odd may well indulge.

V

Writing poems is like the blossoming of flowers;
If there is too much blossom the flowers are generally small;
And all the more, with a man nearing eighty,
Whose powers of invention have long withered away.
Yet all the same, people wanting poems
Continue to clamor for them all day long.
They know that the silkworm, till the moment of its death,
Never ceases to put out fresh threads.
I do my best to turn out something for them,
Though secretly ashamed to show such poor stuff.
Yet oddly enough my good friends that come
All accord in praising what I produce.
I am not the least shaken in my own belief;
But all the same I keep a copy in my drawer.
Can it be that though my body sinks to decay
My writing brush alone is still young?

VI

Now that I am old I get up very early
And feel like God creating a new world.
I come and go, meeting no one on the way;
Wherever I look, no kitchen-smoke rises.
I want to wash, but the water has not been heated;
I want to drink, but no tea has been made.
My boys and girls are behind closed doors;
My man-servants and maid-servants are all fast asleep.
At first I am cross and feel inclined to shout;
But all of a sudden remember my young days—
How I, too, in those early morning hours
Lay snoring, and hated to leave my bed.

VII

The east wind again has brought the splendor of spring flowers;
The willows gradually turn more green, the grass gradually sprouts.
When I look into the stream I must not repine at the snow on my two
    brows;
How few people have lived to see the flowers of four reigns!
Every moment I am now given comes as a gift from Heaven;
There is no limit to the glorious things that happen in the spring.
If you want to call, you need only pause outside the hedge and listen;
The place from which most laughter comes is certain to be my house!

Rabbi Ben Ezra

Robert Browning

I

    Grow old along with me!
    The best is yet to be,
The last of life, for which the first was made:
    Our times are in His hand
    Who saith, "A whole I planned,
Youth shows but half; trust God: see all, nor be afraid!"

II

Not that, amassing flowers,
Youth sighed, "Which rose make ours,
Which lily leave and then as best recall?"
Not that, admiring stars,
It yearned, "Nor Jove, nor Mars;
Mine be some figured flame which blends, transcends them all!"

III

Not for such hopes and fears
Annulling youth's brief years,
Do I remonstrate: folly wide the mark!
Rather I prize the doubt
Low kinds exist without,
Finished and finite clods, untroubled by a spark.

IV

Poor vaunt of life indeed,
Were man but formed to feed
On joy, to solely seek and find and feast:
Such feasting ended, then
As sure an end to men;
Irks care the crop-full bird? Frets doubt the maw-crammed beast?

V

Rejoice we are allied
To That which doth provide
And not partake, effect and not receive!
A spark disturbs our clod;
Nearer we hold of God
Who gives, than of His tribes that take, I must believe.

VI

Then, welcome each rebuff
That turns earth's smoothness rough,
Each sting that bids nor sit nor stand but go!
Be our joys three-parts pain!
Strive, and hold cheap the strain;
Learn, nor account the pang; dare, never grudge the throe!

VII

For thence—a paradox
Which comforts while it mocks—
Shall life succeed in that it seems to fail:
What I aspired to be,
And was not, comforts me:
A brute I might have been, but would not sink i' the scale.

VIII

What is he but a brute
Whose flesh has soul to suit,
Whose spirit works lest arms and legs want play?
To man, propose this test—
Thy body at its best,
How far can that project thy soul on its lone way?

IX

Yet gifts should prove their use:
I own the Past profuse
Of power each side, perfection every turn:
Eyes, ears took in their dole,
Brain treasured up the whole;
Should not the heart beat once, "How good to live and learn"?

X

Not once beat, "Praise be Thine!
I see the whole design,
I, who saw power, see now love perfect too:
Perfect I call Thy plan:
Thanks that I was a man!
Maker, remake, complete—I trust what Thou shalt do!"

XI

For pleasant is this flesh;
Our soul, in its rose-mesh
Pulled ever to the earth, still yearns for rest;
Would we some prize might hold
To match those manifold
Possessions of the brute—gain most, as we did best!

XII

Let us not always say,
    "Spite of this flesh today
I strove, made head, gained ground upon the whole!"
    As the bird wings and sings,
    Let us cry, "All good things
Are ours, nor soul helps flesh more, now, than flesh helps soul!"

XIII

Therefore I summon age
    To grant youth's heritage,
Life's struggle having so far reached its term:
    Thence shall I pass, approved
    A man, for aye removed
From the developed brute; a god though in the germ.

XIV

And I shall thereupon
    Take rest, ere I be gone
Once more on my adventure brave and new:
    Fearless and unperplexed,
    When I wage battle next,
What weapons to select, what armor to indue.

XV

Youth ended, I shall try
    My gain or loss thereby;
Leave the fire ashes, what survives is gold:
    And I shall weigh the same,
    Give life its praise or blame:
Young, all lay in dispute; I shall know, being old.

XVI

For note, when evening shuts,
    A certain moment cuts
The deed off, calls the glory from the gray:
    A whisper from the west
    Shoots—"Add this to the rest,
Take it and try its worth: here dies another day."

XVII

So, still within this life,
Though lifted o'er its strife,
Let me discern, compare, pronouce at last,
"This rage was right i' the main,
That acquiescence vain:
The Future I may face now I have proved the Past."

XVIII

For more is not reserved
To man, with soul just nerved
To act tomorrow what he learns today:
Here, work enough to watch
The Master work, and catch
Hints of the proper craft, tricks of the·tool's true play.

XIX

As it was better, youth
Should strive, through acts uncouth,
Toward making, then repose on aught found made:
So, better, age, exempt
From strife, should know, than tempt
Further. Thou waitedst age: wait death nor be afraid!

XX

Enough now, if the Right
And Good and Infinite
Be named here, as thou callest thy hand thine own,
With knowledge absolute,
Subject to no dispute
From Fools that crowded youth, nor let thee feel alone.

XXI

Be there, for once and all,
Severed great minds from small,
Announced to each his station in the Past!
Was I, the world arraigned,
Were they, my soul disdained,
Right? Let age speak the truth and give us peace at last!

XXII

Now, who shall arbitrate?
Ten men love what I hate,
Shun what I follow, slight what I receive;
Ten, who in ears and eyes
Match me: we all surmise,
They this thing, and I that: whom shall my soul believe?

XXIII

Not on the vulgar mass
Called "work," must sentence pass,
Things done, that took the eye and had the price;
O'er which, from level stand,
The low world laid its hand,
Found straightway to its mind, could value in a trice:

XXIV

But all, the world's coarse thumb
And finger failed to plumb,
So passed in making up the main account;
All instincts immature,
All purposes unsure,
That weighed not as his work, yet swelled the man's amount:

XXV

Thoughts hardly to be packed
Into a narrow act,
Fancies that broke through language and escaped;
All I could never be,
All, men ignored in me,
This, I was worth to God, whose wheel the pitcher shaped.

XXVI

Aye, note that Potter's wheel,
That metaphor! and feel
Why time spins fast, why passive lies our clay—
Thou, to whom fools propound,
When the wine makes its round,
"Since life fleets, all is change; the Past gone, seize today!"

XXVII

Fool! All that is, at all,
  Lasts ever, past recall;
Earth changes, but thy soul and God stand sure:
    What entered into thee,
    That was, is, and shall be:
Time's wheel runs back or stops: Potter and clay endure.

XXVIII

He fixed thee 'mid this dance
  Of plastic circumstance,
This Present, thou, forsooth, wouldst fain arrest:
    Machinery just meant
    To give thy soul its bent,
Try thee and turn thee forth, sufficiently impressed.

XXIX

What though the earlier grooves
  Which ran the laughing loves
Around thy base, no longer pause and press?
    What though, about thy rim,
    Skull-things in order grim
Grow out, in graver mood, obey the sterner stress?

XXX

Look not thou down but up!
  To uses of a cup,
The festal board, lamp's flash, and trumpet's peal,
    The new wine's foaming flow,
    The Master's lips a-glow!
Thou, heaven's consummate cup, what need'st thou with earth's wheel?

XXXI

But I need, now as then,
  Thee, God, who moldest men;
And since, not even while the whirl was worst,
    Did I—to the wheel of life
    With shapes and colors rife,
Bound dizzily—mistake my end, to slake Thy thirst:

XXXII

So, take and use Thy work:
Amend what flaws may lurk,
What strain o' the stuff, what warpings past the aim!
My times be in Thy hand!
Perfect the cup as planned!
Let age approve of youth, and death complete the same!

Part Four

Loss

UNLIKE OTHER TIMES IN THE LIFE CYCLE, OLD AGE IS MOST CLEARLY characterized as a time of loss. Some loss is of course desirable, such as the loss of worries and of the kinds of responsibilities that once may have resulted in states of high anxiety and tension. But most of the losses of the elderly are experienced as undesirable, unwelcome, and depressing, such as the loss of health, friends, spouse, prestige, income, satisfying activity, and so on. These are difficult losses with which to cope in later life because, according to the psychologist Else Frenkel-Brunswik, losses at this time are less likely to be replaced than at other times in life.[1]

When a spouse dies at a younger age, the surviving spouse is more likely to remarry. Not so in later life. Friends who die are also more likely to be replaced. This type of loss is a hardship and a sad occasion, but one that can be handled without undue burden to the individual who survives because that individual, if young or middle-aged, might find new friends. One is less inclined to do that when older and feeling less energetic; instead, one might be more inclined to substitute less meaningful and less involving new acquaintances for the more involved and deeper friendships. That would, however, add enormously to the person's feelings of loneliness. A job, also, is less likely to be replaced by most who are fired or who retire in later life, although, increasingly, older persons are taking on part-time voluntary work. As yet there is little evidence to indicate how the degree and kinds of satisfactions found there compare with those found in the prior full-time paid jobs. Further, one experiences genuine decline and sadness with the loss of certain aspects of health, for, depending on the situation and the individual, there may be many previously enjoyed activities that one can no longer do—run, read extensively, hear others in conversation without difficulty, attend to shopping easily, continue to enjoy certain foods, and so on.

When several losses, such as the death of a spouse, death of some other close family member, personal injury or illness, retirement, change in the health of a family member, change in financial state, or death of a close friend, occur within a year or two, as they often do in the lives of the elderly, the result is likely to be any of a number of illnesses. Researchers T. H. Holmes and M. Masuda found, among persons of various ages who had experienced a number of losses, a higher incidence of colds, tuberculosis, heart disease, skin disease, hernias, infections, allergies, bone and muscle injuries, psychosomatic illnesses, leukemia, cancer, schizophrenia, menstrual difficulties, warts, and even, among football players, a much higher incidence of injuries during the season.[2] They believe that the activity of coping with a crisis itself lowers resis-

[1] Else, Frenkel-Brunswik, "Adjustment and Re-orientation in the Course of the Life Span," in Neugarten, *Middle Age and Aging,* pp. 77–84.

[2] T. H. Holmes and M. Masuda, "Psychosomatic Syndrome," *Psychology Today,* April 1972, pp. 71–72, 106.

tance to disease because we have only so much energy with which to cope with anything.

The elderly and persons who work with the elderly can do much to limit the number and severity of crises the elderly individual has to deal with in a particular period of time. If an older woman loses her husband, for example, it would probably be best if she did not accept the offer of well-meaning sons or daughters to immediately move in with them. To do so would involve a whole chain of additional losses: neighborhood; friends; familiar streets and stores; habits; club, church or synagogue activities; objects within the home or apartment; familiar persons throughout the day; and general routine. It might be better to wait for about a year until she has adjusted to the loss of the spouse before making any additional changes.

Author and lecturer Irene Mortenson Burnside, in writing about loss, suggests that, at least in institutions, small groups meeting weekly, informally or for group therapy, are beneficial to many elderly.[3] Peer groups of aged patients help each other to cope with loss by developing friendships and close relationships, by finding role models in other similarly disabled patients making progress toward independence, and in supporting each other with similar experiences.

The powerful poem "Old People's Home" by W. H. Auden (1907–1973) conveys the experiences of a reluctant visitor who has painfully seen a person he felt close to decline dramatically, so much more painfully because he remembers "who she was in the pomp and sumpture of her hey-day." Each person there is limited; and those who are most aware of their situation, who have not declined to the point where they've become physically and mentally incapacitated, are likely to be the most depressed. Moreover, according to Auden, these elderly, unlike those of the past, have lost their place in society and their place and importance with their families. Instead, they have wound up in a "numbered frequent ward."

When we were young, we never imagined that all of these losses would happen to us, suggests Matthew Arnold (1822–1888) in "Growing Old." Perhaps the worst of it is that we can't even remember exactly what we were like before or even that we were ever young, so great is the change and so profound are the losses. It is not only the physical losses that are hard to take, but also the loss of feelings because our emotional capabilities become less intense. We cannot even feel deeply about these terrible changes. (Unlike Plato, noted in Part 3, Arnold does not see the diminution of emotion positively.)

Memories of good experiences in the past are all that sustain the old woman in Robinson Jeffers's 1928 poem, "Fawn's Foster-Mother." Those memories involve fullness and life and an earth-mother's giving. Now she is dried and decayed, deformed and furrowed, and ready to be shed. There is nothing left.

The loss of physical attractiveness and beauty saddens "The Old Men Ad-

[3] Irene Mortenson Burnside, "Loss: A Constant Theme in Group Work with the Aged," *Hospital and Community Psychiatry* 21, no. 6 (June 1970), pp. 173–77.

miring Themselves in the Water,'' the 1903 poem by William Butler Yeats (1865–1939). No one is skipped by this process, and it makes no difference how good or bad a person has been, according to ''Youth and Age,'' by Mimnermus of Greece, dated 620 B.C. Everyone is afflicted equally with the tragedy of old age. Youth is lovely, and old age is ugly. It is cares (or crises or worries) that hasten the onset of old age.

In old age, at the end of life, there is nothing left but ''Dregs,'' worthless remnants of what used to be, wrote Ernest Dowson (1867–1900; he died of tuberculosis at the age of thirty-two). Health, hope, and love are replaced by lethargy. This view is similar to the image of ''Old Women'' given by Babette Deutsch (born 1895), old women who are so weak, fragile, and whose destruction is almost complete to the extent that they can barely move, gossip, or remember. The bouncy spirit of ''Young and Old'' by Charles Kingsley (1819–1875) belies its biting statement of old age as stale, run down, spent, maimed, while youth alone is enjoyable, vibrant, and attractive.

Keen and interesting insights into the thought, perceptions, and attitudes of the elderly were written by Baldassare Castiglione (1478–1529) in an essay called either ''The Praise of Times Past'' or ''The Second Book,'' Parts 1 through 4, in *The Book of the Courtier,* which he finished in 1528. He suggests that the changes, disillusionment, and destruction of age can have consequences for the way the elderly evaluate the period in which they live. They do not recognize that these changes are really occurring in themselves and they falsely perceive the world outside themselves as decaying. The debilities of aging give them the impression that life around them is getting worse when, in truth, only they are declining. They remember the pleasures of their past, and they think that life generally in the past was much better for everyone than life in the present. They do not recognize that they have declined to the extent that they cannot and do not enjoy life in the present, and therefore exalt life in the past. Perhaps this is why, Castiglione says, the elderly tend to be somewhat more conservative politically, attitudinally, and behaviorally than the rest of a population.

Oliver Wendell Holmes (1809–1894) wrote ''The Last Leaf'' as a young man of twenty-three and had this to say about it.

> The poem was suggested by the sight of a figure well known to Bostonians (in 1831 or 1832), that of Major Thomas Melville, ''the last of the cocked hats,'' as he was sometimes called. The Major had been a personable young man, very evidently, and retained evidence of it in
> ''The monumental pomp of age,''—
> which had something imposing and something old about it for youthful eyes like mine. He was often pointed at as one of the 'Indians' of the famous ''Boston Tea-Party'' of 1774. His aspect among the crowds of a later generation reminded me of a withered leaf which has held to its stem through the storms of autumn and winter, and finds itself still clinging to

its bough while the new growths of spring are bursting their buds and spreading their foliage all around it.[4]

When he was eighty-five and the poem was to be published again in 1894, the last year of his life, Dr. Holmes wrote to his publishers:

> I have read the proof you sent me and find nothing in it which I feel called upon to alter or explain.
>
> I have lasted long enough to serve as an illustration of my own poem. I am one of the very last of the leaves which still cling to the bough of life that budded in the spring of the nineteenth century. The days of my years are threescore and twenty, and I am almost half way up the steep incline which leads me toward the base of the new century so near to which I have already climbed.
>
> I am pleased to find that this poem, carrying with it the marks of having been written in the jocund morning of life, is still read and cared for. It was with a smile on my lips that I wrote it; I cannot read it without a sigh of tender remembrance. I hope it will not sadden my older readers, while it may amuse some of the younger ones to whom its experiences are as yet only floating fancies.[5]

Poets who write about aging, and not all do, frequently tend to limit the topic to the single theme of loss. There are a seemingly infinite number of poems about losses that occur with increasing age, and, generally, aging is seen as a tragedy by these poets. So prevalent is the theme of loss with age in poetry that it was difficult to select a few poems to include in this section out of the abundance of excellent ones available.

Within the theme of loss there are several different types of losses, as we have seen. The next seven poems revolve around one type, the single syndrome of loss of romance, loss of physical and sexual attractiveness, and loss of desire. It is especially interesting that this theme is found in poems written by quite different poets in a wide range of cultures and times.

The poignant "What Lips My Lips Have Kissed" by Edna St. Vincent Millay (1892–1950, American) expresses wistful and tender memories of past loves, while observing that the present contains only the memories. The best part of life is long over. This thought is similar to that expressed in "Outlived Desire," by Alexander Pushkin (1799–1837, Russian), in that the person no longer experiences the desires and pleasures he had treasured in the past. However, much more than in the Millay poem, these memories are now painful, for they remind him of his current inadequacies. He wonders why life continues now that he no longer experiences desire. However, Pushkin says, as long as life continues there is always hope, for there is still the one shuddering leaf.

---

[4] Oliver Wendell Holmes, *The Complete Poetical Works of Oliver Wendell Holmes* (Boston: Houghton Mifflin, 1908), pp. 4–5.

[5] Holmes, *Complete Poetical Works*, pp. 4–5.

The possibility still remains, and that possibility is all the speaker has to relieve the intense pain of the present—pain because love might be over for him.

"An Elegy on the Impermanence of Human Life" by Yamanoe No Okura (660–733, Japanese) is about an aging samurai warrior who bemoans the aging changes: the wrinkles and the white hair, the pains and the tottering, and the end of virility. This poet says that all of these are inevitable in life, and we are unable to do anything about it. It is all part of life, painful as the decline may be.

A similar theme is found in "Old Age" by Al-Aswad Son of Ya'fur (6th century, Arabian). He wants it known that even though he is a worn-out wreck now, without strength and unable to love, he was quite something else in the past. He drank and played freely every night and enjoyed everything around him. He saw and heard much then and savors it all now, even though he can no longer have any of it. All that is good is in the past.

The end of physical and sexual attractiveness, the loss of romance and all that is romantic, the abuse from others because one is no longer handsome, the yearning for it to continue—all of these are the cries of "Lucius Atherton" in *Spoon River Anthology* by Edgar Lee Masters (1868–1950, American). He continues to desire but is no longer desired. He has been discarded. When young, handsome, passionate, and virile, he was loved; but when old, ugly, passionate, and virile, he is scorned. Now he subsists only on leftovers and short orders. It is a far cry from the way it used to be.

Desire continues and all is as it used to be, with the one difference that performance is no longer possible, in "So, We'll Go No More A-Roving" by George Gordon, Lord Byron (1788–1824, English). One is worn out physically even though mentally one wants to continue. Advice to young women that anticipates these changes well in advance of their occurrence is found in the familiar poem "To the Virgins, To Make Much of Time," by Robert Herrick (1591–1674, English). Herrick suggests that since passion and romance are best when young, one should not waste time by waiting, for they only diminish after youth.

The consistency of this message from such different cultures and times is intriguing. Make the most of youth, for all romance, physical and sexual attractiveness, and desire are, in old age, either absent altogether or compare unfavorably with the virility, desire, and ability in the earlier years, according to these otherwise quite diverse poets. The truth or falsity of this belief (gerontologists and many elderly persons have found that desire, attractiveness, and performance can continue with considerable satisfaction) is not the main point here; rather, it is important that this has been believed to have been true in such different times and places.

The 1885 short story "Old Age" by Anton Chekhov (1860–1904) captures the ambivalence of old age: the mellowing and openness of old men—for close to death one does not need to be dishonest anymore—but also the nostalgia for the daring, the competition, and the excitement of earlier years. What is lost is the sense of vitality and vigor that goes with acquisitiveness, cheating, envy, and meanness. One was alive then, though mean and dishonest. As a fighter, one had something to be rotten about. Now, in old age, one is mellow, quiet, humble, and open. Chekhov suggests that the former vitality and zest might have been preferable, no matter how nasty they were.

"The Letter" is by Dhumketu, pseudonym of Gaurishanker Goverdhanram Joshi (born 1892), and was published in 1961. This author from India has written insightfully of the feelings of separation, loss, and loneliness that many old men experience. The story is a common portrait of an old man when he is alone (Ali was apparently a widower) in many cultures, an image of loneliness, loss, and sometimes confusion (see also "The Lost Phoebe" by Theodore Dreiser in Part 6). Ali has lost everything except the one hope of receiving a letter from his daughter, a hope he never gives up.

Ali was independent as a young man; but now, in old age, all he has are memories. He has no friends, no wife, no hunting, no fishing, and he has neither heard from nor seen his daughter in five years. Though he has been a hunter of considerable skill and involvement, he can no longer hunt in his old age because, once his daughter has left with her husband, he identifies with and feels compassion for the young birds who are left alone when he kills their parents. Later, the haughty and previously indifferent postmaster comes to experience empathy and compassion for him when the postmaster feels a similar helplessness.

"The Gold Watch," published in 1961, by Indian writer Mulk Raj Anand (born 1905), captures the older individual's dread of retirement, especially when retirement is imposed suddenly rather than freely chosen. For Srijut Sharma, the anticipated loss is mainly financial, which will be devastating to his family (for he lives in a country in which he will not be able to find another job because of the rigid system restricting job opportunities to particular castes). He has no alternative job opportunities once he is retired. Generally, besides the financial one, there is a chain of other losses associated with the loss of a job one has had for many years: the loss of useful activity, routine developed over the years, the myriad habits associated with the job, prestige in society and power over others, and control over one's own plans, hopes, dreams, and expectations for the future when one is forcibly and hastily retired. Voluntary and gradual retirement are generally preferable, at least in giving the individual the chance to handle gradually the additional free time in ways that are meaningful and comfortable.

Srijut Sharma is understandably upset, but he cannot express his frustration overtly, for he is afraid his employer will take away the small concession he has made or remind him of his failings as a clerk. Certainly Candace Whitcomb (in "A Village Singer" in Part 1) would have handled the situation differently. Where Sharma is passive, she would have fought back fiercely. Had the boss suggested poor job performance, she would have vigorously denied any failings, just as she denies that her voice has at all diminished in quality. Her response, from what we know of her and of the characteristics of females in later life, would surely have been argumentative and vigorous. It also would have been honest in emanating from her own sense of self-worth and integrity. Sharma, on the other hand, though he has been mistreated, is still unwilling to say anything in his own behalf lest it be considered offensive. To a certain extent, the Indian caste system would account for his lack of response; and it is also due to that male-female difference in later life that we saw in Part 1.

Old People's Home

W. H. Auden

All are limitory, but each has her own
nuance of damage. The elite can dress and decent themselves,
    are ambulant with a single stick, adroit
to read a book all through, or play the slow movements of
    easy sonatas. (Yet, perhaps their very
carnal freedom is their spirit's bane: intelligent
    of what has happened and why, they are obnoxious
to a glum beyond tears.) Then come those on wheels, the average
    majority, who endure T.V. and, led by
lenient therapists, do community-singing, then
    the loners, muttering in Limbo, and last
the terminally incompetent, as improvident,
    unspeakable, impeccable as the plants
they parody. (Plants may sweat profusely but never
    sully themselves.) One tie, though, unites them: all
appeared when the world, though much was awry there, was more
    spacious, more comely to look at, its Old Ones
with an audience and secular station. Then a child,
    in dismay with Mamma, could refuge with Gran
to be revalued and told a story. As of now,
    we all know what to expect, but their generation
is the first to fade like this, not at home but assigned
    to a numbered frequent ward, stowed out of conscience
as unpopular luggage.
                        As I ride the subway
    to spend half-an-hour with one, I revisage
who she was in the pomp and sumpture of her hey-day,
    when week-end visits were a presumptive joy,
not a good work. Am I cold to wish for a speedy
    painless dormition, pray, as I know she prays,
that God or Nature will abrupt her earthly function?

Growing Old

Matthew Arnold

What is it to grow old?
Is it to lose the glory of the form,
The lustre of the eye?
Is it for beauty to forego her wealth?
—Yes, but not this alone.

Is it to feel our strength—
Not our bloom only, but our strength—decay?
Is it to feel each limb
Grow stiffer, every function less exact,
Each nerve more loosely strung?

Yes, this, and more; but not—
Ah, 'tis not what in youth we dreamed 'twould be!
'Tis not to have our life
Mellowed and softened as with sunset glow,
A golden day's decline.

'Tis not to see the world
As from a height, with rapt prophetic eyes,
And heart profoundly stirred;
And weep, and feel the fulness of the past,
The years that are no more.

It is to spend long days
And not once feel that we were ever young;
It is to add, immured
In the hot prison of the present, month
To month with weary pain.

It is to suffer this,
And feel but half, and feebly, what we feel.
Deep in our hidden heart
Festers the dull remembrance of a change,
But no emotion—none.

It is!—last stage of all—
When we are frozen up within, and quite
The phantom of ourselves,
To hear the world applaud the hollow ghost
Which blessed the living man.

Fawn's Foster-Mother

Robinson Jeffers

The old woman sits on a bench before the door and quarrels
With her meager pale demoralized daughter.
Once when I passed I found her alone, laughing in the sun
And saying that when she was first married
She lived in the old farmhouse up Garapatas Canyon.
(It is empty now, the roof has fallen
But the log walls hang on the stone foundation; the redwoods
Have all been cut down, the oaks are standing;
The place is now more solitary than ever before.)
"When I was nursing my second baby
My husband found a day-old fawn hid in a fern-brake
And brought it; I put its mouth to the breast
Rather than let it starve, I had milk enough for three babies.
Hey, how it sucked, the little nuzzler,
Digging its little hoofs like quills into my stomach.
I had more joy from that than from the others."
Her face is deformed with age, furrowed like a bad road
With market-wagons, mean cares and decay.
She is thrown up to the surface of things, a cell of dry skin
Soon to be shed from the earth's old eyebrows,
I see that once in her spring she lived in the streaming arteries,
The stir of the world, the music of the mountain.

The Old Men Admiring Themselves in the Water

William Butler Yeats

I heard the old, old men say,
"Everything alters,
And one by one we drop away."
They had hands like claws, and their knees
Were twisted like the old thorn trees
By the waters.
I heard the old, old men say,
"All that's beautiful drifts away
Like the waters."

Youth and Age

Mimnermus

Translated from the Greek by J. A. Symonds, M.D.

Ah! fair and lovely bloom the flowers of youth;
    On men and maids they beautifully smile:
But soon comes doleful eld, who, void of ruth,
    Indifferently afflicts the fair and vile;
Then cares wear out the heart: old eyes forlorn
    Scarce reck the very sunshine to behold—
Unloved by youths, of every maid the scorn—
    So hard a lot God lays upon the old.

Dregs

Ernest Dowson

The fire is out, and spent the warmth thereof,
(This is the end of every song man sings!)
The golden wine is drunk, the dregs remain,
Bitter as wormwood and as salt as pain;
And health and hope have gone the way of love
Into the drear oblivion of lost things.
Ghosts go along with us until the end;
This was a mistress, this, perhaps, a friend.
With pale, indifferent eyes, we sit and wait
For the dropped curtain and the closing gate:
This is the end of all the songs man sings.

Old Women

Babette Deutsch

Old women sit, stiffly, mosaics of pain,
Framed in drab doorways looking on the dark.
Rarely they rouse to gossip or complain
As dozing bitches break their dream to bark.
And then once more they fold their creaking bones
In silence, pulled about them like a a shawl.
Their memories: a heap of tumbling stones,
Once builded stronger than a city wall.
Sometimes they mend the gaps with twitching hand,—
Because they see a woman big with child,
Because a wet wind smells of grave-pocked land,
Because a train wailed, because troops defiled.

Sometimes old women limp through altered streets
Whose hostile houses beat them down to earth;
Now in their beds they fumble at the sheets
That once were spread for bridal, once for birth,
And now are laid for women who are cold
With difficult plodding or with sitting still.
Old women, pitying all that age can kill,
Lie quiet, wondering that they are old.

Young and Old

Charles Kingsley

When all the world is young, lad,
    And all the trees are green;
And every goose a swan, lad,
    And every lass a queen;
Then hey for boot and horse, lad,
    And round the world away;
Young blood must have its course, lad,
    And every dog his day.

When all the world is old, lad,
    And all the trees are brown;
And all the sport is stale, lad,
    And all the wheels run down:
Creep home, and take your place there,
    The spent and maimed among:
God grant you find one face there
    You loved when all was young.

From

The Book of the Courtier

Baldassare Castiglione

Translated from the Italian by Charles S. Singleton

To Messer Alfonso Ariosto

[1] I have often considered—and not without wonder—how a certain error arises which, as it is universally present in old people, can be thought to be proper and natural to them. And this is that they nearly all praise bygone times and denounce the present, railing against our doings and our ways and at everything that they, in their youth, did not do; affirming too that every good custom and good way of life, every virtue, all things, in short, are continually going from bad to worse.

And truly it seems quite contrary to reason and a cause for wonder that a ripe age, which in all other respects is wont to make men's judgment more perfect, should so corrupt it in this respect that they do not see that if the world were always growing worse, and if fathers were generally better than their children, we should long since have reached that lowest grade of badness beyond which it is impossible to go. And yet we see that, not only in our own time, but in the past as well, this fault was ever peculiar to old age, which is something we clearly gather from the writings of many ancient authors, and especially the writers of comedy who, more than the others, set forth the image of human life.

Now, for my part, I do believe that the cause of this mistaken opinion among old people is that the passing years take with them many of the good things of life and, among others, deprive the blood a great part of the vital spirits; wherefore the constitution is changed, and these organs through which the soul exercises its powers become weak. Thus, in old age the sweet flowers of contentment fall from our hearts, as in autumn the leaves fall from their trees, and in place of bright and clear thoughts there comes a cloudy and turbid sadness attended by a thousand ills. So that not only the body but the mind also is enfeebled, and retains of past pleasures merely a lingering memory and the image of that precious time of tender youth in which (while we are enjoying it), wherever we look, heaven and earth and everything appear merry and smiling, and the sweet springtime of happiness seems to flower in our thoughts as in a delightful and lovely garden.

Therefore, when the sun of our life enters the cold season and begins to go down in the west, divesting us of such pleasures, it would perhaps be well if along with them we might lose their memory too; and, as Themistocles said, discover an art that could teach us to forget. For the senses of our body are so deceitful that they often beguile the judgment of our minds as well. Hence, it seems to me that old people in their situation resemble people who, as they sail out of the port, keep their eyes fixed upon the shore and think that their ship is standing still and that the shore is receding, although it is the other way round. For the port, and similarly time and its pleasures, stay the same, while one after the other we in our ship of mortality go scudding across that stormy sea which takes all things to itself and devours them; nor are we ever permitted to touch shore again, but, tossed by conflicting winds, we are finally shipwrecked upon some reef.

Since the senile spirit is thus an unfit vessel for many pleasures, it cannot enjoy them; and even as to those who, when sick with a fever and with a palate spoiled by corrupt vapors, all wines seem bitter, though they be rare and delicate—so to old people in their indisposition (in which, however, there is still the desire) pleasures seem insipid and cold and very different from those which they remember enjoying once, although the pleasures in themselves are still the same. Hence, feeling themselves deprived of them, they complain and denounce present times as bad, not perceiving that the change is in themselves and not in the times; and, contrariwise, they call to mind the past pleasures along with the time in which they had those pleasures; and so they praise that time as good because it seems to carry with it a savor of what they felt when it was present. For our minds, in fact, hate all things that have accompanied our sorrows, and love those things that have accompanied our joys.

This is why sometimes to a lover it is a thing most dear to look upon a window, even if it is shuttered, because there it was that he once knew the bliss of gazing upon his lady love; and similarly, to see a ring, a letter, a garden or other place, or anything whatever that may seem to have been a conscious witness of his joys; and, on the contrary, a room that is most splendid and beautiful will often be distasteful to one who has been a prisoner there or has suffered there some other unhappiness. And I have known persons who would never again drink from a cup like the one from which they had taken medicine when sick. For just as, to the one, the window or ring or letter brings back the sweet memory that is so delightful and seems a part of bygone joy, so, to the other, the room or the cup seems to bring back to the memory the sickness or the imprisonment. For this same reason, I think, old people are brought to praise bygone times and to condemn the present.

[2] Of courts therefore they speak as of all else, declaring those they remember to have been far more excellent and full of outstanding men than those we see nowadays. And when such discussions get under way, they begin at once to extol with boundless praise the courtiers of Duke Filippo or Duke Borso; and they recount the sayings of Niccolò Piccinino, and remind us that in those days there were no murders (or rarely), that there were no fights, no ambushes, no deceits, but only a certain loyal and kindly good will among all men, and a loyal trust; and that in the courts of that time so many good customs prevailed along with such goodness, that the courtiers were all like monks; and woe unto him who spoke a bad word to another or so much as paid some less than honor-

able attention to a woman. And, on the contrary, they say that everything is the reverse these days, and that not only have courtiers lost that fraternal love and that sober manner of life, but that in the courts nothing prevails save envy, malevolence, corrupt manners, and a most dissolute life given over to every kind of vice—the women lascivious and shameless, the men effeminate. They condemn our dress also as indecent and too womanish.

In short, they censure a multitude of things, among which there are many actually deserving of censure, for it cannot be denied that there are many evil and wicked men among us, or that our times abound much more in vices than the times they praise. But I do believe they ill discern the cause of this difference, and that they are foolish. For they would have the world contain all good things, and nothing evil—which is impossible; because, since evil is the opposite of good, and good the opposite of evil, it is necessary that, by way of opposition and a certain counterbalance, the one sustain and reinforce the other, and that if the one diminishes or increases, so must the other, because there is no contrary without its contrary.

Who does not know that there would be no justice in the world if there were no wrongs? No magnanimity, if none were pusillanimous? No continence, if there were no incontinence? No health if there were no sickness? No truth, if there were no falsehood? No happiness, if there were no misfortunes? Thus, Socrates puts it very well when, as Plato has it, he expresses his wonder that Aesop did not write a fable imagining that, as God had never been able to unify pleasure and pain, He had joined them end to end, so that the beginning of the one should be the end of the other; for we know that we can never enjoy any pleasure if something unpleasant does not precede it. Who can appreciate rest without first feeling the weight of fatigue? Who relishes food, drink, or sleep, unless he has first endured hunger, thirst, or want of sleep? Therefore I think that sufferings and sickness were given to man by nature, not chiefly to make him subject to them (since it does not seem right that she who is mother of every good should give us so many ills by her own deliberate design), but as nature created health, pleasure, and other goods, so sickness, vexation, and other ills followed as consequents. Thus, when virtues were bestowed upon the world through grace and as a gift of nature, at once the vices necessarily joined company with them by way of that conjoined opposition; so that whenever the one waxes or wanes, so must the other.

[3] Therefore, when our old men praise bygone courts for not having such vicious men in them as some that are in our courts, they overlook the fact that their courts did not contain some men as virtuous as ours—which is no marvel, since no evil is as evil as that which is born of the corrupted seed of good; hence, as nature produces much greater talents now than she did then, so those who aim at the good do far better now than did those of former times, and those who aim at the bad do far worse. Hence, we must not say that those who refrained from doing evil because they did not know how deserve any praise for this; for, though they did little harm, they did the worst they could. And that

the talents of those times were, on the whole, far inferior to those of our own time is evident enough in all that we see of theirs, in letters as well as in paintings, statues, buildings, and everything else.

These old men also condemn many things that we do (which things are in themselves neither good nor bad) simply because they did not do them. And they say it is unseemly for young men to ride about the city on horseback, especially in slippers, or to wear fur linings or long garments in winter, or wear a cap before the age of eighteen, at least, and the like: in which they are quite wrong, because these customs, besides being convenient and useful, are established by usage and appeal to all, as once to go about in gala dress with uncovered breeches and dainty slippers and, in order to be dashing, to carry always a sparrow hawk on the wrist (to no purpose), to dance without touching the lady's hand, and to follow many other customs that were as much prized then as they would be outlandish now.

Therefore, let it be permitted us to follow the customs of our time without being slandered by these old men who, in their desire to praise themselves will often say: "I was still sleeping with my mother and sisters when I was twenty, and for a long time after that I didn't know what women were; and now boys are hardly dry behind the ears when they know more mischief than grown men did in those days." Nor do they see that in saying this they are confirming the fact that boys today are more talented than old men were then.

Therefore, let them leave off censuring our times as being full of vices, because to take away these would mean to take away the virtues. And let them remember that among the worthy ancients, in the age when those more than human talents and those spirits lived who were glorious and truly divine in every virtue, many vicious men were also to be found, who, if they were alive today, would surpass our wicked men in evil deeds, even as the good men of that age would in good deeds. And to this all history bears ample witness.

[4] But this I think must suffice as a rejoinder to these old men. Hence, we will end this argument, already too lengthy, no doubt, but surely not beside the purpose; and, since it is enough to have shown that the courts of our time are no less deserving of praise than those which are so much praised by old men, we will attend to the discussion that took place concerning the Courtier, from which we readily understand the rank held by the Court of Urbino among other courts, and what manner of Prince and Lady they were who were served by such noble spirits, and how fortunate all could count themselves to live in such a society.

The Last Leaf

Oliver Wendell Holmes

I saw him once before,
As he passed by the door,
  And again
The pavement stones resound,
As he totters o'er the ground
  With his cane.

They say that in his prime,
Ere the pruning-knife of Time
  Cut him down,
Not a better man was found
By the Crier on his round
  Through the town.

But now he walks the streets,
And he looks at all he meets
  Sad and wan,
And he shakes his feeble head,
That it seems as if he said,
  "They are gone."

The mossy marbles rest
On the lips that he has prest
  In their bloom,
And the names he loved to hear
Have been carved for many a year
  On the tomb.

My grandmamma has said—
Poor old lady, she is dead
  Long ago—
That he had a Roman nose,
And his cheek was like a rose
  In the snow;

But now his nose is thin,
And it rests upon his chin
  Life a staff,
And a crook is in his back,
And a melancholy crack
  In his laugh.

I know it is a sin
For me to sit and grin
    At him here;
But the old three-cornered hat,
And the breeches, and all that,
    Are so queer!

And if I should live to be
The last leaf upon the tree
    In the spring,
Let them smile, as I do now,
At the old forsaken bough
    Where I cling.

What Lips My Lips Have Kissed

Edna St. Vincent Millay

What lips my lips have kissed, and where, and why,
I have forgotten, and what arms have lain
Under my head till morning; but the rain
Is full of ghosts tonight, that tap and sigh
Upon the glass and listen for reply;
And in my heart there stirs a quiet pain
For unremembered lads that not again
Will turn to me at midnight with a cry.

Thus in the winter stands the lonely tree,
Nor knows what birds have vanished one by one,
Yet knows its boughs more silent than before:
I cannot say what loves have come and gone;
I only know that summer sang in me
A little while, that in me sings no more.

Outlived Desire

Alexander Pushkin

Translated from the Russian by Frances Cornford and Esther Polianowski Salaman

Outlived desire how departs,
    My dreams I cannot love again;
I reap the fruit of empty hearts,
    The fruit of pain.

The tempest of a cruel fate
    My fair and flowery garlands rend;
Unhappy and alone I wait:
    When comes the end?

So, stricken by the early cold,
    The whistling, bitter gales of grief,
Still the autumnal branches hold
    One shuddering leaf.

An Elegy on the Impermanence of Human Life

Yamanoe No Okura

We are helpless before time
Which ever speeds away.
And pains of a hundred kinds
Pursue us one after another.
Maidens joy in girlish pleasures,
With ship-borne gems on their wrists,
And hand in hand with their friends;
But the bloom of maidenhood,
As it cannot be stopped,
Too swiftly steals away.
When do their ample tresses
Black as a mud-snail's bowels
Turn white with the frost of age?
Whence come those wrinkles
Which furrow their rosy cheeks?
The lusty young men, warrior-like,
Bearing their sword-blades at their waists,
In their hands the hunting bows,
And mounting their bay horses,
With saddles dressed with twill,
Ride about in triumph;
But can their prime of youth
Favour them for ever?
Few are the nights they keep,
When, sliding back the plank doors,
They reach their beloved ones
And sleep, arms intertwined,
Before, with staffs at their waists,
They totter along the road,
Laughed at here, and hated there.
This is the way of the world;
And, cling as I may to life,
I know no help!

Envoy

Although I wish I were thus,
Like the rocks that stay for ever,
In this world of humanity
I cannot keep old age away.

Old Age

Al-Aswad Son of Ya'fur

Translated from the Arabic by Sir Charles Lyall

If now thou seest me a wreck, worn out and minished of sight, and all my
limbs without strength to bear my body along,
And I am deaf to the calls of love and lightness of youth, and follow wisdom in meekness, my steps easy to guide—
Time was I went every night, hair combed, to sellers of wine, and squan-
dered lightly my wealth, compliant, easy of mood.
Yea, once I played, and enjoyed the sweetest flavor of youth, my wine
the first of the grape, mingled with purest of rain—
Wine bought from one with a twang in his speech, and rings in his ears, a
belt girt round him: he brought it forth for good silver coin.
A boy deals it to our guests, girt up, two pearls in his ears, his fingers
ruddy, as though stained deep with mulberry juice,
And women white like the moon or statues stately to see, that softly carry
around great cups filled full with the wine—
White women, dainty, that shoot the hearts of men with their eyes, fair as
a nest full of ostrich eggs betwixt rock and sand.
Kind words they speak, and their limbs are soft and smooth to the touch,
their faces bright, and their hearts to lovers gentle and mild.
Low speech they murmur, in tones that bear no secrets abroad: they gain
their ends without toil, and need no shouting to win.

Lucius Atherton

Edgar Lee Masters

When my moustache curled,
And my hair was black,
And I wore tight trousers
And a diamond stud,
I was an excellent knave of hearts and took many a trick.
But when the gray hairs began to appear—
Lo! a new generation of girls
Laughed at me, not fearing me,
And I had no more exciting adventures
Wherein I was all but shot for a heartless devil,
But only drabby affairs, warmed-over affairs
Of other days and other men.
And time went on until I lived at Mayer's restaurant,
Partaking of short-orders, a gray, untidy,
Toothless, discarded, rural Don Juan. . . .
There is a mighty shade here who sings
Of one named Beatrice;
And I see now that the force that made him great
Drove me to the dregs of life.

So, We'll Go No More A-Roving

George Gordon, Lord Byron

So, we'll go no more a-roving
    So late into the night,
Though the heart be still as loving,
    And the moon be still as bright.

For the sword outwears its sheath,
    And the soul wears out the breast,
And the heart must pause to breathe,
    And Love itself have rest.

Though the night was made for loving,
    And the day returns too soon,
Yet we'll go no more a-roving
    By the light of the moon.

To the Virgins, To Make Much of Time

Robert Herrick

Gather ye rosebuds while ye may,
    Old Time is still a-flying:
And this same flower that smiles today
    To-morrow will be dying.

The glorious lamp of heaven, the sun,
    The higher he's a-getting,
The sooner will his race be run,
    And nearer he's to setting.

That age is best which is the first,
    When youth and blood are warmer;
But being spent, the worse, and worst
    Times still succeed the former.

Then be not coy, but use your time,
    And while ye may, go marry:
For having lost but once your prime,
    You may for ever tarry.

Old Age

Anton Chekhov

State-Councillor Uzelkov, architect, arrived in his native town, where he had been summoned to restore the cemetery church. He was born in the town, he had grown up and been married there, and yet when he got out of the train he hardly recognised it. Everything was changed. For instance, eighteen years ago, when he left the town to settle in Petersburg, where the railway station is now boys used to hunt for marmots: now as you come into the High Street there is a four storied "Hôtel Vienna," with apartments, where there was of old an ugly grey fence. But not the fence or the houses, or anything had changed so much as the people. Questioning the hall-porter, Uzelkov discovered that more than half of the people he remembered were dead or paupers or forgotten.

"Do you remember Uzelkov?" he asked the porter. "Uzelkov, the architect, who divorced his wife. . . . He had a house in Sviribev Street. . . . Surely you remember."

"No, I don't remember anyone of the name."

"Why, it's impossible not to remember. It was an exciting case. All the cab-men knew, even. Try to remember. His divorce was managed by the attorney, Shapkin, the swindler. . . . the notorious sharper, the man who was thrashed at the club. . . ."

"You mean Ivan Nikolaich?"

"Yes. . . . Is he alive? dead?"

"Thank heaven, his honour's alive. His honour's a notary now, with an office. Well-to-do. Two houses in Kirpichny Street. Just lately married his daughter off."

Uzelkov strode from one corner of the room to another. An idea flashed into his mind. From boredom, he decided to see Shapkin. It was afternoon when he left the hotel and quietly walked to Kirpichny Street. He found Shapkin in his office and hardly recognised him. From the well-built, alert attorney with a quick, impudent, perpetually tipsy expression, Shapkin had become a modest, grey-haired, shrunken old man.

"You don't recognise me . . . You have forgotten . . ." Uzelkov began. "I'm your old client, Uzelkov."

"Uzelkov? Which Uzelkov? Ah!"

Remembrance came to Shapkin: he recognised him and was confused. Began exclamations, questions, recollections.

"Never expected . . . never thought . . ." chuckled Shapkin. "What will you have? Would you like champagne? Perhaps you'd like oysters. My dear man, what a lot of money I got out of you in the old days—so much that I can't think what I ought to stand you."

256

"Please don't trouble," said Uzelkov. "I haven't time. I must go to the cemetery and examine the church. I have a commission."

"Splendid. We'll have something to eat and a drink and go together. I've got some splendid horses! I'll take you there and introduce you to the churchwarden. . . . I'll fix up everything. . . . But what's the matter, my dearest man? You're not avoiding me, not afraid? Please sit nearer. There's nothing to be afraid of now. . . . Long ago, I really was pretty sharp, a bit of a rogue . . . but now I'm quieter than water, humbler than grass. I've grown old; got a family. There are children. . . . Time to die!"

The friends had something to eat and drink, and went in a coach and pair to the cemetery.

"Yes, it was a good time," Shapkin was reminiscent, sitting in the sledge. "I remember, but I simply can't believe it. Do you remember how you divorced your wife? It's almost twenty years ago, and you've probably forgotten everything, but I remember it as though I conducted the petition yesterday. My God, how rotten I was! Then I was a smart, casuistical devil, full of sharp practice and devilry . . . and I used to run into some shady affairs, particularly when there was a good fee, as in your case, for instance. What was it you paid me then? Five—six hundred. Enough to upset anybody! By the time you left for Petersburg you'd left the whole affair completely in my hands. 'Do what you like!' And your former wife, Sofya Mikhailovna, though she did come from a merchant family, was proud and selfish. To bribe her to take the guilt on herself was difficult—extremely difficult. I used to come to her for a business talk, and when she saw me, she would say to her maid: 'Masha, surely I told you I wasn't at home to scoundrels.' I tried one way, then another . . . wrote letters to her, tried to meet her accidentally—no good. I had to work through a third person. For a long time I had trouble with her, and she only yielded when you agreed to give her ten thousand. She succumbed. . . . She began to weep, spat in my face, but she yielded and took the guilt on herself."

"If I remember it was fifteen, not ten thousand she took from me," said Uzelkov.

"Yes, of course . . . fifteen, my mistake." Shapkin was disconcerted. "Anyway, it's all past and done with now. Why shouldn't I confess, frankly? Ten I gave to her, and the remaining five I bargained out of you for my own share. I deceived both of you. . . . It's all past, why be ashamed of it? And who else was there to take from, Boris Petrovich, if not from you? I ask you. . . . You were rich and well-to-do. You married in caprice: you were divorced in caprice. You were making a fortune. I remember you got twenty thousand out of a single contract. Whom was I to tap, if not you? And I must confess, I was tortured by envy. If you got hold of a nice lot of money, people would take off their hats to you: but the same people would beat me for shillings and smack my face in the club. But why recall it? It's time to forget."

"Tell me, please, how did Sofya Mikhailovna live afterwards?"

"With her ten thousand? *On ne peut plus* badly. . . . God knows whether it was frenzy or pride and conscience that tortured her, because she had sold herself for money—or perhaps she loved you; but, she took to drink, you know. She received the money and began to gad about with officers in troikas. . . . Drunkenness, philandering, debauchery. . . . She would come into a tavern with an officer, and instead of port or a light wine, she would drink the strongest cognac to drive her into a frenzy.''

"Yes, she was eccentric. I suffered enough with her. She would take offence at some trifle and then get nervous. . . . And what happened afterwards?''

"A week passed, a fortnight. . . . I was sitting at home writing. Suddenly, the door opened and she comes in. 'Take your cursed money,' she said and threw the parcel in my face. . . . She could not resist it. . . . Five hundred were missing. She had only got rid of five hundred.''

"And what did you do with the money?''

"It's all past and done with. What's the good of concealing it? . . . I certainly took it. What are you staring at me like that for? Wait for the sequel. It's a complete novel, the sickness of a soul! Two months passed by. One night I came home drunk, in a wicked mood. . . . I turned on the light and saw Sofya Mikhailovna sitting on my sofa, drunk too, wandering a bit, with something savage in her face as if she had just escaped from the mad-house. 'Give me my money back,' she said. 'I've changed my mind. If I'm going to the dogs, I want to go madly, passionately. Make haste, you scoundrel, give me the money.' How indecent it was!''

"And you . . . did you give it to her?''

"I remember. . . . I gave her ten rubles.''

"Oh . . . is it possible?'' Uzelkov frowned. "If you couldn't do it yourself, or you didn't want to, you could have written to me. . . . And I didn't know . . . I didn't know.''

"My dear man, why should I write, when she wrote herself afterwards when she was in a hospital?''

"I was so taken up with the new marriage that I paid no attention to letters. . . . But you were an outsider; you had no antagonism to Sofya Mikhailovna. . . . Why didn't you help her?''

"We can't judge by our present standards, Boris Petrovich. Now we think in this way; but then we thought quite differently. . . . Now I might perhaps give her a thousand rubles; but then even ten rubles . . . she didn't get them for nothing. It's a terrible story. It's time to forget. . . . But here you are!''

The sledge stopped at the churchyard gate. Uzelkov and Shapkin got out of the sledge, went through the gate and walked along a long, broad avenue. The bare cherry trees, the acacias, the grey crosses and monuments sparkled with hoar-frost. In each flake of snow the bright sunny day was reflected. There was the smell you find in all cemeteries of incense and fresh-dug earth.

"You have a beautiful cemetery,'' said Uzelkov. "It's almost an orchard.''

"Yes, but it's a pity the thieves steal the monuments. Look, there, behind that cast-iron memorial, on the right, Sofya Mikhailovna is buried. Would you like to see?''

The friends turned to the right, stepping in deep snow towards the cast-iron memorial.

"Down here," said Shapkin, pointing to a little stone of white marble. "Some subaltern or other put up the monument on her grave."

Uzelkov slowly took off his hat and showed his bald pate to the snow. Eyeing him, Shapkin also took off his hat, and another baldness shone beneath the sun. The silence round about was like the tomb, as though the air were dead, too. The friends looked at the stone, silent, thinking.

"She is asleep!" Shapkin broke the silence. "And she cares very little that she took the guilt upon herself and drank cognac. Confess, Boris Petrovich!"

"What?" asked Uzelkov, sternly.

"That, however loathsome the past may be, it's better than this." And Shapkin pointed to his grey hairs.

"In the old days I did not even think of death. . . . If I'd met her, I would have circumvented her, but now . . . well, now!"

Sadness took hold of Uzelkov. Suddenly he wanted to cry, passionately, as he once desired to love. . . . And he felt that these tears would be exquisite, refreshing. Moisture came out of his eyes and a lump rose in his throat, but . . . Shapkin was standing by his side, and Uzelkov felt ashamed of his weakness before a witness. He turned back quickly and walked towards the church.

Two hours later, having arranged with the churchwarden and examined the church, he seized the opportunity while Shapkin was talking away to the priest, and ran to shed a tear. He walked to the stone surreptitiously, with stealthy steps, looking round all the time. The little white monument stared at him absently, so sadly and innocently, as though a girl and not a wanton divorcée were beneath.

"If I could weep, could weep!" thought Uzelkov.

But the moment for weeping had been lost. Though the old man managed to make his eyes shine, and tried to bring himself to the right pitch, the tears did not flow and the lump did not rise in his throat. . . . After waiting for about ten minutes, Uzelkov waved his arm and went to look for Shapkin.

The Letter

Dhumketu

Translated from the Gujerati * by the author

In the grey sky of early dawn stars still glowed, as happy memories light up a life that is nearing its close. An old man was walking through the town, now and again drawing his tattered cloak tighter to shield his body from the cold and biting wind. From some houses standing apart came the sound of grinding mills and the sweet voices of women singing at their work, and these sounds helped him along his lonely way. Except for the occasional bark of a dog, the distant steps of a workman going early to work or the screech of a bird disturbed before its time, the whole town was wrapped in deathly silence. Most of its inhabitants were still in the arms of sleep, a sleep which grew more and more profound on account of the intense winter cold; for the cold used sleep to extend its sway over all things even as a false friend lulls his chosen victim with caressing smiles. The old man, shivering at times but fixed of purpose, plodded on till he came out of the town gate to a straight road. Along this he now went at a somewhat slower pace, supporting himself on his old staff.

On one side of the road was a row of trees, on the other the town's public garden. The night was darker now and the cold more intense, for the wind was blowing straight along the road and on it there only fell, like frozen snow, the faint light of the morning star. At the end of the garden stood a handsome building of the newest style, and light gleamed through the crevices of its closed doors and windows.

Beholding the wooden arch of this building, the old man was filled with the joy that the pilgrim feels when he first sees the goal of his journey. On the arch hung an old board with the newly painted letters: POST OFFICE. The old man went in quietly and squatted on the veranda. The voices of the two or three people busy at their routine work could be heard faintly through the wall.

"Police Superintendent," a voice inside called sharply. The old man started at the sound, but composed himself again to wait. But for the faith and love that warmed him he could not have borne the bitter cold.

Name after name rang out from within as the clerk read out the English addresses on the letters and flung them to the waiting postmen. From long practice he had acquired great speed in reading out the titles—Commissioner, Superintendent, Diwan Sahib, Librarian—and in flinging out the letters.

In the midst of this procedure a jesting voice from inside called, "Coachman Ali!"

The old man got up, raised his eyes to Heaven in gratitude and, stepping forward, put his hand on the door.

---

* the language of the people of Gujerat, a region on the west coast of India.

"Godul Bhai!"

"Yes. Who's there?"

"You called out Coachman Ali's name, didn't you? Here I am. I have come for my letter."

"It is a madman, sir, who worries us by calling every day for letters that never come," said the clerk to the postmaster.

The old man went back slowly to the bench on which he had been accustomed to sit for five long years.

Ali had once been a clever shikari. As his skill increased so did his love for the hunt, till at last it was as impossible for him to pass a day without it as it is for the opium eater to forego his daily portion. When Ali sighted the earth-brown partridge, almost invisible to other eyes, the poor bird, they said, was as good as in his bag. His sharp eyes would see the hare crouching in its form. When even the dogs failed to see the creature cunningly hidden in the yellow-brown scrub, Ali's eagle eyes would catch sight of its ears; and in another moment it was dead. Besides this, he would often go with his friends, the fishermen.

But when the evening of his life was drawing in, he left his old ways and suddenly took a new turn. His only child, Miriam, married and left him. She went off with a soldier to his regiment in the Punjab, and for the last five years he had had no news of this daughter for whose sake alone he dragged on a cheerless existence. Now he understood the meaning of love and separation. He could no longer enjoy the sportsman's pleasure and laugh at the bewildered terror of the young partridges bereft of their parents.

Although the hunter's instinct was in his very blood and bones, such a loneliness had come into his life since the day Miriam had gone away that now, forgetting his sport, he would become lost in admiration of the green corn fields. He reflected deeply and came to the conclusion that the whole universe is built up through love and that the grief of separation is inescapable. And seeing this, he sat down under a tree and wept bitterly. From that day he had risen each morning at four o'clock to walk to the post office. In his whole life he had never received a letter, but with a devout serenity born of hope and faith he continued and was always the first to arrive.

The post office, one of the most uninteresting buildings in the world, became his place of pilgrimage. He always occupied a particular seat in a particular corner of the building, and when people got to know his habit they laughed at him. The postmen began to make a game of him. Even though there was no letter for him, they would call out his name for the fun of seeing him jump and come to the door. But with boundless faith and infinite patience he came every day—and went away empty-handed.

While Ali waited, peons would come for their firms' letters and he would hear them discussing their masters' scandals. These smart young peons in their spotless turbans and creaking shoes were always eager to express themselves. Meanwhile the door would be thrown open and the postmaster, a man with a head as sad and inexpressive as a pumpkin, would be seen sitting on his chair inside. There was no glimmer of animation in his features; and such men usually prove to be village schoolmasters, office clerks or postmasters.

One day he was there as usual and did not move from his seat when the door was opened.

"Police Commissioner!" the clerk called out, and a fellow stepped forward briskly for the letters.

"Superintendent!" Another peon came; and so the clerk, like a worshipper of Vishnu, repeated his customary thousand names.

At last they had all gone. Ali too got up and, saluting the post office as though it housed some precious relic, went off, a pitiable figure, a century behind his time.

"That fellow," asked the postmaster, "is he mad?"

"Who, sir? Oh yes," answered the clerk. "No matter what sort of weather, he has been here every day for the last five years. But he doesn't get many letters."

"I can well understand that! Who does he think will have time to write to him every day?"

"But he's a bit touched, sir. In the old days he committed many sins; and maybe he shed blood within some sacred precincts and is paying for it now," the postman added in support to his statement.

"Madmen are strange people," the postmaster said.

"Yes. Once I saw a madman in Ahmedabad who did absolutely nothing but make little heaps of dust. Another had a habit of going every day to the river in order to pour water on a certain stone!"

"Oh, that's nothing," chimed in another. "I knew one madman who paced up and down all day long, another who never ceased declaiming poetry, and a third who would slap himself on the cheek and then begin to cry out because he was being beaten."

And everyone in the post office began talking of lunacy. All working-class people have a habit of taking periodic rests by joining in general discussion for a few minutes. After listening a little, the postmaster got up and said:

"It seems as though the mad live in a world of their own making. To them, perhaps, we too appear mad. The madman's world is rather like the poet's, I should think!"

He laughed as he spoke the last words, looking at one of the clerks who wrote indifferent verse. Then he went out and the office became still again.

For several days Ali had not come to the post office. There was no one with enough sympathy or understanding to guess the reason, but all were curious to know what had stopped the old man. At last he came again; but it was a struggle for him to breathe, and on his face were clear signs of his approaching end. That day he could not contain his impatience.

"Master Sahib," he begged the postmaster, "have you a letter from my Miriam?"

The postmaster was in a hurry to get out to the country.

"What a pest you are, brother!" he exclaimed.

"My name is Ali," answered Ali, absent-mindedly.

"I know! I know! But do you think we've got your Miriam's name registered?"

"Then please note it down, brother. It will be useful if a letter should come when I am not here." For how should the villager who had spent three quarters of his life hunting know that Miriam's name was not worth a pice to anyone but her father?

The postmaster was beginning to lose his temper. "Have you no sense?" he cried. "Get away! Do you think we are going to eat your letter when it comes?" And he walked off hastily. Ali came our very slowly, turning after every few steps to gaze at the post office. His eyes were filling with tears of helplessness, for his patience was exhausted, even though he still had faith. Yet how could he still hope to hear from Miriam?

Ali heard one of the clerks coming up behind him and turned to him.

"Brother!" he said.

The clerk was surprised, but being a decent fellow he said, "Well?"

"Here, look at this!" and Ali produced an old tin box and emptied five golden guineas into the surprised clerk's hands. "Do not look so startled," he continued, "they will be useful to you, and they can never be so to me. But will you do one thing?"

"What?"

"What do you see up there?" said Ali, pointing to the sky.

"Heaven."

"Allah is there, and in His presence I am giving you this money. When it comes, you must forward my Miriam's letter to me."

"But where—where am I to send it?" asked the utterly bewildered clerk.

"To my grave."

"What?"

"Yes. It is true. Today is my last day: my very last, alas! And I have not seen Miriam, I have had no letter from her." Tears were in Ali's eyes as the clerk slowly left him and went on his way with the five golden guineas in his pocket.

Ali was never seen again and no one troubled to inquire after him.

One day, however, trouble came to the postmaster. His daughter lay ill in another town and he was anxiously waiting for news from her. The post was brought in and the letters piled on the table. Seeing an envelope of the color and shape he expected, the postmaster eagerly snatched it up. It was addressed to coachman Ali, and he dropped it as though it had given him an electric shock. The haughty temper of the official had quite left him in his sorrow and anxiety and had laid bare his human heart. He knew at once that this was the letter the old man had been waiting for: it must be from his daughter Miriam.

"Lakshmi Das!" called the postmaster, for such was the name of the clerk to whom Ali had given his money.

"Yes, sir?"

"This is for your old coachman Ali. Where is he now?"

"I will find out, sir."

The postmaster did not receive his own letter all that day.

He worried all night and, getting up at three, went to sit in the office. "When Ali comes at four o'clock," he mused, "I will give him the letter myself."

For now the postmaster understood all Ali's heart, and his very soul. After spending but a single night in suspense, anxiously waiting for news of his daughter, his heart was brimming with sympathy for the poor old man who had spent his nights for the last five years in the same suspense. At the stroke of five he heard a soft knock on the door: he felt sure it was Ali. He rose quickly from his chair, his suffering father's heart recognizing another, and flung the door wide open.

"Come in, brother Ali," he cried, handing the letter to the meek old man, bent double with age, who was standing outside. Ali was leaning on a stick and the tears were wet on his face as they had been when the clerk left him. But his features had been hard then and now they were softened by lines of kindliness. He lifted his eyes and in them was a light so unearthly that the postmaster shrank in fear and astonishment.

Lakshmi Das had heard the postmaster's words as he came towards the office from another quarter. "Who was that, sir? Old Ali?" he asked. But the postmaster took no notice of him. He was staring with wide-open eyes at the doorway from which Ali had disappeared. Where could he have gone? At last he turned to Lakshmi Das. "Yes, I was speaking to Ali," he said.

"Old Ali is dead, sir. But give me his letter."

"What! But when? Are you sure, Lakshmi Das?"

"Yes, it is so," broke in a postman who had just arrived. "Ali died three months ago."

The postmaster was bewildered. Miriam's letter was still lying near the door; Ali's image was still before his eyes. He listened to Lakshmi Das' recital of the last interview, but he could still not doubt the reality of the knock on the door and the tears in Ali's eyes. He was perplexed. Had he really seen Ali? Had his imagination deceived him? Or had it perhaps been Lakshmi Das?

The daily routine began. The clerk read out the addresses—Police Commissioner, Superintendent, Librarian—and flung the letters deftly.

But the postmaster now watched them as though each contained a warm, beating heart. He no longer thought of them in terms of envelopes and postcards. He saw the essential, human worth of a letter.

That evening you might have seen Lakshmi Das and the postmaster walking with slow steps to Ali's grave. They laid the letter on it and turned back.

"Lakshmi Das, were you indeed the first to come to the office this morning?"

"Yes, sir, I was the first."

"Then how . . . No, I don't understand . . ."

"What, sir?"

"Oh, never mind," the postmaster said shortly. At the office he parted from Lakshmi Das and went in. The newly-waked father's heart in him was reproaching him for having failed to understand Ali's anxiety. Tortured by doubt and remorse, he sat down in the glow of the charcoal sigri to wait.

The Gold Watch

Mulk Raj Anand

There was something about the smile of Mr. Acton when he came over to Srijut Sudarshan Sharma's table which betokened disaster. But as the Sahib had only said, "Mr. Sharma, I have brought something specially for you from London—you must come into my office on Monday and take it. . . ," the poor old despatch clerk could not surmise the real meaning of the General Manager's remark. The fact that Mr. Acton should come over to his table at all, fawn upon him and say what he had said was, of course, most flattering, for very rarely did the head of the firm condescend to move down the corridor where the Indian staff of the distribution department of the great Marmalade Empire of Henry King & Co. worked.

But that smile on Mr. Acton's face! Specially as Mr. Acton was not known to smile too much, being a morose old Sahib, hard working, conscientious, and a slave driver, famous as a shrewd businessman, so devoted to the job of spreading the monopoly of King's Marmalade and sundry other products that his wife had left him after a three months' spell of marriage and never returned to India, though no one quite knew whether she was separated or divorced from him or merely preferred to stay away. So the fact that Acton Sahib should smile was enough to give Srijut Sharma cause for thought. But then Srijut Sharma was, in spite of his nobility of soul and fundamental innocence, experienced enough in his study of the vague, detached faces of the white Sahibs by now and had clearly noticed the slight awkward curl of the upper lip, behind which the determined tobacco-stained long teeth showed for the briefest moment a snarl suppressed by the deliberation which Acton Sahib had brought to the whole operation of coming over and pronouncing those kind words. And what could be the reason for his having been singled out from among the twenty-five odd members of the distribution department? In the usual way, he, the despatch clerk, only received an occasional greeting: "Hello, Sharma—how you getting on?" from the head of his own department, Mr. West Sahib, or a reprimand because some letters or packets had gone astray; otherwise, he himself being the incarnation of clockwork efficiency and well-versed in the routine of his job, there was no occasion for any break in the monotony of that anonymous, smooth-working Empire, so far at least as he was concerned.

To be sure, there was the continual gossip of the clerks and the accountants, the bickerings and jealousies of the people above him for grades and promotions and pay, but he, Sharma, had been employed twenty years ago as a special favor, was not even a matriculate, but had picked up the work somehow and, though unwanted and constantly reprimanded by West Sahib in the first few years, had been retained in his job because of the general legend of saintliness which he had acquired . . . He had five more years of service to do, because then he would be fifty-five and the family-raising, *grhst* portion of his life in the fourfold scheme, prescribed by religion, finished. He hoped to retire to his home town, Jullundhur, where his father still ran the confectioner's shop off the Mall Road.

"And what did Acton Sahib have to say to you, Mr. Sharma?" asked Miss Violet Dixon, the plain snub-nosed Anglo-Indian typist in her sing-song.

Since he was an old family man of fifty who had greyed prematurely, she considered her virginity safe enough with this "gentleman" and freely conversed with him, specially during the lunch hour.

"Han," he said, "he has brought something for me from England," Srijut Sharma answered.

"There are such pretty things in U.K.," she said. "My! I wish I could go there! . . . My sister is there, you know! Married! . . ."

She had told Sharma all these things before. So he was not interested. Specially today, because all his thoughts were concentrated on the inner meaning of Mr. Acton's sudden visitation and the ambivalent smile.

"Well, half day today, I am off," said Violet and moved away with the peculiar snobbish agility of the Mem Sahib she affected to be.

Srijut Sharma stared at her blankly, though taking her regular form into his subconscious with more than the old uncle's interest he had always pretended. It was only her snub nose, like that of Sarup-naka, the sister of the demon king, Ravana, that stood in the way of her being married, he felt sure, for otherwise she had a tolerable figure. And his obsession about the meaning of Acton Sahib's words returned, from the pent-up curiosity, with greater force now that he realized the vastness of the space of time during which he would have to wait in suspense before knowing what the boss had brought for him and why.

He took up his faded sola topee, which was, apart from the bush shirt and trousers, one of the few concessions to modernity which he had made throughout his life as a good Brahmin, got up from his chair, beckoned Dugdu from the verandah on his way out and asked: "Has Acton Sahib gone you know?"

"Abhi-Sahib in lift, going down," Dugdu said.

Srijut Sharma made quickly for the stairs and, throwing all caution about slipping on the polished marble steps to the winds, hurtled down. There were three floors below him and he began to sweat, both through fear of missing the Sahib and the heat of mid-April. As he got to the ground floor he saw Acton Sahib already going out of the door.

It was now or never.

Srijut Sharma rushed out. But he was conscious that quite a few employees of the firm would be coming out of the two lifts and he might be seen talking to the Sahib. And that was not done—outside the office. The Sahibs belonged to their private world where no intrusion was tolerated, for they refused to listen to pleas for advancement through improper channels.

Mr. Acton's uniformed driver opened the door of the polished Buick and the Sahib sat down, spreading the shadow of grimness all around him.

Srijut Sharma hesitated, for the demeanor of the Goanese chauffeur was frightening.

By now the driver had smartly shut the back door of the car and was proceeding to his seat.

That was his only chance.

Taking off his hat, he rushed up to the window of the car and rudely thrust his face into the presence of Mr. Acton.

Luckily for him the Sahib did not brush him aside, but smiled a broader smile than that of a few minutes ago and said: "You want to know what I have brought for you—well, it is a gold watch with an inscription on it. See me Monday morning . . ." The Sahib's initiative in anticipating his question threw Srijut Sharma further off his balance. The sweat just poured down from his forehead, even as he mumbled, "Thank you, Sir, thank you . . ."

"Chalo, driver!" the Sahib ordered.

And the chauffeur turned and looked hard at Srijut Sharma.

The despatch clerk withdrew with a sheepish, abject smile on his face and stood, hat in left hand, the right hand raised to his forehead in the attitude of a nearly military salute.

The motor car moved off.

But Srijut Sharma stood still, as though he had been struck dumb. He was neither happy nor sad at this moment—only numbed by the shock of surprise. Why should he be singled out from the whole distribution department of Henry King & Co. for the privilege of the gift of a gold watch! . . . He had done nothing brave that he could remember. "A gold watch, with an inscription on it!" Oh, he knew now—the intuitive truth rose inside him—the Sahib wanted him to retire . . .

The revelation rose to the surface of his awareness from the deep obsessive fear which had possessed him for nearly half an hour, and his heart began to palpitate against his will, and the sweat sozzled his body. He reeled a little, then adjusted himself and got onto the pavement, looking after the car which had already turned the corner into Nicol Road.

He turned and began to walk towards Victoria Terminus Station to take his train to Thana, thirty miles out, where he had resided for cheapness almost all the years he had been in Bombay. His steps were heavy, for he was reasonably sure now that he would get notice of retirement on Monday. He tried to think of some other possible reason why the Sahib may have decided to give him the gift of a gold watch with an inscription. There was no other explanation. His doom was sealed. What would he say to his wife? And his son had still not passed his Matric. How would he support the family? The provident fund would not amount to very much, specially in these days of rising prices . . .

He felt a pull at his heart. He paused for breath and tried to calm himself. The old blood pressure! Or was it merely wind? . . . He must not get into a panic at any cost. He steadied his gait and walked along muttering to himself, "Shanti! Shanti! Shanti!" as though the very incantation of the formula of peace would restore him to calm and equanimity.

During the weekend, Srijut Sharma was able to conceal his panic and confusion behind the façade of an exaggerated *bonhomie* with the skill of an accomplished actor. On Saturday night he went with his wife and son to see Professor Ram's circus which was performing opposite the Portuguese Church. He spent a little longer on his prayers, but otherwise seemed normal enough on the surface. Only he ate very little of the gala meal of the rice kichri put before him by his wife and seemed lost in thought for a few moments at a time. And his illiterate but shrewd wife noticed that there was something on his mind.

"Thou has not eaten at all today," she said as he left the tasty papadum and the mango pickle untouched. "Look at Hari! He has left nothing in his thali!"

"Hoon," he answered abstractedly. And then, realizing that he might be found out for the worried, unhappy man he was, he tried to bluff her. "As a matter of fact, I was thinking of some happy news that the Sahib gave me yesterday: he said he had brought a gold watch as a gift for me from Vilayat . . ."

"Then, Papaji, give me the silver watch you are using now," said Hari, his young son, impetuously. "I have no watch at all and am always late everywhere."

"Not so impatient, son!" counseled Hari's mother. "Let your father get the gold watch first and then . . . he will surely give you his silver watch!"

In the ordinary way, Srijut Sharma would have endorsed his wife's sentiments. But today he felt that, on the face of it, his son's demand was justified. How should Hari know that the silver watch, the gold watch and a gold ring would be all the jewelry he, the father, would have for security against hard days if the gold watch was, as he prognosticated, only a token being offered by the firm to sugarcoat the bitter pill they would ask him to swallow— retirement five years before the appointed time! He hesitated, then lifted his head, smiled at his son and said:

"Acha, Kaka, you can have my silver watch . . ."

"Can I have it really, Papaji, hurry!" the boy said, getting up to fetch it from his father's pocket. "Give it to me now, today!"

"Vay, son, you are so selfish!" his mother exclaimed. For, with the peculiar sensitiveness of the woman, she had surmised from the manner in which her husband had hung his head and then tried to smile as he lifted his face to his son that the father of Hari was upset inside him or at least not in his usual mood of accepting life evenly, accompanying this acceptance with the pious invocation, "Shanti! Shanti! Shanti!"

Hari brought the silver watch, adjusted it to his left ear to see if it ticked and, happy in the possession of it, capered a little caper.

Srijut Sharma did not say anything, but pushing his thali away got up to wash his hands.

The next day it happened as Srijut Sharma had anticipated.

He went in to see Mr. Acton as soon as the Sahib came in, for the suspense of the weekend had mounted to a crescendo by Monday morning and he had been trembling with trepidation, pale and completely unsure of himself. The General Manager called him in immediately and the peon Dugdu presented the little slip with the despatch clerk's name on it.

"Please sit down," said Mr. Acton, lifting his grey-haired head from the papers before him. And then, pulling his keys from his trousers pocket by the gold chain to which they were adjusted, he opened a drawer and fetched out what Sharma thought was a beautiful red case.

"Mr. Sharma, you have been a loyal friend of this firm for many years . . . and . . . you know, your loyalty has been your greatest asset here . . . because . . . er . . . otherwise, we could have got someone with better quali-fications to do your work! Now . . . we are thinking of increasing the ef-ficiency of the business all around! And, well, we feel that you would also like, at your age, to retire to your native Punjab . . . So, as a token of our apprecia-tion for your loyalty to Henry King & Co., we are presenting you this gold watch . . ." And he pushed the red case towards him.

"Sahib! . . ." Srijut Sharma began to speak, but though his mouth opened, he could not go on. "I am only fifty years old," he wanted to say, "and I still have five years to go." His facial muscles seemed to contract, his eyes were dimmed with the fumes of frustration and bitterness, his forehead was covered with sweat. At least they might have made a little ceremony of the presenta-tion. He could not even utter the words, "Thank you, Sir."

"Of course, you will also have your provident fund and one month's leave with pay before you retire . . ."

Again Srijut Sharma tried to voice his inner protest in words which would convey his meaning without seeming to be disloyal, for he did not want to obliterate the one concession the Sahib had made to the whole record of his ser-vice with his firm. It was just likely that Mr. Acton might remind him of his failings as a despatch clerk if he should as much as indicate that he was unamenable to the suggestion made by the Sahib on behalf of Henry King & Co.

"Look at the watch—it has an inscription on it which will please you," said Mr. Acton to get over the embarrassment created by the silence of the despatch clerk.

These words hypnotized Sharma and, stretching his hands across the large table, he reached out heavily for the gift.

Mr. Acton noticed the unsureness of his hand and pushed it gently forward.

Srijut picked up the red box, but, in his eagerness to follow the Sahib's behests, dropped it even as he had held it aloft and tried to open it.

The Sahib's face was livid as he picked up the box and hurriedly opened it. Then, lifting the watch from its socket, he wound it and applied it to his ear. It was ticking. He turned it round and showed the inscription to the despatch clerk.

Srijut Sharma put both his hands out, more steadily this time, and took the gift in the manner in which a beggar receives alms. He brought the glistening object within the orbit of his eyes, but they were dimmed with tears and he could not read anything. He tried to smile, however, and then, with a great heave of his will which rocked his body from side to side, pronounced the words, "Thank you, Sir . . ."

Mr. Acton got up, took the gold watch from Srijut Sharma's hands and put it back in the socket of the red case. Then he stretched his right hand towards the despatch clerk with a brisk shake-hand gesture and offered the case to him with his left hand.

Srijut Sharma instinctively took the Sahib's right hand gratefully in his two sweating hands and then opened the palms out to receive the case.

"Good luck, Sharma," Mr. Acton said. "Come and see me after your leave is over. And when your son matriculates let me know if I can do something for him . . ."

Dumb and with bent head, the fumes of his violent emotions rising above the mouth which could have expressed them, he withdrew in the abject manner of his ancestors going out of the presence of a feudal lord.

Mr. Acton saw the danger to the watch and went ahead to open the door so that the clerk could go out without knocking his head against the door or falling down.

As Srijut Sharma emerged from the General Manager's office, tears involuntarily flowed from his eyes and his lower lip fell in a pout that somehow controlled him from breaking down completely.

The eyes of the whole office staff were on him. In a moment, a few of the men clustered around his person. One of them took the case from his hands, opened it and read the inscription out loud: "In appreciation of the loyal service of Mr. Sharma to Henry King & Co. on his retirement."

The curiosity of his colleagues became a little less enthusiastic though the watch passed from hand to hand.

Unable to stand because of the waves of dizziness that swirled in his head, Srijut Sudarshan Sharma sat down on his chair with his head hidden in his hands and allowed the tears to roll down. One of his colleagues, Mr. Banaji, the accountant, patted his back understandingly. But the pity was too much for him.

"To be sure, Seth Makanji, the new partner, has a relation to fill Sharma's position," one said.

"No, no," another refuted him. "No one is required to kill himself with work in our big concern . . . We are given the Sunday off! And a fat pension years before it is due. The bosses are full of love for us! . . ."

"Damn fine gold watch, but it does not go!" said Shri Raman the typist.

Mr. Banaji took the watch from Srijut Raman and, putting it in the case, placed it before Srijut Sharma as he signed the others to move away.

As Srijut Sharma realized that his colleagues had drifted away, he lifted his morose head, took the case, as well as his hat, and began to walk away. Mr. Banaji saw him off to the door, his hand on Sharma's back. "Sahibji," the parsi accountant said as the lift came up and the liftman took Sharma in.

On the way home he found that the gold watch only went when it was shaken. Obviously some delicate part had broken when he had dropped it on Mr. Acton's table. He would get it mended, but he must save all the cash he could get hold of and not go spending it on the luxury of having a watch repaired now. He shouldn't have been weak with his son and given him his old silver watch. But as there would be no office to attend, he would not need to look at the time very much, specially in Jullundhur where time just stood still and no one bothered about keeping appointments.

Part Five

Dying
and Death

POPULAR AND PROFESSIONAL INTEREST IN AGING AND IN DYING IS NOT NEW, but much of it prior to the past few decades was limited to myths about long life and to ways of achieving longevity.[1] This interest is still prevalent in the field of gerontology. (Contemporary attempts to achieve longevity include beliefs about life after life or life after death, certainly an age-old issue, as well as various rejuvenation methods.)

Current professional interest in the topic of dying focuses on the ways we think about death; the experiences of the individual while dying, such as feelings of loneliness, anger, peace, and acceptance (explored in the research of psychiatrist Elisabeth Kübler-Ross);[2] relationships of the dying person to others, such as distant and close family, friends, and institution or hospital staff members. It is concerned with questions concerning the usage or non-usage of life-extending equipment. It is interested in the types of environments that are most beneficial, both medically and experientially, to the dying person, such as the hospice, the nursing home, the hospital, and the person's own home. Current professional interest also focuses on the issues surrounding the many influences of the dying person on the living by considering such topics as grief: consequences to the individual when grief is or is not expressed and fully experienced, its various dimensions, and the importance to both the individual and to the family of the period of mourning, functions of the funeral, and so on. Professional interest in aging and in dying now goes well beyond earlier concerns, though those earlier concerns continue to be of interest.

One of the current explicit issues—and it probably always was at least an implicit issue—is "What is a good death?" Repeatedly when one asks students this question, many respond with "a quick death, not long, not drawn out—you get it over with quickly," or "it doesn't involve a lot of suffering," or "the person is with loved ones" or "it happens when a person is old, not young," or "when someone is still functioning and enjoying life, not on the skids," and so on. Newspaper surveys have found these to be fairly typical responses. Probably the reasons for the prevalence of the response indicating a preference for a quick death and little suffering have to do with the frequent occurrence of the opposite. So many persons go through lengthy ordeals in which dying becomes a long-drawn-out and painful process, in which the person becomes increasingly weaker, more dependent, and less able to function without drugs and equipment, and functions at a level that frightens the living relatives and friends. The living and fully functioning are reminded of their own mortality, and they become frightened when death is observed as an arduous and painful process.

[1] James E. Birren, and Vivian Clayton, "History of Gerontology," in *Aging: Scientific Perspectives and Social Issues,* ed. Diana S. Woodruff and James E. Birren (New York: D. Van Nostrand, 1975), pp. 15–27.
[2] Kübler-Ross, *On Death and Dying.*

By some of these criteria, the main character in "The Gentleman from San Francisco" by Ivan Bunin (1870–1953) dies a good death; although at 58, by the criterion of age, he dies too young. But he dies quickly; he does not suffer (except briefly as he tries to button his collar button); death occurs while he is still functioning (he has not experienced a decline); he has been enjoying himself (it is the author, not he, who thinks that his life is decadent). Is his a good death? Probably, when measured by the current preference for a quick death with little suffering.

Was his a good life? Bunin clearly thought not. Writing in 1915, this Russian poet and novelist (who won the Nobel Prize for literature in 1933) clearly hated the decadence of the wealthy, their dishonesty, their conspicuous consumption, and their shameless use and abuse of people who were socially beneath them. The social-class differences were enormous. The wealthy expected their overworked employees to be totally deferential, punctual, respectful, sincere, courteous, and single-minded in their behalf. The nameless Gentleman has to have anything and everything expensive, ostentatious—to show that he can afford it, false, and unnatural. He is constantly dressing in the most formal and uncomfortable of attire—which finally chokes him. Perhaps it is his money that chokes him. His values are materialistic, devoid of the spiritual, the emotional, the aesthetic, and all else that humans throughout history have valued. He is trapped, mired, in his materialism. Once he has wealth, nothing unpleasant is permitted, or so he and his family and acquaintances think. That includes old age, unpleasant weather, the sight of poverty, the sight of hard work, sweat, an unkempt appearance—and death. Death is real (and female!) and thus to be ignored and avoided in the artificial and pretentious world of the wealthy. Death and all else that is unpleasant are for lesser persons, not for the Gentleman and those around him. Any reminder of such things is to be ignored.

In contrast to this tone and attitude, Mark Twain (Samuel Langhorne Clemens, 1835–1910) wrote in his notebook on his deathbed:

> Death, the only immortal who treats us all alike, whose pity and whose peace and whose refuge are for all—the soiled and the pure, the rich and the poor, the loved and the unloved.

Death is described by a medical-doctor–poet, K. D. Beernink (1938–1969, who died of leukemia at the age of thirty-one), in "Gino Spinelli." Gino Spinelli has worked hard and put all his hopes in the future. But then the future becomes the present and he dies. Death cruelly cancels his plans.

Dr. Beernink expresses the despair that many medical doctors, who see themselves primarily as healers, experience when they "lose" a patient to death. This loss conflicts with their involvement in being healers. From the public's point of view, it is of course highly desirable that they do see themselves as healers and that they take seriously and personally the death of a patient, for they are thus highly motivated toward cure and control of disease and disorder. However, that self-perception makes it difficult for the doctor to cope with the death of a patient. It is a dilemma that causes some medical doctors to avoid their terminally ill patients and to over-use life-extending equipment.

Dylan Thomas (1914–1953) wrote "Do Not Go Gentle into That Good Night" during the final illness of his father. There is quite an interesting contrast between the fighting spirit urged by Thomas and the sense of acceptance and peace that Küber-Ross encourages in her patients who are dying. She urges them to deal with their unfinished business, their unresolved problems and conflicts, so that they can experience peace. She views the reduction of their involvements and relationships as a positive step by the terminally ill in their acceptance of inevitable death. Kübler-Ross, a physician and psychiatrist, views death as a natural part of life.[3] To the poet Thomas also, death is natural, but it is also insulting, an outrage, an interruption, and a tragedy; and one should not take it lightly but should protest vehemently.

A view of death similar to that of Kübler-Ross is given in "The Odd Old Lady" by Thyra Samter Winslow. Mrs. Quillan's work is done. She has straightened out the important problems of various members of her family. There is nothing more for her to do; now she can die in peace. Moreover, she chooses the time of her death. As in the other story by Winslow in this anthology, "Grandma," we meet in this character a strong, self-confident, insightful, and assertive old woman.

Through intuition and a keen understanding of the individuals involved, Mrs. Quillan anticipates that certain events will happen in certain kinds of situations. She picks up the cues that others do not see. She experiences an interesting confusion of time—confusion of past, present, and future as they blur together in her thoughts. Now that she does not work (is not involved) and her children are adults, she has more time to think; and with this additional time, the past, present, and future became intertwined.

Note that the solution offered by the doctor (whom she trusted and regarded as a friend) is to consider her senile and put her in a sanitarium or a nursing home (despite the fact that he knows her and knows she is competent). He intends to commit her "unless she wants to go voluntarily." Daughter Julia asks about the possibility of giving her drugs. Both of them jump to the conclusion that there is something wrong with her, and that she has to be sent away because of it, even after both daughter and doctor see her predictions come true. Decades later, these attitudes toward the elderly are still alive and well.

In 44 B.C. the Roman philosopher Cicero (106–43 B.C.) wrote the dialogue "Of Death and Old Age" (he was murdered a year later). Cicero believed that death is natural to life and that its certainty results in rest, peace, and security. The certainty of death gives us courage and strength in old age, while, if we fear death, we cannot live or feel secure. We do not know the hour of death; we only know that it is a certainty. It is best to retain one's wits and senses until death. Death is desirable inasmuch as the world is the vale of all misery, and we can escape that misery only through death. One lives on after death

---

[3] Kübler-Ross, *On Death and Dying*.

both in one's reputation and because, according to Cicero, the soul lives on after the death of the body.

The historian Will Durant says, in interpreting Cicero's thoughts on old age:

> An honorable life is the best guarantee of a pleasant old age. An indulgent and intemperate youth delivers to age a body prematurely worn out; but a life well spent can leave both body and mind sound to a hundred years; witness Masinissa. Devotion to study may make one "unaware of the stealthy approach of old age." Age as well as youth has its glories—a tolerant wisdom, the respectful affection of children, desire and ambition's fever cooled. Age may fear death, but not if the mind has been formed by philosophy. Beyond the grave there will be, at the best, a new and happier life; and at the worst there will be peace.[4]

A full description of a Chinese funeral, in which each detail of behavior is strictly prescribed, is given by Ning Lao T'ai-t'ai ("Old Mrs. Ning") in this excerpt from *A Daughter of Han: The Autobiography of a Chinese Working Woman,* edited by Ida Pruitt. The account is based on interviews and conversations with Mrs. Ning in 1937 and 1938 in Peking. Her husband is disliked by his aunt and uncle because he is an opium addict who not only has failed to provide food for his family but also has sold one of his children to support his habit. Hence the family chooses the wife as the chief mourner rather than the husband because they regard him as a disgrace to the family.

---

[4] Will Durant, *Caesar and Christ, The Story of Civilization,* Vol. 3 (New York: Simon & Schuster, 1944), p. 166.

The Gentleman from San Francisco

Ivan Bunin

Alas, alas, that great city Babylon, that mighty city!
——The Apocalypse

The Gentleman from San Francisco—neither at Naples nor at Capri had anyone remembered his name—was journeying to the Old World for two full years, with wife and daughter, wholly for recreation.

He felt firmly assured that he had every right to take a rest, pleasure, in a prolonged and comfortable journey, and other things besides. For such an assurance he had the good reason that, in the first place, he was rich, and that, in the second, in spite of his fifty-eight years, he was only just taking his first plunge into life. Before this he had not lived but merely existed—to be sure, not so badly, but none the less putting all his hopes in the future. He had laboured diligently—the coolies, whom he had employed by the thousands, knew well what this meant!—and at last he saw that much had been achieved, that he was now equal to those he had at one time appointed as his models, and he decided to give himself a well-earned rest. It was a custom among his kind of people to begin the enjoyment of life with a journey to Europe, to India, to Egypt. He proposed to follow their example. Before all, of course, he desired to reward himself for his years of hard toil; nevertheless, he was happy also for his wife's and daughter's sakes. His wife had never been distinguished for any particular susceptibility to fresh impressions, but then all elderly American women are ardent travellers. As for his daughter, a girl no longer young and somewhat ailing, the journey would do her positive good: to say nothing of the benefits her health would derive, was there not always the likelihood of happy encounters during journeys? While travelling one may indeed, at times, sit at the same table with a multi-millionaire, or enjoy looking at frescoes in his company.

The itinerary planned by the gentleman from San Francisco was an extensive one. In December and January he hoped to enjoy the sun of Southern Italy, the monuments of antiquity, the *tarantella,* the serenades of strolling singers, and another thing for which men of his age have a peculiar relish: the love of young Neapolitan women, conferred—let us admit—not with wholly disinterested motives; he planned to spend the Carnival in Nice, in Monte Carlo, toward which the most select society gravitated at this season—that society upon which all the blessings of civilization depend: not alone the cut of the smoking jacket, but also the stability of thrones, and the declaration of wars, and the welfare of hotels—where some devote themselves with ardour to automobiles and sail races, others to roulette, while a third group engages in what is called flirting; a fourth in shooting pigeons which, emerging from their shelters, gracefully soar upward above emerald-green lawns, against the background of a sea of the colour of forget-me-nots, only in the next instant to strike the ground as crumpled little shapes of white. The beginning of March he wanted to devote to Florence; on the eve of the Passion of Our Lord to arrive at Rome, in order to hear the *Miserere* there; his plans also included Venice, and Paris, and bull-fights in Seville, and sea-bathing in the British Isles, and Athens, and Constantinople, and Palestine, and Egypt, and even Japan—naturally, on the return journey . . . And everything went splendidly at first.

It was the end of November; almost to Gibraltar itself the ship proceeded now through an icy mist, now through a storm with wet snow; but it sailed on unperturbed and even without rolling; the passengers on the steamer were many, and all of them persons of consequence; the ship—the famous *Atlantis*—resembled the most expensive of European hotels, with all conveniences; an all-night bar, Turkish baths, a newspaper of its own,—and life upon it flowed in accordance with a splendid system of regulations: the passengers rose early, to the sound of bugles, sharply reverberating through the passages at the yet dark hour when day was so slowly and reluctantly dawning above the gray-green watery desert, ponderously restless in the mist. They put on their flannel pajamas, drank coffee, chocolate, cocoa; then they reclined in marble bath-tubs, performed exercises, awakening an appetite and a sense of well-being, attended to their daily toilet and went to breakfast. Until eleven they were supposed to promenade the decks lustily, breathing in the cool freshness of the ocean, or to play at shuffleboard and other games for a renewed stimulation of the appetite; and at eleven, to seek refreshment in bouillon and sandwiches; after which they read their newspaper with pleasure and calmly awaited lunch, a meal even more nourishing and varied than the breakfast; the following two hours were dedicated to repose; all the decks were then arranged with *chaises longues,* upon which the travellers reclined, covered up with plaid rugs, contemplating the cloudy sky and the foaming billows flashing by beyond the rail, or else gently drowsing. At five o'clock, enlivened and refreshed, they were served with strong fragrant tea and pastries; at seven the bugle call announced dinner, consisting of nine courses. . . . At this point the gentleman from San Francisco, greatly cheered, would hurry to his magnificent *cabin de luxe,* to dress.

In the evening the tiers of the *Atlantis* gaped through the dusk as with fiery, countless eyes, and a great multitude of servants worked with especial feverishness in the kitchens, sculleries, and wine vaults. The ocean, heaving on the other side of the walls, was terrifying, but none gave it a thought, firmly believing it under the sway of the captain,—a red-haired man of monstrous bulk and ponderousness, always seeming sleepy, resembling, in his uniform frock-coat, with its golden chevrons, an enormous idol; it was only very rarely that he left his mysterious quarters to appear in public. A siren on the forecastle howled ceaselessly in hellish sullenness and whined in frenzied malice, but not many of the diners heard the siren,—it was drowned by the strains of a splendid stringed orchestra, playing exquisitely and without pause in the two-tiered hall, decorated with marble, its floors covered with velvet rugs; festively flooded with the lights of crystal lustres and gilded *girandoles,* filled to capacity with diamond-bedecked ladies in *décolleté* and men in smoking jackets, graceful waiters and deferential *maîtres d'hôtel,*—among whom one, who took orders for wines exclusively, even walked about with a chain around his neck, like a lord mayor. A smoking jacket and perfect linen made the gentleman from San Francisco appear very much younger. Spare, not tall, awkwardly but strongly built, groomed until he shone and moderately animated, he sat in the aureate-pearly refulgence of this palatial room, at a table with a bottle of amber Johannesberg, with countless goblets, small and large, of the thinnest glass, with a fragrant bouquet of curly hyacinths. There was something Mongolian about his yellowish face with clipped silvery moustache; his large teeth gleamed with gold fillings; his stalwart, bald head glistened like old ivory. Rich, yet in keeping with her years, was the attire of his wife,—a big, broad, calm woman; elaborate, yet light and diaphanous, with an innocent frankness, was that of his daughter,—a girl innocently frank, tall, slender, with magnificent hair, exquisitely dressed, with breath aromatic from violet cachous and with the tenderest of tiny moles about her lips and between her shoulder blades, slightly powdered. . . .

The dinner went on for two whole hours; after dinner there was dancing in the ball-room, during which the men—the gentleman from San Francisco among their number, of course—with their feet cocked up, decided, upon the basis of the latest political and stock-exchange news, the destinies of nations, smoking Havana cigars and drinking *liqueurs* until their faces were flushed, while seated in the bar, where the waiters were Negroes in red jackets, the whites of their eyes resembling peeled, hard-boiled eggs. The ocean, with a dull roar, was moving in black mountains on the other side of the wall; the snow-gale whistled fiercely through the soaked rigging; the whole ship quivered as it mastered both the gale and the mountains, sundering to either side, as though with a plough, their shifting masses, which again and again boiled up and flung themselves high, with tails of foam; the siren, stifled by the fog, was moaning with a deathly anguish; the lookouts up in their crow's-nest froze with the cold and grew dazed from straining their attention beyond their strength. Akin to the grim sultry depths of the infernal regions, akin to their ultimate, their ninth circle, was the womb of the steamer, below the water line,—that womb where dully gurgled the gigantic furnaces, devouring with their fiery maws mountains of hard coal, cast into them by men stripped to the waist, purple from the flames, and with smarting, filthy sweat pouring over them; while here, in the bar, men threw their legs over the arms of their chairs with never a care, sipping cognac and *liqueurs,* and were wafted among clouds of spicy smoke as they indulged in refined conversation; in the ball-room everything was radiant with light and warmth and joy; couples were now whirling in waltzes, now swaying in the tango,—and the music insistently, in some delectably shameless melancholy, supplicated always of one, always of the same thing. . . . There was an ambassador among this brilliant throng,—a lean, modest little old man; there was a rich man,—clean-shaven, lanky, of indeterminate years, and with the appearance of a prelate, in an old-fashioned frock coat; there was a well-known Spanish writer; there was a world-celebrated beauty, already just the very least trifle faded and of an unenviable morality; there was an exquisite couple in love with each other, whom all watched with curiosity and whose happiness was unconcealed: *he* danced only with *her;* sang—and with great ability—only to *her* accompaniment; everything they did was carried out so charmingly; and only the captain knew that this pair was hired by Lloyd's to play at love for good money, and that they had been sailing for a long time, now on one ship, now on another.

At Gibraltar everybody was gladdened by the sun,—it seemed like early spring; a new passenger, whose person aroused the general interest, made his appearance on board the *Atlantis,*—he was the hereditary prince of a certain Asiatic kingdom, travelling incognito; a little man who somehow seemed to be all made of wood, even though he was agile in his movements; broad of face, with narrow eyes, in gold-rimmed spectacles; a trifle unpleasant owing to the fact that his skin showed through his coarse black moustache like that of a corpse; on the whole, however, he was charming, simple, and modest. On the Mediterranean Sea there was a whiff of winter again; the billows ran high, were as multi-coloured as the tail of a peacock, and had snowy-white crests, due, in spite of the sparklingly bright sun and perfectly clear sky, to a *tramontana,* a chill northern wind from beyond the mountains, that was joyously and madly rushing to meet the ship. . . . Then, on the second day, the sky began to pale, the horizon became covered with mist, land was nearing; Ischia, Capri appeared; through the binoculars, Naples—lumps of sugar strewn at the foot of some dove-coloured mass—could be seen; while over it and this dove-coloured object were visible the ridges of distant mountains, vaguely glimmering with the dead whiteness of snow. There was a great number of people on deck; many of the ladies and gentlemen had already put on short, light fur coats, with the fur outside; Chinese boys, patient and always speaking in a whisper, bow-legged striplings with pitch-black queues reaching to their heels and with eyelashes as long and thick as those of young girls were already dragging, little by little, sundry plaids, canes, and portmanteaux and grips of alligator hide toward the companion-ways. . . . The daughter of the gentleman from San Francisco was standing beside the prince, who had been, by a happy chance, presented to her yesterday evening, and she pretended to be looking intently into the distance, in a direction he was pointing out to her, telling, explaining something or other to her, hurriedly and quietly. On account of his height he seemed a boy by contrast with others,—he was odd and not at all prepossessing of person, with his spectacles, his bowler, his English greatcoat, while his scanty moustache looked just as if it were of horse-hair, and the swarthy, thin skin seemed to be drawn tightly over his face, and somehow had the appearance of being lacquered,—but the young girl was listening to him, without understanding, in her perturbation, what he was saying; her heart was thumping from an incomprehensible rapture in his presence and from pride that he was speaking with her, and not someone else; everything about him that was different from others,—his lean hands, his clear skin, under which flowed the ancient blood of kings, even his wholly unpretentious, yet somehow singularly neat, European dress,—everything held a secret, inexplicable charm, evoked a feeling of amorousness. As for the gentleman from San Francisco himself,—he, in a high silk hat, in gray spats over patent-leather shoes, kept on glancing at the famous beauty, who was standing beside him,—a tall blonde of striking figure, with eyes painted in the latest Parisian fashion; she was holding a diminutive, hunched-up, mangy lap dog on a silver chain and was chattering to it without pause. And the daughter, in some vague embarrassment, tried not to notice her father.

Like all Americans of means, he was very generous while travelling, and, like all of them, believed in the full sincerity and good-will of those who brought him food and drink with such solicitude, who served him from morn till night, anticipating his slightest wish; of those who guarded his cleanliness and rest, lugged his things around, summoned porters for him, delivered his trunks to hotels. Thus had it been everywhere, thus had it been on the ship, and thus it had to be in Naples as well. Naples grew, and drew nearer; the musicians, the brass of their instruments flashing, had already clustered upon the deck, and suddenly deafened everybody with the triumphant strains of a march; the gigantic captain, in his full-dress uniform, appeared upon his stage, and, like a gracious pagan god, waved his hand amiably to the passengers,—and to the gentleman from San Francisco it seemed that it was for him alone that the march so beloved by proud America was thundering, that it was he whom the captain was felicitating upon a safe arrival. And every other passenger felt similarly about himself—or herself. And when the *Atlantis* finally entered the harbour, heaved to at the wharf with her many-tiered mass, black with people, and the gang-planks clattered down,—what a multitude of porters and their helpers in caps with gold braid, what a multitude of different *commissionaires,* whistling gamins, and strapping ragamuffins with packets of coloured postal cards in their hands, made a rush toward the gentleman from San Francisco, with offers of their services! And he smiled, with a kindly contemptuousness, at these ragamuffins, as he went toward the automobile of precisely that hotel where there was a likelihood of the prince's stopping. He drawled through his teeth, now in English, now in Italian:

"Go away! *Via!*"

Life at Naples at once assumed its wonted, ordered routine: in the early morning, breakfast in the gloomy dining-room with its damp draught from windows opening on some sort of a stony little garden. The sky was overcast, holding out little promise, and there was the usual crowd of guides at the door of the vestibule; then came the first smiles of a warm, rosy sun. From the high hanging balcony Vesuvius came into view, enveloped to its foot by radiant morning mists, and the silver-and-pearl eddies on the surface of the Bay, and the delicate contour of Capri against the horizon. One could see tiny burros, harnessed in twos to little carts, running down below over the quay, sticky with mire, and detachments of diminutive soldiers, marching somewhere to lively and exhilarating music. Next came the procession to the waiting automobile and the slow progress through the populous, narrow, and damp corridors of streets, between tall, many-windowed houses; the inspection of lifelessly-clean museums, evenly and pleasantly, yet bleakly, lighted, seemingly illuminated by snow; or of cool churches, smelling of wax, which everywhere and always contain the same things; a majestic portal, screened by a heavy curtain of leather, and inside,—empty vastness, silence, quiescent tiny flames of a seven-branched candle-stick glowing redly in the distant depths, on an altar bedecked with laces; a solitary old woman among the dark wooden pews; slippery tombstones underfoot; and someone's "Descent from the Cross,"—it goes without saying, a celebrated one. At one o'clock there was luncheon upon the mountain of San Marino, where, toward noon, not a few people of the very first quality gathered, and where the daughter of the gentleman from San Francisco had once almost fainted away for joy, because she thought she saw the prince sitting in the hall, although she already knew through the newspapers that he had left for a temporary stay at Rome. At five came tea at the hotel, in the showy salon, so cosy with its rugs and flaming fireplaces; and after that it was already time to prepare for dinner,—and once more came the mighty clamour of the gong reverberating through the hotel; once more the moving queues of ladies in *décolleté,* rustling in their silks upon the staircases and reflected in all the mirrors; once more the palatial dining-room, widely and hospitably opened, and the red jackets of the musicians upon their platform, and the black cluster of waiters about the *maître d'hôtel,* who, with inordinate skill, was ladling some sort of thick, reddish soup into plates. . . . The dinners, as everywhere else, were the crowning glory of each day; the guests dressed for them as for a party, and those dinners were so abundant in edibles, and wines, and mineral waters, and sweets, and fruits, that toward eleven o'clock at night the chambermaids were distributing through all the rooms rubber bags with hot water to warm the stomachs.

As it happened, the December of that year proved to be not a wholly successful one for Naples; the porters grew confused when one talked with them of the weather, and merely shrugged their shoulders guiltily, muttering that they could not recall such a year,—although it was not the first year that they had been forced to mutter this, and to base their statement on that "something terrible is happening everywhere"; there were unheard of storms and torrents of rain on the Riviera; there was snow in Athens; Etna was also all snowed over and was aglow at night; tourists were fleeing from Palermo in all directions, to escape from the cold. The morning sun deceived the Neapolitans every day that winter: toward noon the sky became gray and a fine rain began falling, but grew heavier and colder all the time; then the palms near the entrance of the hotel glistened as though they were of tin, the town seemed especially dirty and cramped, the museums curiously alike; the cigar stumps of the corpulent cab-men, whose rubber coats flapped in the wind like wings, seemed to have an in-sufferable stench, while the energetic snapping of their whips over their scrawny-necked nags was patently false; the footgear of the *signori* sweeping the rails of the tramways seemed horrible; the women, splashing through the mud, their black-haired heads bared to the rain, appeared hideously short-legged; as for the dampness, and the stench of putrid fish from the sea foaming at the quay,—there was nothing to be said. The gentleman and the lady from San Francisco began quarreling in the morning; their daughter either walked about pale, with a headache, or, coming to life again, went into raptures over everything, and was, at times both charming and beautiful: beautiful were those tender and complex emotions which had been awakened within her by meeting that unsightly man through whose veins flowed uncommon blood; for, after all is said and done, perhaps it is of no actual importance just what it is, precisely, that awakens a maiden's soul,—whether it be money, or fame, or illustrious ancestry. . . . Everybody asserted that things were quite different in Sorrento, in Capri,—there it was both warmer and sunnier, and the lemons were in blos-som, and the customs were more honest, and the wine was better. And so the family from San Francisco resolved to set out with all its trunks to Capri, and, after seeing it all, after treading the stones where the palace of Tiberius had once stood, after visiting the faery-like caverns of the Blue Grotto, and hearing the bag-pipers of Abruzzi, who for a whole month preceding Christmas wander over the island and sing the praises of the Virgin Mary, they meant to settle in Sorrento.

On the day of departure,—a most memorable one for the family from San Francisco!—there was no early morning sun. A heavy fog hid Vesuvius to the very base; this gray fog spread low over the leaden swell of the sea that was lost to the eye at a distance of a half a mile. Capri was quite invisible,—as if there had never been such an island in the world. And the tiny steamer that set out for it was so tossed from side to side that the family from San Francisco was laid prostrate upon the divans in the sorry general cabin of this tiny steamer, their feet wrapped up in plaid rugs, and their eyes closed. The mother suffered,—so she thought,—more than anybody; she was overcome by sea-sickness several times; it seemed to her that she was dying, while the steward-ess, who always ran up to her with a small basin,—she had been, for many years, day in and day out, rolling on these waves, in sultry weather and in cold, and yet was still tireless and kind to everybody,—merely laughed. The daugh-ter was dreadfully pale and held a slice of lemon between her teeth; now she could not have been comforted even by the hope of a chance meeting with the prince at Sorrento, where he intended to be about Christmas. The father, who was lying on his back, in roomy overcoat and large cap, never opened his jaws all the way over; his face had grown darker and his moustache whiter, and his head ached dreadfully: during the last days, thanks to the bad weather, he had been drinking too heavily of evenings, and had too much admired the "living pictures" in the haunts of manufactured libertinage. But the rain kept on lashing against the jarring windows, the water from them running down on the divans; the wind, howling, bent the masts, and at times, aided by the onslaught of a wave, careened the little steamer entirely to one side, and then something in the hold would roll with a rumble. During the stops at Castellamare, at Sorrento, things were a trifle more bearable, but even then the rocking was fearful,—the shore, with all its cliffs, gardens, pine-groves, its pink and white hotels and hazy mountains clad in wavy greenery, swayed up and down as if on a swing; boats bumped up against the sides of the ship; sailors and steerage passengers were shouting fiercely; somewhere, as if it had been crushed, a baby was wailing and smothering; a raw wind was blowing in at the door; and, from a swaying boat with the flag of the Hotel Royal, a lisping gamin was screaming, luring travellers: "Kgoya-al! Hôtel Kgoya-al! . . ." And the gentleman from San Francisco, feeling himself to be incredibly old,—which was as it should be,—was already thinking with sadness and loathing of all these Royals, Splendids, Excelsiors, and of these greedy, insignificant little men, reeking of garlic, called Italians. Once, having opened his eyes and raised himself from the divan, he saw, underneath the craggy barrier on the shore, a cluster of stone hovels mouldy through and through, stuck one on top of another near the very edge of the water, near boats, near all sorts of rags, tins, and brown nets,—hovels so wretched, that, at the recollection this was the very Italy he had come here to enjoy, he felt despair. . . . Finally, at twilight, the dark mass of the island began to draw near, seemingly bored through and through by little red lights near its base; the wind became softer, warmer, more fragrant; over the abating waves, as opalescent as black oil, golden serpents flowed from the lanterns on the wharf. . . . Then came the sudden rumble of the anchor, and it fell with a splash into the water; the savage shouts of the boatmen, vying with one another, floated in from all quarters,—and at once the heart grew lighter, the lamps in the general cabin shone more brightly, a desire arose to eat, to drink, to smoke, to be stirring. . . .

Ten minutes later the family from San Francisco had descended into a large boat; within fifteen minutes it had set foot upon the stones of the wharf, and had then got into a bright little railway car and to its buzzing started the ascent of the slope, amid the stakes of the vineyards, half-crumbled stone enclosures, and wet, gnarled orange trees, some of them under coverings of straw,—trees with thick, glossy foliage, aglimmer with the orange fruits; all these objects were sliding downward, past the open windows of the little car, toward the base of the mountain. . . . Sweetly smells the earth of Italy after rain, and her every island has its own, its especial aroma!

On this evening the island of Capri was damp and dark. But now for an instant it came into life; lights sprang up here and there, as always on the steamer's arrival. At the top of the mountain, where stood the station of the *funicular,* there was another throng of those whose duty it was to receive fittingly the gentleman from San Francisco. There were other arrivals, but they merited no attention,—several Russians, who had settled in Capri,—absentminded because of their bookish meditations, unkempt, bearded, spectacled, the collars of their old frayed overcoats turned up; and a group of long-legged, long-necked, round-headed German youths in Tyrolean costumes, with canvas knapsacks slung over their shoulders; these stood in no need of anybody's services, feeling themselves at home everywhere, and knowing how to practise the strictest economies. The gentleman from San Francisco, on the other hand, who was calmly keeping aloof from both the one group and the other, was immediately observed. He and his ladies were promptly helped out, some men running ahead of him to show him the way. Again he was surrounded by urchins, and by those stalwart Caprian wives who bear on their heads the portmanteaux and trunks of respectable travellers. The wooden pattens of these women clattered over a little square, which seemed to belong to some opera, an electric globe swaying above it in the damp wind. The rabble of urchins burst into sharp, bird-like whistles,—and, as if on a stage, the gentleman from San Francisco proceeded in their midst toward some mediaeval arch underneath houses that had become merged into one mass, beyond which a little echoing street,—with the tuft of a palm above flat roofs on its left, and with blue stars in the black sky overhead,—led slopingly to the now visible grand entrance of the hotel, all agleam with light. . . . And again it seemed that it was in honour of the guests from San Francisco that this damp little town of stone on a craggy little island of the Mediterranean Sea had come to life, that it was they who had made the proprietor of the hotel so happy and affable, that it was only for them that the Chinese gong began to sound the summons to dinner through all the stories of the hotel, the instant they had set foot in the vestibule.

The proprietor, a young man of courtly elegance, who had met them with a polite and exquisite bow, for a minute dumbfounded the gentleman from San Francisco. After a glance at him, the gentleman from San Francisco suddenly remembered that just the night before, among the confusion of numerous images which had beset him in his sleep, he had seen precisely this gentleman,—just like him, down to the least detail: in the same sort of frock with rounded skirts, and with the same pomaded and painstakingly combed head. Startled, he almost paused. But since, from long, long before, there was not even a mustard seed of any sort of so-called mystical emotions left in his soul, his astonishment was dimmed the same instant; as he proceeded through a corridor of the hotel, he spoke jestingly to his wife and daughter of this strange coincidence of dream and reality. And only his daughter glanced at him with alarm at that moment: her heart suddenly contracted from sadness, from a feeling of their loneliness upon this dark alien island,—a feeling so strong that she almost burst into tears. Nevertheless, she said nothing of her feelings to her father,—as always.

An exalted personage—Rais XVII—who had been visiting Capri, had just taken his departure. And now the guests from San Francisco were conducted to the same apartments that he had occupied. To them was assigned the ablest and handsomest chambermaid, a Belgian, whose waist was slenderly and firmly corseted, and whose tiny starched cap looked like a scalloped crown; also, the best-looking and most dignified of flunkies, a fiery-eyed Sicilian, black as coal, and the nimblest of bell-boys, the short and stout Luigi,—a fellow who was very fond of a joke, and who had served many masters in his time. And a minute later there was a slight tap at the door of the room of the gentleman from San Francisco,—the French *maître d'hôtel* had come to find out if the newly arrived guests would dine, and, in event of an answer in the affirmative,—of which, of course, there was no doubt,—to inform them that the *carte de jour* consisted of crawfish, roast beef, asparagus, pheasants, and so forth. The floor was still rocking under the gentleman from San Francisco,—so badly had the atrocious little Italian steamer tossed him about,—but, without hurrying, with his own hands, although somewhat awkwardly from being unaccustomed to such things, he shut a window that had banged when the *maître d'hôtel* had entered and had let in the odours of the distant kitchen and of the wet flowers in the garden, and with a lingering deliberateness replied that they would dine, that their table must be placed as far as possible from the door, at the other end of the dining-room, that they would drink local wine and champagne,— moderately dry and only slightly chilled. The *maître d'hôtel* approved every word of his, in most varied intonations, having in any case, but one significance,—that there was never a doubt, nor could there possibly be any, about the correctness of the wishes of the gentleman from San Francisco, and that everything would be carried out with precision. In conclusion he inclined his head, and asked deferentially:

"Will that be all, sir?"

And, having received in answer a leisurely "Yes," he added that the *tarantella* would be danced in the vestibule tonight,—the dancers would be Carmella and Giuseppe, known to all Italy, and to "the entire world of tourists."

"I have seen her on postcards," said the gentleman from San Francisco in a wholly inexpressive voice. "As for this Giuseppe,—is he her husband?"

"Her cousin, sir," answered the *maître d'hôtel*.

And, after a brief pause, during which he appeared to be considering something, the gentleman from San Francisco dismissed him with a nod.

And then he once more began his preparations, as if for a wedding ceremony: he turned on all the electric lights, filling all the mirrors with reflections of light and glitter, of furniture and opened trunks; he began shaving and washing, ringing the bell every minute, while other impatient rings from his wife's and daughter's rooms sounded through the entire corridor and interrupted his. And Luigi, in his red apron, was rushing forward to answer the bell, with an agility peculiar to many stout men, not omitting grimaces of horror that made the chambermaids, running by with glazed porcelain pails in their hands, laugh till they cried. He knocked on the door with his knuckles, and asked with an assumed timidity, with a deference which verged on idiocy:

"*Ha sonato, signore?*"

And from the other side of the door came an unhurried, grating voice, humiliatingly polite:

"Yes, come in. . . ."

What were the thoughts, what were the emotions of the gentleman from San

Francisco on this evening, that was to be of such significance to him? He felt nothing exceptional,—for the trouble in this world is just that everything is apparently all too simple! And even if he had sensed within his soul that something was impending, he would, nevertheless, have thought that this thing would not occur for some time to come,—in any case, not immediately. Besides that, like everyone who has experienced the rocking of a ship, he wanted very much to eat, was looking forward to the first spoonful of soup, the first mouthful of wine, and performed the usual routine of dressing, even with a certain degree of exhilaration that left no time for reflections.

After shaving and washing himself, after inserting several artificial teeth properly, he remained standing before a mirror, while he wetted the remnants of his thick, pearly-gray hair and plastered it down around his swarthy yellow skull, with brushes set in silver; drew a suit of cream-coloured silk underwear over his strong old body, beginning to be full at the waist from excesses in food, and put on silk socks and dancing slippers on his shrivelled, splayed feet; sitting down, he put in order his black trousers, drawn high by black silk braces, as well as his snowy-white shirt, with the bosom bulging out; put the links through the glossy cuffs, and began the agonizing manipulation of the collar-button underneath the stiffly starched collar. The floor was still swaying beneath him, the tips of his fingers pained him greatly, the collar-button at times nipped hard the flabby skin in the hollow under his Adam's-apple, but he was persistent and at last, his eyes glittering from the exertion, his face all livid from the collar that was choking his throat,—a collar far too tight,—he did succeed in accomplishing his task, and sat down in exhaustion in front of the pier glass. He was reflected in it from head to foot, a reflection that was repeated in all the other mirrors.

"Oh, this is dreadful!" he muttered, lowering his strong bald head, and without trying to understand, without considering, just what, precisely, was dreadful; then, with an accustomed and attentive glance, he inspected his stubby fingers, with gouty hardenings at the joints, and his convex nails of an almond colour, and repeated, with conviction: "This is dreadful. . . ."

At this point the second gong, sonorously, as in some pagan temple, dinned through the entire house. And, getting up quickly from his seat, the gentleman from San Francisco drew his collar still tighter with the necktie and his stomach by means of the low-cut vest, put on his smoking-jacket, arranged his cuffs, surveyed himself once more in the mirror. . . . This Carmella, swarthy, with eyes which she knew well how to use tellingly, resembling a mulatto woman, clad in a dress of many colours, with the colour of orange predominant, must dance exceptionally, he imagined. And, stepping briskly out of his room and walking over the carpet to the next one,—his wife's—he asked loudly, if they would be ready soon.

"In five minutes, Dad!" a girl's voice, ringing and by now gay, responded from the other side of the door.

"Very well," said the gentleman from San Francisco.

And, leisurely, he walked through red-carpeted corridors and down staircases, in quest of the reading room. The servants he met stood aside and hugged the wall to let him pass, but he kept on his way as though he had never even noticed them. An old woman who was late for dinner, already stooping, with milky hair but *décolleté* in a light-gray gown of silk, was hurrying with all her might, but drolly, in a hen-like manner, and he easily outstripped her. Near the glass doors of the dining-room, where all the guests had already assembled, and were beginning their dinner, he stopped before a little table piled with boxes of cigars and Egyptian cigarettes, took a large Manila cigar, and flung three *lire* upon the little table. Walking on the terrace, he glanced, in passing, through the open window; out of the darkness he felt a breath of the balmy air upon him, thought he saw the tip of an ancient palm. Its gigantic fronds seemed to reach out across the stars. He heard the distant, measured din of the sea. . . . In the reading room,—snug, quiet, and illuminated only above the tables, some gray-haired German was standing, rustling the newspapers,—unkempt, resembling Ibsen, in round silver spectacles and with mad, astonished eyes. After scrutinizing him coldly, the gentleman from San Francisco sat down in a deep leather chair in a corner near a green-shaded lamp, put on his *pince-nez*, twitching his head because his collar was choking him, and hid himself completely behind the newspaper. He rapidly ran through the headlines of certain items, read a few lines about the never-ceasing Balkan war, with an accustomed gesture turned the newspaper over,—when suddenly the lines flared up before him with a glassy glare, his neck became taut, his eyes bulged out, the *pince-nez* flew off his nose. . . . He lunged forward, tried to swallow some air,—and made a wild hoarse sound; his lower jaw sank, lighting up his entire mouth with the reflection of the gold fillings; his head dropped back on his shoulder and began to sway; the bosom of his shirt bulged out like a basket,— and his whole body, squirming, his heels catching the carpet, slid downward to the floor, desperately struggling with someone.

Had the German not been in the reading room, the hotel attendants would have managed, quickly and adroitly, to hush up this dreadful occurrence; instantly, through back passages, seizing him by the head and feet, they would have rushed off the gentleman from San Francisco as far away as possible,— and not a soul among the guests would have found out what he had been up to. But the German had dashed out of the reading room with a scream,—he had aroused the entire house, the entire dining-room. And many jumped up from their meal, overturning their chairs; many, paling, ran toward the reading room. "What—what has happened?" was heard in all languages,—and no one gave a sensible answer, no one comprehended anything, since even to this day men are amazed most of all by death, and will not, in any circumstances, believe in it. The proprietor dashed from one guest to another, trying to detain those who were running away and to pacify them with hasty assurances that this was just a trifling occurrence, a slight fainting spell of a certain gentleman from San Francisco. . . . No one listened to him; many had seen the flunkeys and corridor attendants tearing the necktie, the vest, and the rumpled smoking-jacket off this gentleman, and even, for some reason or other, the dancing slippers off his splayed feet, clad in black silk. He was still struggling. He was still obdurately wrestling with death; he absolutely refused to yield to her, who had so unexpectedly and inconsiderately fallen upon him. His head was swaying, he rattled hoarsely, like one with his throat cut; his eyes had rolled up, like a drunkard's. . . . When he was hurriedly carried in and laid upon a bed in room Number Forty-three,—the smallest, the poorest, the dampest and the coldest, situated at the end of the bottom corridor,—his daughter ran in, with her hair down, in a little dressing-gown that had flown open, her bosom, raised up by the corset, uncovered; then his wife, big and ponderous, already dressed for dinner,—her mouth rounded in terror. . . . But by now he had ceased even wagging his head.

A quarter of an hour later everything in the hotel had assumed a semblance of order. Nevertheless, the evening was irreparably spoiled. Some guests, re-turning to the dining-room, finished their dinner, but in silence, with aggrieved faces, while the proprietor would approach now one group, now another, shrugging his shoulders in polite yet impotent irritation, feeling himself guilty without guilt, assuring everybody that he understood very well "how unpleas-ant all this was," and pledging his word that he would take "all measures within his power" to remove this unpleasantness. The *tarantella* had to be called off, all superfluous electric lights were extinguished, the majority of the guests withdrew into the bar, and it became so quiet that one heard distinctly the ticking of the clock in the vestibule, whose sole occupant was a parrot, dully muttering something, fussing in his cage before going to sleep, contriving to doze off at last with one claw ludicrously stretched up to the upper berth. . . . The gentleman from San Francisco was lying upon a cheap iron bed, under coarse woolen blankets, upon which the dull light of a single bulb beat down from the ceiling. An ice-bag was askew on his moist and cold forehead. The livid face, already dead, was gradually growing cold; the hoarse rattling, expelled from the open mouth, illuminated by the reflection of gold, was grow-ing fainter. This was no longer the gentleman from San Francisco rattling,—he no longer existed,—but some other. His wife, his daughter, the doctor and the servants were standing, gazing at him dully. Suddenly, that which they awaited and feared was consummated,—the rattling ceased abruptly. And slowly, slowly, before the eyes of all, a pallor suffused the face of the man who had died, and his features seemed to grow finer, to become irradiated with a beauty which had been rightfully his in the long ago. . . .

The proprietor entered. *"Già è morto,"* said the doctor to him in a whisper. The proprietor, with dispassionate face, shrugged his shoulders. The wife, down whose cheeks the tears were quietly coursing, walked up to him and timidly said that the deceased ought now to be carried to his own room.

"Oh, no, madam," hastily, correctly, but now without any amiability and not in English, but in French, retorted the proprietor, who was not at all inter-ested now in such trifling sums as the arrivals from San Francisco might leave in his coffers. "That is absolutely impossible, madam," he said, and added in explanation that he valued the apartments occupied by them very much; that, were he to carry out her wishes, everybody in Capri would know it and the tourists would shun those apartments.

The young woman, who had been all this time gazing at him strangely, sat down on a chair, and, pressing a handkerchief to her mouth, burst into sobs. The wife dried her tears immediately, her face flaring up. She adopted a louder tone, making demands in her own language, and still incredulous of the fact that all respect for them had been completely lost. The proprietor, with polite dignity, cut her short: if madam was not pleased with the customs of the hotel, he would not venture to detain her; and he firmly announced that the body must be gotten away this very day, at dawn, that the police had already been notified, and one of the police officers would be here very soon and would carry out all the necessary formalities. Was it possible to secure even a common coffin in Capri?—madam asked. Regrettably, no,—it was beyond possibility, and no one would be able to make one in time. It would be necessary to have recourse to something else. . . . He had a suggestion.—English soda water came in large and long boxes. . . . It was possible to knock the partitions out of such a box. . . .

At night the whole hotel slept. The window in room Number Forty-three was opened,—it gave out upon a corner of the garden where, near a high stone wall with broken glass upon its crest, a consumptive banana tree was growing; the electric light was switched off; the key was turned in the door, and everybody went away. The dead man remained in the darkness,—the blue stars looked down upon him from the sky, a cricket with a pensive insouciance began his song in the wall. . . . In the dimly lit corridor two chambermaids were seated on a window sill, at some darning. Luigi, in slippers, entered with a pile of clothing in his arms.

"*Pronto?*" he asked solicitously, in an audible whisper, indicating with his eyes the fearsome door at the end of the corridor. And, he waved his hand airily in that direction. . . . "*Partenza!*" he called out in a whisper, as though he were speeding a train, the usual phrase used in Italian depots at the departure of trains,—and the chambermaids, choking with silent laughter, let their heads sink on each other's shoulder.

Thereupon, hopping softly, he ran up to the very door, gave it the merest tap, and, inclining his head to one side, in a low voice, asked with the utmost deference:

"*Ha sonato, signore?*"

And, squeezing his throat, thrusting out his lower jaw, in a grating voice, slowly and sadly, he answered his own question, in English, as though from the other side of the door:

"Yes, come in. . . ."

And at dawn, when it had become light beyond the window of room Number Forty-three, and a humid wind had begun to rustle the tattered leaves of the banana tree; when the blue sky of morning had lifted and spread out over the Island of Capri, and the pure and clear-cut summit of Monte Solaro had grown golden against the sun that was rising beyond the distant blue mountains of

Italy; when the stone masons, who were repairing the tourists' paths on the island, had set out to work,—a long box that had formerly been used for soda water was brought to room Number Forty-three. Soon it became very heavy, and was pressing hard against the knees of the junior porter, who bore it off briskly on a one horse cab over the white paved highway that was sinuously winding over the slopes of Capri, among the stone walls and the vineyards, ever downwards, to the sea itself. The cabby, a puny little man with reddened eyes, in an old jacket with short sleeves and in much-worn shoes, was suffering the after-effects of drink,—he had spent the whole night long in playing with dice in a *tratoria,* and kept on lashing his sturdy little horse, rigged out in Sicilian fashion, with all sorts of little bells livelily jingling upon the bridle with its tufts of colored wool, and upon the brass points of its high pad; with a yard-long feather stuck in its cropped forelock,—a feather that shook as the horse ran. The cabby kept silent; he was oppressed by his shiftlessness, his vices,—by the circumstance that he had, that night, lost to the last mite all those coppers with which his pockets had been filled. But the morning was fresh; in air such as this, with the sea all around, under the morning sky, the after-effects of drink quickly evaporate, and a man is soon restored to a care-free mood, and the cabby was furthermore consoled by that unexpected wind-fall, conferred upon him by some gentleman from San Francisco, whose life-less head was bobbing from side to side in the box at his back. . . . The little steamer,—a beetle lying far down below, against the tender and vivid deep-blue with which the Bay of Naples is so densely and highly flooded,—was already blowing its final whistles, that reverberated loudly all over the island, whose every bend, every ridge, every stone, was as distinctly visible from every point as if there were absolutely no such thing as atmosphere. Near the wharf the junior porter was joined by the senior, who was speeding with the daughter and wife of the gentleman from San Francisco in his automobile,—they were pale, with eyes hollow from tears and a sleepless night. And ten minutes later the little steamer was again noisily making its way through the water, again running toward Sorrento, toward Castellamare, carrying away from Capri, for all time, the family from San Francisco. . . . And again peace and quiet reigned upon the island.

Upon this island, two thousand years ago, had lived a man who had become completely enmeshed in his cruel and foul deeds, who had for some reason seized the power over millions of people in his hands, and who, having himself lost his head at the senselessness of this power and from the fear of death by assassination by some one, lurking round the corner, had committed cruelties beyond all measure,—and humankind has remembered him for all time; and those who, in their collusion, just as incomprehensibly and, in substance, just as cruelly as he, reign at present in power over this world, gather from all over the earth to gaze upon the ruins of that stone villa where he had dwelt on one of the steepest ascents of the island. On this marvellous morning all those who had come to Capri for just this purpose were still sleeping in the hotels, although, toward the entrances, were already being led little mouse-gray burros with red saddles, upon which, after awaking and sating themselves with food, Americans and Germans, men and women, young and old, would again ponderously clamber up the steep paths this day, and after whom would again run the old Caprian beggar women, with sticks in their gnarled hands,—would run over stony paths, and always up-hill, up to the very summit of Mount Tiberio. Comforted by the knowledge that the dead old man from San Francisco, who had likewise been planning to go with them but instead of that had only frightened them with a reminder of death, had already been shipped off to Naples, the travellers slept on heavily, and the quiet of the island was still undisturbed, the shops in the town were still shut. The market place in the little square alone was carrying on traffic,—in fish and greens; and the people there were all simple folk, among whom, without anything to do, as always, was standing Lorenzo the boatman, famous all over Italy,—a tall old man, a care-free rake and a handsome fellow, who had served more than once as a model to many artists; he had brought, and had already sold for a trifle, two lobsters that he had caught that night and which were already rustling in the apron of the cook of that very hotel where the family from San Francisco had passed the night, and now he could afford to stand in calm idleness even until the evening, looking about him with a kingly bearing, consciously and flauntingly picturesque with his tatters, clay pipe, and a red woolen *beretta* drooping over one ear.

And, along the precipices of Monte Solaro, upon the ancient Phoenician road, hewn out of the crags, down its stone steps, two mountaineers of Abruzzi were descending from Anacapri. One had bag-pipes under his leathern mantle,—a large bag made from the skin of a she-goat, with two pipes; the other had something in the nature of wooden Pan's-reeds. They went on,—and all the land, joyous, lovely, sun-swept, spread out below them: the stony humps of the island, which was lying almost in its entirety at their feet; and that faery-like deep-blue in which it was afloat; and the shining morning vapours over the sea, toward the east, under the blinding sun, that was now beating down hotly, rising ever higher and higher; and, still in their morning vagueness, the mistily blue massive outlines of Italy, of her mountains near and far, whose beauty human speech is impotent to express. . . . Half way down the pipers slackened their pace: over the path, within a grotto in the craggy side of Monte Solaro, all bright in the sun, all bathed in its warmth and glow, in snowy-white raiment of gypsum, and in a royal crown, golden-rusty from inclement weathers, stood the Mother of God, meek and gracious, her orbs lifted up to heaven, to the eternal and happy abodes of Her thrice-blessed Son. The pipers bared their heads, put their reeds to their lips,—and there poured forth their naïve and humbly-jubilant praises to the sun, to the morning, to Her, the Immaculate Intercessor for all those who suffer in this evil and beautiful world, and to Him Who had been born of Her womb in a cavern at Bethlehem, in a poor shepherd's shelter in the distant land of Judaea. . . .

Meanwhile, the body of the dead old man from San Francisco was returning to its home, to a grave on the shores of the New World. Having gone through many humiliations, through much human neglect, having wandered for a week from one port warehouse to another, it had finally gotten once more on board that same famous ship upon which but lately, with so much deference, he had been borne to the Old World. But now he was already being concealed from the quick,—he was lowered in his tarred coffin deep into the black hold. And once more the ship was sailing on and on upon its long sea voyage. By night it sailed past the Island of Capri, and, to one watching them from the island, there was something sad about the ships' lights, slowly disappearing over the dark sea. But, upon the ship itself, in its brilliant *salons* resplendent with lustres and marble, there was, as usual, a crowded ball that night.

There was a ball on the second night, and also on the third,—again in the midst of a raging snow gale, whirling over an ocean booming like a burial mass, and rolling in mountains arrayed in mourning by the silvery foam. The innumerable fiery eyes of the ship were barely visible, because of the snow, to the Devil watching from the crags of Gibraltar, from the stony gateway of two worlds, the ship receding into the night and the snow gale. The Devil was as enormous as a cliff, but even more enormous was the ship, many-tiered, many-funnelled, created by the pride of the New Man with an ancient heart. The snow gale smote upon its rigging and wide-throated funnels, white from the snow, but the ship was steadfast, firm, majestic—and terrifying. Upon its top-most deck were reared, in their solitude among the snowy whirlwinds, those snug, dimly lighted chambers where, plunged in a light and uneasy slumber, was its ponderous guide who resembled a pagan idol, reigning over the whole ship. He heard the pained howlings and the ferocious squealings of the storm-stifled siren, but comforted himself by the proximity of that which, in the final summing up, was incomprehensible even to himself, that which was on the other side of his wall: that large cabin, which had the appearance of being ar-moured, and was being constantly filled by the mysterious rumbling, quivering, and crisp sputtering of blue flames, flaring up and exploding around the pale-faced operator with a metal half-hoop upon his head. In the very depths, in the submerged womb of the *Atlantis,* were the thirty-thousand-pound masses of boilers and of all sorts of other machinery—dully glittering with steel, hissing out steam and exuding oil and boiling water,—of that kitchen, made red hot from infernal furnaces underneath, wherein was brewing the motion of the ship. Forces, fearful in their concentration, were bubbling, were being trans-mitted to its very keel, into an endlessly long dungeon, into a tunnel, illumi-nated by electricity, wherein slowly, with an inexorableness that was crushing to the human soul, was revolving within its oily couch the gigantic shaft, ex-actly like a living monster that had stretched itself out in this tunnel.

Meanwhile, amidship the *Atlantis,* its warm and luxurious cabins, its dining halls and ball-rooms, poured forth radiance and joyousness, were humming with the voices of a well-dressed gathering, were fragrant with fresh flowers, and the strains of the stringed orchestra were their song. And again excruci-atingly coiled and at intervals feverishly came together among this throng, among this glitter of lights, silks, diamonds and bared feminine shoulders, the pliant pair of hired lovers: the sinfully modest, very pretty young woman, with eyelashes cast down, with a chaste coiffure, and the well-built young man, with black hair that seemed to be pasted on, with his face pale from powder, shod in the most elegant of patent-leather foot-gear, clad in a tight-fitting dress coat with long tails,—a handsome man who resembled a huge leech. And none knew that, already for a long time, this pair had grown weary of languishing dissemblingly in their blissful torment to the sounds of the shamelessly sad music,—nor that far, far below, at the bottom of the black hold, stood a tarred coffin, neighbouring on the gloomy, sultry depths of the ship that was ponderously overcoming the darkness, the ocean, the gale. . . .

Gino Spinelli
Acute Lymphocytic Leukemia

K. D. Beernink, M.D.

"No next of kin," you'd said that night
They carried you onto my ward, but you smiled
At the grey-haired lady whose hand you held. Though I failed
That night to see her love for you, it wasn't long
Before you'd told us all that "you're as young
As you feel," and that's what made you feel like a child
Again, because you were in love.

                I paled
The color of my suit when first I heard
Your marriage plans. Unless the lab had erred,
You shouldn't have had the strength to grin
At me the way you did. Chaste
Mistress, Cancer, but she'd had her taste
Of the body you'd pledged to another.

                "So thin
"He's gotten, Doctor; that must be what made him faint."
(Maria was certain that "thin" was "cause.")

              "Too bad things went
Like this, but we can wait till he gets out.
Been waiting all our lives for this, can wait
A little longer; haven't really set a date."

You'd spent your youthful energy on poverty,
The youngest of eleven in southern Italy,
And couldn't say hello in English when you arrived
At twenty-four, to find a fortune and some dignity.

They thought you always a fool, they contrived
Explanation for why you could not understand
The English too well, and why you would never demand
A higher price for a pound of tomatoes, and how
You could live through the New Haven winters alone
Without a regular job. Had they known
Of your loneliness would they have reasoned so?

You were cheerful as always the next Sunday morning.
You talked to the priest of Maria, and read him the sports page
And asked about all your old roommates.

                                      Your wheezing
Began after lunch, I recall. You sat on the edge
Of your bed trying so hard to smile, and explained
That your breathing was suddenly hard.
I could hear in your lungs what we all had feared,
And before I completed the cultures you leaned
On my shoulder—I saw that your smile had turned blue,
And quietly you
Convulsed.
I broke two of your teeth with the laryngoscope, but
In my fight to place the tube your cords stayed taught.
To the surgeon laryngospasm was nothing new,
And I helped him open your tubes too late
To mend your mind or move your sick white blood.
The nurses left and the priest arrived, and I made him wait
While I pumped your chest—
But your pupils never shrank.
                         Quietly
He mumbled, ''Doctor, you did your best.''
And I gave you to him reluctantly.

I dialed the number for next of kin.
''Come right away, the turn is for the worse.''
I fingered my sweaty lip and smelled
Your terminal vomitus. The day nurse
Shoved the death certificate before me, spelled
Your name in pencil, and left to join the outside world
Where life is three score and ten. I'd often called
To say the turn is for the worse—a deceit
To further compromise the already effete
Self-image of a healer that lay
Weeping in this wrinkled white.

But I had never called a fiancée.

Do Not Go Gentle into That Good Night

Dylan Thomas

Do not go gentle into that good night,
Old age should burn and rave at close of day;
Rage, rage against the dying of the light.

Though wise men at their end know dark is right,
Because their words had forked no lightning they
Do not go gentle into that good night.

Good men, the last wave by, crying how bright
Their frail deeds might have danced in a green bay,
Rage, rage against the dying of the light.

Wild men who caught and sang the sun in flight,
And learn, too late, they grieved it on its way,
Do not go gentle into that good night.

Grave men, near death, who see with blinding sight
Blind eyes could blaze like meteors and be gay,
Rage, rage against the dying of the light.

And you, my father, there on the sad height,
Curse, bless, me now with your fierce tears, I pray.
Do not go gentle into that good night.
Rage, rage against the dying of the light.

The Odd Old Lady

Thyra Samter Winslow

The first time that old Mrs. Quillan knew anything was, well, different, was the night at dinner when Winnie came into the dining room wearing her new blue dress.

Winnie was seventeen and the prettiest of the old lady's grandchildren. She had soft, light hair and a tip-tilted nose, and had just got over the sloppy-sweater stage. Now she wore a dress that fitted closely her slim, young body.

"I'm so glad you got the spot out of your dress," the old lady said, in her gentle voice with just a suggestion of a quaver in it.

"What spot do you mean, Grandma?" asked Winnie. "This is my new dress. I never had a spot on it."

"Why, didn't Ralph Miller spill chocolate ice-cream soda on it and we couldn't . . ." Grandma began and stopped suddenly.

"You must have dreamed that, Mother," said Julia Latham a bit uncertainly. It wasn't like Mrs. Quillan to imagine things. Everybody was always saying how clear her mind was.

"Of course, I . . . I guess I dreamed it," said the old lady quickly. She put some raspberry jam on a piece of bread for Bobby and was glad he didn't say anything. Bobby was a great one for repeating things. So was Evan, her son-in-law. They never meant anything by it, Grandma knew that. But they liked family jokes. If . . . if they took this up . . . Grandma gave a sigh of relief when they began talking about something else.

For, as soon as she had said it, Grandma knew! She knew as definitely as she knew that on the table stood the old teapot and sugar bowl that Grandpa had brought her when he'd gone to St. Louis many years ago. It wasn't a dream! She knew something no one else could know. And it had never happened to her before. Winnie didn't know about the spot on her dress because she hadn't yet spotted her dress! Ralph Miller hadn't yet spilled the chocolate soda down the front of it. Poor Winnie! Her lovely new dress to be ruined like that! Grandma couldn't warn her.

There was nothing she could do, for Grandma didn't know how she knew about the spot. Sometimes, here of late, she'd got sort of mixed up about things. Like when she thought she'd seen Mrs. Willis on the street—and Mrs. Willis had been dead for three years! Oh, Grandma knew, all right, when she thought hard. And she tried to think before she said things, but this had sort of tumbled out. Oh, well, maybe she was wrong! Maybe Winnie wouldn't spot her dress after all.

Grandma tried to pretend to herself that she hadn't said anything.

There were lots of things to do. Dishes to wash. Beds to make. Helping her daughter, Julia, so that Julia could have time for the things she liked to do. Doing the things Winnie was supposed to do, because Winnie hated housework. A young girl has to have some fun!

Three days later Winnie flew into the house.

"That awkward goon of a Ralph Miller!" she wailed. "He spilled a whole glass of chocolate ice-cream soda all over my dress! He said Chester Alden shoved his arm. It never will come out, I know!"

"You'd better take it right to the cleaners," her mother said, "unless Grandma . . ."

"I'm afraid I can't," said Grandma, knowing the spot would always show.

"It's my new dress!" said Winnie. And then she remembered. "Grandma, didn't you say I'd get chocolate soda on my dress?"

"Oh, Grandma was just imagining things. She wasn't even with you. Rush out to the cleaners with that dress," Julia said.

Winnie ran away and Grandma took a deep breath of thankfulness. Maybe they wouldn't mention what she'd said about the spot ever again. It was too bad, though, it's coming true. Winnie didn't get many pretty things. Grandma made a resolution to be more careful.

It was odd about life, anyway. One time everything had run along so smoothly. There'd been the little cottage and Grandpa, and then the children. There wasn't even time to think about things, then. Everything was in its right order—just the way it happened. Breakfast to get—hearty breakfasts, for Grandpa worked hard and liked hot biscuits and a nice piece of fried ham in the morning. And there was bread to bake—fat, fragrant loaves, and coffee roasting in the oven and bacon frying. Grandma liked nice smells. And sewing for the whole family—you couldn't buy good, ready-made things in those days. And long rides with Grandpa in the surrey behind Nelly, the steady, old mare. And then this big house, and a girl to help with the cleaning, though Grandma liked to do the cooking herself. And the children growing up . . .

And now Grandpa was dead and little Josephine was dead. And Arthur was married and living in Chicago, and he never forgot to send a check every month and a letter, too, though being married to a wife none of them knew very well sort of separated them.

Grandma shook her head. Everything was all right! Here she was, living with Julia and Evan, who were so good to her. Of course the house was hers, and Arthur's check went into the family coffers, but she knew Evan did the best he could. Grandma did her share, too. And she was glad she could help in the house and with the neighbors when she had a chance. Dr. Clement was mighty good about coming by, and picking her up, and letting her do things when he had a patient who was too poor to hire a nurse.

Yes, everything was all right, except knowing things. And even that might be all right, if she could remember to keep things straight in her mind.

It was last year when things began to get mixed up. Things that had happened a long time ago seemed to have happened only yesterday. And things that had happened only yesterday she couldn't remember at all. She asked Dr. Clement about it—as if it were happening to someone else, and he said that's the way it was sometimes when you got old.

It wasn't much fun getting old. Grandma knew she took little, short steps, and the others had to walk slowly when they went to church. And there were her teeth . . . and her eyes. And it was lonely without Grandpa, though she never let the others know. There weren't many men like Grandpa. She'd been lucky having him all those years. The year they planted the lilac bush . . . It seemed odd when she forgot it had been planted many years ago.

But that was all right, remembering things that happened so long ago and forgetting the things that happened just yesterday. It was this new thing that worried Grandma, knowing things before they happened at all. But maybe it was an accident—knowing about the stain on the blue dress. She must be careful and keep her mind on what she was saying.

But she forgot that day at breakfast. The rest of the family drank coffee, but Grandma liked tea.

"Bring in Grandma's tea," Julia called to Winnie, who was carrying things in from the kitchen.

"Just bring my tea in a cup," said Grandma, "as long as the teapot's broken." But she was sorry about the teapot, for she loved it.

"The teapot's not broken, Mother," said Julia.

"But Bobby broke it," said Grandma. "Don't you remember? I don't mind, really. He couldn't help it."

"Here's your teapot," said Winnie and put it on the table in front of Grandma.

"I'm sorry," Grandma said, "I just imagined it, I guess."

But she hadn't imagined it. She just hadn't realized that the teapot hadn't yet been broken! She picked it up lovingly and watched the clear amber stream pour into her cup.

"You're getting odd notions, Mother," said Evan, "the way you imagine things!"

"I know," said Grandma, "maybe things that I dream of. . . ."

She put her hands into her lap suddenly. They were trembling so she couldn't have held the pot another minute.

A couple of days later, Bobby came home from school and reached for the cookie jar, high on the shelf, and the teapot careened onto the floor and lay there, broken.

"I couldn't help it!" wailed Bobby. "Maybe, because what Grandma said about my breaking the teapot . . ."

"Of course," comforted Grandma, "I sort of put it into your mind. You couldn't help it at all." She gave Bobby some of the Jordan almonds Mrs. Rogers had brought her on her birthday. No one said anything else about the teapot—after all, it was just an old teapot that only Grandma cared about.

"I'll be more careful after this!" Grandma told herself. But it worried her. It was all right the days she took an umbrella when the skies were still clear, because old ladies were apt to carry umbrellas. And going to see old Mrs. Hodges when she was lying alone and ill, because Grandma always had gone to see Mrs. Hodges. Only that day Grandma took a basket of provisions and wore her old clothes, the way she did when Dr. Clement took her to see sick people. But no one thought anything about it, because no one but Grandma was interested in Mrs. Hodges.

It was different about Winnie's new beau. Grandma knew about him as if it had already happened. But she couldn't seem to see clearly the people he was mixed up with. It couldn't be Winnie! Winnie couldn't get into anything like that!

Grandma thought it over and she knew she had to warn Evan, though she usually stayed out of things.

"That new boy from Chicago—I wouldn't let Winnie go out with him," she said.

"Why, Mother, he's a cousin of the Dillmans," Evan said. "He's been ill, came here to build up. A fine young man!"

"He's not a fine young man," Grandma said. "He'll . . . he'll get into trouble. I don't want Winnie . . ."

"The way you talk!" said Winnie. "Honest, Grandma, he couldn't be nicer—not like these dull home-town boys I'm used to."

The others agreed—a nice young man, Sid Forrest.

They never knew that when Sid telephoned, and Grandma answered the call, she didn't tell Winnie. And she gave Winnie the wrong directions the day Sid was to meet her at the library.

But when Winnie continued to see Sid, Grandma knew she had to do something. She even worried about it at night in bed.

Finally, she made up her mind. One day she put on her best black dress, with a little, white-embroidered collar, and the brooch Grandpa had given her, and her rather shapeless little black hat, and went to see Morris Dillman.

Mr. Dillman was a tall, lanky gentleman, with a lined face. He had known Grandma Quillan all of his life.

"What can I do for you, Mrs. Quillan?" he asked kindly.

"It's about Sid Forrest," Grandma said. "He's going with Winnie, my granddaughter. I don't want him to come to the house any more."

"Why, Mrs. Quillan, he's my own second cousin. We're very fond of him. Did the family send you?"

"Oh, no, they don't know anything about it. I thought, if we talked it over . . ."

"I'll see what I can do," said Dillman, as if he were talking to a child. "Now, you go home and forget all about it."

"Oh, thank you," Grandma said. And stayed on to talk about little things, so Mr. Dillman wouldn't think she was odd or anything.

Morris Dillman must have gone right over to see Evan Latham, for by the time Grandma got home—she had stopped in to see Mrs. Morrison and the twins—the whole family knew about her call.

"Why, Mama," Julia said, "I don't know what's got into you lately. It isn't like you at all."

"Dillman thought it was odd," said Evan, who looked worried, too, "his cousin and all . . ."

"Why, Mother," Julia said sternly, "you'll ruin Winnie's chances . . ."

"I've never done anything like this before. And she'll have other chances. She's only seventeen."

Winnie was in tears. She didn't say anything.

But Sid kept on seeing Winnie. Grandma didn't know what to do. If there were only some way she could tell them what she knew. And right on the heels of that, there was that thing she said, without thinking, on the way to church.

"They're certainly neglecting the Kerner house since old man Kerner died," Grandma said.

They all looked at her curiously.

"Why, what makes you think he's dead?" Evan asked.

"Why, he died that day we had the rainstorm . . ." She began, then stopped, remembering!

"He's alive as any of us," Evan said. "But they do neglect their place, all right—too lazy to keep it up. You mustn't get notions like that in your mind, Mother."

Old man Kerner died a few weeks later, and it rained hard the day he died. It was funny, Grandma saying that.

And when she said that about the Bates's apple tree being struck by lightning, weeks beforehand. Just a coincidence, of course, but it was odd . . .

Grandma began to be afraid to say anything. She had to think over carefully what she was going to say, and try to remember if a thing had happened twenty years ago—or yesterday—or was going to happen tomorrow. It was like, well, being up in a balloon, or maybe an airplane. Grandma didn't know about airplanes. She'd never been up in a balloon, either. But an airplane winged so swiftly through the sky, surely it couldn't get a view of the whole country at one time. A balloon seemed sort of stationary. She could see everything all stretched out at one time, though not too clearly, sometimes.

Yesterdays, a long way back, were clear. But recent yesterdays were dimmed, with just a few things plain. Today was clear enough. And tomorrow was like yesterday—certain things standing out bright and real and shining, the rest of it sort of dim, as if it were still in Time.

Sometimes Grandma knew, by the way the family looked at her, that she had said things she didn't mean to say, even when she didn't know what she had said. Only Bobby didn't seem to care. She loved Bobby; she loved all her children and grandchildren. If there was only something she could do . . .

If she'd only cared about big events! If only she'd been smarter when she was young! And had read the first pages of the newspapers and all of the serious books Grandpa had read, instead of darning children's stockings in the evening. If she knew about things, maybe now she'd be able to see things ahead that would help people. But when she tried to see ahead—to big things— she saw only confusion, and never anything she could tell anyone. But, if the little things just stayed in their proper places . . .

Julia Latham was awfully worried about her mother. She talked things over with Evan.

"I don't know what we can do," she said. "Mother acts all right most of the time, but some of the things she says . . . And she has such odd explanations . . ."

"It's too bad," Evan said. "She's been such a wonderful person, but now . . . she's odd. There's no denying it. Perhaps if you saw Dr. Clement . . ."

"That's what I thought I'd do," Julia said. "He's known Mother longer than any of us, and being a doctor and all. . . ."

Julia sat in the doctor's office and pretended to read the magazines that were as old as the cartoons said magazines in doctors' offices were. She tried to keep her mind on what she was reading and on the people in the office, until the nurse said Dr. Clement could see her.

Dr. Clement was hearty and red-faced, kind and wise.

"Nothing wrong, I hope," he said. "I saw Evan yesterday. He looked fine. And Grandma Quillan. . . ."

It's about Mother I want to see you," Julia said. "She's not really ill. She's always been so well, but here lately . . . we're worried about her."

"But she seemed fine! She stopped in just a few weeks ago, to tell me about the Bosleys down on Graham Road. Said the older boy was going to die, but that we could save the other two. As good a diagnosis as a doctor could have given. The boy died of rheumatic fever, but we're getting the other two on their feet. With the right care. . . . She's a remarkable woman, Grandma Quillan. Many's the time she's helped me out."

"Mother is wonderful," said Julia. "You don't have to tell me that. But, well, like knowing about the Bosley boy. . . . Maybe that isn't just what I mean. But her mind is all confused. She doesn't remember what happened yesterday, but something that happened twenty years ago. . . ."

"Sure!" Dr. Clement said. "A lot of old people get that way. She asked me about that condition some time ago, but I wasn't certain she meant herself.

Usually people don't realize their own condition. But I don't think that's serious.''

"I'm glad of that," Julia said. "But that isn't all. She gets all kinds of hallucinations. She imagines things.''

"What kind of things?''

"She thinks they've happened. But they haven't happened at all.''

"Oh, I see!'' Dr. Clement was more serious now.

"Sometimes she tries to pretend she didn't say them, and then gets more mixed up than ever. And sometimes she frightens us—things happen just the way she says they've already happened. I don't know if you see what I mean. A coincidence, of course, but it worries us.''

"Of course," Dr. Clement said.

"And there's Bobby. She's devoted to him and he loves her, too, but he's only seven. And after school she's frequently alone with him . . .''

"Oh, I feel she's perfectly safe.''

"I hope so, doctor. But we can't help worrying. The other day she said Bobby would cut himself with a new knife somebody had given him. And the next day he did cut himself. It may be the power of suggestion on a child, for Bobby hangs on every word she says. And she went to a friend of ours and complained about one of Winnie's boy friends. Isn't there something, doctor?''

"There aren't any drugs, if that's what you mean. I'm afraid it's senile dementia. But let me come in and look her over. She ought to have a good physical and mental check-up. And it may be, if you can't take care of her at home, that she ought to go to a sanitarium or a nursing home.''

"There must be some other way!'' Julia began to sob.

"Don't cry, child," said Dr. Clement. "If the old lady is . . . odd, it might be the best way all around. She'd be perfectly comfortable. There's a place just out of town run by trained nurses—a series of little white cottages and very pleasant. There are some old schoolteachers there—a nice class of people. I could send her to a hospital for observation, or have a couple of psychiatrists pass on her, unless she wants to go voluntarily. But don't worry about it until I talk to her. And don't let her know; I'll just drop in. . . .''

The next afternoon, Dr. Clement came to call. Grandma liked and admired him. She gave him a glass of sherry and some homemade cookies.

"You work too hard," she said. "But I could have helped with Mrs. Bronson. She told me what you did for her.''

"I didn't think you were up to it.''

"I'm as good as I was twenty years ago.''

"I hope you are, but you look . . . peaked. Maybe you need a good overhauling—a good tonic.''

"Nonsense, never felt better!''

"Well, I'm going to look you over anyhow.''

"If you've nothing better to do with your time.''

He listened to Grandma's heart and her lungs. He asked her questions. And Grandma sat on the sofa, very still, like a little girl, and answered everything. Some of the questions were peculiar, but after all, he was her friend. When he'd first come to town, she'd thought he was a fine young man. Grandpa had thought so, too.

She hoped she said the right things. A couple of times she got so interested in what he was saying she sort of forgot. . . . Oh, well, he knew her pretty well. He'd understand.

They talked about little things then, people they both knew, the weather, spring was nearly here . . .

"I see you found your bag all right," said Grandma when Dr. Clement picked it up and started to leave.

"Found my bag?"

"Why, yes. Didn't you leave it at the Plunketts' out on Talbot Road?"

"Why, yes, of course," said Dr. Clement. But when he was in his car he had to admit that Mrs. Latham was right. For the old lady was odd when she spoke of old man Brewster, who had been dead for ten years, and of the Corning boy having measles when he wasn't sick, and the lost bag. Why, he hadn't been near the Plunketts' in a couple of months! Maybe it would be better if the old lady went to a nursing home. The psychiatrists could examine her there. He'd make arrangements. . . .

Grandma was in her room when she heard a lot of excitement downstairs. She went down at once to find the family assembled in the living room, and Winnie in tears.

"It's Sid Forrest!" she sobbed.

"So, they found out about him!" said Grandma.

"What do you mean?" Evan asked.

"About the checks and the girl in the bakery shop . . ."

"That's not it, Grandma! He eloped with Irene Jessup. If I'd only treated him nicer," Winnie wailed.

"Then they don't know about the checks?"

"What checks?" asked Julia.

"Why . . . why . . ." Grandma didn't go on.

"It's bad enough that he eloped," said Winnie, "without your saying terrible things . . ."

"Just forget him!" said her father. "There's other good fish!"

"Not in this town!" Winnie sobbed.

"You're only seventeen! You're just a child!" Julia said.

Grandma put her arms around her granddaughter and drew her down on the couch next to her.

"You'll meet someone else," she said, "a fine man, you'll see!"

"Will he be good-looking?"

"Yes," said Grandma, "and you'll be very much in love."

It wasn't until two days later that the family found out about the forged checks.

The very next day Grandma woke up earlier than usual. She dressed quickly, not in her neat housedress, but in her best black dress, with a fresh collar, and Grandpa's pin to hold it in place. There were so many things to do. . . .

She straightened her bureau drawers, though they were already in apple-pie order—the pile of clean handkerchiefs; her collars; her decent, plain underthings.

"What are you doing?" Julia called. She was so worried about her mother—about Winnie—about so many things. But there was nothing she could do. . . .

"I thought I'd go over to Mrs. Hodges. Take her a few things. . . ."

"If you feel well enough. . . ."

"Never felt better in my life!"

Grandma made half a dozen neat little bundles, her pearl beads—not real, but mighty pretty; the cameo pin Julia thought old-fashioned; the bracelet with the onyx ornament. After the breakfast dishes were finished, and she'd made her bed, she'd give these little packets to some of her old friends. They weren't much. She didn't have much to give—for she wanted Julia and Winnie to have her ring and her gold bracelet, her other things. Well, these would bring a little pleasure—folks didn't have too much pleasure these days.

She was tired when she came home, but not too tired to help get dinner. She'd had a bite of lunch with Mrs. Burgess, to whom she'd given her real-lace collar-and-cuff set. Mrs. Burgess had always admired it, and she didn't have a lot, poor thing. Grandma smiled. She herself always had had nice things; not grand, exactly, but nice—the moonstone pin Julia liked to wear, the little, enameled watch Arthur's wife had given her, and the house . . . Wouldn't it be awful to be old and not have things to give anyone?

In the excitement of finding out about Sid Forrest's activities, Winnie had already got over her heartbreak. She was a bit tragic at dinner, but Grandma gathered she was rather enjoying herself.

Grandma went to her room as soon as the dishes were in the cupboard. All of the running around and the excitement and all. . . .

She heard the telephone ring and Julia's voice answering:

"Dr. Clement, you went to the Plunketts' on Talbot Road? And you left your bag there. And you didn't know where you left it when you stopped in to see the Corning boy who had the measles. And then you remembered what Grandma Quillan had said. I don't quite understand, but of course I'll tell her. She's gone to bed now, but in the morning. . . ."

Grandma smiled to herself. So Dr. Clement had found out about the bag and the measles. They'd find out a lot of things. . . .

The telephone rang again. This time it was for Winnie. Her voice was excited and loud.

"Isn't it dreadful!" she said. "But I'm not surprised at all. Grandma told me

weeks ago what would happen—warned me! She's got second sight or something. She can tell fortunes. She told me I was going to marry a rich, handsome
man and be happy! Sure! Come over tomorrow and she'll tell you everything. . . .''

That would be terrible, almost the last straw! Grandma smiled wryly. But
she knew she wouldn't have to worry about it. There didn't have to be a last
straw!

Julia and Evan were fine . . . and Winnie, once she got some sense into her
head . . . and Arthur's family . . . none of them needed her any more . . .
not even Bobby, who was growing up.

Grandma puttered around the room, arranging things the way she wanted
them, climbed into the old-fashioned double bed she'd kept for herself when
Julia refurnished the house.

Very carefully, so as not to break them—as if it mattered any more—she put
her glasses on the little bed table, turned out the light and closed her eyes. She
was never one for reading in bed or lying awake at night. She'd always been
too tired for that. And then she said the prayers she'd learned from her own
mother, the way she always said them, ''Our Father, which art in Heaven'' and
''Now I lay me down to sleep.''

She wished she could have helped them more . . . Julia and Evan . . .
Winnie, with her new idea about fortune-telling . . . all of them . . . if there
only had been some way . . .

She wiped a tear from her cheek with the back of her hand. The views from
the balloon—a long-ago view of yesterday, and the view of today, and tomorrow—all began to merge and grow dim. Grandma gave a long sigh of relief
as she fell asleep. There wasn't a thing she had to worry about any more.

Of Death and Old Age

Marcus Tullius Cicero

Translated from the Latin by Thomas Newton

For all things which come by course of nature are to be reckoned and ac-
compted among good things; and what is so much according to natural course
as for an old aged man to die? Which doth happen to young men, as it were,
maugre nature's good-will. Therefore, young men, in mine opinion, seem so to
die as when a raging and violent flame of fire is quenched, with a great quantity
or effusion of water; but old men die as it were fire, which, lacking wood and
combustible matter to nourish it, goeth out quietly and is quenched, as though

it were of his own accord, not forcibly. And as apples which are green and unripe are not plucked from the tree but by a certain violent plucking, but if they be ripe and mellow, they fall voluntarily down from the tree; so likewise, young men depart out of their life by violent force and painful struggling, but old men die by a certain ripeness and maturity. And as often as I [Cato] think thereon, I am rapt with such joy and comfort, that the nearer I draw and approach to death, the sooner, methink, I see the dry land, and (as it were, after a long navigation and seafaring voyage) shall at length arrive at the quiet haven and port of all rest and security. All other ages have a certain number of years appointed, how long every one continueth, but unto old age there are no determinate and certain times limited and prefixed, and therefore thou livest therein well and laudably, as long as thou canst execute thy office, discharge thy duty, and defend thine authority, and yet, nevertheless, contemn death. And for this cause, it happeneth that old age is endued with greater courage and animosity than adolescency and youth is. And this is the cause, that when the tyrant Peisistratus demanded of Solon how he durst be so bold, or wherein he reposed his trust, so wilfully and boldly to gainsay and disobey his proceedings: Solon answered him that he trusted to his old age, and that was it that made him full of courage, and gave him boldness to resist him; forasmuch as he with lawless force and monstrous tyranny had attempted to oppress the commonwealth, miserably frushed through his unbridled and tyrannical invasions.

But the best end of life is this: when nature, which compacted and framed the body, doth likewise dissolve and bring to death the same, being in good and perfect remembrance, the use of the wits and senses in no part appaired nor diminished. For even as the shipwright which made the ship knoweth best how to undo and pull the same asunder again, and as none hath better skill to unjoint or take down a house than the carpenter that made it; even so nature, which fashioned the feature of the body and set the same in a most decent symmetry, doth best dissolve and end it by natural death. For every conglutination when it is fresh and newly glued together, will not easily be pulled asunder but by violent haling and forcible rupture, but when it is inveterate and old, it may easily be divelled and severed. Thus, you see that the small remnant and time of our race and life which is behind unrun, is neither affectuously to be desired, nor without cause to be left and forsaken. And the famous philosopher, Pythagoras, giveth us a sore charge, that we should not depart out of the garrison and wardhouse of this life unless we have commission and commandment from our general-captain which is God. Solon his wise saying is very notable and praiseworthy, for he would not that his death should be unbewailed and unlamented of his friends. His meaning, I think, was because he would not seem to be forgotten, but rather entirely to be beloved and remembered of his friends, which thing their dolorous plaints and inward griefs at his last end and funeral obsequies should bewray and evidently witness. But yet Ennius his opinion in like case may, in my judgment, be better allowed, for he would not have his friends to moan and lament for him after his death, and these are his words:

'Surcease from tears, when I am dead,
And let not them for me be shed,
When death shall with his deadly dart
My corpse and soul asunder part!
And why? the clanging trump of fame
Shall ever sound abroad my name.'

This noble poet would not have the death of them to be lamented and with feminine blubbering and screeches to be bewailed, whose praise and virtue is immortalized and enrolled in the book of fame, and their worthy deeds registered in the scroll of eternity. As touching the bitter pangs and extreme agonies which they suffer that lie in dying (if there may any such be), truly it continueth but for a short while, specially in an old man; and after death, the sense is either such as is blessed and optable, or else it is none at all. But all young men ought to imprint this in their minds, and meditate the same, that they be not in any servile and distardly fear of death, but to stand at defiance and contemn it. For whatsoever enureth not himself with this meditation cannot have a quiet mind. We are most sure that we must die, and we know not whether our hour will come even that same very day. Therefore he that every hour standeth in fear of death, how can his mind be in any rest or tranquillity? Whereof there needeth no very long disputation to be had, sith I do well remember not only Lucius Brutus, who in the quarrel of his country, which was despoiled and with tyranny oppressed, most manfully was slain; the two Decii, who, being armed at all pieces and mounted on horseback, galloped and gave themselves willingly to death for their country's sake; Marcus Regulus, who (rather than he would forswear himself and break promise with his most deadly and bloody enemies) went willingly to his most certain torment and punishment (where he well knew that he should suffer death after a strange and terrible manner), and would not in any wise by his kinsfolks and friends be altered and removed from his determination; the two Scipios, who with their own bodies chose rather to stop the passage of the fresh succours (which, under the conduct of Hasdrubal, came to aid Hannibal and the proud Carthaginians, for infesting and afflicting Italy with sword, famine, and fire), than to suffer and permit them to set any foot within the territories and precincts of the Roman dition; your grandfather, Lucius Paulus, who, through the temerity and folly of his fellow-in-office, Terentius Varro, was in that ignominious overthrow and shameful discomfiture in the conflict and battle of Cannae, slain and brought to confusion; and Marcus Marcellus, whose valiance and magnanimity was so great and so well tried, that his and our cruel enemy, Hannibal, when he had slain him in the field, caused his dead corse with all funeral pomp and solemnity of sepulture to be interred; but also how our legions and armies courageously adventured to take such voyages and venturous expeditions into such dangerous places, from whence they looked [not] to return alive again; whereof I have written in my book of *Originals*.

Shall, therefore, old men, which have great knowledge and experience, fear that which young striplings, and the same not only unskilful, but also blunt and rustical, do contemn and care not for? But, methinks satiety of all things causeth satiety of life. There are some fantastical and childish plays whereat young children in their childhood delight to play; shall, therefore, young men and tall fellows addict themselves to the same semblably? There are some exercises and affections wherein youthly years do enure themselves: shall the ripe and constant age (which is called the middle age of man) look to play at the same? And of this middle age there are some studies, wills, and appetites which old age careth not for. And there be some studies and exercises belonging and appropriate to old age. And therefore as the pleasure and delight of the studies and exercises in fresher and lustier ages doth in time wear away and come to an end, so doth the studies of old age in continuance and tract of time also die and vanish. And when this pleasure and delightful contentation begin in old men once to decrease, then doth satiety of life bring to them a convenable and mature time to die. For verily I cannot see why I should not be bold to utter and declare to you twain the very entire cogitations of my heart, and the opinion which I have of death, and the rather because I suppose that I do better know and see it, as one that now am near the pit's brink having one of my feet already in the grave.

And I am in this belief, O Publius Scipio and Caius Laelius, that your noble fathers, men for their virtuous manners and worthy demerit immortalized, who also were my most dear and loving friends, do yet live, yea, and such a life as is worthy only to be called a life, which is immortal and not transitory, for as long as we dwell and be included within this lumpish body, proportioned with joints, sinews, flesh, bone, and other parts, which may be called the prison or case of our soul, we are driven and by a necessity enforced to do some actions (will we or nill we) as to sleep, eat, drink, etc., and to do some cumbersome works which are inevitable. But the mind or soul, which is divine and celestial, sent down from God out of heaven and infused into man, is depressed and as it were forcibly dejected or thrust down to the earth, being a place quite contrary to divine nature and eternity, because it is mortal and visible, whereas the other is immortal and invisible. But I do think that the immortal Gods inspired minds into human bodies because there should be some to inhabit the earth, who, beholding and considering the orders of the celestial bodies, and weighing how duly they observe their courses and motions, might imitate and follow the same right order in the trades of their life and constancy. And not only reason and frequent disputation moveth me thus to believe, but also the profound doctrine and authorities of most noble and approved philosophers. For I have been in places where I heard that Pythagoras and his disciples which inhabited within our country, and were in manner free denizens within our precinct and dominion (for they were once named Italian Philosophers) affirmed and said that they were never otherwise persuaded nor never held opinion to the contrary, but that our minds were formed and derived from the universal divinity of God. Furthermore, it was told me what Socrates disputed and spake concerning the immortality of the soul, and what he openly said, being an ancient philosopher, and one whom Apollo his oracle judged the wisest man in the whole world, even the last day of his life, a little before his death.

What needeth many words? I am so firmly persuaded, and on this point so wholly resolved, seeing there is so great celerity of the mind, so good remembrance of things past, and so great forecast and produce in things to come, so many arts, so many sciences, so many inventions and ingenious devices, that the nature which understandeth and containeth the knowledge of all these things is not mortal. And sith the mind is ever moved, having no beginning of motion because it moveth itself, and shall never have any end of motion, because it is eternal, and shall never leave itself, and sith the nature of the mind is simple, having nothing mixed to it which is unlike and discrepant to it, I thereby know that it is indivisible, whereupon it confrequently followeth that forasmuch as it is indivisible it can never die and perish utterly.

And these reasons following make much for the probation thereof, that men know many things before they be born; that children (notwithstanding the abstruse and painful difficulty of arts) do so quickly learn and, as who would say, snatchingly conceive innumerable things, that they seem not then at the first to learn them, but rather repeat and call them again to memory. These be for the most part the arguments and reasons which the divine philosopher Plato allegeth and bringeth for his proof of the immortality of the souls. Also Xenophon writeth that King Cyrus, the elder, lying on his death-bed, spake these words following to his children:

'I would not, my children, that you should think, when I am departed out of this life and gone from you, that I shall be nowhere or brought to nothing. For you never saw with your bodily eyes my mind, during all this while that I lived here with you: but as long as I dwelled in this body you well perceived and knew by my valiant exploits and acts that I had a mind. Therefore think you not otherwise but that I am the very same still, and my said mind shall still remain as before, although you see it not visibly. For neither should the noble memorial and honourable monuments of princes and worthy personages remain after their death, if in their lifetime, by the policy and prowess of their minds, they did not achieve some worthy enterprises, whereby their fame and honour might be remembered and magnified of their posterity. Truly it would never sink in my brain that the minds or souls did live only while they remained in mortal bodies, and being departed out of them utterly to die, that no more of them should remain. Nor that the soul and mind of sots and fools is doltish and blockish when it is set at liberty and departed out of their foolish bodies; but when it is purified from the filthy admixtion and drossy impurity of the same body, and fined from imperfection and beginning to be sound, perfect, and clear, then is it wise, sapient, and incorrupt.

'And man's nature being by death dissolved, it is apparent and well enough to all men known to what place all the other parts do go, for they do all return to that matter whereof they had their first and original beginning; but the mind only is never with any bodily eyes seen nor perceived, neither when it is in the body, nor when it goeth and departeth out of the body.

'Now, you see that nothing is so like to death as sleep. And yet the minds of them that are asleep do greatly declare their divinity; for when they be at quietness and rest and with no careful cogitations overwhelmed, they do foresee many things to come, whereby it may plainly be perceived how and in what happy state they shall be, when they be dismissed and discharged out of their dungeon or goal of their mortal bodies. If, therefore, these things be true, then reverence and honour me as a god for the participation of the divine nature which is in my mind. But if the soul do die together with the body (as some ass-headed philosophers, flattering themselves in their bestial living and wallowing like swine in the filthy puddle of their epicurial sensuality, have affirmed) yet you, ever dreading the gods, being the protectors, disposers and governors of all the beautiful ornament and furniture of this wide world, shall not miss, but godly and inviolably solemnize and keep the memorial of me.'

These advertisements and exhortations Cyrus gave to his sons, lying on his deathbed. Now let us, if you think good, take a survey of our own selves, and see whether the same opinion and belief be not to be found in us and in other of our countrymen. I will be plain with thee, Scipio: no man in the world shall ever be able to persuade me that either thy father, Paulus Æmilius, or thy two grandfathers, Paulus and Africanus, or Publius Scipio, the brother of Africanus, or Caius Scipio, his uncle, or many more famous and worthy men which here need not to be rehearsed, would ever have attempted such perilous adventures (only to leave a noble and worthy memorial of their fame and valiance of their sequel whom they wished should take example of their fortitude and tread in the foot-steps of their laudable virtues, whereby they might achieve like success in their glorious affairs, and not fear to die in the quarrel of their country when foreign hostility invadeth it), if with the quick understanding of their minds they had not well seen and considered that their posterity appertained and belonged to them. Do you think that I (for I may, I trust, somewhat vaunt and boast of myself, as old men are wont to do) would ever have undertaken so many labours and painful travails night and day, both in the time of peace and also of war, if I had had this opinion fixed and rooted in my mind, that my glory and fame should extend no further than my natural life, and that when the one ceased the other should die also? For if that were so, were it not, I pray you, a great deal better to lead a quiet life, sequestered and exempt from all hurly-burly and toiling business, and never to intermeddle with contentious matters and the laborious affairs of the weal public? But the mind of noble personages, I know not how it chanceth, erecting itself and taking courage, had ever such a careful respect to their succession, as though when they were departed out of this life, they should then at length, and never till then, live and flourish, their incomparable gifts triumphing over cankered oblivion and their virtuous lives over mortal death. For if it were not so that the souls should be immortal, the mind of every good and virtuous man would not so earnestly with all his study and devoir seek to attain and aspire to immortal glory and per-petual renown.

Furthermore, every good and wise man dieth willingly, and rejoiceth therein exceedingly, taking death to be a joyful messenger to summon him to endless felicity: on the other side, every foolish man dieth unwillingly. Do you not think that the mind which seeth better and further off, doth well perceive and know that he goeth to a far better state than in this world is to be found? Again, the mind of the foolish sort, whose sight is dimmer and duller, doth not see nor understand so much. But, verily, I have a great desire to see and behold your fathers, whom I entirely loved, and had for their singular virtues in great admi-ration. And not them only am I so earnestly affected to see, with whom I was very familiarly acquainted, but others also of whom I have both heard, read, and also written. And when I am in my journey to them (which I so greatly desire) there should no man bring me back again, though he would and also could; neither to make me to retire to the place from whence I came, like to a ball which tennis players toss and strike to their counter players, and they again to the other side, yea, though he would undertake to renew my youth again, as we read that Pelias was in his old age.

I will say more, if God would grant me now in this age to return again to my infancy and to be as young as a child that lieth crying in his cradle, I would re-fuse and forsake the offer with all my might; neither would I when I have al-ready in a manner run the whole race and won the goal, be again revoked from the end marks to the lists, or place where I took my course at the first setting out. For who would be contented, when he hath gotten the best game, to be forced to run again for the same? What pleasure and commodity hath life? yea, rather, what pain, toil, and labour hath it not? But let us admit that it had great commodity, yet, undoubtedly, it hath either an end or else satiety. For I mean not to lament and deplore the lack of the pleasant and fresh time of my youth, as diverse and the same right well-learned men have done; neither do I repent that I have lived, because I have so lived and led my life that I may judge of myself that I was not born in vain, but rather for great utility and special con-sideration. And I depart out of this life as out of an inn, and not out of a dwelling-house. For nature hath given to us a lodging to remain and sojourn in for a time, and not to dwell in continually.

O lucky and blessed day wherein I shall take my journey to appear before the blissful troop and convocation of happy minds, and leave this troublesome world, being the vale of all misery and the filthy sink of all mischief. For I shall not only go to those worthy men of whom I spake a little before, but also to my dear son Cato, who was a man of such sanctity and goodness as none more, of such sincere and unstained honesty as none better, whose body was with funeral rites put into the fire and burned to ashes by me his father, whereas it had been more meet and more agreeable to the course of nature that my body should have been with semblable obsequies and ceremonies first burnt and in-tumulate by him. But his mind and soul not utterly forsaking me, but ever look-ing and expecting my coming, is gone before into those places of joy whither

he perceived that I myself, ere it be long, must also come. Which brunt of calamity and heavy chance of sorrow I seemed patiently to sustain, not because I
did take the matter so patiently indeed; but I comforted myself thinking and
deeming that we should not be long asunder, but after a time again to have a
joyful meeting. These are the causes and the very reasons, Scipio (because you
and Laelius said you much marvelled thereat) which make my old age to me
easy and tolerable, and not only without all grievance and disturbation, but also
replenished with all expedient pleasures.

And if I do err because I think that the souls of men be immortal, verily I am
well contented in the same error still to continue, and as long as I live I will
never renounce nor recant the same, wherein I take such singular pleasure and
comfort; and if it were not so, that after death I should feel nothing nor have no
sense at all (as certain pettifoggers and bastard philosophers hold opinion) I fear
not a whit least these lip-labourers and idiotical philosophers, when they themselves be dead, should scoff and make a mockingstock at this mine assertion
and belief, because they themselves shall also be without sense, and like to
brute beasts. But admit that after death we should not be immortal, yet it is
both convenient and also optable for a man, when he hath honestly played his
part in the pageant of this life, to die and pay his debt to nature. For nature as
she hath an end of all other things, so also of living. And old age is, as it were,
the peroration or final end of a man's time in this world, much like to the epi-
logue or catastrophe of an interlude, the wearisome repetition or defatigation
whereof we ought to avoid and eschew, and especially when we are fully
cloyed with satiety.

This much at your request I had to say concerning old age, unto the which
God grant you may arrive, that the things which you have heard of me by
mouth, you may prove true by certain trial and actual experiment.

From

A Daughter of Han: The Autobiography of a Chinese Working Woman

Ida Pruitt

Across the west wall from us lived an old uncle and aunt. He was a cousin to
my husband's father. They were an old couple with no children and they were
very fond of me. They had land and houses. They wove baskets of willow
withes and boiled sea water for salt.

This old uncle was over seventy, a strong old man who loved his wine. He was good to me and hated my husband. The old aunt was a little old woman, over fifty.

I often went to their house and they fed me many meals when my husband brought home nothing for me to eat.

When I was about twenty the old aunt died. I nursed her. She was ill for a month and very ill for half a month.

"I don't want Liu-Yi-tze to be my chief mourner." Liu-Yi-tze was my husband's baby name, the one his family knew him by. By rights he should have been the chief mourner as he was the nearest nephew. They asked me to be the chief mourner and carry the Heredity Jar. This is a small earthen jar into which all the members of the family, of the next generation, put food—rice, chiaotze, bread. They stuff the jar full that there may be many descendants and that there may be food for the person about to go on the long journey, also that there may be luck for those who put in the food. The child who stuffs in the most food will have the greatest fortune. The youngest son puts the round loaf of bread on the top of the jar and sticks a pair of chopsticks into it. I had to be all the children and stuff the jar, and also the youngest son and stick in the chopsticks, and the oldest son and carry the jar. Carrying the jar is the sign of the chief mourner. It is placed in the grave at the coffin head.

I was by the old aunt's side when she died. It is said that those who die alone, who die with no one beside them, will come back after transmigration as single people, people who have no descendants. The family must be there when anyone dies.

I made the little red bag which was to provide her with comforts for the journey and hung it on her buttonhole. I cut a piece of silver from an earring that she might have silver to buy what she needed, and put it in the bag with a pinch of tea and a piece of candy and a bit of salt vegetable to make her food more palatable. And, according to custom, as my old aunt died, as the breath left her body, I stuffed the little red bag into her mouth that she might have food to eat on her journey. I placed in her hand the small bundle of food which she needed to feed the dogs as she crossed the great Dog Mountain. I bound her feet together so that her body should not get up again. I did all the things for her that a son or a daughter-in-law or a daughter should do.

As soon as the breath had left her body we went to the Tu Ti Miao, the Temple of the Earth God. I pounded with my rolling pin three times on the ground to knock at the gate of Hades and pointed three times to the sky to knock at the gates of Heaven.

On the second morning all the family, male and female, went to the Cheng Huang Miao, the Temple of the City God, for by this time the Earth God had brought the spirit to this temple and we must feed it. We took a bowl of gruel and poured it in the court and we all kowtowed and wept. And on the third day all these things were done at the Temple of the Tien Chun Lao Yeh, the Master of the Hosts of Heaven. All the relatives and friends go there.

The funeral was on the fifth day. Old people should be kept at least seven days and young people at least three, but we buried her on the fifth day. All the night before we knelt around the coffin in our unbleached and unhemmed white clothes and wept, and the musicians played. This was to help the spirit start on its journey. It is natural that the spirit should linger by the body several days and find it difficult to leave and start on the unknown journey.

We put the ashes of all the paper money and clothes and the paper servants that had been burned for her into an earthen basin. As the coffin was lifted, to carry it away, the basin was thrown to the ground and broken and we all wailed.

I wore sackcloth and my head was bound with the rope of the chief mourner, and I walked in front of the coffin with the Heredity Jar in my arms.

Part Six

Alone and with Peers

LONELINESS IS ONE OF THE MORE PAINFUL OF THE PROBLEMS MANY ELDERLY experience and one of the most difficult to alleviate. It is a problem that is likely to increase in the future because many elderly persons depend on siblings as close friends and fewer are likely to have siblings. Given the reduced birth rates in this century that have accompanied industrialization and urbanization, the future elderly will include an increasing percentage of "only" offspring who are likely to be even more dependent on peers, in the absence of sibling relationships. Yet, peer relationships are fragile and are often difficult to replace. Many elderly persons also depend on close ties with daughters and sons; yet, given the lower birth rates since the 1930s—interrupted by increases in the latter 1940s and '50s—the present and future elderly are likely to have fewer sons and daughters than did prior generations. The absence or reduced number of family relationships, both siblings and offspring, is a likely contributor to the feelings of loneliness expressed by many elderly persons today and is likely to be an increasing problem in the future.

Elderly persons may have taken peer relationships for granted when younger, only to find those relationships ending or diminishing because of death, geographical mobility, conflict, physical difficulties in getting about, hearing losses, and so on. It is often difficult to find new friends to replace those lost, although, increasingly, organizational and institutional settings (such as community centers and apartment complexes for the well and independent elderly) are providing the types of environments in which new friendships can develop. I hope that there will be more such attempts in the future. What is needed are societally encouraged, developed, and assisted peer relationships, such as those described by sociologist Arlie Russell Hochschild as "social siblings" in her perceptive study of Merrill Court.[1]

Pa Minick in "Old Man Minick" (in Part 1) finds that he cannot fit in and participate comfortably in the lives of his son and daughter-in-law. He feels alone with them even though they are physically present. The differences between them and him cause him to feel that he is an outsider. He feels comfortable only when with his peers from the Grant Home for Aged Gentlemen whom he meets in the park; he is one of them and one with them. Loneliness is experienced in other ways by some elderly. The ostracism experienced by "The Widow," Sister Hsiang-lin (in Part 2), sets her apart in a negative way and makes her feel as unwelcome as the other characters intend her to be. She is isolated emotionally and socially from all others at an early age, has no one with whom to express and share her grief, and ages rapidly while relatively young. The absence of a close relationship that is emotionally supportive is del-

[1] Arlie Russell Hochschild, *The Unexpected Community*. Merrill Court was an apartment complex for the well and independent elderly. It was highly cohesive; individuals shared and did much for each other. There was a close sense of community—the residents really were social siblings. To Hochschild, this was unexpected. (See also Part 1.)

eterious to her. All those around her are either neutral or negative toward her.

In this section ''An Old Man's Winter Night'' (1916) by Robert Frost (1875–1963) conveys the sense of loneliness of the ''one aged man.'' Not only is the house a lonely place, with its empty rooms and barrels, and he all alone in it, but the old man is also alone as ''a light . . . to no one but himself.'' No one depends on him, needs him; he is important to no one but himself; he matters to no one.

This is quite unlike the situation of ''Isaac and Archibald'' (1902) by Edwin Arlington Robinson (1869–1935). While they live apart from each other, these two men are emotionally close and dependent. Since they care about each other, each is not alone. This is a poem about the close friendship of two elderly men, comfortable with and concerned and worried about each other; each worried about losing the other and being left alone; being mutually happy. Isaac is concerned that Archibald has not cut his oats (he has) and that Archibald is declining. Walking the five miles to see Archibald, ostensibly to check on Archibald and to remind him to cut the oats, gives Isaac a goal, a sense of purpose, which enlivens the walk. He is going somewhere definite, and he also has the company of a twelve-year-old boy who listens to him and takes him seriously. It is likely that without his feeling that the walk is important to the three of them and will accomplish something, Isaac would not be as spirited and vigorous as he is during it. Archibald, too, is concerned that his friend of many decades is declining. Isaac fears that Archibald will die first, and when that happens, that he will change drastically. Meanwhile, life in the present is perfect, with close friendship, purpose, excellent cider, and the spirited card game.

Mrs. Vernor, of ''Games'' by Howard Webber (first published in 1963), loses all that is familiar to her when she moves to her daughter's home. Her own home was familiar, comfortable, to her, and she has had the whole house to herself to do with as she wished. Her daughter and son-in-law play games with her that she goes along with, pretending that she has not changed, ignoring signs that she is aging and declining, and blaming others for her failures. But this pretense makes her feel even more lonely. Apparently she cannot be honest with the two of them, though the pretense saddens her both because she likes them and does not want to hurt them and because she too is bothered by her losses and her decline.

It is only with Mrs. Hartwell, her peer, that she can be herself and only with her that she can play an actual game rather than a symbolic game, and eventually stop playing games altogether. Even though formal with each other (they call each other ''Mrs.'' since they have not known each other in the past), they feel free in sharing problems, reminiscing, and playing the game they both enjoyed and were competent at much earlier in their lives. Old age has not hindered their competence in this one actual game. Moreover, they feel comfortable with each other and understand each other. It is only with a peer that each can feel comfortable, gradually stop playing games, and feel better, for each is in the same boat.

Hattie and Alice in "The Cries of Love" (1968) by Patricia Highsmith (born 1921) also understand each other: each knows what will hurt the other. Hattie feels jealous whenever Alice has anything nice and attempts to destroy it and Alice's enjoyment of it. She does this successfully several times. Only a masochist would continue to endure it. Alice, however, finds that she is dependent on Hattie for companionship; she fears being alone; and Hattie finds that she too is lonely and unhappy without Alice. Without each other, their routine, the order and stability of their lives, dissolves, in addition to the loss of their mutual physical presence. Though they are both proud and strong-willed, they are also dependent and lonely. Further, they both lack alternative close relationships, which makes them even more dependent on each other.

This is a different kind of relationship than is found among adolescent peers. Adolescents are also dependent on and jealous of each other; but they are trusting of each other, which Hattie and Alice are not. Adolescents band together to move through a difficult period, for they need the emotional and social support of their peers to help them break their ties of dependence on their parents (and their parents' ties of dependence on them). Hattie and Alice, in contrast, are competitive, individualistic, distant, ambivalent, jealous, and secretive with each other. Unlike adolescents, they are not trusting and open with each other, for they lack the common external enemy that adolescents have. Their reasons for friendship are different. They simply need each other to combat loneliness and to maintain the orderly routine of their respective lives. Their common enemy is loneliness rather than parents. Theirs is a more difficult battle.

A different kind of relationship appears in "The Lost Phoebe" (1912) by Theodore Dreiser (1871–1945). Henry experiences the loss of Phoebe, who has been both his wife and his best friend. His life, his habits, and his purpose have been determined by this relationship. He is, as is usual with elderly males, more dependent on her than she on him (she has threatened to leave *him*—never vice versa). He is single-minded in his dependence on their lives together. Given his intense dependence, it is surprising that he lives for as many as seven years after her death.

"The Lost Phoebe" was rejected by nineteen magazines before it was finally bought. Dreiser had successively reduced his price for it from $600 to $400, for awhile his bottom price, to, finally, $200, the purchase price.[2] Despite the rejections, and the frustration that accompanied each of them, Dreiser persisted, and this is now considered one of his best-known and best short stories. James T. Farrell referred to "The Lost Phoebe" as one of Dreiser's acknowledged classics, and wrote of it:

> Henry and Phoebe lived together on their farm for forty-eight years. Their love had changed into a condition of habit and mutual need. Then, Phoebe died. Henry lived alone, and in time his mind became deranged. Day after day, he tramped the countryside searching for his lost wife. He could not accept the fact that she was dead—she had merely gone away.

[2] W. A. Swanberg, *Dreiser* (New York: Charles Scribner's Sons, 1965), pp. 184, 185, 189–90, 268.

He would find her. The memory of Phoebe when young returns to him vividly. His search is not for the old woman who died, but for the young girl who had been his bride: his search is for dreams long since faded. He dies in deranged happiness, seeking the beautiful young Phoebe he knew years ago. In this story, it is as though life itself were speaking to us through the author. And it is a tale not only of the sad end which comes to us in old age; also, it is a tale of a lost dream, a dream that once endowed life with a beauty that was akin to poetry. Time, the enemy of all men, has eaten away beauty and rendered dreams obsolete. And yet the dreams remain. Dreiser's handling of this theme is truly poetic.[3]

One question that is of practical interest to those who work with the elderly is: Should the persons Henry encounters when he goes out to search for Phoebe introduce reality to him, repeating that she is dead, or should they allow him to continue in his fantasy world of thinking that she is still alive? The more basic question is: Could he have changed from his dependence on his life with Phoebe or is he hopelessly locked into his existing personality and needs? The farmer, Dodge, tries to introduce reality to him; the others do not. Persons who work with elderly individuals who are confused are divided on this point. Some contend that those elderly who live in worlds of their own creation are happy and, in the absence of any genuine alternatives, that is the best they can obtain from life. Others claim that growth and change are always possible, and are not likely to occur if they are not nurtured. Henry, of course, would need a great deal of social and emotional support for any change to be initiated and be satisfying and lasting. His neighbors would have to help him create a new style of living. Peers would have been needed to help him find new inner resources and try to tap whatever other strengths were latent within him, as well as to develop new capacities. These of course are very emotionally demanding, time-consuming, and personally involving tasks; it is much easier to let him be. There is also considerable risk in attempting to effect change, for attempts to introduce reality to Henry could make him miserable. He is happy as he is, and at least he died happy. It is extremely difficult to anticipate results in advance and to create consequences that will not be worse than the status quo.

Another kind of relationship and event that an elderly person sometimes experiences and which results in being left alone is the death of a son or daughter. It is especially devastating when the younger generation dies first, leaving the older completely alone. In this case, both a son and a daughter-in-law are lost by Osumi in ''A Clod of Soil'' by Ryunosuke Akutagawa (1892–1927). Osumi loses her son and, nine years later, her hard-working daughter-in-law. Initially she experiences relief after the deaths of each of them, but then the relief is mixed with the realization of her profound loss.

[3] James T. Farrell, *The Best Short Stories of Theodore Dreiser* (Cleveland: World, 1956), p. 11.

An Old Man's Winter Night

Robert Frost

All out of doors looked darkly in at him
Through the thin frost, almost in separate stars,
That gathers on the pane in empty rooms.
What kept his eyes from giving back the gaze
Was the lamp tilted near them in his hand.
What kept him from remembering what it was
That brought him to that creaking room was age.
He stood with barrels round him—at a loss.
And having scared the cellar under him
In clomping there, he scared it once again
In clomping off;—and scared the outer night,
Which has its sounds, familiar, like the roar
Of trees and crack of branches, common things,
But nothing so like beating on a box.
A light he was to no one but himself
Where now he sat, concerned with he knew what,
A quiet light, and then not even that.
He consigned to the moon, such as she was,
So late-arising, to the broken moon
As better than the sun in any case
For such a charge, his snow upon the roof,
His icicles along the wall to keep;
And slept. The log that shifted with a jolt
Once in the stove, disturbed him and he shifted,
And eased his heavy breathing, but still slept.
One aged man—one man—can't keep a house,
A farm, a countryside, or if he can,
It's thus he does it of a winter night.

Isaac and Archibald

Edwin Arlington Robinson

To Mrs. Henry Richards

Isaac and Archibald were two old men.
I knew them, and I may have laughed at them
A little; but I must have honored them
For they were old, and they were good to me.

I do not think of either of them now,
Without remembering, infallibly,
A journey that I made one afternoon
With Isaac to find out what Archibald
Was doing with his oats. It was high time
Those oats were cut, said Isaac; and he feared
That Archibald—well, he could never feel
Quite sure of Archibald. Accordingly
The good old man invited me—that is,
Permitted me—to go along with him;
And I, with a small boy's adhesiveness
To competent old age, got up and went.

I do not know that I cared overmuch
For Archibald's or anybody's oats,
But Archibald was quite another thing,
And Isaac yet another; and the world
Was wide, and there was gladness everywhere.
We walked together down the River Road
With all the warmth and wonder of the land
Around us, and the wayside flash of leaves,—
And Isaac said the day was glorious;
But somewhere at the end of the first mile
I found that I was figuring to find
How long those ancient legs of his would keep
The pace that he had set for them. The sun
Was hot, and I was ready to sweat blood;
But Isaac, for aught I could make of him,
Was cool to his hat-band. So I said then
With a dry gasp of affable despair,
Something about the scorching days we have
In August without knowing it sometimes;
But Isaac said the day was like a dream,

323

And praised the Lord, and talked about the breeze.
I made a fair confession of the breeze,
And crowded casually on his thought
The nearness of a profitable nook
That I could see. First I was half inclined
To caution him that he was growing old,
But something that was not compassion soon
Made plain the folly of all subterfuge.
Isaac was old, but not so old as that.

So I proposed, without an overture,
That we be seated in the shade a while,
And Isaac made no murmur. Soon the talk
Was turned on Archibald, and I began
To feel some premonitions of a kind
That only childhood knows; for the old man
Had looked at me and clutched me with his eye,
And asked if I had ever noticed things.
I told him that I could not think of them,
And I knew then, by the frown that left his face
Unsatisfied, that I had injured him.
'My good young friend,' he said, 'you cannot feel
What I have seen so long. You have the eyes—
Oh, yes—but you have not the other things:
The sight within that never will deceive,
You do not know—you have no right to know;
The twilight warning of experience,
The singular idea of loneliness,—
These are not yours. But they have long been mine,
And they have shown me now for seven years
That Archibald is changing. It is not
So much that he should come to his last hand,
And leave the game, and go the old way down;
But I have known him in and out so long,
And I have seen so much of good in him
That other men have shared and have not seen,
And I have gone so far through thick and thin,
Through cold and fire with him, that now it brings
To this old heart of mine an ache that you
Have not yet lived enough to know about.
But even unto you, and your boy's faith,
Your freedom, and your untried confidence,
A time will come to find out what it means
To know that you are losing what was yours,
To know that you are being left behind;

And then the long contempt of innocence—
God bless you, boy!—don't think the worse of it
Because an old man chatters in the shade—
Will all be like a story you have read
In childhood and remembered for the pictures.
And when the best friend of your life goes down,
When first you know in him the slackening
That comes, and coming always tells the end,—
Now in a common word that would have passed
Uncaught from any other lips than his,
Now in some trivial act of every day,
Done as he might have done it all along
But for a twinging little difference
That nips you like a squirrel's teeth—oh, yes,'
Then you will understand it well enough.
But oftener it comes in other ways;
It comes without your knowing when it comes;
You know that he is changing, and you know
That he is going—just as I know now
That Archibald is going, and that I
Am staying . . . Look at me, my boy,
And when the time shall come for you to see
That I must follow after him, try then
To think of me, to bring me back again,
Just as I was to-day. Think of the place
Where we are sitting now, and think of me—
Think of old Isaac as you knew him then,
When you set out with him in August once
To see old Archibald.'—The words come back
Almost as Isaac must have uttered them,
And there comes with them a dry memory
Of something in my throat that would not move.

If you had asked me then to tell just why
I made so much of Isaac and the things
He said, I should have gone far for an answer;
For I knew it was not sorrow that I felt,
Whatever I may have wished it, or tried then
To make myself believe. My mouth was full
Of words, and they would have been comforting
To Isaac, spite of my twelve years, I think;
But there was not in me the willingness
To speak them out. Therefore I watched the ground;
And I was wondering what made the Lord
Create a thing so nervous as an ant,

When Isaac, with commendable unrest,
Ordained that we should take the road again—
For it was yet three miles to Archibald's,
And one to the first pump. I felt relieved
All over when the old man told me that;
I felt that he had stilled a fear of mine
That those extremities of heat and cold
Which he had long gone through with Archibald
Had made the man impervious to both;
But Isaac had a desert somewhere in him,
And at the pump he thanked God for all things
That He had put on earth for men to drink,
And he drank well,—so well that I proposed
That we go slowly lest I learn too soon
The bitterness of being left behind,
And all those other things. That was a joke
To Isaac, and it pleased him very much;
And that pleased me—for I was twelve years old.

At the end of an hour's walking after that
The cottage of old Archibald appeared.
Little and white and high on a smooth round hill
It stood, with hackmatacks and apple-trees
Before it, and a big barn-roof beyond;
And over the place—trees, houses, fields and all—
Hovered an air of still simplicity
And a fragrance of old summers—the old style
That lives the while it passes. I dare say
That I was lightly conscious of all this
When Isaac, of a sudden, stopped himself,
And for the long first quarter of a minute
Gazed with incredulous eyes, forgetful quite
Of breezes and of me and of all else
Under the scorching sun but a smooth-cut field,
Faint yellow in the distance. I was young,
But there were a few things that I could see,
And this was one of them.—'Well, well!' said he;
And 'Archibald will be surprised, I think,'
Said I. But all my childhood subtlety
Was lost on Isaac, for he strode along
Like something out of Homer—powerful
And awful on the wayside, so I thought.
Also I thought how good it was to be
So near the end of my short-legged endeavor
To keep the pace with Isaac for five miles.

Hardly had we turned in from the main road
When Archibald, with one hand on his back
And the other clutching his huge-headed cane,
Came limping down to meet us.—'Well! well! well!'
Said he; and then he looked at my red face,
All streaked with dust and sweat, and shook my hand,
And said it must have been a right smart walk
That we had had that day from Tilbury Town.—
'Magnificent,' said Isaac; and he told
About the beautiful west wind there was
Which cooled and clarified the atmosphere.
'You must have made it with your legs, I guess,'
Said Archibald; and Isaac humored him
With one of those infrequent smiles of his
Which he kept in reserve, apparently,
For Archibald alone. 'But why,' said he,
'Should Providence have cider in the world
If not for such an afternoon as this?'
And Archibald, with a soft light in his eyes,
Replied that if he chose to go down cellar,
There he would find eight barrels—one of which
Was newly tapped, he said, and to his taste
An honor to the fruit. Isaac approved
Most heartily of that, and guided us
Forthwith, as if his venerable feet
Were measuring the turf in his own door-yard,
Straight to the open rollway. Down we went,
Out of the fiery sunshine to the gloom,
Grateful and half sepulchral, where we found
The barrels, like eight potent sentinels,
Close ranged along the wall. From one of them
A bright pine spile stuck out alluringly,
And on the black flat stone, just under it,
Glimmered a late-spilled proof that Archibald
Had spoken from unfeigned experience.
There was a fluted antique water-glass
Close by, and in it, prisoned, or at rest,
There was a cricket, of the brown soft sort
That feeds on darkness. Isaac turned him out,
And touched him with his thumb to make him jump,
And then composedly pulled out the plug
With such a practised hand that scarce a drop
Did even touch his fingers. Then he drank
And smacked his lips with a slow patronage
And looked along the line of barrels there

With a pride that may have been forgetfulness
That they were Archibald's and not his own.
'I never twist a spigot nowadays,'
He said, and raised the glass up to the light,
'But I thank God for orchards.' And that glass
Was filled repeatedly for the same hand
Before I thought it worth while to discern
Again that I was young, and that old age,
With all his woes, had some advantages.

'Now, Archibald,' said Isaac, when we stood
Outside again, 'I have it in my mind
That I shall take a sort of little walk—
To stretch my legs and see what you are doing.
You stay and rest your back and tell the boy
A story: Tell him all about the time
In Stafford's cabin forty years ago,
When four of us were snowed up for ten days
With only one dried haddock. Tell him all
About it, and be wary of your back.
Now I will go along.'—I looked up then·
At Archibald, and as I looked I saw
Just how his nostrils widened once or twice
And then grew narrow. I can hear to-day
The way the old man chuckled to himself—
Not wholesomely, not wholly to convince
Another of his mirth,—as I can hear
The lonely sigh that followed.—But at length
He said: 'The orchard now's the place for us;
We may find something like an apple there,
And we shall have the shade, at any rate.'
So there we went and there we laid ourselves
Where the sun could not reach us; and I champed
A dozen of worm-blighted astrakhans
While Archibald said nothing—merely told
The tale of Stafford's cabin, which was good,
Though 'master chilly'—after his own phrase—
Even for a day like that. But other thoughts
Were moving in his mind, imperative,
And writhing to be spoken: I could see
The glimmer of them in a glance or two,
Cautious, or else unconscious, that he gave
Over his shoulder: . . . 'Stafford and the rest—
But that's an old song now, and Archibald
And Isaac are old men. Remember, boy,

That we are old. Whatever we have gained,
Or lost, or thrown away, we are old men.
You look before you and we look behind,
And we are playing life out in the shadow—
But that's not all of it. The sunshine lights
A good road yet before us if we look,
And we are doing that when least we know it;
For both of us are children of the sun,
Like you, and like the weed there at your feet.
The shadow calls us, and it frightens us—
We think; but there's a light behind the stars
And we old fellows who have dared to live,
We see it—and we see the other things,
The other things . . . Yes, I have seen it come
These eight years, and these ten years, and I know
Now that it cannot be for very long
That Isaac will be Isaac. You have seen—
Young as you are, you must have seen the strange
Uncomfortable habit of the man?
He'll take my nerves and tie them in a knot
Sometimes, and that's not Isaac. I know that—
And I know what it is: I get it here
A little, in my knees, and Isaac—here.'
The old man shook his head regretfully
And laid his knuckles three times on his forehead.
'That's what it is: Isaac is not quite right.
You see it, but you don't know what it means:
The thousand little differences—no,
You do not know them, and it's well you don't;
You'll know them soon enough—God bless you, boy!—
You'll know them, but not all of them—not all.
So think of them as little as you can:
There's nothing in them for you, or for me—
But I am old and I must think of them;
I'm in the shadow, but I don't forget
The light, my boy,—the light behind the stars.
Remember that: remember that I said it;
And when the time that you think far away
Shall come for you to say it—say it, boy;
Let there be no confusion or distrust
In you, no snarling of a life half lived,
Nor any cursing over broken things
That your complaint has been the ruin of.
Live to see clearly and the light will come
To you, and as you need it.—But there, there,

I'm going it again, as Isaac says,
And I'll stop now before you go to sleep.—
Only be sure that you growl cautiously,
And always where the shadow may not reach you.'

Never shall I forget, long as I live,
The quaint thin crack in Archibald's voice,
The lonely twinkle in his little eyes,
Or the way it made me feel to be with him.
I know I lay and looked for a long time
Down through the orchard and across the road,
Across the river and the sun-scorched hills
That ceased in a blue forest, where the world
Ceased with it. Now and then my fancy caught
A flying glimpse of a good life beyond—
Something of ships and sunlight, streets and singing,
Troy falling, and the ages coming back,
And ages coming forward: Archibald
And Isaac were good fellows in old clothes,
And Agamemnon was a friend of mine;
Ulysses coming home again to shoot
With bows and feathered arrows made another,
And all was as it should be. I was young.

So I lay dreaming of what things I would,
Calm and incorrigibly satisfied
With apples and romance and ignorance,
And the still smoke from Archibald's clay pipe.
There was a stillness over everything,
As if the spirit of heat had laid its hand
Upon the world and hushed it; and I felt
Within the mightiness of the white sun
That smote the land around us and wrought out
A fragrance from the trees, a vital warmth
And fullness for the time that was to come,
And a glory for the world beyond the forest.
The present and the future and the past,
Isaac and Archibald, the burning bush,
The Trojans and the walls of Jericho,
Were beautifully fused; and all went well
Till Archibald began to fret for Isaac
And said it was a master day for sunstroke.
That was enough to make a mummy smile,
I thought; and I remained hilarious,
In face of all precedence and respect,

Till Isaac (who had come to us unheard)
Found he had no tobacco, looked at me
Peculiarly, and asked of Archibald
What ailed the boy to make him chirrup so.
From that he told us what a blessed world
The Lord had given us.—'But, Archibald,'
He added, with a sweet severity
That made me think of peach-skins and goose-flesh,
'I'm half afraid you cut those oats of yours
A day or two before they were well set.'
'They were set well enough,' said Archibald,—
And I remarked the process of his nose
Before the words came out. 'But never mind
Your neighbor's oats: you stay here in the shade
And rest yourself while I go find the cards.
We'll have a little game of seven-up
And let the boy keep count.'—'We'll have the game,
Assuredly,' said Isaac; 'and I think
That I will have a drop of cider, also.'

They marched away together towards the house
And left me to my childish ruminations
Upon the ways of men. I followed them
Down cellar with my fancy, and then I left them
For a fairer vision of all things at once
That was anon to be destroyed again
By the sound of voices and of heavy feet—
One of the sounds of life that I remember,
Though I forget so many that rang first
As if they were thrown down to me from Sinai.

So I remember, even to this day,
Just how they sounded, how they placed themselves,
And how the game went on while I made marks
And crossed them out, and meanwhile made some Trojans
Likewise I made Ulysses, after Isaac,
And a little after Flaxman. Archibald
Was injured when he found himself left out,
But he had no heroics, and I said so:
I told him that his white beard was too long
And too straight down to be like things in Homer.
'Quite so,' said Isaac.—'Low,' said Archibald;
And he threw down a deuce with a deep grin
That showed his yellow teeth and made me happy.
So they played on till a bell rang from the door,

And Archibald said, 'Supper.'—After that
The old men smoked while I sat watching them
And wondered with all comfort what might come
To me, and what might never come to me;
And when the time came for the long walk home
With Isaac in the twilight, I could see
The forest and the sunset and the sky-line,
No matter where it was that I was looking:
The flame beyond the boundary, the music,
The foam and the white ships, and two old men
Were things that would not leave me.—And that night
There came to me a dream—a shining one,
With two old angels in it. They had wings,
And they were sitting where a silver light
Suffused them, face to face. The wings of one
Began to palpitate as I approached,
But I was yet unseen when a dry voice
Cried thinly, with unpatronizing triumph,
'I've got you, Isaac; high, low, jack, and the game.'

Isaac and Archibald have gone their way
To the silence of the loved and well-forgotten.
I knew them, and I may have laughed at them;
But there's a laughing that has honor in it,
And I have no regret for light words now.
Rather I think sometimes they may have made
Their sport of me;—but they would not do that,
They were too old for that. They were old men,
And I may laugh at them because I knew them.

Games

Howard R. Webber

My name is Eleanor Vernor, and I am an old woman. I live now with my daughter and her husband. Until my daughter came to get me, I was alone in the house where I had passed nearly my entire adult lifetime. In the last of those years, the house had fallen into some disrepair. Paint was needed on all the wood, the windowpanes were loose in their frames because the putty had become brittle and had fallen away, some of the screens had holes in them, and the corner of one of the porches was sinking. But it was not a disreputable house, though it was too big for me, having held at one time, besides me and my daughter, my husband and an aunt of mine whom we had brought to live with us much as my daughter has brought me to live with her. We had altered the house, worn it down and built it up in a thousand ways, and it was a monument to all of us. I had always assumed I would die in it.

I do not remember having lived in any other house. I remember other rooms, particularly from my childhood, but I can only conceive of them as being arranged in the pattern of that house, so that it is as if the furniture, the decoration, and even the placement of the windows and doors had varied but the essential house had always been with me. I believe that if I had ever become blind, my memory would have served for sight, and as I grew older that thought comforted me. And as long as I was able to see, the appearance of the house would have comforted me also, for it suited the way in which I have come to look at the world. One sloughs off many customs and impostures, and the house as well no longer felt it must hide its naturalness or correct every lapse of posture. It was a good house, full of time.

Then Laura decided I was no longer able to live alone, and I have now a single bedroom to myself in her new house that smells of paint and impermanence. I have wondered who it was who told her—the neighbors, perhaps: Mr. and Mrs. Wrigley, whose Saint Bernard yearned to sleep on my porch swing; the Esmonds, whose voices were so loud; Mrs. Britten, whose yardman was always running her mower into the flower bed that edged my property on her side—and I have wondered which one of the embarrassing little incidents it was she learned of. They were all squabbles of one kind or another. The milkman had begun counting out the wrong change for me. The postman had held back my mail. The paper boy had delivered my newspaper or not, as the inclination struck him. And the clerks at the grocery store had amused themselves by playing petty tricks on me, breaking a few of my eggs as they packed the carton in a bag, or speaking so softly I could not hear them. The milkman wanted money, the postman and the newspaper boy convenience, the clerks amusement. To keep me from insisting on justice and courtesy, they relied on the precariousness of an old person's reputation, on the skepticism with which the word of the old is regarded, on my fear and feebleness. But I caught each of them up, and I did insist.

When I was young, I used to discount what the old ladies I knew said. I heard their tales of injustice with a smile working at the corners of my mouth. Outrage screwed their faces up even more than age had already, and, breathless and palsied, they showed in their passion a presumption that amused me. But now I was discovering that the old ladies were right, having become one myself; there is no end to the advantage people will take of you if they can. I could not let that advantage be taken. So much seemed to depend on standing firm—my self-respect, the possibility for a reasonable life in the years ahead, even the balance of my mind. Yet I recalled my own smiles of years ago, and I was not surprised when Laura came to my door one afternoon.

I was in one way pleased to see her. I had known that the aspect of things changes from year to year, that it is like the examples of optical illusions one used to see in books or magazines—the clever patterns that shifted inward or outward according as one happened to look at them. I could not submit to the milkman's cheating, but I could tell what he was thinking of me. As I ran out and called back the postman, I had the dreadful feeling that when I spoke my words to him they might emerge as noise or light or delicate puffs of smoke. I could picture the wide-mouthed, close-eyed face of the paper boy exploding into a joke-store bouquet of plastic pansies. The clerks I could imagine slowly rising on their billowing aprons into the sky, like Baptist angels. I do not mean that I had lost hold. I do not think one ever loses one's intelligence, and visions play in the attics of everyone's mind. What I mean is that my visions, so far as I could tell, were different now, that maybe I had my own code of justice now, which was unlike Laura's, or my own twenty years ago, or sixty years ago. When she came, I thought, Now I don't have to worry about the meaning of these new illusions. Now Laura will take care of the world outside.

As soon as I opened the door, Laura said she had been struck with a sense of missing me and had decided on impulse to ride up and see me. She talked about the time when she was a little girl, and recalled how she had depended on me. She mentioned the complexity of her present life and the pace of the world. She spoke of doing things for others, and the importance of family. In time, Peter, my son-in-law, came in. "Laura needs you," Peter said. "She won't admit it, but it's really true."

It was clear that Peter and Laura had considered in advance what to do and say—I saw that without difficulty. So that I could think, I went off and made tea for the three of us. By the time I returned, I had understood they were trying to deceive me. Not that the evidence was in any way obscure; I simply couldn't, at first, bring myself to accept their astonishing conviction that I was susceptible to that kind of deceit. They took their tea and began talking again, but I wouldn't allow it. I broke in and made the suggestion myself that I go back with them. It was the only way I saw to cut off the pretense. I did return with Laura and Peter, but the pretense was merely beginning.

It is games, really, that we have played—games about who I am. The aim of them all was that I am as young as Laura and Peter, as free, as carefree, as strong, as recollected. They must soon have known that I knew they were trying to deceive me, and their encouragements and deferences and accommodations became an elegant play among us. I was never tired because I am old but because I had walked too much or there had been a draft upon my legs, and my turn came when I said, "Yes, yes, that is exactly what it is." If I couldn't open the olive jar, the packers of olives were taken to task for affixing the covers too tightly. If I lay awake at night, it was the unseasonable weather that was blamed. Every one of my acquiescences in these pretenses brought me sadness.

The evening I got here—I remember I was wearing a gray suit that I had decided to give to the Salvation Army but that Laura had laid out for me to wear on our trip—I was ill at ease. I stood in their strange kitchen and wondered whether I should sit or offer to make dinner or go to my room. There had been a haste about our departure, and now there was shame in the air. Laura and Peter put on their serious expressions and began again telling me how fond they were of me. I remember wishing they had told me instead that they could imagine how it is to have to give up dreaming and the possibility of justification that the future allows, to have to tolerate a mind that on occasion cannot follow the slight movements of the present moment, and, finally, to have to give up authority and independence. But I said nothing. Later on, we talked again. "Do whatever you like, as you like it," they told me. "Keep your own hours. Go shopping, have friends in." Then they sent me to bed. And I said a pleasant "good night" as I went. I was caught in the trap of the games already.

I stayed in it, even though some of them were quite cruel. I used to paint—water colors—years ago, and they brought down some of my best work, which had been hanging on the walls of my home, and hung these pictures in my bedroom here. Then they bought me brushes and colors and paper, and I, who had vowed that when my hand wavered I would cheerfully give up painting and content myself with admiring what I had done at my best, had no choice but to take it up again, having not painted a stroke for ten or more years. I puttered with the paints, but that was not enough. They made me go on. They went so far as to frame one of my wretched efforts and put it on the wall with the others. They admired it extravagantly, but if I had dared, I would have burned it, and the good ones with it. As it was, I became a little surly, but even that satisfaction was removed, for they ascribed my humor to a new variety of medicine I was taking.

I like my daughter and my son-in-law. There is a lot of my husband in Laura. He has been dead for many years, but I have not forgotten him. To others, I suppose he must have seemed ineffectual. He dressed carelessly, and, whatever he was doing, moved by indirection. He was a master of the precisely inappropriate word, forgot people's names, occasionally fell asleep at parties, and lost his wallet or his car keys time after time. But when he finally blundered into the clear truth about any human situation, he did, during all the years I lived with him, what was kind and right, unfailingly. And Laura's aim is often wide of the mark, but her mark is the same as his was.

As for my son-in-law, the only thing I really know about him is that my daughter loves him. He is very youthful and energetic. He speaks respectfully to me, awkwardly, and frequently. I have the feeling that if I knew him better I would have many more grounds for liking him.

Laura and Peter do not disappoint me. What has disappointed me is the way things are—the subtle conspiracy of my weakening nerves and tendons and of the alteration in my outward flesh and of my changing disposition that has cut me off from the continent of the young and put me on the ancient island where I am. And yet, island and continent are both part of the world of the living. The changeless old are not changeless at all. They live, they are real, authentic, and the same combinations of circumstance form on one side as on the other.

As my months with Laura and Peter passed, and the games thronged our days until it was wearisome to be in one another's presence, I almost began to look upon myself as they did—changeless, timeless, exiled on my island. But happenings go on, even for the old, and the happening that brought me back to myself began with Mrs. Hartwell, who is even older than I.

Mrs. Hartwell—her first name is Eva, but I never call her that—lives four blocks away. She is with her son and his wife and has in their house a room quite like my own. It was Laura who learned about Mrs. Hartwell and from time to time took me to sit in her son's garden with her. She herself is not able to move about much any more. It is a pleasant garden, and when Laura and Mrs. Hartwell's daughter-in-law settled us there and left, we were perfectly alone, not being able to see more than the tops of the surrounding houses above all the trees. In an hour, the young people returned, and Laura and I went home.

"Dear Mrs. Vernor," Mrs. Hartwell always began when we were by ourselves, "how are things with you these days?"

And then we talked about our situations. There are two children in Mrs. Hartwell's house, and that is her advantage in many ways. Her son and his wife do not have as much time to contrive as Laura and Peter do. There is not as much routine. Best of all, the children do not know enough to engage in duplicities, and she and they are friends. On the other hand, she has been quite ill and dreads the time when she may have to go to a hospital. Also, her daughter-in-law somehow has the idea that Mrs. Hartwell's poor health jeopardizes the children, and all the dishes are sterilized whenever she is unwell. She is always trying to seem better than she really feels.

When I first began to visit Mrs. Hartwell, our conversations were limited to those matters one can discuss with an intelligent person about whom one knows almost nothing. They would have sufficed. Mrs. Hartwell was not in my debt, nor was I in hers; we had common problems; and, altogether, we were able to speak freely and enjoyably. Later, though, as we began to learn more about each other, we confided more and ranged further. We talked a great deal about our childhoods. She remembered a school much like the one I went to. She could still call up her teachers' names, the procedures of the classroom, what the children wore and did, what games they played.

"Did you by any chance ever play marbles, Mrs. Vernor?" she said to me one day.

"Why, yes," I said. "I was a champion player."

"What a coincidence," she said.

And for the next few minutes we compared our merits as marbles players. We both, it seemed, had been little girls gifted at the game. I had prided myself on never having to buy any new marbles. I had had a reserve of marbles that I kept in three cloth bags, I remembered. I never used these in play and, in fact, never touched them except occasionally to turn them over in my fingers and admire them. She recalled that the time had come when it was difficult to find any boy who would risk his marbles against her, she won so consistently. She had begun to have to play with a handicap, such as her boulders against someone else's agates.

Our talk moved to other matters, and I thought no more about marbles until I next came to see her. She was waiting for me in the garden, and she had an embroidered purse in her lap. I did not notice it in the beginning, and our conversation at first was quite usual. It lagged after a while, though, and we sat for a time in silence. Mrs. Hartwell broke the pause by holding up her purse and shaking it. I thought she wanted me to admire it, and I passed some compliment, but I saw then that was not what she had in mind.

"What do you suppose is inside?" she asked me.

I had no idea, of course, and said so, but instead of telling me, she put the purse down and started philosophizing in some way about friends and friendship.

"What's wrong?" I said.

"Nothing's wrong," she said. "I'm trying to tell you that this purse is full of marbles."

"Marbles?" I said.

"I got them from the children," she said. "They lent them to me so we could play. I told them you wanted to."

For a minute, I thought I was witnessing some kind of disintegration in Mrs. Hartwell. I was shocked and saddened. But then, seeing her sitting there looking like herself, her hands folded around the purse, her face composed and earnest, I knew that could not be so. "If you want to play, let's play," I said.

"Don't do it unless you really do want to," she said.

"I do," I said, and by that time I did indeed, though it surprised me to discover it.

Our chairs were always set upon a sandy oval where a folding table was sometimes put for outdoor entertainments, and this surface, with a little digging, made an entirely adequate ring. I moved my chair across from Mrs. Hartwell's and scooped out the sand with my hand. We divided the marbles, and hesitantly, as when one takes up a song that others are singing, began a game. We had to crouch in our chairs in order to reach the ring, but we played leisurely, breaking off now and then to rest. Before long, I was enjoying myself, and I believe Mrs. Hartwell was, too. I could not help feeling that what we were doing was a justification of ourselves as reasonable human beings, entitled to our wishes.

Each of us won about as often as the other that day. Allowing for age and lack of practice, Mrs. Hartwell had not exaggerated her prowess, but then, neither had I my own. We were careful to finish playing long before we began to expect the two young people. The marbles were returned to Mrs. Hartwell's purse, I filled in the ring, and when Laura and Mrs. Hartwell's daughter-in-law came, we were exactly as they had found us every other time.

When I visited Mrs. Hartwell again, I felt uneasy about our little indulgence. I looked immediately to see whether the purse was again in her lap, and it was. She, however, behaved so naturally—when we were alone, opening it in the middle of a story she was telling, and counting the marbles into two piles with perfect self-possession—that I could not remain disquieted. Once more we moved our chairs, and once more I prepared the ring.

This day, I won the first few games, but then Mrs. Hartwell, saying "Knuckles down," set out to recoup her losses. She recovered her eye and, when her turn came, fired off a peerless shot. Then she fainted. It was only vertigo, I believe, for she was quite all right in a few minutes, but at the time I could not know she would be, and I had to call for help. At first, though I suppose her daughter-in-law and Laura saw what we had been doing, they were occupied in reviving Mrs. Hartwell. It was after she was herself again that the awkwardness came.

"Mother," Laura said, looking at me. It was an entirely equivocal word in that circumstance, but my conscience led me to take it badly, and I was ashamed.

Laura and I made a hasty departure. My embarrassment did not abate when we were back at her house. Laura and Peter were very kind to me through the evening, but that only made me feel worse. A day passed, and I hardly went out of my room. Another day came, and in the morning Laura told me she would be taking me to see Mrs. Hartwell at three.

I pretended I did not feel well and told her I wouldn't be able to go. She cocked her head at me, the way her father used to, conjuring him into my mind with that small gesture. I gave in.

When I actually got in the car and then got out at Mrs. Hartwell's, when I passed through the house, when I came out on the lawn and saw Mrs. Hartwell sitting in her chair, I was in anguish. The young people left quickly, but at the last moment Laura pressed my hand. I went forward, though I did not look at Mrs. Hartwell.

"Mrs. Vernor," she said to me.

So I looked at her. The purse was in her lap.

"How are things these days?" she said, motioning me to my chair.

On the seat of it was an old evening bag of mine that Laura had stuffed into one of my suitcases when I moved to her house. I opened it, and, of course, it was filled with marbles.

Since then, the pretenses that had confined my life have been receding. My essential situation is the same. I am not free or carefree or strong or recollected. But something has happened at the core of things. I feel better. Mrs. Hartwell and I do not play marbles any more, for that was a silly business. It is not at all silly to feel better, though, and when I am alone I think often how some slight event can shift a whole structure of circumstance so that the balance is somewhat away from distress.

The Cries of Love

Patricia Highsmith

Hattie pulled the little chain of the reading lamp, drew the covers over her shoulders and lay tense, waiting for Alice's sniffs and coughs to subside.

"Alice?" she said.

No response. Yes, she was sleeping already, though she said she never closed an eye before the clock struck eleven.

Hattie eased herself to the edge of the bed and slowly put out a white-stockinged foot. She twisted round to look at Alice, of whom nothing was visible except a thin nose projecting between the ruffle of her nightcap and the sheet pulled over her mouth. She was quite still.

Hattie rose gently from the bed, her breath coming short with excitement. In the semi-darkness she could see the two sets of false teeth in their glasses of water on the bed table. She giggled, nervously.

Like a white ghost she made her way across the room, past the Victorian settle. She stopped at the sewing table, lifted the folding top and groped among the spools and pattern papers until she found the scissors. Then, holding them tightly, she crossed the room again. She had left the wardrobe door slightly ajar earlier in the evening, and it swung open noiselessly. Hattie reached a trembling hand into the blackness, felt the two woollen coats, a few dresses. Finally she touched a fuzzy thing, and lifted the hanger down. The scissors slipped out of her hand. There was a clatter, followed by her half-suppressed laughter. She peeked round the wardrobe door at Alice, motionless on the bed. Alice was rather hard of hearing.

With her white toes turned up stiffly, Hattie clumped to the easy chair by the window where a bar of moonlight slanted, and sat down with the scissors and the angora sweater in her lap. In the moonlight her face gleamed, toothless and demoniacal. She examined the sweater in the manner of a person who toys with a piece of steak before deciding where to put his knife.

It was really a lovely sweater. Alice had received it the week before from her niece as a birthday present. Alice would never have indulged herself in such a luxury. She was happy as a child with the sweater and had worn it every day over her dresses.

The scissors cut purringly up the soft wool sleeves, between the wristbands and the shoulders. She considered. There should be one more cut. The back, of course. But only about a foot long, so it wouldn't be immediately visible.

A few seconds later, she had put the scissors back into the table, hung the sweater in the wardrobe, and was lying under the covers. She heaved a tremendous sigh. She thought of the gaping sleeves, of Alice's face in the morning. The sweater was quite beyond repair, and she was immensely pleased with herself.

They were awakened at eight-thirty by the hotel maid. It was a ritual that never failed: three bony raps on the door and a bawling voice with a hint of insolence, "Eight-thirty! You can get breakfast now!" Then Hattie, who always woke first, would poke Alice's shoulder.

Mechanically they sat up on their respective sides of the bed and pulled their nightgowns over their heads, revealing clean white undergarments. They said nothing. Seven years of co-existence had pared their conversation to an economical core.

This morning, however, Hattie's mind was on the sweater. She felt self-conscious, but she could think of nothing to say or do to relieve the tension, so she spent more time than usual with her hair. She had a braid nearly two feet long that she wound around her head, and every morning she undid it for its hundred strokes. Her hair was her only vanity. Finally, she stood shifting uneasily, pretending to be fastening the snaps on her dress.

Alice seemed to take an age at the washbasin, gargling with her solution of tepid water and salt. She held stubbornly to water and salt in the mornings, despite Hattie's tempting bottle of red mouthwash setting on the shelf.

"What are you giggling at now?" Alice turned from the basin, her face wet and smiling a little.

Hattie could say nothing, looked at the teeth in the glass on the bed table and giggled again. "Here's your teeth." She reached the glass awkwardly to Alice. "I thought you were going down to breakfast without them."

"Now when did I *ever* go off without my teeth, Hattie?"

Alice smiled to herself. It was going to be a good day, she thought. Mrs. Crumm and her sister were back from a weekend, and they could all play gin rummy together in the afternoon. She walked to the wardrobe in her stockinged feet.

Hattie watched as she took down the powder-blue dress, the one that went best with the beige angora sweater. She fastened all the little buttons in front. Then she took the sweater from the hanger and put one arm into a sleeve.

"Oh!" she breathed painfully. Then like a hurt child her eyes almost closed and her face twisted petulantly. Tears came quickly down her cheeks. "H-Hattie—"

Hattie smirked, uncomfortable yet enjoying herself thoroughly. "Well, I do know!" she exclaimed. "I wonder who could have done a trick like that!" She went to the bed and sat down, doubled up with laughter.

"Hattie, you did this," Alice declared in an unsteady voice. She clutched the sweater to her. "Hattie, you're just wicked!"

Lying across the bed, Hattie was almost hysterical. "You know I didn't now, Alice . . . hah-haw! . . . Why do you think I'd—" Her voice was choked off by incontrollable laughing.

Hattie lay there several minutes before she was calm enough to go down to breakfast. And when she left the room, Alice was sitting in the big chair by the window, sobbing, her face buried in the angora sweater.

Alice did not come down until she was called for lunch. She chatted at the table with Mrs. Crumm and her sister and took no notice of Hattie. Hattie sat opposite her, silent and restless, but not at all sorry for what she had done. She could have endured days of indifference on Alice's part without feeling the slightest remorse.

It was a beautiful day. After lunch, they went with Mrs. Crumm, her sister, and the hotel hostess, Mrs. Holland, and sat in Gramercy Park.

Alice pretended to be absorbed in her book. It was a detective story by her favorite author, borrowed from the hotel's circulating library. Mrs. Crumm and her sister did most of the talking. A weekend trip provided conversation for several afternoons, and Mrs. Crumm was able to remember every item of food she had eaten for days running.

The monotonous tones of the voices, the warmth of the sunshine, lulled Alice into half-sleep. The page was blurred to her eyes.

Earlier in the day, she had planned to adopt an attitude toward Hattie. She should be cool and aloof. It was not the first time Hattie had committed an out-rage. There had been the ink spilt on her lace tablecloth months ago, the day before she was going to give it to her niece . . . And her missing volume of Tennyson that was bound in morocco. She was sure Hattie had it, somewhere. She decided that that evening she should calmly pack her bag, write Hattie a note, short but well worded, and leave the hotel. She would go to another hotel in the neighborhood, let it be known through Mrs. Crumm where she was, and have the satisfaction of Hattie's coming to her and apologizing. But the fact was, she was not at all sure Hattie would come to her, and this embarrassing possibility prevented her from taking such a dangerous course. What if she had to spend the rest of her life alone? It was much easier to stay where she was, to have a pleasant game of gin rummy in the afternoons, and to take out her revenge in little ways. It was also more ladylike, she consoled herself. She did not think beyond this, of the particular times she would say or do things calculated to hurt Hattie. The opportunities would just come of themselves.

Mrs. Holland nudged her. "We're going to get some ice cream now. Then we're going to play some gin rummy."

"I was just at the most exciting part of the book." But Alice rose with the others and was almost cheerful as they walked to the drugstore.

Alice won at gin rummy, and felt pleased with herself. Hattie, watching her uneasily all day, was much relieved when she decreed speaking terms again.

Nevertheless, the thought of the ruined sweater rankled in Alice's mind, and prodded her with a sense of injustice. Indeed, she was ashamed of herself for being able to take it as lightly as she did. It was letting Hattie walk over her. She wished she could muster a really strong hatred.

They were in their room reading at nine o'clock. Every vestige of Hattie's shyness or pretended contrition had vanished.

"Wasn't it a nice day?" Hattie ventured.

"Um-hm." Alice did not raise her head.

"Well," Hattie made the inevitable remark through the inevitable yawn, "I think I'll be going off to bed."

And a few minutes later they were both in bed, propped up by four pillows, Hattie with the newspaper and Alice with her detective story. They were silent for a while, then Hattie adjusted her pillows and lay down.

"Good night, Alice."

"Good night."

Soon Alice pulled out the light, and there was absolute silence in the room except for the soft ticking of the clock and the occasional purr of an automobile. The clock on the mantel whirred and began to strike ten.

Alice lay open-eyed. All day her tears had been restrained, and now she began to cry. But they were not the childish tears of the morning, she felt. She wiped her nose on the top of the sheet.

She raised herself on one elbow. The darkish braid of hair outlined Hattie's neck and shoulder against the white bedclothes. She felt very strong, strong enough to murder Hattie with her own hands. But the idea of murder passed from her mind as swiftly as it had entered. Her revenge had to be something that would last, that would hurt, something that Hattie must endure and that she herself could enjoy.

Then it came to her, and she was out of bed, walking boldly to the sewing table, as Hattie had done twenty-four hours before . . . and she was standing by the bed, bending over Hattie, peering at her placid, sleeping face through her tears and her shortsighted eyes. Two quick strokes of the scissors would cut through the braid, right near the head. But Alice lowered the scissors just a little, to where the braid was tighter. She squeezed the scissors with both hands, made them chew on the braid, as Hattie slowly awakened with the touch of cold metal on her neck. *Whack,* and it was done.

"What is it? . . . What—?" Hattie said.

The braid was off, lying like a dark gray snake on the bed cover.

"Alice!" Hattie said, and groped at her neck, felt the stiff ends of the braid's stump. "Alice!"

Alice stood a few feet away, staring at Hattie who was sitting up in bed, and suddenly Alice was overcome with mirth. She tittered, and at the same time tears started in her eyes. "You did it to me!" she said. "You cut my sweater!"

Alice's instant of self-defense was unnecessary, because Hattie was absolutely crumpled and stunned. She started to get out of bed, as if to go to the mirror, but sat back again, moaning and weeping, feeling of the horrid thing at the end of her hair. Then she lay down again, still moaning into her pillow. Alice stayed up, and sat finally in the easy chair. She was full of energy, not sleepy at all. But toward dawn, when Hattie slept, Alice crept between the covers.

Hattie did not speak to her in the morning, and did not look at her. Hattie put the braid away in a drawer. Then she tied a scarf around her head to go down to breakfast, and in the dining room, Hattie took another table from the one at which Alice and she usually sat. Alice saw Hattie speaking to Mrs. Holland after breakfast.

A few minutes later, Mrs. Holland came over to Alice, who was reading in a corner of the lounge.

"I think," Mrs. Holland said gently, "that you and your friend might be happier if you had separate rooms for a while, don't you?"

This took Alice by surprise, though at the same time she had been expecting something worse. Her prepared statement about the spilt ink, the missing Tennyson, and the ruined angora subsided in her, and she said quite briskly, "I do indeed, Mrs. Holland. I'm agreeable to anything Hattie wishes."

Alice offered to move out, but it was Hattie who did. She moved to a smaller room three doors down on the same floor.

That night, Alice could not sleep. It was not that she thought about Hattie particularly, or that she felt in the least sorry for what she had done—she decidedly didn't—but that things, the room, the darkness, even the clock's ticking, were so different because she was alone. A couple of times during the night, she heard a footstep outside the door, and thought it might be Hattie coming back, but it was only people visiting the W.C. at the end of the hall. It occurred to Alice that she could knock on Hattie's door and apologize but, she asked herself, why should she?

In the morning, Alice could tell from Hattie's appearance that she hadn't slept either. Again, they did not speak or look at each other all day, and during the gin rummy and tea at four, they managed to take different tables. Alice slept very badly that night also, and blamed it on the lamb stew at dinner, which she was having trouble digesting. Hattie would have the same trouble, perhaps, as Hattie's digestion was, if anything, worse.

Three more days and nights passed, and the ravages of Hattie's and Alice's sleepless nights became apparent on their faces. Mrs. Holland noticed, and offered Alice some sedatives, which Alice politely declined. She had her pride, she wasn't going to show anyone she was disturbed by Hattie's absence, and besides, she thought it was weak and self-indulgent to yield to sleeping pills—though perhaps Hattie would.

On the fifth day, at three in the afternoon, Hattie knocked on Alice's door. Her head was still swathed in a scarf, one of three that Hattie possessed, and this was one Alice had given her last Christmas.

"Alice, I want to say I'm sorry, if *you're* sorry," Hattie said, her lips twisting and pursing as she fought to keep back the tears.

This was or should have been a moment of triumph for Alice. It was, mainly, she felt, though something—she was not sure what—tarnished it a little, made it not quite pure victory. "I am sorry about your braid, if you're sorry about my sweater," Alice replied.

"I am," said Hattie.

"And about the ink stain on my tablecloth and . . . where is my volume of Alfred Lord Tennyson's poems?"

"I have not got it," Hattie said, still tremulous with tears.

"You haven't *got* it?"

''No,'' Hattie declared positively.

And in a flash, Alice knew what had really happened: Hattie had at some point, in some place, destroyed it, so it was in a way true now that she hadn't ''got'' it. Alice knew, too, that she must not stick over this, that she ought to forgive and forget it, though neither emotionally nor intellectually did she come to this decision: she simply knew it, and behaved accordingly, saying, ''Very well, Hattie. You may move back, if you wish.''

Hattie then moved back, though at the card game at four-thirty they still sat at separate tables.

Hattie, having swallowed the biggest lump of pride she had ever swallowed in knocking on Alice's door and saying she was sorry, slept very much better back in the old arrangement, but suffered a lurking sense of unfairness. After all, a book of poems and a sweater could be replaced, but could her hair? Alice had got back at her all right, and then some. The score was not quite even.

After a few days, Hattie and Alice were back to normal, saying little to each other, but outwardly being congenial, taking meals and playing cards at the same table. Mrs. Holland seemed pleased.

It crossed Alice's mind to buy Hattie some expensive hair tonic she saw in a Madison Avenue window one day while on an outing with Mrs. Holland and the group. But Alice didn't. Neither did she buy a ''special treatment'' for hair which she saw advertised in the back of a magazine, guaranteed to make the hair grow thicker and faster, but Alice read every word of the advertisements.

Meanwhile, Hattie struggled in silence with her stump of braid, brushed her hair faithfully as usual, but only when Alice was having her bath or was out of the room, so Alice would not see it. Nothing in Alice's possession now seemed important enough for Hattie's vengeance. But Christmas was coming soon. Hattie determined to wait patiently and see what Alice got then.

The Lost Phoebe

Theodore Dreiser

They lived together in a part of the country which was not so prosperous as it had once been, about three miles from one of those small towns that, instead of increasing in population, is steadily decreasing. The territory was not very thickly settled; perhaps a house every other mile or so, with large areas of corn- and wheat-land and fallow fields that at odd seasons had been sown to timothy and clover. Their particular house was part log and part frame, the log portion being the old original home of Henry's grandfather. The new portion, of now rain-beaten, time-worn slabs, through which the wind squeaked in the chinks at

times, and which several overshadowing elms and a butternut tree made picturesque and reminiscently pathetic, but a little damp, was erected by Henry when
he was twenty-one and just married.

That was forty-eight years before. The furniture inside, like the house outside, was old and mildewy and reminiscent of an earlier day. You have seen
the what-not of cherry wood, perhaps, with spiral legs and fluted top. It was
there. The old-fashioned four poster bed, with its ball-like protuberances and
deep curving incisions, was there also, a sadly alienated descendant of an early
Jacobean ancestor. The bureau of cherry was also high and wide and solidly
built, but faded-looking, and with a musty odor. The rag carpet that underlay
all these sturdy examples of enduring furniture was a weak, faded, lead-and-
pink-colored affair woven by Phoebe Ann's own hands, when she was fifteen
years younger than she was when she died. The creaky wooden loom on which
it had been done now stood like a dusty, bony skeleton, along with a broken
rocking-chair, a worm-eaten clothes-press—Heaven knows how old—a lime-
stained bench that had once been used to keep flowers on outside the door, and
other broken-down furniture were about this place; an antiquated clothes-horse,
cracked in two of its ribs; a broken mirror in an old cherry frame, which had
fallen from a nail and cracked itself three days before their youngest son, Jerry,
died; an extension hat-rack, which once had had porcelain knobs on the ends of
its pegs; and a sewing-machine, long since outdone in its clumsy mechanism by
rivals of a newer generation.

The orchard to the east of the house was full of gnarled old apple-trees,
worm-eaten as to trunks and branches, and fully ornamented with green and
white lichens, so that it had a sad, greenish-white, silvery effect in moonlight.
The low outhouses, which had once housed chickens, a horse or two, a cow,
and several pigs, were covered with patches of moss as to their roof, and the
sides had been free of paint for so long that they were blackish gray as to color,
and a little spongy. The picket-fence in front, with its gate squeaky and askew,
and the side fences of the stake-and-rider type were in an equally run-down
condition. As a matter of fact, they had aged synchronously with the persons
who lived here, old Henry Reifsneider and his wife Phoebe Ann.

They had lived here, these two, ever since their marriage, forty-eight years
before, and Henry had lived here before that from his childhood up. His father
and mother, well along in years when he was a boy, had invited him to bring
his wife here when he had first fallen in love and decided to marry; and he had
done so. His father and mother were the companions of himself and his wife
for ten years after they were married, when both died; and then Henry and
Phoebe were left with their five children growing lustily apace. But all sorts of
things had happened since then. Of the seven children, all told, that had been
born to them, three had died; one girl had gone to Kansas; one boy had gone to
Sioux Falls, never even to be heard of after; another boy had gone to Washington; and the last girl lived five counties away in the same State, but was so burdened with cares of her own that she rarely gave them a thought. Time and a
commonplace home life that had never been attractive had weaned them

thoroughly, so that, wherever they were, they gave little thought as to how it might be with their father and mother.

Old Henry Reifsneider and his wife Phoebe were a loving couple. You perhaps know how it is with simple natures that fasten themselves like lichens on the stones of circumstance and weather their days to a crumbling conclusion. The great world sounds widely, but it has no call for them. They have no soaring intellect. The orchard, the meadow, the cornfield, the pig-pen, and the chicken-lot measure the range of their human activities. When the wheat is headed it is reaped and threshed; when the corn is browned and frosted it is cut and shocked; when the timothy is in full head it is cut, and the hay-cock erected. After that comes winter, with the hauling of grain to market, the sawing and splitting of wood, the simple chores of fire-building, meal-getting, occasional repairing, and visiting. Beyond these and the changes of weather—the snows, the rains, and the fair days—there are no immediate, significant things. All the rest of life is a far-off, clamorous phantasmagoria, flickering like northern lights in the night, and sounding as faintly as cow-bells tinkling in the distance.

Old Henry and his wife Phoebe were as fond of each other as it is possible for two old people to be who have nothing else in this life to be fond of. He was a thin old man, seventy when she died, a queer, crotchety person with coarse gray-black hair and beard, quite straggly and unkempt. He looked at you out of dull, fishy, watery eyes that had deep-brown crow's-feet at the sides. His clothes, like the clothes of many farmers, were aged and angular and baggy, standing out at the pockets, not fitting about the neck, protuberant and worn at elbow and knee. Phoebe Ann was thin and shapeless, a very umbrella of a woman, clad in shabby black, and with a black bonnet for her best wear. As time had passed, and they had only themselves to look after, their movements had become slower and slower, their activities fewer and fewer. The annual keep of pigs had been reduced from five to one grunting porker, and the single horse which Henry now retained was a sleepy animal, not over-nourished and not very clean. The chickens, of which formerly there was a large flock, had almost disappeared, owing to ferrets, foxes, and the lack of proper care, which produces disease. The former healthy garden was now a straggling memory of itself, and the vines and flower-beds that formerly ornamented the windows and dooryard had now become choking thickets. A will had been made which divided the small tax-eaten property equally among the remaining four, so that it was really of no interest to any of them. Yet these two lived together in peace and sympathy, only that now and then old Henry would become unduly cranky, complaining almost invariably that something had been neglected or mislaid which was of no importance at all.

"Phoebe, where's my corn knife? You ain't never minded to let my things alone no more."

"Now you hush, Henry," his wife would caution him in a cracked and squeaky voice. "If you don't, I'll leave yuh. I'll git up and walk out of here some day, and then where would y' be? Y'ain't got anybody but me to look after yuh, so yuh just behave yourself. Your corn knife's on the mantel where it's allus been unless you've gone an' put it summers else."

Old Henry, who knew his wife would never leave him in any circumstances, used to speculate at times as to what he would do if she were to die. That was the one leaving that he really feared. As he climbed on the chair at night to wind the old, long-pendulumed, double-weighted clock, or went finally to the front and the back door to see that they were safely shut in, it was a comfort to know that Phoebe was there, properly ensconced on her side of the bed, and that if he stirred restlessly in the night, she would be there to ask what he wanted.

"Now, Henry, do lie still! You're as restless as a chicken."

"Well, I can't sleep, Phoebe."

"Well, yuh needn't roll so, anyhow. Yuh kin let me sleep."

This usually reduced him to a state of somnolent ease. If she wanted a pail of water, it was a grumbling pleasure for him to get it; and if she did rise first to build the fires, he saw that the wood was cut and placed within easy reach. They divided this simple world nicely between them.

As the years had gone on, however, fewer and fewer people had called. They were well-known for a distance of as much as ten square miles as old Mr. and Mrs. Reifsneider, honest, moderately Christian, but too old to be really interesting any longer. The writing of letters had become an almost impossible burden too difficult to continue or even negotiate via others, although an occasional letter still did arrive from the daughter in Pemberton County. Now and then some old friend stopped with a pie or cake or a roasted chicken or duck, or merely to see that they were well; but even these kindly-minded visits were no longer frequent.

One day in the early spring of her sixty-fourth year Mrs. Reifsneider took sick, and from a low fever passed into some indefinable ailment which, because of her age, was no longer curable. Old Henry drove to Swinnerton, the neighboring town, and procured a doctor. Some friends called, and the immediate care of her was taken off his hands. Then one chill spring night she died, and old Henry, in a fog of sorrow and uncertainty, followed her body to the nearest graveyard, an unattractive space with a few pines growing in it. Although he might have gone to the daughter in Pemberton or sent for her, it was really too much trouble and he was too weary and fixed. It was suggested to him at once by one friend and another that he come to stay with them awhile, but he did not see fit. He was so old and so fixed in his notions and so accustomed to the exact surroundings he had known all his days, that he could not think of leaving. He wanted to remain near where they had put his Phoebe; and the fact that he would have to live alone did not trouble him in the least. The living children were notified and the care of him offered if he would leave, but he would not.

"I kin make a shift for myself," he continually announced to old Dr. Morrow, who had attended his wife in this case. "I kin cook a little, and besides, it don't take much more'n coffee an' bread in the mornin's to satisfy me. I'll get along now well enough. Yuh just let me be." And after many pleadings and proffers of advice, with supplies of coffee and bacon and baked bread duly offered and accepted, he was left to himself. For a while he sat idly outside his door brooding in the spring sun. He tried to revive his interest in farming, and to keep himself busy and free from thought by looking after the fields, which of late had been much neglected. It was a gloomy thing to come in of an evening, however, or in the afternoon and find no shadow of Phoebe where everything suggested her. By degrees he put a few of her things away. At night he sat beside his lamp and read in the papers that were left him occasionally or in a Bible that he had neglected for years, but he could get little solace from these things. Mostly he held his hand over his mouth and looked at the floor as he sat and thought of what had become of her, and how soon he himself would die. He made a great business of making his coffee in the morning and frying himself a little bacon at night; but his appetite was gone. The shell in which he had been housed so long seemed vacant, and its shadows were suggestive of immedicable griefs. So he lived quite dolefully for five long months, and then a change began.

It was one night, after he had looked after the front and the back door, wound the clock, blown out the light, and gone through all the selfsame motions that he had indulged in for years, that he went to bed not so much to sleep as to think. It was a moonlight night. The green-lichen-covered orchard just outside and to be seen from his bed where he now lay was a silvery affair, sweetly spectral. The moon shone through the east windows, throwing the pattern of the panes on the wooden floor, and making the old furniture, to which he was accustomed, stand out dimly in the room. As usual he had been thinking of Phoebe and the years when they had been young together, and of the children who had gone, and the poor shift he was making of his present days. The house was coming to be in a very bad state indeed. The bed-clothes were in disorder and not clean, for he made a wretched shift of washing. It was a terror to him. The roof leaked, causing things, some of them, to remain damp for weeks at a time, but he was getting into that brooding state where he would accept anything rather than exert himself. He preferred to pace slowly to and fro or to sit and think.

By twelve o'clock of this particular night he was asleep, however, and by two had waked again. The moon by this time had shifted to a position on the western side of the house, and it now shone in through the windows of the living-room and those of the kitchen beyond. A certain combination of furniture—a chair near a table, with his coat on it, the half-open kitchen door casting a shadow, and the position of a lamp near a paper—gave him an exact representation of Phoebe leaning over the table as he had often seen her do in life. It gave him a great start. Could it be she—or her ghost? He had scarcely ever believed in spirits; and still—He looked at her fixedly in the feeble half-light, his old hair tingling oddly at the roots, and then sat up. The figure did not move. He put his thin legs out of the bed and sat looking at her, wondering if this could really be Phoebe. They had talked of ghosts often in their life-time, of apparitions and omens; but they had never agreed that such things could be.

It had never been a part of his wife's creed that she could have a spirit that could return to walk the earth. Her after-world was quite a different affair, a vague heaven, no less, from which the righteous did not trouble to return. Yet here she was now, bending over the table in her black skirt and gray shawl, her pale profile outlined against the moonlight.

"Phoebe," he called, thrilling from head to toe and putting out one bony hand, "have yuh come back?"

The figure did not stir, and he arose and walked uncertainly to the door, looking at it fixedly the while. As he drew near, however, the apparition resolved itself into its primal content—his old coat over the high-backed chair, the lamp by the paper, the half-open door.

"Well," he said to himself, his mouth open, "I thought shore I saw her." And he ran his hand strangely and vaguely through his hair, the while his nervous tension relaxed. Vanished as it had, it gave him the idea that she might return.

Another night, because of this first illusion, and because his mind was now constantly on her and he was old, he looked out of the window that was nearest his bed and commanded a hen-coop and pig-pen and a part of the wagon-shed, and there, a faint mist exuding from the damp of the ground, he thought he saw her again. It was one of those little wisps of mist, one of those faint exhalations of the earth that rise in a cool night after a warm day, and flicker like small white cypresses of fog before they disappear. In life it had been a custom of hers to cross this lot from her kitchen door to the pig-pen to throw in any scrap that was left from her cooking, and here she was again. He sat up and watched it strangely, doubtfully, because of his previous experience, but inclined, because of the nervous titillation that passed over his body, to believe that spirits really were, and that Phoebe, who would be concerned because of his lonely state, must be thinking about him, and hence returning. What other way would she have? How otherwise could she express herself? It would be within the province of her charity so to do, and like her loving interest in him. He quivered and watched it eagerly; but, a faint breath of air stirring, it wound away toward the fence and disappeared.

A third night, as he was actually dreaming, some ten days later, she came to his bedside and put her hand on his head.

"Poor Henry!" she said. "It's too bad."

He roused out of his sleep, actually to see her, he thought, moving from his bed-room into the one living-room, her figure a shadowy mass of black. The weak straining of his eyes caused little points of light to flicker about the outlines of her form. He arose, greatly astonished, walked the floor in the cool room, convinced that Phoebe was coming back to him. If he only thought sufficiently, if he made it perfectly clear by his feeling that he needed her greatly, she would come back, this kindly wife, and tell him what to do. She would perhaps be with him much of the time, in the night, anyhow; and that would make him less lonely, this state more endurable.

In age and with the feeble it is not such a far cry from the subtleties of illusion to actual hallucination, and in due time this transition was made for Henry. Night after night he waited, expecting her return. Once in his weird mood he thought he saw a pale light moving about the room, and another time he thought he saw her walking in the orchard after dark. It was one morning when the details of his lonely state were virtually unendurable that he woke with the thought that she was not dead. How he had arrived at this conclusion it is hard to say. His mind had gone. In its place was a fixed illusion. He and Phoebe had had a senseless quarrel. He had reproached her for not leaving his pipe where he was accustomed to find it, and she had left. It was an aberrated fulfillment of her old jesting threat that if he did not behave himself she would leave him.

"I guess I could find yuh ag'in," he had always said. But her cackling threat had always been:

"Yuh'll not find me if I ever leave yuh. I guess I kin git some place where yuh can't find me."

This morning when he arose he did not think to build the fire in the customary way or to grind his coffee and cut his bread, as was his wont, but solely to meditate as to where he should search for her and how he should induce her to come back. Recently the one horse had been dispensed with because he found it cumbersome and beyond his needs. He took down his soft crush hat after he had dressed himself, a new glint of interest and determination in his eye, and taking his black crook cane from behind the door, where he had always placed it, started out briskly to look for her among the nearest neighbors. His old shoes clumped soundly in the dust as he walked, and his gray-black locks, now grown rather long, straggled out in a dramatic fringe or halo from under his hat. His short coat stirred busily as he walked, and his hands and face were peaked and pale.

"Why, hello, Henry! Where're yuh goin' this mornin'?" inquired Farmer Dodge, who, hauling a load of wheat to market, encountered him on the public road. He had not seen the aged farmer in months, not since his wife's death, and he wondered now, seeing him looking so spry.

"Yuh ain't seen Phoebe, have yuh?" inquired the old man, looking up quizzically.

"Phoebe who?" inquired Farmer Dodge, not for the moment connecting the name with Henry's dead wife.

"Why, my wife Phoebe, o' course. Who do yuh s'pose I mean?" He stared up with a pathetic sharpness of glance from under his shaggy, gray eyebrows.

"Wall, I'll swan, Henry, yuh ain't jokin', are yuh?" said the solid Dodge, a pursy man, with a smooth, hard, red face. "It can't be your wife yuh're talkin' about. She's dead."

"Dead! Shucks!" retorted the demented Reifsneider. "She left me early this mornin', while I was sleepin'. She allus got up to build the fire, but she's gone now. We had a little spat last night, an' I guess that's the reason. But I guess I kin find her. She's gone over to Matilda Race's; that's where she's gone."

He started briskly up the road, leaving the amazed Dodge to stare in wonder after him.

"Well, I'll be switched!" he said aloud to himself. "He's clean out'n his head. That poor old feller's been livin' down there till he's gone outen his mind. I'll have to notify the authorities." And he flicked his whip with great enthusiasm. "Geddap!" he said, and was off.

Reifsneider met no one else in this poorly populated region until he reached the whitewashed fence of Matilda Race and her husband three miles away. He had passed several other houses en route, but these not being within the range of his illusion were not considered. His wife, who had known Matilda well, must be here. He opened the picket-gate which guarded the walk, and stamped briskly up to the door.

"Why, Mr. Reifsneider," exclaimed old Matilda herself, a stout woman, looking out of the door in answer to his knock, "What brings yuh here this mornin'?"

"Is Phoebe here?" he demanded eagerly.

"Phoebe who? What Phoebe?" replied Mrs. Race, curious as to this sudden development of energy on his part.

"Why, my Phoebe, o' course. My wife Phoebe. Who do yuh s'pose? Ain't she here now?"

"Lawsy me!" exclaimed Mrs. Race, opening her mouth. "Yuh pore man! So you're clean out'n your mind now. Yuh come right in and sit down. I'll git yuh a cup o' coffee. O' course your wife ain't here; but yuh come in an' sit down. I'll find her fer yuh after a while. I know where she is."

The old farmer's eyes softened, and he entered. He was so thin and pale a specimen, pantalooned and patriarchal, that he aroused Mrs. Race's extremest sympathy as he took off his hat and laid it on his knees quite softly and mildly.

We had a quarrel last night, an' she left me," he volunteered.

"Laws! laws!" sighed Mrs. Race, there being no one present with whom to share her astonishment as she went to her kitchen. "The pore man! Now some-body's just got to look after him. He can't be allowed to run around the country this way lookin' for his dead wife. It's turrible."

She boiled him a pot of coffee and brought in some of her new-baked bread and fresh butter. She set out some of her best jam and put a couple of eggs to boil, lying whole-heartedly the while.

"Now yuh stay right there, Uncle Henry, till Jake comes in, an' I'll send him to look for Phoebe. I think it's more'n likely she's over to Swinnerton with some o' her friends. Anyhow, we'll find out. Now yuh just drink this coffee an' eat this bread. Yuh must be tired. Yuh've had a long walk this mornin'." Her idea was to take counsel with Jake, "her man," and perhaps have him no-tify the authorities.

She bustled about, meditating on the uncertainties of life, while old Reif-sneider thrummed on the rim of his hat with his pale fingers and later ate ab-stractedly of what she offered. His mind was on his wife, however, and since she was not here, or did not appear, it wandered vaguely away to a family by the name of Murray, miles away in another direction. He decided after a time that he would not wait for Jake Race to hunt his wife but would seek her for himself. He must be on, and urge her to come back.

"Well, I'll be goin'," he said, getting up and looking strangely about him. "I guess she didn't come here after all. She went over to the Murrays', I guess. I'll not wait any longer, Mis' Race. There's a lot to do over to the house today." And out he marched in the face of her protests taking to the dusty road again in the warm spring sun, his cane striking the earth as he went.

It was two hours later that this pale figure of a man appeared in the Murrays' doorway, dusty, perspiring, eager. He had tramped all of five miles, and it was noon. An amazed husband and wife of sixty heard his strange query, and realized also that he was mad. They begged him to stay to dinner, intending to notify the authorities later and see what could be done; but though he stayed to partake of a little something, he did not stay long, and was off again to another distant farmhouse, his idea of many things to do and his need of Phoebe impelling him. So it went for that day and the next and the next, the circle of his inquiry ever widening.

The process by which a character assumes the significance of being peculiar, his antics weird, yet harmless, in such a community is often involute and pathetic. This day, as has been said, saw Reifsneider at other doors, eagerly asking his unnatural question, and leaving a trail of amazement, sympathy, and pity in his wake. Although the authorities were informed—the county sheriff, no less—it was not deemed advisable to take him into custody; for when those who knew old Henry, and had for so long, reflected on the condition of the county insane asylum, a place which, because of the poverty of the district, was of staggering aberration and sickening environment, it was decided to let him remain at large; for, strange to relate, it was found on investigation that at night he returned peaceably enough to his lonesome domicile there to discover whether his wife had returned, and to brood in loneliness until the morning. Who would lock up a thin, eager, seeking old man with iron-gray hair and an attitude of kindly, innocent inquiry, particularly when he was well known for a past of only kindly servitude and reliability? Those who had known him best rather agreed that he should be allowed to roam at large. He could do no harm. There were many who were willing to help him as to food, old clothes, the odds and ends of his daily life—at least at first. His figure after a time became not so much a common-place as an accepted curiosity, and the replies, "Why, no, Henry; I ain't seen her," or "No, Henry; she ain't been here today," more customary.

For several years thereafter then he was an odd figure in the sun and rain, on dusty roads and muddy ones, encountered occasionally in strange and unexpected places, pursuing his endless search. Undernourishment, after a time, although the neighbors and those who knew his history gladly contributed from their store, affected his body; for he walked much and ate little. The longer he roamed the public highway in this manner, the deeper became his strange hallu-

cination; and finding it harder and harder to return from his more and more distant pilgrimages, he finally began taking a few utensils with him from his
home, making a small package of them, in order that he might not be compelled to return. In an old tin coffee-pot of large size he placed a small tin cup,
a knife, fork, and spoon, some salt and pepper, and to the outside of it, by a
string forced through a pierced hole, he fastened a plate, which could be released, and which was his woodland table. It was no trouble for him to secure
the little food that he needed, and with a strange, almost religious dignity, he
had no hesitation in asking for that much. By degrees his hair became longer
and longer, his once black hat became an earthen brown, and his clothes
threadbare and dusty.

For all of three years he walked, and none knew how wide were his peram-
bulations, nor how he survived the storms and cold. They could not see him,
with homely rural understanding and forethought, sheltering himself in hay-
cocks, or by the sides of cattle, whose warm bodies protected him from the
cold, and whose dull understandings were not opposed to his harmless presence. Overhanging rocks and trees kèpt him at times from the rain, and a
friendly hay-loft or corn-crib was not above his humble consideration.

The involute progression of hallucination is strange. From asking at doors
and being constantly rebuffed or denied, he finally came to the conclusion that
although his Phoebe might not be in any of the houses at the doors of which he
inquired, she might nevertheless be within the sound of his voice. And so, from
patient inquiry, he began to call sad, occasional cries, that ever and anon
waked the quiet landscapes and ragged hill regions, and set to echoing his thin
"O-o-o Phoebe! O-o-o Phoebe!" It had a pathetic, albeit insane, ring, and
many a farmer or plowboy came to know it even from afar and say, "There
goes old Reifsneider."

Another thing that puzzled him greatly after a time and after many hundreds
of inquiries was, when he no longer had any particular dooryard in view and no
special inquiry to make, which way to go. These cross-roads, which occasionally led in four or even six directions, came after a time to puzzle him.
But to solve this knotty problem, which became more and more of a puzzle,
there came to his aid another hallucination. Phoebe's spirit or some power of
the air or wind or nature would tell him. If he stood at the center of the parting
of the ways, closed his eyes, turned thrice about, and called "O-o-o Phoebe!"
twice, and then threw his cane straight before him, that would surely indicate
which way to go for Phoebe, or one of these mystic powers would surely gov-
ern its direction and fall! In whichever direction it went, even though, as was
not infrequently the case, it took him back along the path he had already come,
or across fields, he was not so far gone in his mind but that he gave himself
ample time to search before he called again. Also the hallucinations seemed to
persist that at some time he would surely find her. There were hours when his
feet were sore, and his limbs weary, when he would stop in the heat to wipe his
seamed brow, or in the cold to beat his arms. Sometimes, after throwing away
his cane, and finding it indicating the direction from which he had just come,

he would shake his head wearily and philosophically, as if contemplating the unbelievable or an untoward fate, and then start briskly off. His strange figure came finally to be known in the farthest reaches of three or four counties. Old Reifsneider was a pathetic character. His fame was wide.

Near a little town called Watersville in Green County, perhaps four miles from that minor center of human activity, there was a place or precipice locally known as the Red Cliff, a sheer wall of red sandstone, perhaps a hundred feet high, which raised its sharp face for half a mile or more above the fruitful corn-fields and orchards that lay beneath, and which was surmounted by a thick grove of trees. The slope that slowly led up to it from the opposite side was covered by a rank growth of beech, hickory, and ash, through which threaded a number of wagon-tracks crossing at various angles. In fair weather it had become old Reifsneider's habit, so inured was he by now to the open, to make his bed in some such patch of trees as this to fry his bacon or boil his eggs at the foot of some tree before laying himself down for the night. Occasionally, so light and inconsequential was his sleep, he would walk at night. More often, the moonlight or some sudden wind stirring in the trees or a reconnoitering animal arousing him, he would sit up and think, or pursue his quest in the moonlight or the dark, a strange, unnatural, half wild, half savage-looking but utterly harmless creature, calling at lonely road crossings, staring at dark and shuttered houses, and wondering where, where Phoebe could really be.

That particular lull that comes in the systole-diastole of this earthly ball at two o'clock in the morning invariably aroused him, and though he might not go any farther he would sit up and contemplate the darkness or the stars, wondering. Sometimes in the strange processes of his mind he would fancy that he saw moving among the trees the figure of his lost wife, and then he would get up to follow, taking his utensils, always on a string, and his cane. If she seemed to evade him too easily he would run, or plead, or, suddenly losing track of the fancied figure, stand awed or disappointed, grieving for the moment over the almost insurmountable difficulties of his search.

It was in the seventh year of these hopeless peregrinations, in the dawn of a similar springtime to that in which his wife had died, that he came at last one night to the vicinity of this self-same patch that crowned the rise to the Red Cliff. His far-flung cane, used as a divining-rod at the last cross-roads, had brought him hither. He had walked many, many miles. If was after ten o'clock at night, and he was very weary. Long wandering and little eating had left him but a shadow of his former self. It was a question now not so much of physical strength but of spiritual endurance which kept him up. He had scarcely eaten this day, and now exhausted he set himself down in the dark to rest and possibly to sleep.

Curiously on this occasion a strange suggestion of the presence of his wife surrounded him. It would not be long now, he counseled with himself, although the long months had brought him nothing, until he should see her, talk to her. He fell asleep after a time, his head on his knees. At midnight the moon began to rise, and at two in the morning, his wakeful hour, was a large silver disk shining through the trees to the east. He opened his eyes when the radiance became strong, making a silver pattern at his feet and lighting the woods with strange lusters and silvery, shadowy forms. As usual, his old notion that his wife must be near occurred to him on this occasion, and he looked about him with a speculative, anticipatory eye. What was it that moved in the distant shadows along the path by which he had entered—a pale, flickering will-o'-the-wisp that bobbed gracefully among the trees and riveted his expectant gaze? Moonlight and shadows combined to give it a strange form and a stranger reality, this fluttering of bogfire or dancing of wandering fire-flies. Was it truly his lost Phoebe? By a circuitous route it passed about him, and in his fevered state he fancied that he could see the very eyes of her, not as she was when he last saw her in the black dress and shawl but now a strangely younger Phoebe, gayer, sweeter, the one whom he had known years before as a girl. Old Reifsneider got up. He had been expecting and dreaming of this hour all these years, and now as he saw the feeble light dancing lightly before him he peered at it questioningly, one thin hand in his gray hair.

Of a sudden there came to him now for the first time in many years the full charm of her girlish figure as he had known it in boyhood, the pleasing, sympathetic smile, the brown hair, the blue sash she had once worn about her waist at a picnic, her gay, graceful movements. He walked around the base of the tree, straining with his eyes, forgetting for once his cane and utensils, and following eagerly after. On she moved before him, a will-o'-the-wisp of the spring, a little flame above her head, and it seemed as though among the small saplings of ash and beech and the thick trunks of hickory and elm that she signaled with a young, a lightsome hand.

"O Phoebe! Phoebe!" he called. "Have yuh really come? Have yuh really answered me?" And hurrying faster, he fell once, scrambling lamely to his feet, only to see the light in the distance dancing illusively on. On and on he hurried until he was fairly running, brushing his ragged arms against the trees, striking his hands and face against impeding twigs. His hat was gone, his lungs were breathless, his reason quite astray, when coming to the edge of the cliff he saw her below among a silvery bed of apple-trees now blooming in the spring.

"O Phoebe!" he called. "O Phoebe! Oh, no, don't leave me!" And feeling the lure of a world where love was young and Phoebe as this vision presented her, a delightful epitome of their quondam youth, he gave a gay cry of "Oh, wait, Phoebe!" and leaped.

Some farmer-boys, reconnoitering this region of bounty and prospect some few days afterward, found first the tin utensils tied together under the tree where he had left them, and then later at the foot of the cliff, pale, broken, but elated, a molded smile of peace and delight upon his lips, his body. His old hat was discovered lying under some low-growing saplings the twigs of which had held it back.

No one of all the simple population knew how eagerly and joyously he had found his lost mate.

A Clod of Soil

Ryunosuke Akutagawa

Translated from the Japanese by Takashi Kojima

It was the beginning of the tea-picking season and Osumi was sorely grieved by the loss of her son, Nitaro, who had been lying practically crippled for over eight years. The death of her son did not bring unmixed grief to this old widow, whose soul, the neighbors said, would be born to live a blessed life in the Land of Bliss after her death. When she burned an incense stick to pray for the peaceful repose of his soul now laid in his coffin, she felt as if she had at last managed to cross the steep mountain pass.

After the funeral service of Nitaro was over, the first question that came up was what should be done with his wife, Otami, and her little son. This young widow had taken upon herself most of the family farm work from the hands of her husband who was bedridden. If she left, the family would be burdened not only with the care of the little child but would have no means left for earning a living. Osumi had a good mind to seek a husband for the widowed Otami after the lapse of forty-nine days and to have her work for the family as she did when he was living. In her heart she thought that her late son's cousin, Yoki-chi, might be a suitable husband for the young widow.

"Are you thinking of leaving this child and me already? It's wrong of me to have been silent about a plan for your future," extraordinarily shocked, Osumi asked in a tone of more appeal than reprimand when she saw Otami tidying up the room on the morning of the eighth day after the death of her husband. Osumi was looking after the grand-child on the verandah adjoining the back room. The plaything she gave him was a spray of cherry-blossoms in full bloom which she had taken from the school playground.

"What are you talking about?" Otami answered with a smile, without even looking at her. What a relief it was to Osumi.

"I just imagined so. Sure you're not leaving us, are you?" Osumi kept harping on her solicitous entreaty in a whining voice. Presently her own words made her sentimental, until tears flowed freely down her cheeks.

"Why, really I mean to stay here for good, if you wish." Otami also grew tearful before she was aware of it, and took up her child, Koji, on her lap. "I've got this child. Why should I ever go anywhere else?" Koji, looking strangely shy, appeared attracted to the spray of cherry-blossoms lying upon the old mat of the back room.

* * * * * * *

Otami kept on working as hard as she did while Nitaro was living. However, the problem of her taking a husband could not be as easily settled as had been expected. She did not seem to have any interest at all in this matter. Osumi of course took every opportunity to arouse Otami's interest in her remarriage and to approach her with a proposal. However, Otami gave only evasive answers like "Maybe next year, please." Doubtless this was as much a joy as a worry to Otami, who finally decided to wait for the turn of the year, yielding to her daughter-in-law's wishes. However, she took seriously to heart what other people might think of them.

The following year came and Otami seemed to give no thought to anything but working out in the fields. The old woman began more persistently and even prayerfully to persuade the young widow to take a husband. This was partly because she worried over criticism leveled by her relatives and backbiting by people.

"But you see, you're so young you can't go along without a man for good, I'm afraid," appealed Osumi.

"Good heavens!" answered Otami. "Can't I get along without a man? How can I help it? If you bring in a stranger among us, Hiro will have a hard time, you'll be under pressure, and I'll have no end of cares and troubles."

"This is why I urge you. Take Yokichi for your husband, won't you? He's given up gambling forever, I understand," persuaded Osumi.

"Why, he's a relative of yours, but, after all, he's a stranger to me," replied the younger woman.

"But you'll have to be patient for years and years," Osumi argued.

"Why not? It's for the sake of my dear Hiro. If I only suffer now, the whole of our farm will pass undivided into his hands," Otami thoughtfully replied.

"Well," Osumi said lowering her voice, as she always did when she talked of this matter. "In any case people will talk, you see. I pray you, Otami, tell others exactly what you've just said to me."

How often they had questions and answers like these! But each time only added to the strength of Otami's determination. Really, without the help of a male hand, she worked harder than ever, planting potatoes and reaping barley. Moreover, during the summers she kept cows, and even on rainy days she went out mowing. This hard work was in itself her strong resistance against admitting a stranger into her home. At last Osumi gave up the idea of getting a husband for Otami. However, her resignation was not altogether unpleasant to her.

*　　　*　　　*　　　*　　　*　　　*　　　*

Otami continued to support the family by her own hands. There was no doubt that her toil was motivated by her whole-hearted desire to work for the sake of her little son, Hiro. Another more inherent cause was traceable to the power of heredity that ran deep in her blood. She was a daughter of a so-called migrant family that had formerly moved into this district from a sterile mountainous province.

"Your Otami is much stronger than she looks," from time to time the next-door old woman was heard to say to Osumi. "The other day I saw her carrying four huge bundles of rice-plants on her back."

Osumi tried to translate her thanks to Otami by taking over the management of the daily household chores: looking after her grandson, taking care of the cows, cooking meals, washing clothes, going to the neighbor's house to draw water, etc. Bent with age, she found happiness and pleasure in taking over all sorts of household tasks herself.

One night in the late autumn, Otami came home with difficulty, carrying bulky bundles of pine-needles under her arms. Just then Osumi with Hiroji fastened to her back, was stoking a fire in the furnace in a corner of the small earthen floor.

"You must be cold. You're back late," Osumi said.

"I did a bit of extra work today," Otami replied wearily.

Tossing down the bundles of pine-needles below the sill, without even taking off her muddy straw sandals, she came in and sat down right by the side of the open fireplace, where an oak stump was burning with a cheery flame. Osumi tried to rise to her feet at once, but burdened with Hiroji on her back, she had to hold on to the edge of the bathtub before she could slowly raise herself.

"Have a bath right away, won't you?"

"I'm too hungry for a bath. I'd rather eat sweet potatoes first. You've got some boiled sweet potatoes, haven't you?"

Osumi toddled along to the sill, and brought back the pot of boiled sweet potatoes. "I've had them waiting for you for a long time. I'm afraid they're cold now."

They roasted the sweet potatoes over the fire in the open fireplace.

"Hiro's fast asleep. Lay the tot in bed."

"No, it's so awful cold tonight and he won't go to sleep," Osumi replied.

While talking, Otami began cramming her mouth full of the sweet potatoes which had begun steaming. Her manner of eating could only be observed among farmers who come back home after the day's tiresome labors. She ravenously gulped down one sweet potato after another which she had removed from the spit. Osumi, feeling the weight of the faintly snoring Hiroji on her back, busily kept broiling more sweet potatoes.

"Anyway working as hard as you do, you must feel twice as hungry as anyone else." Time and again Osumi looked admiringly into the face of Otami, as she kept cramming the sweet potatoes into her mouth in the dim light of the sooty fire.

*   *   *   *   *   *   *

Otami toiled on all the harder at a man's work without sparing herself. Sometimes even at night she walked around, thinning out greens by the light of a lantern. Osumi always had respect for her daughter-in-law. Really it was more a sense of awe than respect. Except for labor in the fields and hills, Otami thrust all work upon her mother-in-law, without washing even her own clothes. Nevertheless, without breathing a word of complaint, Osumi worked on straightening herself up now and then.

Osumi never saw the old woman next door without extolling her daughter-in-law to the skies, saying, "Anyway Otami's like that. So no matter when I die, my family will have nothing to worry about."

However, Otami's mania for work seemed too far gone to be thrown off. When another year had passed she began to speak of extending the sphere of her labor to the mulberry field across the irrigation ditch. She asserted that it was absurd to tenant out the land covering a quarter of an acre for only ten dollars a year. She went on to reason that if they planted mulberry trees there and raised silkworms at odd times, their labor would be sure to yield them about 150 dollars net yearly, barring fluctuations in the silkworm market. Although money was their greatest consideration, it was more than Osumi could bear to be pressed with extra labor. Above all, raising silkworms was an exacting demand upon their time and far beyond the limit of her capacity and endurance. At last she offered a querulous remonstrance.

"You see, Otami. I'm not shirking. We haven't got a man—just a little crying child to look after. Even now the work is too much for me. So your idea's too absurd. How could I ever take up raising silkworms? Think of me a little. I pray you!"

In the face of her mother-in-law's plaintive protest, Otami did not have the heart to insist on having her own way. So she gave up the idea of raising silkworms, but insisted on carrying her point in planting the mulberry field.

"Never mind. Only I've got to work out in the fields." Casting a determined look at Osumi, she grumbled out the insinuating remark.

From this time on, Osumi again thought of adopting a son. Formerly she had entertained this idea out of her anxiety over her family's living and out of her regard for what people might think of her family. But now she wished to adopt a son out of her impatience to be released from her painful duty of taking care of the house work. So now how more intense and irresistible than ever before was her desire to receive a son-in-law into her family!

Just at the time when the tangerine fields were tinged with full-blown blossoms, Osumi seated in front of the oil-lamp, ventured to bring up the proposal, eyeing Otami over the rims of her spectacles, which she wore while doing her needlework at night.

"Talking of my taking a husband again! That's no concern of mine," Otami, sitting cross-legged and munching salted peas, turned a deaf ear. Formerly Osumi might, in all probability, have dropped the proposal.

"But you shouldn't altogether say, 'No,' now." This particular night she persistently tried her best to persuade Otami. "Tomorrow at the funeral service of the Miyashita family, our family is assigned the duty of digging the grave. At a time like this I wish we had a man."

"Don't worry. I'll do the digging," Otami interjected.

"Sure not. Bein' a woman, you don't mean it." Osumi thought of laughing it off. But looking into Otami's face, she dared not.

"Granny, you want to retire now, don't you?" Otami, with her hands on the knees of her crossed legs, coldly touched Osumi on her sensitive spot.

"Oh, no, Otami, why should I ever . . . ?" Osumi, who was caught off balance took off her spectacles in spite of herself. But she could not tell why she did so.

"You remember what you said when Hiro's father died, don't you?" persisted Otami. "It would be a sin against our ancestors ever to divide up the estate of our family . . ."

"Well, yes, I said so. But we have to take things as they are. This can't be helped." Osumi tried hard to plead in favor of bringing a man into their family. Nevertheless, her argument did not sound plausible or convincing even to her own ears. First of all, this was because she could not bring up her real underlying motive to live an easier life.

"It may be all very well for you, as you'll die earlier than I." Continuing to munch salted peas, Otami, who had discovered Osumi's vulnerability, began taking her severely to task. Her natural glib tongue lent force to her reprimand. "In the situation I'm in, how can I shirk my responsibility? I haven't remained a widow for any show or pride. At nights when my limbs are too painful for me to go to sleep, I often feel that it's no good being stubborn. But I'm doing all this though, thinking this is for the sake of our family and Hiro."

In a stupid daze, Osumi looked Otami in the face. In the course of time, her mind clearly began to grasp a certain fact. It was that struggle as she might, she could never ease up until she closed her eyes forever. After Otami's outburst was over, she put on her spectacles again.

"But Otami," Osumi concluded her talk as if she were talking to herself. "Things in life don't go only according to reason. Think it over carefully, won't you? I won't say anything more about it."

Twenty minutes later some village youngster walked past the house, singing in a tenor voice:

> "The young bride's out on her mowing work today,
> Grass bend low, scythe be sharp!"

When the singing died away, Osumi gave another glance at Otami's face over the rims of her spectacles. Otami, on the other side of the lamp, was only yawning heavily, with her legs fully outstretched.

"Now I'll get off to bed. I must get up nice and early in the morning." Muttering these words, Otami snatched a handful of salted peas, and stood up languidly by the fireside.

Osumi silently continued to endure her sufferings for the subsequent three or four years. These were the sufferings an old horse experiences when teamed up with a young spirited one. Otami persevered with her arduous work and toiled in the fields like a bee. To outsiders Osumi seemed to be as happy as ever, taking care of the house. But the shadow of an invisible whip constantly harassed her. She was apt to be scolded or indirectly rebuked by the spirited Otami, sometimes for failing to heat the bath, and at others for forgetting to air unhulled rice or letting the cows out. Nevertheless, without answering back, she continued to endure her sufferings. For one thing, it was because her spirit was accustomed to submission; and for another, because her grandson, Hiro, was attached more to her than to his mother.

Actually to outsiders, Osumi had hardly changed in any way. If she had, it was that she did not praise her son's wife as she had done previously. However, such a trivial change did not attract any special notice from others. At least to the old woman next door, she remained the same blessed woman as ever.

At high noon one summer when the blazing hot sun was beating straight down upon the earth, Osumi was talking with the next-door old woman under the shadow of the grape-vine trellis spreading all over in front of the cow-shed. The old woman talked while smoking cigarette butts. She had carefully collected the cigarette butts left by her son.

"Hm. Otami-san's out mowing hay. She's so young, and yet she does all work without complaining," observed the old woman.

"Well, house work is best for women," responded Osumi.

"No, there's nothing you should enjoy more than farming. My son's wife hasn't ever been out weeding much less farming for even a single day in the seven years since they got married. She spends all her livelong days washing her kids' clothes and remaking her own."

"Tidying up your kids and keeping yourself neat and attractive is an adornment to life," chimed Osumi.

"But the young today don't like to work in the fields. Oh, dear! What's the noise now?" asked the neighbor.

"That noise? Why, it's just the cow breaking wind."

"Oh, the cow breaking wind! Really? When young, it's awful trying to weed, with your back blistered under the scorching rays of the sun," concluded the neighbor.

The two old women generally chatted like that in a familiar and friendly way.

For more than eight years after the death of Jintaro, Otami continued to support her family single-handed. In the course of time her name had spread all over the village and beyond. In the eyes of the villagers, she was no longer a young widow, who, seized by a mania for work, toiled night and day. Much less was she a young "missus" to the village youngsters. Instead she was an example to all brides. She was a present-day paragon of female virtue and fidelity. Such spontaneous eulogies were upon everyone's lips. As for Osumi, she did not divulge her sufferings or her innermost thoughts to anyone. Nor did she want to. From the depths of her heart she placed her faith in Providence, although she was not clearly conscious of God. Now that her faith was dashed to pieces, her only and last hope was her grandson, Hiro. She desperately poured her love out to her darling twelve-year-old grandson. But this last hope of hers was often blighted.

One fine fall afternoon Hiro came home hurriedly from school in a state of agitation, holding a sheaf of books under his arm. Osumi, sitting in front of the stable, using her knife quite dexterously, was cording persimmons to dry them.

He skipped nimbly over one of the mats, on which unhulled millet was airing, and smartly arranged his feet and raised his hand in a crisp salute.

"Say, granny," he abruptly asked her earnestly, "Is Mama a very great woman?"

"Why?" Resting her hand which had just been using the knife, she could not help staring at her grandson's face.

"Because the teacher told us in the morals lesson that she was greater than any other woman in this neighborhood."

"Eh? The teacher? Who?" First she was upset. "Even the school teacher tells my grandson such a shocking lie." Really nothing was a greater surprise to her. After a moment's confusion, she was seized with a fit of anger, and began berating Otami as if she were a changed being.

"That's a lie. A black lie. Your mama works hard only outdoors, so she seems extraordinary and wonderful to others. But she's real wicked at heart. She drives granny hard, and is so headstrong."

Astonished, Hiroji watched his grandmother's face which was livid with anger. In the course of time a reaction must have overtaken her, for she had tears in her eyes.

"So your granny's living with you as her only hope in life. Always keep this in mind. By and by as soon as you're seventeen, get married and let your granny breathe freely. Your mama takes it easy and says you should get married after you're through with your military service. But how could I ever wait that long? You understand. Be doubly kind to granny so as to do your daddy's share of duty, and I'll be very good to you. You shall have everything," Osumi said persuasively.

"Will you give me these persimmons when they're ripe?" Koji was fingering and coveting a basket of persimmons.

"Sure, why not?" Osumi hiccuped her laughter through her tears. "You're just a little tyke, but you understand everything. Now don't change your mind."

The night following this outburst, Osumi had a rowdy squabble with Otami about a trifling matter which arose from Osumi's alleged eating of Otami's share of boiled sweet potatoes. As they became heated in their argument Otami said with a grin, "If you don't want to work, you have no choice but to die."

This incensed Osumi and she unexpectedly raved like an insane woman.

"Hiro, here, wake up!" Osumi aroused Hiroji, who had been asleep all this while with his head on her lap, and continued to howl with rage. "Hiro, wake up! Hiro,—wake up! Listen to what your mama says. She tells me to die. Do you hear? Listen real well, will you? In mama's days we've got a bit more money, but grandpa and granny cleared our three acres of farm and all between ourselves. And yet mama tells me I should die if I want to take things easy . . . Otami, I'll die. Why should I be afraid of dying? I won't be dictated to by you. Oh, I'll die by all means. I'll die and haunt you . . ."

Osumi continued to rave and revile in a loud voice, holding her grandson who had started to cry in her arms. Otami all this while lay by the fireside, turning a deaf ear to the ravings of Osumi.

＊　　　　＊　　　　＊　　　　＊　　　　＊　　　　＊　　　　＊

However, Osumi did not die, while on the other hand Otami, who boasted of her excellent health, caught typhoid fever and died a week later. At that time the disease took an appalling toll of life in the village. The day before she fell ill, she took her turn at the task of digging a grave for the funeral of the iron-smith who had fallen victim to the same disease. At the smith's she saw the young apprentice who was to be sent to the isolation hospital on the very day of the funeral.

"You must've caught it then," after the doctor left, Osumi dropped a hint of her censure to the patient, who lay in bed with her face burning with fever.

The day of Otami's funeral it rained heavily. Nevertheless, her funeral was attended by all the villagers including the village mayor. All those who were there mourned the early death of Otami and expressed their sympathy to Osumi and Hiroji who had lost their breadwinner. The village representative told Osumi that the county office had been contemplating an official commendation for Otami shortly. At these words Osumi could do nothing but bow her head.

"Well, Osumi," went on the good-hearted representative, nodding his bald head. "You'd better resign yourself to your great misfortune. To get the official recommendation of Otami-san, we've sent in petitions to the county office, and I've been there to see the county commissioner five times. But we're going to resign ourselves to the tragedy, so you'd better be resigned, too." His preaching adulterated with levity made the grade-school teachers stare at him with a look of obvious displeasure.

The night after the funeral of Otami, found Osumi sleeping with Hiroji inside the same mosquito net in the corner of the back room where the Buddhist altar had been erected. At other times they used to sleep in the dark room with the light out. That night, however, the altar was still lit with candles and, the mats seemed to have been permeated with the peculiar odor of the usual disinfectant, which kept Osumi awake in bed for a long time. Without doubt, Otami's death had at last brought her a great happiness. Now it was no longer necessary for her to work. Besides, she was also free from the fear of being rebuked.

She now had a bank deposit of a thousand dollars and three acres of farm land. She and Hiroji would be free, from now on to eat delicious boiled rice together, instead of having to endure the less-appetizing mixture of boiled barley and rice, and she would also be free to purchase her favorite salted cod by the bale. Never in her life had she felt so relieved from cares as at that moment. Presently her memory vividly recalled a certain night nine years ago. On that night she heaved the same sigh of relief as she did now. That was the night after the funeral of the only son of her flesh and blood. This was the night the funeral of her son's wife who bore her only grandson was also just over.

Osumi opened her eyes of her own accord, and found her grandson asleep close by her with his innocent face turned upward. While she was gazing fondly into his relaxed and restful face, it gradually occurred to her that she was a wretched creature and that at the same time both her son, Jintaro, and his wife, Otami, who formed an ill-fated union with her, were also to be pitied. The change in her feelings helped to instantly erase nine years of hatred and bitterness. The parent and her children, all three, were to be pitied. Osumi, who survived the other two to live such a disgraceful life was the most pitiable of them all.

"Otami, why did you die?" she whispered faintly to the departed. Suddenly in spite of herself an endless stream of tears flowed down her cheeks.

After she heard the clock strike four, the sleep of the weary fell upon her, as the sky, over her thatched roof on the eastern horizon was greeting the first chilly grey streaks of dawn.

Part Seven

The Life Cycle

MOST CURRENT IDEAS ABOUT THE LIFE CYCLE ASSUME A CONTINUITY OF COG-
nitive styles and personality configurations, in that the preceding periods and
experiences in a person's life are believed to influence subsequent periods.
Thus, according to Freud, personality is formed early and, while some changes
occur all through the life cycle, the middle-aged and elderly individual is quite
similar to and consistent with himself or herself when younger. Freud thought
that we become used to ourselves as we age, as well as used to our repressions,
rationalizations, projections, and other defense or adaptive mechanisms which
are part of our personalities, creating greater self-acceptance with increasing
age. It is a self-acceptance based on habit rather than on self-understanding.
The increased self-acceptance can make it difficult for the individual to benefit
from therapy, if therapy is needed, for therapy requires the self-dissatisfaction
that provides the motivation for a person to want to change. Even though an individual might benefit from the changes that occur with therapy, the individual
is unlikely to do so if he or she is comfortable with existing personality characteristics, including personality quirks, hostility toward other persons, compul-
sive habits, bitterness with the past, and an angry view of life itself. All of
these, as well as positive attitudes and characteristics, are included in the tendency toward greater self-acceptance with increasing age.

Plato, as we noted in Part 3, believed that reason is possible only in the later
years, for by then one is done with the emotions or passions that earlier interfered with the ability to reason clearly and deeply. His is one of the few
theories that ascribes positive growth to old age. Although one might argue that
the decline of intense emotions is not particularly positive, it is clear that the
increased ability to reason is a positive change.

Middle age is often seen as the period of stability, evenness, and calmness,
after a period of experimentation, excitement, adventure, and novelty. The person has come to understand himself, his sense of who he is becomes stable, and
the wild searching and constant need for excitement diminishes. Erik Erikson
suggests, however, that middle age has the potential for *too much* stability to
the extent that a person can fall into a rut and come to prefer routine to novelty
in all things, stability to change, the "tried and true" instead of challenges,
sameness and habit to growth, with the result that the person stagnates rather
than lives fully. Not a great deal is known about the kinds of and develop-
mental histories of individuals who come to prefer stagnation in middle age.
The evenness, calmness, and greater stability of middle age can also result in
greater productivity and insight rather than stagnation. In other words, stagnation is not an inevitable result of stability. Much depends on the individual's
over-all characteristics.

Some poets (as well as some social scientists) see aging positively, such as
William Butler Yeats in his 1924 poem, "Youth and Age." Because we lack
control of our lives when we are young, Yeats says, we feel put upon and frus-

trated. As we age we gain control. Other poets, sometimes unconsciously rather than overtly, see it as a most undesirable time of life. At times both of these are contained in the same poem, reflecting a basic ambivalence about aging. This is especially true of the satirical "You Are Old, Father William," by Lewis Carroll.

In 1799, Robert Southey (1774–1843) wrote "The Old Man's Comforts and How He Gained Them," a poem that contains much that is optimistic about old age. Father William is old, healthy, age-accepting, sagacious, and cheerful. This poem inspired a parody by Lewis Carroll (pen name of Charles Lutwidge Dodgson, 1832–1898), found in Chapter 5 of *Alice in Wonderland* (1865). Carroll's Father William is old, fat, and something of a humbug. Southey was put down by Carroll perhaps as much for the attitudes Father William expressed— his acceptance of the aging process and death and his lack of a sense of loss and self-pity—as for Southey's sing-song style, which created a Pollyanna-like impression. Apart from the style, was it the boundless optimism Southey's Father William expresses that so annoyed Carroll? Should the old man have been mired in pity, decrepitude, sickness, and regrets? Perhaps it was unseemly and inappropriate for an older man to be so buoyant and life-accepting. Or perhaps it was the style that inspired Carroll to parody it. Even so, the content of his satire is decidedly negative toward aging.

Several of the poems in Part 7 pertain to the entire life cycle, notably "Of The Four Ages of Man" (1650) by Anne Bradstreet (1612–1672). In it we find the four humors, or body fluids, described by Hippocrates about 400 B.C. He applied them to personality types, relating temperament and physique. His four temperaments—phlegmatic, sanguine, choleric, and melancholic—Bradstreet applies, not to different types of individuals but to changes throughout the life cycle. Phlegmatic has to do with the Child who is undeveloped and, hence, unstable; sanguine refers to frolicking and merrymaking Youth; choleric of the Manly explains why he angers easily and is emotionally intense; while Old Age is characterized by melancholy or gloominess and, she adds, seriousness. In addition, death is possible at any time of life.

"The Four Ages of Man" (1935) by William Butler Yeats, who wrote many poems about aging, old age, and death, conveys the various crises or struggles at each age throughout the life cycle.

William Shakespeare's familiar lines from *As You Like It* (c. 1600) divide the life cycle into seven ages. As most all poetic and psychological conceptions of the life cycle, his pertains to males only. While the last age has been quoted extensively as most clearly conveying the sense of loss in old age, and as a rather pessimistic observation of old age, the earlier ages are also not especially attractive. The puking infant and the whining schoolboy are not pleasant images, and one should view Jaques' perception of the last age in that context.

The text of Ecclesiastes 3 in the Old Testament has been attributed to King Solomon as an old man by Jonathan, in his commentary in *Canticles Rabbah* (Midrash), 1.1.10, who says: "Solomon wrote first the *Song of Songs,* then *Proverbs,* then *Ecclesiastes,* and this is the way of the world. When young, we compose songs; when older, we make sententious remarks; and when old, we speak of the vanity of things.'' Seen from another point of view, this portion of Ecclesiastes conveys the basic continuity and wholeness of life. Life flows easily, always back to the original source, away again, and back again. A similar thought is expressed by Leonardo da Vinci (1452–1519): There is a natural rhythm to life in which the future is related to the past and present, death is related to life, youth is related to old age. Nonetheless, in these excerpts from his notebooks, Leonardo expresses much ambivalence about old age.

Death is important to life and living, suggests Yoshida Kenkō, who became a Buddhist monk in 1324 at the age of 41 (note his extremely negative references to the ''fortieth year'' and beyond in the text). He wrote ''Essays in Idleness'' around 1340.

An exceedingly positive attitude toward old age is expressed by Isaac Disraeli (1766–1848), father of the British statesman Benjamin Disraeli, in ''The Progress of Old Age in New Studies'' from his *Curiosities of Literature* (1791). Enthusiasm for and productivity in art, science, and literature persist in old age. According to Disraeli, creativity and curiosity do not diminish as one ages: many older people continue to want to know; they enjoy the world of ideas, perhaps even more than previously; they continue to learn, to study, to write, and to create. It often happens that we do not learn or accomplish certain things when we are young, perhaps because we do not have the opportunity or are not motivated to do so then. It is by no means too late to accomplish them when we are older. Disraeli gives many examples of persons who started and completed noteworthy accomplishments well beyond the ages when these things are usually attempted.

''Let Me Grow Lovely'' by Karle Wilson Baker (Charlotte Wilson, born 1878) expresses the often forgotten point that we value many fine objects as they age and consider them even more precious and pleasing with age. Some that are highly valued greatly increase in beauty with age and inspire a positive attitude in us. So, too, it might be with persons.

Perhaps we could say that the message of ''Middle Age'' by Rudolph Chambers Lehmann (1856–1929) is that whatever one's age is at present appears to be the best of all possible ages. ''Middle Age'' expresses the feeling that we are the very center of life itself when we are young. The world appears made for us, wide open to us, there are no limitations, we are in total control of life. We look at those who are older as has-beens who are in no way similar to ourselves, for they are over the hill while we are still full of strength and vitality and are open to challenges. But once we reach forty-two we have a quite different perception of ourselves and of the young. Youth appears wasteful of time and energy because of a lack of knowledge. Youth flounders, makes false starts, wastes time, is restless, becomes intense—all of which waste its vitality. By forty-two, however, we have the perspective that comes only with experience and with our reflection on and assessment of that experience. Perspective comes slowly and painfully. We make mistakes and only much later recognize them as mistakes. It is the greater perspective in middle age that gives us our vitality then, and, to Lehmann, this is preferable to the vitality of the young.

Life is out of joint, protests Walter Learned (1847–1915) in "To Critics." He saw what today we would call age-appropriate behavior as mostly restrictive and prohibiting one from doing, rather than as permissive and enhancing.[1]

The French poet Pierre Jean de Béranger (1780–1857), in his "Fifty Years," characterized age 50 as a time of ill health, the end of casual and spontaneous sex, the end of reason and hope, and the recognition of moments lost. The only escape from the ravages of time is provided by a relationship with a woman who is young. This is a belief that some men have had in a great many cultures over the past few thousand years. Both rejuvenation through sexual rites and the fountain of youth legend have been common beliefs. Many of the techniques are based on the idea that a man absorbs youth from a young woman. Some versions of the belief do not involve direct sexual contact but only the influence, the breath, or the heat obtained simply by the man's proximity to the young female body.

Experimenters have found that this works with rats. One young female was put among aging males, and she regularly groomed them. They did live longer than a control group. (So far, no one has tried to put a young male rat among aging female rats. That is probably seen both as much less important and as obscene.) Parabiosis experiments have also produced some reversals and control of the aging processes among elderly male cockroaches and rats.

Since old age is a time for reminiscing, anticipate that you also will reminisce in your later years, suggests French poet Pierre de Ronsard (1524–1585) to his lady, in the poem "When You are Very Old." Live now so that you will not look back later and be disappointed with your past. Ronsard had love in mind as the specific experience to enjoy both in the present and in later reminiscing. He suggests to the young lady that she not spurn him now only to regret it in old age. In a most unique and interesting argument, he assures her that if she accepts him now her memories in old age will be most pleasant.

"When You Are Old" by William Butler Yeats was adapted from Ronsard's poem, but is quite different in its purpose. Both assume that in the sleepy later years *all* one has are memories. This of course need not be the case. These poets' perceptions of the limitations of old age are somewhat stereotypical and are automatically assumed to apply to everyone, and that assumption in itself might prevent an individual from attempting to transcend them. The point that Ronsard makes is, however, an important one: When younger, one should live in the present in such a way that one does not look back on one's youth with regrets.

[1] For a discussion of age-appropriate behavior and the importance of on-time events from a particular social-science point of view, see "Adaptation and the Life Cycle" by Bernice L. Neugarten in *Counseling Adults,* ed. Nancy K. Schlossberg and Alan D. Entine (Belmont, Calif.: Books/Cole, 1977), pp. 34–46, or *The Journal of Geriatric Psychiatry* 4 (1970), 71–87 and "The Changing Age-Status System" by Bernice L. Neugarten and Joan W. Moore in Neugarten, *Middle Age and Aging.*

Some interesting observations on the life cycle are provided by the Duc de La Rochefoucauld (1613–1680) from his book of maxims (1665). Another interesting assessment of the life cycle is found in the words of the important Chinese philosopher Confucius (551–479 B.C.) whose ideas were implemented as norms in Chinese society through the examination system for two thousand years. His emphasis on filial piety, together with the gerentocracy produced by the examination system, created a paradise for many elderly persons.

Finally, a verse from the Apocrypha: "Dishonor not the old: we shall all be numbered among them." It is included here to remind us that no one has a monopoly on old age; all of us, if we are lucky enough to live a long life, will be old and older; and that ought to be an important consideration in our thoughts about old age and in our relationships with older persons.

Youth And Age

William Butler Yeats

Much did I rage when young,
Being by the world oppressed,
But now with flattering tongue
It speeds the parting guest.

The Old Man's Comforts

And How He Gained Them

Robert Southey

"You are old, Father William," the young man cried,
    "The few locks which are left you are grey;
"You are hale, Father William, a hearty old man,
    Now tell me the reason, I pray."

"In the days of my youth," Father William replied,
    "I remember'd that youth would fly fast,
And abused not my health and my vigour at first,
    That I never might need them at last."

"You are old, Father William," the young man cried,
    "And pleasures with youth pass away;
And yet you lament not the days that are gone,
    Now tell me the reason, I pray."

"In the days of my youth," Father William replied,
    "I remember'd that youth could not last;
I thought of the future, whatever I did,
    That I never might grieve for the past."

"You are old, Father William, the young man cried,
    "And life must be hastening away;
You are cheerful, and love to converse upon death,
    Now tell me the reason, I pray."

"I am cheerful, young man," Father William replied,
    "Let the cause thy attention engage;
In the days of my youth I remember'd my God!
    And He hath not forgotten my age."

You Are Old, Father William

After Southey

Lewis Carroll

"You are old, father William," the young man said,
    "And your hair has become very white;
And yet you incessantly stand on your head—
    Do you think, at your age, it is right?"

"In my youth," father William replied to his son,
    "I feared it might injure the brain;
But now that I'm perfectly sure I have none,
    Why, I do it again and again."

"You are old," said the youth, "as I mentioned before,
    And have grown most uncommonly fat;
Yet you turned a back-somersault in at the door—
    Pray, what is the reason for that?"

"In my youth," said the sage, as he shook his grey locks,
    "I kept all my limbs very supple
By the use of this ointment—one shilling the box—
    Allow me to sell you a couple?"

"You are old," said the youth, "and your jaws are too weak
    For anything stronger than suet;
Yet you finished the goose, with the bones and the beak:
    Pray, how did you manage to do it?"

"In my youth," said his father, "I took to the law,
    And argued each case with my wife;
And the muscular strength which it gave to my jaw,
    Has lasted the rest of my life."

"You are old," said the youth, "one would hardly suppose
    That your eye was as steady as ever;
Yet you balanced an eel on the end of your nose—
    What made you so awfully clever?"

"I have answered three questions, and that is enough,"
    Said his father; "don't give yourself airs!
Do you think I can listen all day to such stuff?
    Be off, or I'll kick you downstairs!"

Of the Four Ages of Man

Anne Bradstreet

Lo, now, four other acts upon the stage,
Childhood and Youth, the Manly and Old Age:
The first, son unto phlegm, grandchild to water,
Unstable supple, moist and cold's his nature.
The second, frolic, claims his pedigree
From blood and air, for hot and moist is he.
The third of fire and choler is composed,
Vindicative and quarrelsome disposed.
The last, of earth and heavy melancholy,
Solid, hating all lightness and all folly.
Childhood was clothed in white and given to show
His spring was intermixèd with some snow:
Upon his head a garland nature set
Of daisy, primrose, and the violet.
Such cold mean flowers as these blossom betime
Before the sun hath thoroughly warmed the clime.
His hobby striding did not ride but run,
And in his hand an hour-glass new begun,
In dangers every moment of a fall,
And when 'tis broke then ends his life and all.
But if he hold till it have run its last,
Then may he live till threescore years or past.

Next Youth came up in gorgeous attire
(As that fond age doth most of all desire):
His suit of crimson and his scarf of green,
In 's countenance his pride quickly was seen;
Garland of roses, pinks, and gillyflowers
Seemèd to grow on's head bedewed with showers.
His face as fresh as is Aurora fair,
When blushing first she 'gins to red the air.
No wooden horse, but one of metal tried,
He seems to fly or swim, and not to ride.
Then prancing on the stage about he wheels,
But as he went, death waited at his heels.
The next came up in a more graver sort,
As one that carèd for a good report.
His sword by's side, and choler in his eyes,
But neither used as yet, for he was wise;
Of autumn fruits a basket on his arm,
His golden god in's purse, which was his charm.
And last of all to act upon this stage,
Leaning upon his staff comes up Old Age:
Under his arm a sheaf of wheat he bore,
A harvest of the best, what needs he more?
In's other hand a glass ev'n almost run,
This writ about: "This out, then I am done."

The Four Ages of Man

William Butler Yeats

He with body waged a fight,
But body won; it walks upright.

Then he struggled with the heart;
Innocence and peace depart.

Then he struggled with the mind;
His proud heart he left behind.

Now his wars on God begin;
At stroke of midnight God shall win.

From

As You Like It

Act II, scene vii

William Shakespeare

DUKE SENIOR   Thou seest we are not all alone unhappy.
This wide and universal theater
Presents more woeful pageants than the scene
Wherein we play in.
JAQUES   All the world's a stage,
And all the men and women merely players.
They have their exits and their entrances,
And one man in his time plays many parts,
His acts being seven ages. At first the infant,
Mewling and puking in the nurse's arms.
Then the whining schoolboy, with his satchel
And shining morning face, creeping like snail
Unwillingly to school. And then the lover,
Sighing like furnace, with a woeful ballad
Made to his mistress' eyebrow. Then a soldier,
Full of strange oaths and bearded like the pard,
Jealous in honor, sudden and quick in quarrel,
Seeking the bubble reputation
Even in the cannon's mouth. And then the justice,
In fair round belly with good capon lined,
With eyes severe and beard of formal cut,
Full of wise saws and modern instances,
And so he plays his part. The sixth age shifts
Into the lean and slippered Pantaloon
With spectacles on nose and pouch on side,
His youthful hose, well saved, a world too wide
For his shrunk shank, and his big manly voice,
Turning again toward childish treble, pipes
And whistles in his sound. Last scene of all,
That ends this strange eventful history,
Is second childishness and mere oblivion,
Sans teeth, sans eyes, sans taste, sans everything.

From

Ecclesiastes

3:1–8

To every thing there is a season, and a time to every purpose under the
    heaven:
A time to be born, and a time to die;
A time to plant, and a time to pluck up that which is planted;
A time to kill, and a time to heal;
A time to break down, and a time to build up;
A time to weep, and a time to laugh;
A time to mourn, and a time to dance;
A time to cast away stones, and a time to gather stones together;
A time to embrace, and a time to refrain from embracing;
A time to seek, and a time to lose;
A time to keep, and a time to cast away;
A time to rend, and a time to sew;
A time to keep silence, and a time to speak;
A time to love, and a time to hate;
A time for war, and a time for peace.

Notes on Human Life

Leonardo da Vinci

Translated from the Italian by Edward McCurdy

Behold now the hope and desire to go back to our own country, and to return to
our former state, how like it is to the moth with the light! And the man who
with perpetual longing ever looks forward with joy to each new spring and each
new summer, and to the new months and the new years, deeming that the
things he longs for are too slow in coming, does not perceive that he is longing
for his own destruction. But this longing is the quintessence and spirit of the elements, which, finding itself imprisoned with the life of the human body,
desires continually to return ·to its source. And I would have you to know that
this very same longing is that quintessence inherent in nature, and that man is a
type of the world.

In youth acquire that which may requite you for the deprivations of old age; and if you are mindful that old age has wisdom for its food, you will so exert yourself in youth that your old age will not lack sustenance.

As a well-spent day brings happy sleep, so life well used brings happy death.

While I thought that I was learning how to live, I have been learning how to die.

Life well spent is long.

In rivers, the water that you touch is the last of what has passed and the first of that which comes: so with time present.

O Time, thou that consumest all things! O envious age, thou destroyest all things and devourest all things with the hard teeth of the years, little by little, in slow death! Helen, when she looked in her mirror and saw the withered wrinkles which old age had made in her face, wept, and wondered to herself why ever she had twice been carried away. O time, thou that consumest all things! O envious age, whereby all things are consumed.

Essays in Idleness

Yoshida Kenkō

Translated from the Japanese by G. B. Sansom

Were we to live on for ever—were the dews of Adashino never to vanish, the smoke on Toribeyama* never to fade away—then indeed would men not feel the pity of things.

Truly the beauty of life is its uncertainty. Of all living things, none lives so long as man. Consider how the ephemera awaits the fall of evening, and the summer cicada knows neither spring nor autumn. Even a year of life lived peacefully seems long and happy beyond compare; but for such as never weary of this world and are loath to die, a thousand years would pass away like the dream of a single night.

What shall it avail a man to drag out till he becomes decrepit and unsightly a life which some day needs must end? Long life brings many shames. At most before his fortieth year is full, it is seemly for a man to die.

After that age it is pitiful to see how, unashamed of his looks, he loves to thrust himself into the society of others and, cherishing his offspring in the evening of his days, craves to live on and on that he may watch them grow and prosper. So he continues, his heart set on nought but worldliness, and hardening to the pity of things.

* Adashino and Toribeyama were places of cremation.

The Progress of Old Age in New Studies

Isaac Disraeli

Of the pleasures derivable from the cultivation of the arts, sciences, and literature, time will not abate the growing passion; for old men still cherish an affection and feel a youthful enthusiasm in those pursuits, when all others have ceased to interest. Dr. Reid, to his last day, retained a most active curiosity in his various studies, and particularly in the revolutions of modern chemistry. In advanced life we may resume our former studies with a new pleasure, and in old age we may enjoy them with the same relish with which more youthful students commence. Adam Smith observed to Dugald Stewart that "of all the amusements of old age, the most grateful and soothing is a renewal of acquaintance with the favorite studies and favorite authors of youth"—a remark, adds Stewart, which, in his own case, seemed to be more particularly exemplified while he was re-perusing, with the enthusiasm of a student, the tragic poets of ancient Greece. "I have heard him repeat the observation more than once, while Sophocles and Euripides lay open on his table."

Socrates learned to play on musical instruments in his old age; Cato, at eighty, thought proper to learn Greek; and Plutarch, almost as late in his life, Latin.

Theophrastus began his admirable work on the characters of men at the extreme age of ninety. He only terminated his literary labors by his death.

Ronsard, one of the fathers of French poetry, applied himself late to study. His acute genius, and ardent application, rivaled those poetic models which he admired; and Boccaccio was thirty-five years of age when he commenced his studies in polite literature.

The great Arnauld retained the vigor of his genius, and the command of his pen, to the age of eighty-two, and was still the great Arnauld.

Sir Henry Spelman neglected the sciences in his youth, but cultivated them at fifty years of age. His early years were chiefly passed in farming, which greatly diverted him from his studies; but a remarkable disappointment respecting a contested estate disgusted him with these rustic occupations: resolved to attach himself to regular studies, and literary society, he sold his farms, and became the most learned antiquary and lawyer.

Colbert, the famous French minister, almost at sixty, returned to his Latin and law studies.

Dr. Johnson applied himself to the Dutch language but a few years before his death. The Marquis de Saint Aulaire, at the age of seventy, began to court the Muses, and they crowned him with their freshest flowers. The verses of this French Anacreon are full of fire, delicacy, and sweetness.

Chaucer's *Canterbury Tales* were the composition of his latest years; they were begun in his fifty-fourth year, and finished in his sixty-first.

Ludovico Monaldesco, at the extraordinary age of one hundred and fifteen, wrote the memoirs of his times. A singular exertion, noticed by Voltaire, who himself is one of the most remarkable instances of the progress of age in new studies.

The most delightful of autobiographies for artists is that of Benvenuto Cellini; a work of great originality, which was not begun till "the clock of his age had struck fifty-eight."

Koornhert began at forty to learn the Latin and Greek languages, of which he became a master; several students, who afterward distinguished themselves, have commenced as late in life their literary pursuits. Ogilby, the translator of Homer and Vergil, knew little of Latin or Greek till he was past fifty; and Franklin's philosophical pursuits began when he had nearly reached his fiftieth year.

Accorso, a great lawyer, being asked why he began the study of the law so late, answered, beginning it late, he should master it the sooner.

Dryden's complete works form the largest body of poetry from the pen of a single writer in the English language; yet he gave no public testimony of poetic abilities till his twenty-seventh year. In his sixty-eighth year he proposed to translate the whole *Iliad:* and his most pleasing productions were written in his old age.

Michelangelo preserved his creative genius even in extreme old age: there is a device said to be invented by him, of an old man represented in a go-cart, with an hourglass upon it; the inscription *Ancora imparo!*—Yet I Am Learning!

Let Me Grow Lovely

Karle Wilson Baker

Let me grow lovely, growing old—
    So many fine things do:
Laces, and ivory, and gold,
    And silks need not be new;

And there is healing in old trees,
    Old streets a glamour hold;
Why may not I, as well as these,
    Grow lovely, growing old?

Middle Age

Rudolph Chambers Lehmann

When that my days were fewer,
    Some twenty years ago,
And all that is was newer,
    And time itself seemed slow,
With ardor all impassioned,
    I let my hopes fly free,
And deemed the world was fashioned
    My playing-field to be.

The cup of joy was filled then
    With Fancy's sparkling wine;
And all the things I willed then
    Seemed destined to be mine.
Friends had I then in plenty,
    And every friend was true;
Friends always are at twenty,
    And on to twenty-two.

The men whose hair was sprinkled
    With little flecks of gray,
Whose faded brows were wrinkled—
    Sure they had had their day.
And though we bore no malice,
    We knew their hearts were cold,
For they had drained their chalice,
    And now were spent and old.

At thirty, we admitted,
    A man may be alive,
But slower, feebler witted;
    And done at thirty-five.
If Fate prolongs his earth-days,
    His joys grow fewer still;
And after five more birthdays
    He totters down the hill.

We were the true immortals
    Who held the earth in fee;
For us were flung the portals
    Of fame and victory.
The days were bright and breezy,
    And gay our banners flew,
And every peak was easy
    To scale at twenty-two.

And thus we spent our gay time
    As having much to spend;
Swift, swift, that pretty playtime
    Flew by and had its end.
And lo! without a warning
    I woke, as others do,
One fine mid-winter morning,
    A man of forty-two.

And now I see how vainly
    Is youth with ardor fired;
How fondly, how insanely
    I formerly aspired.
A boy may still detest age,
    But as for me I know,
A man has reached his best age
    At forty-two or so.

For youth it is the season
    Of restlessness and strife;
Of passion and unreason,
    And ignorance of life.
Since, though his cheeks have roses,
    No boy can understand
That everything he knows is
    A graft at second hand.

But *we* have toiled and wandered
    With weary feet and numb,
Have doubted, sifted, pondered,—
    How else should knowledge come?
Have seen, too late for heeding,
    Our hopes go out in tears,
Lost in the dim receding,
    Irrevocable years.

Yet, though with busy fingers
    No more we wreathe the flowers,
An airy perfume lingers,
    A brightness still is ours.
And though no rose our cheeks have,
    The sky still shines as blue;
And still the distant peaks have
    The glow of twenty-two.

To Critics

Walter Learned

When I was seventeen I heard
    From each censorious tongue,
"I'd not do that if I were you;
    You see you're rather young."

Now that I number forty years,
    I'm quite as often told
Of this or that I shouldn't do
    Because I'm quite too old.

O carping world! If there's an age
    Where youth and manhood keep
An equal poise, alas! I must
    Have passed it in my sleep.

Fifty Years

Pierre Jean de Béranger

Translated from the French by William Young

Wherefore these flowers? floral applause?
    Ah, no, these blossoms came to say
That I am growing old, because
    I number fifty years to-day.
O rapid, ever-fleeting day!
    O moments lost, I know not how!
O wrinkled cheek and hair grown gray!
    Alas, for I am fifty now!

Sad age, when we pursue no more—
    Fruit dies upon the withering tree:
Hark! some one rapped upon my door.
    Nay, open not. 'Tis not for me—
Or else the doctor calls. Not yet
    Must I expect his studious bow.
Once I'd have called, "Come in, Lizzette"—
    Alas, for I am fifty now!

In age what aches and pains abound:
    The torturing gout racks us awhile;
Blindness, a prison dark, profound;
    Or deafness that provokes a smile.
Then Reason's lamp grows faint and dim
    With flickering ray. Children, allow
Old Age the honor due to him—
    Alas, for I am fifty now!

Ah, heaven! the voice of Death I know,
    Who rubs his hands in joyous mood;
The sexton knocks and I must go,—
    Farewell, my friends the human brood!
Below are famine, plague, and strife;
    Above, new heavens my soul endow:
Since God remains, begin, new life!
    Alas, for I am fifty now!

But no, 'tis you, sweetheart, whose youth,
    Tempting my soul with dainty ways,
Shall hide from it the somber truth,
    This incubus of evil days.
Springtime is yours, and flowers; come then,
    Scatter your roses on my brow,
And let me dream of youth again—
    Alas, for I am fifty now!

When You Are Very Old, at Evening, by Candlelight

Pierre de Ronsard

Translated from the French by Geoffrey de Brereton

When you are very old, at evening, by candlelight,
sitting near the fire spooling and spinning the wool,
you will say, in wonder, as you sing my verses:
'Ronsard praised me in the days when I was beautiful.'
Then not one of your servants who hears that news,
though already half asleep over her work,
but will start awake at the sound of my name,
and bless your name of immortal renown.
I shall be under the ground, a boneless ghost,
taking my rest in the myrtles' shade;
you will be an old woman crouching by the hearth,
regretting my love and your own proud scorn.
Heed me and live now, do not wait till tomorrow.
Gather today the roses of life.

When You Are Old

William Butler Yeats

When you are old and gray and full of sleep,
And nodding by the fire, take down this book,
And slowly read, and dream of the soft look
Your eyes had once, and of their shadows deep;

How many loved your moments of glad grace,
And loved your beauty with love false or true;
But one man loved the pilgrim soul in you,
And loved the sorrows of your changing face.

And bending down beside the glowing bars,
Murmur, a little sadly, how love fled
And paced upon the mountains overhead,
And hid his face amid a crowd of stars.

Maxims

Duc François de La Rochefoucauld

Translated from the French by John Heard

Few men have an intimate knowledge of death. We die not because of resignation, but from stupidity and custom, and most of us die because we cannot help it.

Old people like to give good advice, since they can no longer set bad examples.

It may be said that vices, like the inns where we must sleep, await us along the road of life; and I doubt whether, should we travel the same road twice, experience would teach us to avoid them.

Devoting one's life to keeping well is one of the most tedious of ailments.

The enthusiasm of youth is no more harmful than the indifference of age.

Each age of life is new to us, and we find ourselves hampered by inexperience regardless of our years.

From

The Chinese Classics

Confucius

Translated from the Chinese by James Legge

Confucius said, 'There are three things which the superior man guards against. In youth, when the physical powers are not yet settled, he guards against lust. When he is strong, and the physical powers are full of vigour, he guards against quarrelsomeness. When he is old, and the animal powers are decayed, he guards against covetousness.'

From

The Apocrypha

Ecclesiasticus, 8:6

Dishonor not the old: we shall all be numbered among them.

Copyrights and Acknowledgments

Sources for Further Reading

The following articles from journals and books contain bibliographies of literature on aging.

"The Experiences of Old Age as Depicted in Contemporary Novels," by Mary Sohngen, in *The Gerontologist,* Vol. 17, No. 1 (1977), pp. 70–78, includes summaries of 87 novels published within the past thirty years.

"Novels of Senescence," by Celeste Loughman, in the same issue of *The Gerontologist,* pp. 79–84, is an excellent analytical study of contemporary novels.

"Images of Old Age in Poetry" by Mary Sohngen and Robert J. Smith, in *The Gerontologist,* Vol. 18, No. 2 (1978), pp. 181–86, contains references to 127 poems.

"Interpersonal Communication in Prominent Western Drama," by George Banziger, in *The Gerontologist,* Vol. 19, No. 5 (1979), analyzes intergenerational attitudes and relationships in Greek and Roman drama and in plays by Shakespeare, Molière, G. B. Shaw, Eugene O'Neill, and Arthur Miller.

Robert N. Butler and Myrna I. Lewis, *Aging and Mental Health,* Second Edition (St. Louis: C. V. Mosby, 1977), contains a listing of twentieth-century fiction and films on pages 332 and 333.

In David Hackett Fischer's *Growing Old in America* (New York: Oxford University Press, 1978), Chapter 3, "Gerontophobia: The Cult of Youth in Modern America, 1770–1970," includes Fischer's analysis of the attitudes of Thoreau, Longfellow, Hawthorne, and Whitman on aging. Footnotes throughout the chapter provide a wealth of references to American essays and fiction on old age.

Jon Hendricks and C. Davis Hendricks' *Aging in Mass Society: Myths and Realities* (Cambridge, Mass.: Winthrop, 1977), pp. 48–50, provides references to a number of historical-literary-philosophical works that express attitudes about aging.

The Home Book of Verse, edited by Burton Stevenson (New York: Holt, 1922), is an anthology that contains a lengthy section on "Youth and Age," as does his *Home Book of Modern Verse* (New York: Holt, 1925). Both are excellent sources for poems on the entire life cycle and have appeared in many subsequent editions since their original publication dates.